1 Timothy

1 Timothy

A Charge to God's Missional Household

Volume 1

Paul S. Jeon

☙PICKWICK *Publications* • Eugene, Oregon

1 TIMOTHY
A Charge to God's Missional Household
Volume 1

Copyright © 2017 Paul S. Jeon. All rights reserved. Except for brief quotations in critical publications or reviews, no part of this book may be reproduced in any manner without prior written permission from the publisher. Write: Permissions, Wipf and Stock Publishers, 199 W. 8th Ave., Suite 3, Eugene, OR 97401.

Pickwick Publications
An Imprint of Wipf and Stock Publishers
199 W. 8th Ave., Suite 3
Eugene, OR 97401

www.wipfandstock.com

PAPERBACK ISBN: 978-1-5326-0241-2
HARDCOVER ISBN: 978-1-5326-0243-6
EBOOK ISBN: 978-1-5326-0242-9

Cataloguing-in-Publication data:

Names: Jeon, Paul S.

Title: 1 Timothy : a charge to God's missional household : vol. 1 / by Paul S. Jeon.

Description: Eugene, OR: Pickwick Publications, 2017 | Includes bibliographical references.

Identifiers: ISBN 978-1-5326-0241-2 (paperback) | ISBN 978-1-5326-0243-6 (hardcover) | ISBN 978-1-5326-0242-9 (ebook)

Subjects: LCSH: Bible. Timothy, 1st—Commentaries. | Bible. Timothy, 1st—Criticism, interpretation, etc.

Classification: LCC BS2745.3 J4 2017 (print) | LCC BS2745.3 (ebook)

Manufactured in the U.S.A.   12/13/17

To Timothy J. Keller, True Teacher of
the Gospel and Model of Humility

Contents

Preface | ix
Acknowledgments | xi
Abbreviations | xiii

1 Introduction | 1
   A Explanation of the Overarching Message of the Letter and Title of the Book | 1
   B Authorship, Audience, and Historical Setting of the Letter | 10
   C Approach to 1 Timothy: Text-Centered, Literary-Rhetorical, Audience-Oriented | 22

2 The Chiastic Structures of 1 Timothy | 27
   A Chiasm in 1 Timothy | 27
   B Terminology and Types of Chiasms | 31
   C Translation of 1 Timothy | 36
   D Outline of the Chiastic Structures of 1 Timothy | 45
   E The Six Microchiasms of the 1 Timothy Letter | 45
   F The Macrochiastic Structure of the 1 Timothy Letter | 63

3 1 Timothy 1:1–20: Paul's Charge for Timothy to Preserve the Teaching (A Unit) | 66

4 1 Timothy 2:1–15: Salvation for All through Prayer and Godly Conduct (B Unit) | 142

Bibliography | 217

Preface

I HAD PLANNED TO COMPLETE this book on 1 Timothy not long after completing my dissertation on Titus. At the time, I figured that I had "academic momentum," a rhythm that one picks up from constantly researching and writing in the final season of a PhD. Given that I had worked with the 1 Timothy letter for many years and already developed what I thought was a solid outline, I thought that this book would be churned out in a matter of one or two years. That was the fall of 2011. Between then and now, much has transpired—so much that I wondered if I would ever be able to complete this project. Still, the unexpected delay gave me an extended season to dwell on the letter and gain certain insights that can come only with time. During the intervening years, I had ample opportunities both to lecture on 1 Timothy while teaching at Reformed Theological Seminary and to preach on it at my church (NewCity) and occasional conferences. Regular dialogue with students, colleagues, and parishioners opened new angles into understanding the message of 1 Timothy, a letter that unfortunately tends to be treated somewhat plainly as a sort of church-manual.

I write commentaries in hope that they might be of some service to those who want to better understand the Bible. My desire has never been to write *the* commentary on any given work in the New Testament. Rather, I see myself as entering into a dialogue that has been taking place for many centuries about the meaning of the text. In this sense, I feel deeply privileged to offer my brief comments on 1 Timothy. My goal is that the reader will feel like he or she has a better grasp of the meaning and import of the letter and, in turn, will experience a degree of the benefits that I have experienced from sitting down with this letter—indeed, sitting under it—for almost six years now.

Acknowledgments

First, as always, I want to thank my parents. They know that I have no idea how much they have sacrificed for me. Second, I want to thank my research assistant, Brian Forman, who meticulously reviewed the text and enhanced the overall commentary in more ways than I can fully express. Third, though we have never met, I want to readily acknowledge Philip Towner, who served as both my guide and conversationalist through his wonderful commentary for over six years. In more ways than I can count, he pointed me away from exegetical fallacies and towards more promising interpretations. Finally, I want to thank my church NewCity and my family—especially my wife, Geena—for making life and ministry a delight.

Abbreviations

1 Tim	1 Timothy
AB	Anchor Bible
AGAJU	Arbeiten zur Geschichte des antiken Judentums und des Urchristentums
ANTC	Abingdon New Testament Commentaries
ASE	*Annali di storia dell'esegesi*
ATR	*Anglican Theological Review*
BDAG	W. Bauer, W. F. Arndt, and F. W. Gingrich (3rd ed.; rev. by F. W. Danker), *Greek-English Lexicon of the New Testament*
BDF	F. Blass, A. Debrunner, and R. W. Funk, *A Greek Grammar of the NT*
Bib	*Biblica*
BibInt	*Biblical Interpretation*
BJRL	*Bulletin of the John Rylands University Library of Manchester*
BPC	Biblical Performance Criticism
BrazTCB	Brazos Theological Commentary on the Bible
BSac	*Bibliotheca Sacra*
BSR	*Buddhist Studies Review*
BTB	*Biblical Theology Bulletin*
BTCB	Belief: A Theological Commentary on the Bible
BZ	*Biblische Zeitschrift*
BZNW	Beihefte zur Zeitschrift für die neutestamentliche Wissenschaft

CBC	Cornerstone Biblical Commentary
CBQ	*Catholic Biblical Quarterly*
CC	*Christian Century*
CCSS	Catholic Commentary on Sacred Scripture
COP	Colloquium Oecumenicum Paulinum
CTM	*Concordia Theological Monthly*
CTR	*Criswell Theological Review*
CTST	*Current Trends in Scripture Translation*
DLTH	Daily Life Through History
EBib	Études bibliques
ECL	Early Christianity and Its Literature
EKK	Evangelisch-katholischer Kommentar zum Neuen Testament
ESV	English Standard Version
HB	*Human Biology*
HNTC	Harper's New Testament Commentaries
ICC	International Critical Commentary
ITS	Invitation to Theological Studies
IVPNTC	IVP New Testament Commentary
JBL	*Journal of Biblical Literature*
JETS	*Journal of the Evangelical Theological Society*
JSNT	*Journal for the Study of the New Testament*
JSNTSup	JSNT, Supplement Series
JSOT	*Journal for the Study of the Old Testament*
JTS	*Journal of Theological Studies*
KJV	*King James Version*
LBS	Linguistic Biblical Studies
LPS	Library of Pauline Studies
LNTS	Library of New Testament Studies
LXX	Septuagint
McMBSS	McMaster Biblical Studies Series
MM	J. H. Moulton and G. Milligan, *The Vocabulary of the Greek Testament*

MNTC	MacArthur New Testament Commentary
MSJ	*Master's Seminary Journal*
NASB	New American Standard Bible
NCBC	New Collegeville Bible Commentary
NCBNT	New Clarendon Bible, New Testament
NCCS	New Covenant Commentary Series
NDIEC	New Documents Illustrating Early Christianity
Neot	*Neotestamentica*
NIBC	New International Biblical Commentary
NIDNTT	New International Dictionary of New Testament Theology
NIGTC	New International Greek Testament Commentary
NovT	*Novum Testamentum*
NRSV	New Revised Standard Version
NT	New Testament
NTD	Das Neue Testament Deutsch
NTL	New Testament Library
NTMono	New Testament Monographs
NTOASUNT	Novum Testamentum et Orbis Antiquus, Studien zur Umwelt des Neuen Testaments
OBC	Oxford Bible Commentary
OLAW	Orality and Literacy in the Ancient World
OT	Old Testament
PBM	Paternoster Biblical Monographs
PE	Pastoral Epistles
PP	*Priscilla Papers*
PS	Pauline Studies
PTMS	Princeton Theological Monograph Series
REB	*Revised English Bible*
ResQ	*Restoration Quarterly*
RNBC	Readings: A New Biblical Commentary
RNT	Regensburger Neues Testament
SBL	Society of Biblical Literature

SNT	Supplements to Novum Testamentum
SNTG	Studies in New Testament Greek
SNTSMS	Society for New Testament Studies Monograph Series
STR	*Sewanee Theological Review*
SVTQ	*St Vladimir's Theological Quarterly*
TCGNT	B. M. Metzger, *A Textual Commentary on the Greek New Testament*
TDNT	*Theological Dictionary of the New Testament*
ThF	Trierer Historische Forschungen
TrinJ	*Trinity Journal*
TynBul	*Tyndale Bulletin*
TynNTC	Tyndale New Testament Commentaries
TZ	*Theologische Zeitschrift*
UBS	United Bible Societies lexicon
USQR	*Union Seminary Quarterly Review*
VC	*Vigiliae Christianae*
WA	*World Archaeology*
WBC	Word Biblical Commentary
WesTJ	*Wesleyan Theological Journal*
WUNT	Wissenschaftliche Untersuchungen zum Neuen Testament
ZNW	*Zeitschrift für die Neutestamentliche Wissenschaft*

1

Introduction[1]

Explanation of the Overarching Message of the Letter and Title of the Book

THE TITLE, *1 Timothy: A Charge to God's Missional Household*, was chosen to reflect and summarize what I believe is the main message in Paul's letter to Timothy and the first-century Ephesian church.[2] An explanation for the title follows. When referring to the 1 Timothy text throughout this section, my English translations of the original Greek are often interwoven without quotations;[3] this is to utilize the text of 1 Timothy as much as possible. When specific words or phrases of the 1 Timothy text are being analyzed, they will be marked with quotations and accompanied by the Greek text in parentheses.[4] All translations of 1 Timothy and other biblical texts are my own unless indicated otherwise.[5]

"A Charge"

The title phrase "*A Charge*" is taken directly from the 1 Timothy text. Its seven cognate occurrences throughout the letter establish the overall purpose and tone.[6] From the very outset, Paul underscores the sole reason why

---

1. The organization of this chapter follows in large part the work of Heil (see e.g., *Ephesians*, 1–11).

2. I will briefly address 1 Timothy's authorship and audience in the next section.

3. Many of my English translations are hyphenated words and will be apparent as such.

4. When entire phrases of 1 Timothy are marked with quotations, the Greek text in parentheses applies to the English word that immediately precedes it.

5. For an explanation of my English translations and the methodology thereof, see chapter 2.

6. References to *cognates* throughout this commentary are important. As such, a

Timothy is in Ephesus: "that you might charge (παραγγείλῃς) some not to teach-different" (1:3). Immediately following, Paul states that the purpose and end result "of the charge (παραγγελίας) is love from a pure heart and a good conscience and a without-hypocrisy faith" (1:5). In other words, Paul makes clear that "*A Charge*" intends love and faith for "some" who teach-different. Moreover, Paul's statement, "This charge (παραγγελίαν) I entrust to you" (1:18) further emphasizes that "*A Charge*" is central to the overarching purpose of the 1 Timothy letter. In view of "some" who apostasy from the faith (4:1), in 4:11 Paul commands Timothy, "Charge (παράγγελλε) these-things and teach." To "someone" who does not provide for their own household nor for God's household (5:8; cf. 5:4, 6), Paul declares, "And these charge (παράγγελλε), that they might be irreproachable" (5:7). Finally, in the last section of the letter Paul says to Timothy, "I charge (παραγγέλλω), in the sight of God . . . you to keep the commandment spotless" (6:13–14), and he again instructs Timothy to "charge (παράγγελλε) [the rich] not to be-haughty, nor to hope upon the without-certainty of riches" (6:17).

The overall tone of "*A Charge*" throughout 1 Timothy is not merely thematic but rhetorically assertive to convey an authoritative force.[7] In the greeting of the letter, Paul grounds all of his words—thus "*A Charge*"—in the authority of Christ Jesus and God: Paul is an "*apostle* of Christ Jesus" (1:1)—a chosen representative with the full authority of the sender—and his appointment thereof is "according to the *command* of God" (1:1).[8] Indeed, it is this fundamental emphasis on Paul's authority from Christ Jesus and God that provides the significance of his authoritative language throughout the letter. In 1 Timothy 1, Paul begins: "I exhorted (παρακάλεσά) you to remain in Ephesus . . . that you might charge some not to teach-different" (1:3).[9] In 1 Timothy 2, Paul gives authoritative instructions for the entire church: "I exhort (παρακαλῶ), therefore, first of all to be-done supplications, prayers,

---

brief definition for clarity is in order. Words that are *cognate* terms are related by the original word or linguistic root that they share in common. See discussion in chapter 2 regarding translation methodology.

7. According to the Friberg Lexicon, the verb "charge" (παραγγέλλω) means "issuing a directive from an authoritative source" (20488).

8. Emphasis added. For the authoritative significance of "apostle," see chapter 3 regarding 1 Timothy 1:1.

Towner, *Letters*, 93: "A glance at Paul's letters shows how flexible the greeting might be . . . Variations often reflect directions in which Paul will move as the letter unfolds, as well as the tone he desires to adopt with the readers." See also Aune, *Literary Environment*, 158–82.

9. The more common translation "I urge" (e.g., *ESV*) seems to disregard the authoritative aspect of Paul's greeting as an "*apostle* of Christ Jesus according to *the command* of God" (1:1, emphasis added). See above.

intercessions, thanksgivings on behalf of all humans" (2:1).[10] Similar comments could be said of Paul's specific instructions to the men (2:8) and women (2:9–12). In 1 Timothy 3, Paul begins by outlining the "necessary" qualifications of overseers (3:1–7) and deacons (3:8–13), then he concludes with the statement: "These-things to you I write . . . that you might know how it is necessary to behave in the household of God" (3:14–15). In other words, Paul establishes the code of conduct that Timothy is to implement and to which the Ephesian church must adhere. Moreover, in 1 Timothy 5, Paul specifies that Timothy is to "exhort" (παρακάλει) an elderly-man in the church as a father (5:1), conveying that his authority must be marked by respect and a familial love. Still, it is this sustained theme and tone of authority that Paul reinforces in his direct command to Timothy in 6:1: "Teach and exhort (παρακάλει)."

In sum, the authoritative nature of Paul's language in the 1 Timothy letter is adequately captured by the title phrase "*A Charge.*" It is with a clear awareness and sensitivity to the directive and commanding quality of Paul's letter by which his first-century audience would have experienced and understood it. Significantly, then, it is within this framework that a modern audience of the 1 Timothy text may also hear and experience the authoritative tone that Paul utilizes to communicate both the overarching purpose of "*A Charge*" and the audience's intended response thereof.

"to Preserve the Teaching and Promote Godliness"

A single navigation through the entire letter demonstrates that "*to Preserve the Teaching*" is the explicit reason for "*A Charge.*" From the very beginning in 1 Timothy 1, Paul makes clear that "some" in the Ephesian church "teach-different" (ἑτεροδιδασκαλεῖν, 1:3), namely that which is "different" (ἕτερον) and lies-opposed to "the (τῇ) sound teaching (διδασκαλίᾳ)" (1:10) with which Paul was counted-faithful (1:11). In 1 Timothy 2, in view of the truth (2:4), that is, the testimony concerning Christ Jesus who gave himself as a ransom on behalf of all (2:6), Paul was divinely appointed a proclaimer, apostle, and "teacher" (διδάσκαλος) in faith and truth (2:7);[11] in this way also, his instruction that women in the church are not permitted "to teach" (διδάσκειν) is dependent on "the sound teaching" (1:10) to

---

10. That "I exhort" (2:1) is not merely a suggestion but rather an authoritative command carrying the sense that the church *must* pray on behalf of all humans, see chapter 4.

11. That Paul's appointment as a "teacher" was by the divine activity of God, see discussion in chapter 4 regarding 1 Timothy 2:7.

which he was appointed by God as a "teacher" (2:7). In 1 Timothy 3, regarding the church, which is a pillar and foundation of truth (3:15), Paul indicates that it is necessary for its leader—an overseer—to be "able-to-teach" (διδακτικόν, 3:2), namely that which is consistent with "the sound teaching" of the "teacher" Paul. In 1 Timothy 4, in view of the "teachings" (διδασκαλίαις) of demons to which "some" are holding-toward (4:2), Paul intends for Timothy to continue being-nourished in "the (τῆς) commendable teaching (διδασκαλίας)" that he has followed (4:6), to "teach" (δίδασκε, 4;11) in the church, to hold-toward "the teaching" (τῇ διδασκαλίᾳ, 4:13), and to strongly-hold "the teaching" (τῇ διδασκαλίᾳ) for the sake of his own salvation and those who hear him (4:16). In 1 Timothy 5, with such sustained importance in the relation to teaching and leadership in the church, Paul makes clear that elders who lead commendably in "teaching" (διδασκαλίᾳ) must be considered-worthy of double honor (5:17); indeed, even the most common workers in Ephesus are responsible for ensuring that "the teaching" (ἡ διδασκαλία) might not be-blasphemed (6:1), and Paul commands that Timothy must "teach" (δίδασκε) these-things (6:2). Finally, in 1 Timothy 6, Paul's charge in 6:17 has in view "someone" who "teaches-different" (ἑτεροδιδασκαλεῖ) and does not come-toward the sound words of the Lord Jesus Christ nor to "the teaching" (τῇ . . . διδασκαλίᾳ) (6:3). From beginning to end, therefore, it is the sustained emphasis *"to Preserve the Teaching"* over and against the different teaching of "some" that determines and prompts *"A Charge."*

Still, the phrase *"and Promote Godliness"* reflects the letter's dual and related emphasis that flows from *"A Charge to Preserve the Teaching."*[12] In 1 Timothy 1–2, in contrast to the "without-godly" (ἀσεβέσιν) for whom the law is laid (1:8–10), Paul's exhortation to the church intends for them to live a life in all "godliness" (εὐσεβείᾳ, 2:2); such is why Paul instructs the women

---

12. It may be worth commenting on the use of the term " godliness." In the Bible, the connotation of the terms "godliness" and "obedience" are closely related to each other. Obedience to God, which is the essence of biblical ethics, is essentially the submission of creation to the Creator—this includes obedience to the Creator's intended design for his creation (see discussion in chapter 4 regarding 1 Tim 2:12–13). Hence, children are called to honor and submit themselves to their parents out of reverence for God's design of the family (Exod 20:12; Eph 6:1–3; cf. 1 Tim 5:4, 16, see discussion in volume 3, chapter 2); citizens are to submit themselves to governing authorities (Rom 13:1–5; cf. 1 Tim 6:1–2, see discussion in volume 3, chapter 2); and humanity is to submit its rules and regulations to God's ordinances (Exod 20:3–17). Thus obedience within the church should never be understood as a preference but rather as the fruit of promulgating "the sound teaching, according to the gospel of the glory of the blessed God" (1 Tim 1:10–11), namely "the sound words of our Lord Jesus Christ and the teaching that is according to godliness" (6:3). In this sense, "obedience" and "godliness" are functionally synonymous.

who profess "godliness" (θεοσέβειαν) to cosmetic themselves consistent-with good works (2:10). In 1 Timothy 3, Paul intends the behavior of the church to align with the confessedly great mystery of "godliness" (εὐσεβείας) concerning Christ Jesus (3:16). In 1 Timothy 4, in view of the commendable teaching, Timothy must train himself toward "godliness" (εὐσέβειαν, 4:7), namely because "godliness" (εὐσέβεια) is toward all profitability (4:9). In 1 Timothy 5, the children or those-from-parents in the church must learn "to be-godly" (εὐσεβεῖν) to their own household (5:4). Finally, in 1 Timothy 6, over and against "someone" who does not come-toward the teaching that is according to "godliness" (εὐσέβειαν, 6:3) and thus is supposing "godliness" (εὐσέβειαν) to be a means-of-gain (6:5), Paul remedially declares that "godliness" (εὐσέβεια) with contentment is great gain (6:6), namely the "godliness" (εὐσέβειαν) that Timothy must pursue (6:11).

It is in this way that "*A Charge*" in the sub-title has in mind the phrase "*A Charge to Preserve the Teaching and Promote Godliness*," which summarizes Paul's "*charge*" (1:3, 5, 18; 4:11; 5:7; 6:13, 17) *to promote* a tangible expression of "*godliness*" (2:2, 10; 3:16; 4:7b, 8b; 5:4a; 6:3, 6, 11) as the direct result of agreeing with "*the teaching*" (1:10; 4:6, 13, 16; 6:3; cf. 2:7, 12; 3:2; 5:17; 6:1, 3) that Timothy is *to preserve* over and against different teachings that result in ungodliness (1:3, 10; 4:2; 6:3). The dual, integrated, and sequential emphasis in regard to *the teaching* and the subsequent *godliness* that ensues will be explicated throughout the following chapters.[13]

"God's Missional Household"

The phrase "*God's ... Household*" is taken directly from 3:15, which identifies "the church of the living God" as "the household (οἴκῳ) of God." Indeed, the household imagery plays a critical role in the audience's proper understanding of Paul's "*Charge to Preserve the Teaching and Promote Godliness*" in 1 Timothy.[14] The noun "household" (οἶκος) and its related cognate terms occur repeatedly throughout the letter. In 1 Timothy 1, "some" who teach-different bring-about controversial-speculations rather than "the

---

13. My analysis of 1 Timothy demonstrates that the summarizing theme "A Charge to Preserve the Teaching and Promote Godliness . . ." is itself reflected in the rhetorical arrangement of the letter as a chiasm; see chapter 2. See esp. volume 3, chapter 3 regarding the climactic implications of Paul's rhetorical use of the chiastic arrangement.

14. See discussion in Barcley, "1 Timothy," 373–74. Poythress, "The Church as Family," 235: "The theme of family relationships is particularly prominent in Paul's First Letter to Timothy. Paul repeatedly invokes the analogy of a family in order to enable Timothy better to understand the appropriate order and responsibilities within the Christian church."

household-law (οἰκονομίαν) of God in faith" (1:4). In 1 Timothy 3, Paul discusses the integral relation between one's own household and God's household: it is a necessary qualifications for an overseer to be "leading his own household (οἴκου) commendably" (3:4), namely because "if someone does not know how to lead his own household (οἴκου), how will he care-for the church of God?" (3:5); qualified deacons must be known for "leading children commendably and their own households (οἴκων)" (3:12). In 1 Timothy 5, children and those-from-parents must learn first to be-godly "to their own household (οἶκον) and to give-return repayments to their parents" (5:4); indeed, says Paul, "if someone does not provide-for those of his own"—a person's own biological family—"and especially for household-members (οἰκείων)"—those in God's household, the church—"he has denied the faith and is worse-than the without-faith" (5:8).[15] Clearly, the connection and importance of "household" in 1 Timothy—both one's own and God's own—is unmistakable. It is for this reason that Paul is concerned about younger widows in Ephesus who "learn to be idlers, going-about the houses (οἰκίας)" as gossips and busybodies (5:13) and also why Paul wants them instead "to master-households" (οἰκοδεσποτεῖν, 5:14). Ultimately and finally in 1 Timothy 6, Paul envelopes the theme of household with his praising description of God as the blessed and only Power who is "housing-in" (οἰκῶν) without-approachable light (6:15–16). In other words, where the Ephesian church is "the household of God" (3:15), it is therefore the place where God is "housing-in" (6:16). Most certainly, then, Paul regards "*God's . . . Household*" as an essential aspect of the 1 Timothy letter.

Moreover, even in the absence of explicit references to the term "household" and its cognates, the household imagery is consistently heard in the explicit familial language of the letter.[16] 1 Timothy 1, Paul refers to God as

---

15. That Paul is both distinguishing and connecting an individual's family household ("those of-his-own") and God's family household ("household-members"), see discussion in volume 3, chapter 2 regarding the term "especially" (5:8) in relation to 1 Timothy 4:10.

16. Ibid., 237: "In fact, almost the whole of 1 Timothy may be seen as a catalog of types of behavior and organization needed in a harmonious family. True doctrine is necessary because the family needs to know its own rules (1 Timothy 1:3–11, 18–20). Doctrine is therefore foundational for all the more specific kinds of organization and mutual relations within the family. Mercy and forgiveness bind the family together (1 Timothy 1:12–17). Protection is necessary from destructive outside interference and for the benefit of the family's relations to the larger world (2:1–7). The men in the family must not generate strife among themselves but be united in petitions (2:8). The women must devote themselves to family service and not to frivolities (2:9–10) or to usurping authority over men (2:11–14). The family must have wise, competent overseers (3:1–7). It must have wise care for family rules and examples from the leaders are most important (4:1–16). Family members must all treat one another with the respect and

"Father" (πατρός, 1:2); immediately prior to Paul's exhortation for Timothy to "charge some not to teach-different (1:3), he refers to Timothy as "genuine child (τέκνῳ) in faith" (1:2); similarly, immediately after reiterating "This charge I entrust to you," Paul refers to Timothy as "child (τέκνον) Timothy" (1:18).[17] In 1 Timothy 2, men and women in the Ephesian church are given equal and distinct roles based on God's creational design of the very first household—that of Adam and Eve (2:11-14)—and women who cosmetic themselves consistent-with good works (2:10) do so consistent-with "child-parenting" (τεκνογονίας, 2:15).[18] In 1 Timothy 3, overseers and deacons are qualified based on their marital fidelity and leadership ability within their own household (3:2, 12), particularly toward their "children" (τέκνα, 3:4; τέκνων, 3:12). In 1 Timothy 4, Paul refers to the faithful in the church as "brothers" (ἀδελφοῖς, 4:6), and he underscores that "some" who are "forbidding to marry" are rejecting the truth regarding God's commendable creation (4:3-4). In 1 Timothy 5, Paul is explicit about the familial perspective that Timothy must have toward all members of God's household (5:1-2): "An elderly-man do not rebuke-violently; rather exhort as a father (πατέρα), younger-men as brothers (ἀδελφούς), elderly-women as mothers (μητέρας), younger-women as sisters (ἀδελφάς), in all purity." Paul is equally clear that the familial aspect of God's household applies to the relationship of slaves and their masters who both belong to God's household: "they are brothers (ἀδελφοί)" (6:2). Lastly, in 1 Timothy 6, Paul concludes with Timothy's name (6:20), recalling for the audience Paul's opening reference to "genuine child Timothy" (1:2).[19]

The word "*Missional*" in the title phrase "*God's Missional Household*" underscores the universal offer of salvation to all humans that is expressed and emphasized throughout the 1 Timothy letter. In 1 Timothy 1, Paul's first words of the letter identify God as the "Savior" (σωτῆρος, 1:1) and

---

honor and sensitivity appropriate to their mutual status (5:1–6:2). Those in need must be cared for, preferably by those closest to them (5:3–10). Use of money must support family goals (6:6–10, 17–19)."

17. Paul's specific attention to and association of "child Timothy" (1:2; 1:18) with his duty to "charge" and the "charge" (1:3, 18) is notable as a rhetorical strategy in the letter; see chapter 3 regarding 1 Timothy 1:18. See also volume 3, chapter 3 regarding 1 Timothy 6:17, 20.

18. Regarding the relation of God's creational design of Adam and Eve to roles in the church, see chapter 4 (1 Tim 2:12–13); see esp. discussion regarding the exegetical significance of the term "first" (πρῶτος, 2:13), which refers not to sequence but rather to prominence and the subsequent responsibility thereof. Regarding "child-parenting" (2:15) in reference to God's household, see chapter 4 (1 Tim 2:15).

19. Paul's specific mention of the name "Timothy" notably frames the entire letter (1:2, 18; 6:20) and is part of Paul's rhetorical strategy; see volume 3, chapter 3 regarding 1 Timothy 6:20.

thus the reason why Christ Jesus came into the world "to save" (σῶσαι) sinners (1:15). Christ Jesus granted-mercy to Paul—the former blasphemer, persecutor, and hubristic-person (1:14)—in order to display "all" (ἅπασαν) patience as an example to those who would-inevitably-come to have-faith upon Christ for life eternal (1:16). In 1 Timothy 2, given that Christ intends for mercy and salvation to be displayed for the purpose of salvation, Paul exhorts the church to pray on behalf of "all (πάντων) humans (ἀνθρώπων)" and "all" (πάντων) those being in authority (2:1–2); indeed, Paul indicates that such is commendable and acceptable in the sight of the "Savior (σωτῆρος) God" who desires "all (πάντας) humans (ἀνθρώπους) to be-saved (σωθῆναι)" (2:3–4); moreover, it is for this reason that "the mediator of God and humans (ἀνθρώπων), the human (ἄνθρωπος) Christ Jesus . . . gave himself as a ransom on behalf of all (πάντων)" (2:6). In 1 Timothy 4, Paul asserts that the living God is the "Savior (σωτήρ) of all (πάντων) humans (ἀνθρώπων)" (4:10). In short, Paul's language makes evident that the church, which is the household of God (3:15), is "*Missional*" precisely because God, the Father of the household (1:2), is missional (2:3–4; 4:10).

In this way, the 1 Timothy letter would not be heard by Paul's Ephesian audience as an attempt to maintain an insular community; nor, then, should it be understood as such by a modern audience. Much rather, it is clear that Paul intends "*God's Missional Household*" to attract, welcome, and have a presence in the greater Ephesian community. From top to bottom, that is, from leadership in the church who are to hold a commendable testimony from those-outside (3:7), to widows who have followed "all" (παντί) good work (5:10), to children or those-from-parents in the church who are to be-godly to their-own household (5:4), Paul's concern in the letter is a lifestyle that makes Christ Jesus attractive to any and everyone. It is for this reason that Paul wants men and women in the church to lead-through a peaceful and quiet life (2:2). Namely, men are to pray in "all" (παντί) places without anger or word-quarreling (2:8); women are not to cosmetic themselves in braids and gold or pearls or rich attire (2:9) but rather with what is proper for women who profess godliness, consistent-with good works (2:10), which includes learning in "all" (πάσῃ) submissiveness (2:11). It is "*God's Missional Household*"—the entire church of leaders, children, those-from-parents, men, women, and widows alike who are to draw attention not to themselves but to Christ. For sure, the goal of "*A Charge to Preserve the Teaching and Promote Godliness*" is not to create an isolated Christian household but a "*Missional Household*" that shares "*God's*" desire for all humans to come to a knowing-embrace of the truth (2:4).

Still, it is worth noting that the sustained emphasis on "*God's Missional Household*" is simultaneously oriented toward "some" within the church who explicitly hinder and undermine its missional purpose—namely, "some" (τισίν) who teach-different (1:3), that is, "someone" (τις) who teaches-different and does not come-toward the sound words of the Lord Jesus Christ and the teaching that is according to godliness (6:3).[20] In 1 Timothy 1, "some" (τισίν) who teach-different bring-about controversial-speculations rather than the household-law of God in faith (1:3–4); "some" (τινες) have turned-aside from love and a without-hypocrisy faith for useless-words (1:6); "someone" (τις) does not know the lawful use of the law (cf. 1:8); "some" (τινες) are rejecting faith and a good conscience (1:19) and must be-disciplined not to blaspheme (1:20). In 1 Timothy 3, "someone" (τις) aspires to lead the church as an overseer (3:1), yet Paul rhetorically states that "someone" (τις) does not how to lead his own household and thus cannot care-for the church of God (3:5), which is the household of God (3:15). In 1 Timothy 4, "some" (τινες) are false-worders (4:2), forbidding to marry (4:3); furthermore, the influence and impact of this group upon the church in 1 Timothy 5 is evident: "someone" (τις) does not provide-for his own family members nor for God's own household-members (5:8), and "some" (τις) faithful-woman (5:16) is not assisting "some" (τις) widow (5:4), which is preventing the church from assisting those who are truly widows (5:16).[21] Finally, in 1 Timothy 6, "someone" (τις) who teaches-different is puffed-up, having-an-unhealthy-craving regarding controversies and word-fights (6:4), falling into temptation and harmful longings, which plunge them into ruin and destruction (6:9); indeed, by professing false-named knowledge that results in vile empty-talk and contradictions, "some" (τινες) have swerved regarding the faith (6:20–21). Clearly, "some" in the church do not enable "*God's Missional Household*" to fulfill its purpose. Thus specifically in view of "some" who "teach-different" (1:3; 6:3) and do not come-toward with "the teaching" that is according to "godliness" (6:3), it is clear that "*A Charge to Preserve the Teaching and Promote Godliness*" is vital for the Ephesian church to continue as "*God's Missional Household.*"

In summary, it is the integrated interplay between Paul's *charge*, *the teaching*, *godliness*, and the *missional* activity of *God's household* over and against the different teaching, ungodliness, and anti-missional activity of

---

20. Paul's specific attention to "some" and "someone" (1:3; 6:3) and their specific association with "teach-different" and "teaches-different" (1:3; 6:3) frames the entire arrangement of the 1 Timothy letter. See discussion in chapter 2; see also volume 3, chapter 3 regarding 1 Timothy 6:3 and 6:21.

21. That "some widow" in 5:4 and "some faithful-woman" in 5:16 are interconnected, see volume 3, chapter 2.

"some" in the first-century Ephesian church that lends to the sub-title of this commentary on 1 Timothy: "A Charge to God's Missional Household."

Authorship, Audience, and Historical Setting of the Letter

This section provides a brief overview of background information that is necessary for understanding both the 1 Timothy letter and my analysis that follows in the subsequent chapters of this commentary. Unless noted, all translations of biblical texts in this section are my own and for the purpose of highlighting linguistic commonalities to key words in 1 Timothy, which are accompanied by the Greek text in parentheses.[22]

Authorship

Much discussion has been given to the issue of authorship, and scholars remain divided.[23] Many reputable scholars suggest that the historic apostle Paul did not write 1 Timothy and that the letter is pseudonymous.[24] Others argue the opposite.[25] A few scholars hold to a third position that is best articulated by I. Howard Marshall as "allonymity."[26] Marshall maintains that the apparent linguistic and theological distinctives of the Pastoral Epistles—1 Timothy, 2 Timothy, Titus—make it unlikely that Paul himself was the author of 1 Timothy;[27] yet, he rejects the theory of pseudonymity, given that such practice entailed a level of deception. As such, the middle position that Marshall suggests is that a disciple of the apostle Paul either edited the notes of his deceased teacher or carried the apostle's teaching to the next

---

22. For an explanation of my English translations and the methodology thereof, see chapter 2.

23. For a summary on authorship, see Barcley, "Introduction to the PE," 350–52; Belleville, "Christology, the PE," 317; Wilder, "Pseudonymity," 28–51.

24. For a summary of the main arguments against Pauline authorship, see Dibelius and Conzelmann, *PE*, 1–5; see also Harris, *Paul*, 217–18. For further discussion on pseudonymity, see Puskas and Reasoner, *Letters of Paul*, 220–34; Bauckham, "Pseudo-Apostolic Letters," 469–94; Brox, "Zu den persönlichen Notizen der Pastoralbrief," 76–94.

25. See Mounce, *PE*, 46–130; Fee, *1 & 2 Tim*; Knight, *PE*, 13–52; Wilder "Pseudonymity," 28–29, 34–37, 51.

26. Marshall, *PE*, 83–84.

27. Some scholars protest to the use of the term "Pastorals" (e.g., Towner, *Letters*, 88; cf. Puskas and Reasoner, *Letters of Paul*, 219–20). Still, it is the traditional name for the three letters and will, for conventional purposes, be used in this book.

generation.[28] According to Marshall, "allonymity" explains both the similarities and distinctives that occur between the Pastoral Epistles and the other Pauline letters that are commonly accepted as genuine by scholars.

In this commentary, I take the position that the historical apostle Paul was in fact the author of 1 Timothy. For the sake of brevity, my reasons presented here are based on the 1 Timothy text itself.[29] First, the author identifies himself as "Paul, apostle of Christ Jesus" (1:1). This same self-identification is not only affirmed again in 2:7—"I-myself was appointed proclaimer and apostle"—but also insisted upon through the words "the truth I am saying, I am not falsifying." Similarly, throughout the letter, the author's repetitive use of the grammatically unnecessary first-person pronoun "I-myself" (ἐγώ, 1:11, 15; 2:7) functions to emphasize that "I" is the same person who identified himself as "Paul." That a fictitious author would make such an insistence seems—plainly put—duplicitous. Second, the letter's historical references buttress the position that the historical Paul authored 1 Timothy. Early in the letter, the author indicates that he had exhorted Timothy while-journeying for Macedonia (1:3) and later notes that he hopes to return to Ephesus as soon as possible (3:14; cf. 4:13). That a student of the apostle Paul would have fabricated this journey and travel plans in order to lend credibility to the letter seems rather incredible. Third, the tone of the letter assumes an intimate and authentic relationship between the recipients and author. In particular, Paul's personal charges and exhortations to Timothy, whom he considers his "genuine child" (1:2; cf. 1:18), lose their rhetorical force if the exchange is between fictional characters. Fourth and finally, given that the ultimate goal of the letter is for the audience—and particularly "some"—to respond in faith and obedience to the apostle's authoritative teaching, such a response seems unreasonable unless the actual apostle of Christ Jesus—Paul—authored the letter with his God-given authority (1:1, 11; 2:7).[30]

---

28. This also seems to be the position taken by Long, *1 & 2 Timothy*, 11–12, 20–21.

29. I readily admit that it is impossible to "prove" the authenticity of the letter. Still, from the perspective of the recipients of the letter in the first century, almost all would agree that the implied author—"Paul" (1:1)—is to be understood by the implied audience—Timothy (1:2) and the Ephesian church (6:21)—as the historical apostle Paul who himself established the church. Strange, "'His letters are weighty,'" 127: "Paul's first readers read them as the product of Paul the apostle."

Furthermore, given my personal belief in God's sovereignty (see e.g., 1 Tim 6:15–16), my presupposition is that God only permitted an authentic, truthful inscripturation of his words to the church—here, through Paul, whom God directly commanded (1:1) and divinely appointed to be a proclaimer, apostle, and teacher in faith and truth (2:7).

30. For further reflection on the question of authorship and the related question of interpretation, see Towner, *Letters*, 9–89.

Audience

Although there can be no doubt that Timothy is the primary recipient—"To Timothy" (1:2)—it is evident that Paul's implied audience includes the entire Ephesian church—"you-all" (6:21).[31] To be sure, modern scholarship endorses the fact that as a first-century letter, 1 Timothy was composed and intended to be read aloud publically, that is, performed to a greater audience.[32] Particularly, given the presence of "some" in the Ephesian church and thus *a charge to preserve the teaching and promote godliness as God's missional household*, the public aspect of the letter is heard throughout Paul's rhetorical use of langauage. Not only does Paul repeatedly highlight his apostolic authority and divine appointment (1:1, 11, 12; 2:7) and underscore Timothy's authority and qualifications to lead and represent in Paul's absence (1:2, 18; 4:12-14; 5:11), but Paul consistently employs the Greek language in a sustained and persuasive rhetorical strategy that would be apparent and recognizable to a first-century Greco-Roman audience.[33] In other words, the authoritative content, language, and rhetoric of the letter is most unnecessary if Paul were simply addressing Timothy, who as Paul's "genuine child in faith" (1:2) was already familiar with "the commendable teaching that you have followed" (4:6); indeed, Paul's language and rhetoric

---

31. Mihoc, "Final Admonition to Timothy," 151: "The use of the plural ὑμῶν ["you-all"] in this final blessing in 1 Timothy suggests that Paul expected this letter to be read in the church to all the believers, and that throughout this writing he had them all, not simply Timothy, in view." See Jeon, *To Exhort and Reprove*, 5.

32. Rhoads and Dewey, "Performance Criticism," 15: "Overwhelmingly, those in the first century who experienced the contents of the writings that came to be included centuries later in the New Testament experienced them as oral performances to gathered audiences." Witherington, *New Testament Rhetoric*, 1-2: "So far as we can tell, no documents in antiquity were intended for 'silent' reading . . . They were always meant to be read out loud and usually read out loud to a group . . . This was particularly true of ancient letters . . . They were composed with their aural and oral potential in mind, and they were meant to be orally delivered when they arrive at their destination." Fowler, "Why Everything We Know," 5: "Because we have been reading the Bible in print for 500 years, we naturally assume that that is the way people have always experienced the Bible. But that is not the case: for 2500 years prior to Gutenberg, most people experienced the Bible either through oral/aural performance or in the form of unique and rare handwritten manuscripts." For discussions regarding public versus private ["silent"] reading of NT manuscripts, see Rhoads, "Translating for Oral Performance," 15-16. For further discussion regarding the public performance of the 1 Timothy letter, see below.

33. Paul's rhetorical use of the Greek language and strategy thereof will be analyzed in the following chapters. For an overview, see chapter 2.

For discussion on the rhetorical training that Paul may have received and employed in his letters, see Porter and Dyer, *Paul and Ancient Rhetoric*. See also Dewey, *Oral Ethos*, 16-17.

is most necessary in view of the different-teaching group of "some" who would be listening to the letter's public recitation in the church.[34] Moreover, the relational dynamics within the letter do not merely concern Paul in relation to Timothy (1:2, 18; 3:14; 4:7, 10; 6:11–14) nor only Timothy in relation to the Ephesian church (1:3; 4:6, 11–16; 5:1–2, 7, 20–23; 6:2b, 17, 20). Rather, the 1 Timothy letter clearly concerns the relationships of the people themselves to the church itself: the relation of "some" to the church (1:3–10; 3:5; 4:1–3; 5:24, cf. 5:19–20; 6:4–5, 9–10, 17, 21), to Paul (1:10), to Jesus Christ (6:3), and to God (6:17); the church in relation to all humans (2:1–2); men to other men in the church (2:8); women to the Ephesian community and to men in the church (2:9–15); leaders in relation to their families, households, and those-outside the church (3:1–13); children or those-from-parents in relation to their own widows and parents (5:4); the church in relation to widows (5:3, 16); younger-women in relation to Christ (5:11), to Satan (5:15), and to their own widows (5:16); Christian slaves to their non-Christian masters (6:1); and Christian slaves to their Christian masters, and vice versa (6:2). In sum, the full spectrum of Paul's audience in 1 Timothy supports the practice of first-century letters and New Testament documents as public performances for the intended purpose of persuading the entire audience, perhaps over multiple occasions.[35] As such, 1 Timothy is to be understood as a communal letter with the implied audience including Timothy and everyone in the Ephesian church.[36]

---

34. Towner, *Letters*, 10: ". . . Timothy is not the sole addressee of 1 Timothy but that much of what is conveyed to him is intended for the church in which he is being directed to minister. And on occasion the purpose of this letter could be seen to be that of authorizing Timothy as an apostolic delegate for work in a context where that authority might be challenged." Schreiner, *Interpreting the Pauline Epistles*, 12: "the letters were not merely private individual letters. Paul wrote them as an apostle of Jesus Christ, and he expected them to be read aloud and obeyed by the Christian community." Fee, *Listening to the Spirit in the Text*, 153: "The letter betrays evidences everywhere that it was intended for the church itself, not just Timothy."

35. Rhoads, "Translating for Oral Performance," 26–27: "The New Testament is a collection of Christian narratives and letters . . . that were primarily presented and received as oral performances, each probably presented in its entirety in a performance event . . . by a lector performing from a scroll to a gathered audience in a particular time and place"; the written letters mainly functioned "to enable performances to be repeated on new occasions and in other locations." Sampley, *Ruminations*, x: "after its initial reading-performance . . . it could be referred to and rehearsed in future deliberations within the community. So Pauline letters . . . represented a continuing Pauline presence."

36. Maxey, *From Orality to Orality*, 114: "Written manuscripts circulated and were communicated in community settings."

To be sure, the communal, public, and performative aspect of the letter would be implied, given that the majority of the audience would have been illiterate and, therefore,

Historical Setting of the Letter[37]

In the early to mid-fifties of the first century, Paul established the Ephesian church during one of his missionary journeys. Roughly ten to fifteen years later, in the mid-sixties Paul sent a letter to the same Ephesian church; this is the letter we now call "1 Timothy" and is the subject of this commentary.[38] Much of the historic background to the 1 Timothy letter is recorded in the Acts narrative by Luke, one of Paul's first-century missionary traveling companions, and by Paul himself in his other letters. Together, with the biblical witness in Acts, 1 Timothy provides a clear picture of the specific situation into which Paul was speaking nearly two thousand years ago to the first-century Ephesian church.

---

could gain access to Paul's letters only through oral performance. Rhoads, "Translating for Oral Performance," 27: "It is considered likely that more than 90 to 95 percent of the people in the Mediterranean world, including Israel in Palestine, were nonliterate." Nässelqvist, *Public Reading in Early Christianity*, 60: "Early Christian congregations encompassed a diversity of social levels and Christians with a reading ability were rarely fluent readers. In this aspect, early Christian communities differed markedly from contemporary elite circles, in which literary writings were read and discussed in groups of highly educated individuals." For more on the practice of reading ancient letters to an audience, see Iersel, *Mark*, 71; Shiner, *Proclaiming the Gospel*; Botha, "Verbal Art of the Pauline Letters," 409–28; Stirewalt, *Paul: The Letter Writer*, 13–18; Richards, *Paul and First-Century Letter Writing*, 202–4; Harvey, *Listening to the Text*, 35–56, esp 54; Johnson, *Contested Issues*, 365–66; Aageson, *Paul*, 9; White, "Saint Paul," 437.

It may be worth noting that the size of the community hearing the letter was likely substantial. Nässelqvist suggests that on a scale of four tiers (smallest = a; biggest = d), "public reading in early Christian gatherings probably belongs to b or c . . . b) reading aloud in a small, controlled context, namely in a semi-private setting . . . c) reading aloud in a limited, but less controlled context" (*Public Reading in Early Christianity*, 15).

37. Extant scholarship on the historical setting is massive. My purpose here is not to provide an integrative or exhaustive account of the historical setting surrounding the 1 Timothy letter or Paul's missionary journeys but rather a brief overview for understanding the relationship of Paul, Timothy, and the audience of the Ephesian church.

38. See Barcley, "Introduction to the PE," 352. Merkle, "Biblical Qualifications for Elders," 255: "The church at Ephesus was a somewhat well-established congregation when Paul wrote 1 Timothy. By that time, the church had been in existence for about fifteen years and already had established leaders." Belleville suggests that the church was ten years old ("1 Timothy," 69). Both suggestions are valid, given that Paul first visited Ephesus in the early to mid-fifties (Schnabel, "Paul the Missionary," 41) and 1 Timothy was composed in the mid-sixties (see Carson and Moo, *Introduction*, 572; Blomberg, *From Pentecost to Patmos*, 348; Knight, *PE*, 54).

It may also be worth noting that Paul's other letter to the Ephesian church, which we now call "Ephesians," is also dated to the early to mid-sixties (Carson and Moo, *Introduction*, 486–87). Given the absence of Paul's concern for the false teachers in "Ephesians," it seems likely that it was composed prior to "1 Timothy"; its contents, therefore, and the audience's awareness thereof would provide further historical context for the 1 Timothy letter (e.g., Eph 5:22–33 and 1 Tim 3:2; see volume 2, chapter 2).

Paul and Timothy

Paul is first introduced in the New Testament as a man who approved the death of a Christian named Stephen (Acts 8:1). Immediately following, Luke records that "there arose on that day a great persecution against the church in Jerusalem . . . Saul [Paul] was ravaging the church, and entering house after house, he dragged off men and women and committed them to prison" (8:1, 3 *ESV*). In Acts 9:1–2, Luke continues to recount Paul's history (*ESV*): "But Saul, still breathing threats and murder against the disciples of the Lord," actively sought authoritative permission from Jerusalem's high priest to travel north to the city of Damascus "so that if he found any belonging to the Way [Christians], men or women, he might bring them bound to Jerusalem."[39] In short, Paul is first described in the NT as fiercely determined to compromise, restrain, and effectively exterminate the teaching and lifestyle of a person named Jesus Christ.[40]

It is most unexpected, therefore, that while traveling to Damascus in the early to mid-thirties of the first century, Paul's life is transformed by Jesus Christ: ". . . suddenly shined-around him light from heaven, and falling upon the ground he heard a voice saying to him, 'Saul, Saul, why are you persecuting me? . . . I-myself am Jesus whom you are persecuting; rather, rise and enter into the city, and you will be told what is necessary for you to do'" (Acts 9:4, 6).[41] It is from this single event that the first-century, mid-sixties Ephesian church ever came to exist, as Jesus himself tells: "he [Paul] is to me a chosen vessel to bear my name in the sight of the Gentiles and kings and the sons of Israel. For I-myself will display to him how much it is necessary for him to suffer on behalf of my name" (Acts 9:15–16).[42] That

---

39. For the relevance of Paul's activity of "murder" (φόνου) in Acts 9:1 to his description in 1 Timothy of those "for whom the law is laid"—namely "murders" (ἀνδροφόνοις)—see chapter 3 regarding 1 Timothy 1:9.

40. About 150 miles from Jerusalem, Paul's resolve to walk to Damscus—an entire week's journey—for the sole purpose of arresting Christians further highlights his persistence to stop Christianity.

41. For the relevance of Jesus's statement, "you are persecuting" (διώκεις) me" in Acts 9:4, 6, see Paul's recollection of this event in 1 Timothy 1:13, where Paul refers to himself as "a persecutor" (διώκτην) prior to receiving grace and mercy specifically from Jesus. See chapter 3.

Also, in Acts 9:8, Paul is immediately unable to see after the "light" (φῶς) shown from heaven. That Paul may have this event and its subsequent result in view of 1 Timothy 1, see volume 3, chapter 3 regarding Paul's description of God in 6:16: ". . . without-approachable light (φῶς), which no human has seen nor has power to see."

42. For the relevance that Jesus "will display" (ὑποδείξω) in Acts 9:16, see chapter 3 regarding Paul's statement that "I was granted-mercy, that in me the first Christ Jesus might display (ἐνδείξεται) all patience as an example to those who

is, Paul the persecutor of Christ suddenly became "Paul, apostle of Christ Jesus" (1 Tim 1:1), "proclaimer and apostle . . . teacher of the Gentiles in faith and truth" (2:7).[43]

Nearly fifteen years after his encounter with Jesus, in the mid to late-forties Paul met Timothy on his second missionary journey in the Galatian province at the cities of Derbe and Lystra (Acts 16:1–3). While Timothy was the son of a Jewish Christian woman, his father was Greek, that is, non-Jewish.[44] Given that Timothy was well-testified by the Christians at the cities of Lystra and Iconium (v. 2), Paul recruited Timothy to accompany him on his missionary journeys (v. 3).[45] The rest of Acts and Paul's undisputed letters make it clear that Paul considered Timothy to be a trustworthy "fellow-worker of mine" (Rom 16:21).[46] Indeed, Timothy knew Paul's teaching and lifestyle comprehensively, so much in fact that Paul says to the troubled church at Corinth: "I am sending to you-all Timothy, who is a beloved and faithful child of mine in the Lord, who is to remind you-all of the ways of mine that are in Christ, just-as I teach everywhere in every church" (1 Cor 4:17).[47] In less tumultuous but equally demanding situations, Timothy was repeatedly commissioned to act as an emissary; to the church in Thessalonica, Paul says, "we sent Timothy, our brother and fellow-worker of God in the gospel of Christ, to establish and to exhort you-all on behalf of your faith" (1 Thess 3:2).[48] Furthermore, in addition to regularly being identified

---

would-inevitably-come to have-faith upon him for life eternal" (1 Tim 1:16).

43. So significant was Paul's encounter with Jesus and subsequent conversion that the event is recounted by Paul on two other occasions in Acts (22:6–16; 26:12–20). Given the lasting importance in his life, it seems likely that Paul alludes to this life-changing event in 1 Timothy 1:12–16; see chapter 3.

44. For a discussion regarding Timothy's mother and father, see Meiser, "Timothy in Acts," 326–27.

45. Acts 16:3 also indicates that Paul circumsized Timothy. Much has been written about Timothy's circumcision and whether or not he was Jewish; for further discussion, see ibid., 327–32.

46. Merkle, "Ecclesiology in the PE," 196: "Timothy was one of Paul's most faithful and trusted missionary companions." See ibid., n. 89.

47. For the relevance of Timothy as Paul's "child" (τέκνον) who is thoroughly acquainted and able to represent Paul "just as I teach (διδάσκω)" (1 Cor 4:17), see Paul's statements in 1 Timothy 1:2, 18 ("child"; τέκνῳ, 1:2; τέκνον, 1:18) and 4:6 ("being-nourished in the words of the faith and of the commendable teaching (διδασκαλίας) you have followed"), respectively.

48. For the relevance of Timothy's authority "to exhort" (παρακαλέσαι, 1 Thess 3:2) in relation to Timothy's authority in 1 Timothy, see chapter 3 (1 Tim 1:3), chapter 4 (1 Tim 2:1), and volume 3, chapter 2 (1 Timothy 6:2). Where Timothy is identified as a fellow-worker of God in "the gospel" (τῷ εὐαγγελίῳ, 1 Thess 3:2), the implication is that in 1 Timothy he was thoroughly familiar with "the sound teaching, according to

as a coauthor of Paul's letters (Phil 1:1; Col 1:1; 1 Thess 1:1; Phlm 1:1), Timothy was regularly praised by Paul; in his letter to the Philippian church, Paul says of Timothy: "For I have no-one like-souled, who regarding you-all will be genuinely concerned. For all those seek things of themselves, not things of Jesus Christ. But you-all know the esteem of him, because, as a son to a father, with me he has slaved for the gospel" (Phil 2:20–22).[49] Still, Paul cared for and protected Timothy; to the Corinthian church, Paul commands: "But if Timothy comes, see that he might be without-fear to you-all; for the work of the Lord he is working as I also; therefore, someone may not despise him. But you must help him in peace, that he might come to me; for I am waiting-for him with the brothers" (1 Cor 16:10–11).[50] Unsurprisingly, then, after nearly twenty years of collaborative missionary work together, in the 1 Timothy letter Paul maintains his high estimation of Timothy as a reliable representative (1:3, 18) and co-laborer (4:10) who is qualified to carry out Paul's *charge to preserve the teaching and promote godliness as God's missional household*, particularly in view of "some" who teach-different in the mid-sixties Ephesian church (1:3; 10; 6:3).[51]

The Church in Ephesus

In Acts 19, Luke describes Paul's missionary work in the early to mid-fifties that established the church in the city of Ephesus.[52] The narrative highlights

---

the gospel (τὸ εὐαγγέλιον)" (1:10–11). See chapter 3.

49. For relevance of "genuinely" (γνησίως) and "child" (τέκνον) in Phil 2:20–22, see Paul's statement in 1 Timothy 1:2: "To Timothy, genuine (γνησίῳ) child (τέκνον) in faith." Significantly, where Timothy has slaved with Paul in "the gospel" (τὸ εὐαγγέλιον, Phil 2:22), the clear implication in 1 Timothy is that Timothy was thoroughly familiar with "the sound teaching, according to the gospel (τὸ εὐαγγέλιον)" (1:10–11). See chapter 3.

50. It is also worth noting that 2 Timothy represents the capstone of Paul's high estimation of Timothy.

51. Paul met Timothy in the mid to late forties; the 1 Timothy letter was composed in the mid-sixties. Similarly, MacArthur, *1 Timothy*, 6: "By the time 1 Timothy was written, he had been with Paul for about fifteen years as the apostle's constant companion." Witherington aptly observes: "We have seen, then, that Timothy had previous connections with Ephesus, and certainly Paul had assigned him difficult tasks before. Thus it is not at all improbable that Paul would call on Timothy to deal with the trouble in Ephesus, as he had been called upon to do in Thessalonike and Corinth earlier" (*Letters*, 185).

52. The city of Ephesus began as a seaport but became a rich and pluralistic city. For a description of first-century Ephesus, see Trebilco, *Early Christians in Ephesus*, 11–18. For a summary of the ancient history and setting of Ephesus, see O'Connor, *St. Paul's Ephesus*, 7–35.

Paul's sustained determination to share the Christian message to all: to the Jews in Ephesus, "he entered into the synagogue openly for three months discussing and persuading regarding the kingdom of God" (Acts 19:8); to the Gentiles in Ephesus, Paul went to a public philosophical lecture arena, "discussing daily in the hall of Tyrannus. This was happening for two years" (Acts 19:8–9). Notably, the intensity and resolve that Paul had used to persecute the church in the thirties (Acts 8:1–3; 9:1–2) was now used to advance it in the fifties. As a result of Paul's daily work for several years in Ephesus, "all the householders in Asia heard the word of the Lord, Jews and Greeks" (Acts 19:10).[53] Soon thereafter, the church in Ephesus was established: "the name of the Lord Jesus was magnified" (Acts 19:17), there were "many of those now-having-faith" (19:18), and "according to the strength of the Lord, the word increased and was mighty" (19:20).[54]

Timothy himself was present in Ephesus during the establishment of the church (Acts 19:22).[55] However, after sending Timothy west across the Aegean Sea to the province of Macedonia, Paul was soon met with opposition by the Ephesian society. Demetrius, "a silversmith who made temple silver" for the worship of the goddess Artemis (Acts 19:24), stirred the craftsmen in Ephesus against Paul; Demetrius claimed that the numerous conversions to Christianity were disrupting the source of their wealth—"from this work is our abundant-prosperity" (Acts 19:25).[56] Moreover, in response to

---

53. "Asia" refers to the Asia Minor province wherein Ephesus was located, immediately west of the Galatian province. For the relevance of "the word of the Lord" (τὸν λόγον τοῦ κυρίου, Acts 19:10), see volume 3, chapter 3 regarding 1 Timothy 6:3: "If someone does not come-toward the sound words (λόγοις) of our Lord (κυρίου) Jesus Christ."

54. For the combined relevance of "strength" (κράτος) and "Lord" (κυρίου) in Acts 19:20, see volume 3, chapter 3 regarding 1 Timothy 6:15b–16: ". . . Lord (κύριος) of those who-are-lords . . . to him honor and eternal strength (κράτος), amen."

55. Witherington, *Letters*, 183: "What we can say with more certainty is that Timothy is in Ephesus during Paul's rather lengthy stay there during his so-called missionary journey in the mid-50s."

56. The topic of wealth in relation to the false teachers in 1 Timothy is explicit. Given this historical situation in Ephesus, therefore, it is worth noting the contextual significance of Paul's word choice in 1 Timothy. Where the riot in Ephesus was caused by those who were concerned with money and clearly did not worship God—namely, a "silversmith" (ἀργυροκόπος) who made temple "silver" (ἀργυροῦς)" for the worship of Artemis (Acts 19:24)—Paul's repeated use of these several terms would likely be highly meaningful and connotative for Paul's Ephesian audience. In 1 Timothy 3:3, Paul states that it is necessary for a qualified overseer to be "without-affection-of-money" (ἀφιλάργυρον, 3:3)—literally, "without-affection-of-silver." Furthermore, Paul defines the false teachers by their "affection-of-money" (ἀφιλάργυρον, 6:10)—literally, "affection-of-silver." In this way, the historical context in Acts 19 combined with Paul's word choice in 1 Timothy would have a specific polemical implication against the false

Demetrius's instigations that Paul was dishonoring the worship of "the great goddess Artemis" (19:27), the craftsmen attacked Paul's companions and rioted for two hours while crying out, "Great is Artemis of the Ephesians" (Acts 19:34).[57] Although the town clerk succeeded in calming and dispelling the crowd, Paul's memory of his experience at Ephesus remained strong.

Paul clearly indicates in 1 Timothy that the church within the historic city of Ephesus is both the intended destination of the letter and the place where Timothy is called to action: "I exhorted you to remain in Ephesus . . . that you might charge some not to teach-different" (1:3). In other words, the 1 Timothy letter is not an abstraction but is addressed to real people in a real setting.

The Problem in the Ephesian Church

Heard within the text of the 1 Timothy letter itself and corroborated by the text of Acts, the historical situation of the first-century Ephesian church can be described as a definitive circumstance, namely one that prompted Paul to both exhort Timothy to remain in Ephesus (1:3) and then to send a letter regarding his own plans to personally come to Timothy in Ephesus (3:15; 4:13). Here, Fee's observation is astute: "The key to its [1 Timothy] purpose . . . is to take with full seriousness three pieces of data: Paul's own statements of purpose in 1 Tim 1:3 and 3:15 and the content of Paul's farewell address as given by Luke in Acts 20:17–35, especially 20:30."[58] Timothy is exhorted to remain Ephesus for the explicit purpose that he might "charge some not to teach-different" (1:3), and Paul sends the 1 Timothy letter for the explicit purpose of defining "how it is necessary to behave in the household of God, which is the church of the living God" (3:15). In other words, it is evident that the presence of "some" who teach-different in the Ephesian church and their ungodly influence therein prompted the composition and delivery

---

teachers, namely to underscore that, like Demetrius, the false teachers are motivated by wealth, not by Christ. See volume 2, chapter 2 (1 Tim 3:3) and esp. volume 3, chapter 3 (1 Tim 6:5, 9, 10, 17).

57. For the relevance of "great" (μεγάλης) in the context of worship in Acts 19:27, see chapters 5 regarding 1 Timothy 3:16, wherein "great" (μέγα) is applied to the church's confession of Christ. Hooker, "Artemis of Ephesus," 43: "her [Artemis's] cult was the source of the city's wealth. Paul's gospel was inevitably regarded as an attack on the goddess, but since it was her worship that attracted the crowds to the city, it would have been seen also as a threat to the livelihood of the inhabitants." For more on the identity and long-standing influence of Artemis on the Ephesian community, see Glahn, "Identity of Artemis," 316–34; Brinks, "'Great is Artemis,'" 776–94; Trebilco, *Early Christians in Ephesus*, 19–29; Glahn, "First-Century Ephesian Artemis," 450–69.

58. Fee, *Listening to the Spirit in the Text*, 149.

of the 1 Timothy letter to the first-century church in Ephesus. Still, more specifically, roughly ten years prior to the 1 Timothy letter, Paul's final words to the Ephesian overseers before he left the Ephesian church in the early to mid-fifties both identify and corroborate the historic situation regarding "some" who were teaching-different (1:3, 10; 6:3) in the mid-sixties Ephesian church. In Acts 20, Paul calls together the "elders" (πρεσβυτέρους) of the church in Ephesus (20:17) to whom he specifically addresses at length:[59]

> 20:28 Hold-toward yourselves and all the flock, in which the Holy Spirit has appointed you-all overseers (ἐπισκόπους) to care-for the church of God, which he made-about through his own blood. [29] I know that with my departure fierce wolves will come into you-all, not sparing the flock, [30] and from you-all yourselves will arise men saying twisted-things pulling-away the disciples after themselves.

Paul is speaking directly to the Ephesian "elders" (πρεσβυτέρους, 20:17) whom he synonymously calls "you-all overseers (ἐπισκόπους)" (20:28). Moreover, he asserts that fierce wolves will come specifically into this group of overseers ("you-all," 20:29) and that from this group of overseers ("from you-all yourselves," 20:30) will arise men saying twisted-thing and pulling-away the disciples after "themselves" (20:30). This is precisely the historic situation that Paul describes roughly ten years later in the 1 Timothy letter.[60] This is why Paul is concerned with "someone" who aspires to the work of an "overseer" (ἐπισκοπῆς, 3:1) and, therefore, explicitly states the necessary qualifications for "the overseer" (τὸν ἐπίσκοπον, 3:2);[61] indeed, this is why Paul is specifically concerned that "elders" (πρεσβύτεροι) who toil in the teaching—teaching elders, that is, overseers—must be those who lead commendably in the church (5:17; cf. 3:5). In sum, the historical situation in Ephesus involved men who were overseers in the Ephesian church, who were saying twisted-things and pulling-away the disciples after themselves;

---

59. The following is my English translation according to the methodology outlined in chapter 2. The words accompanied by the Greek text in parentheses are relevant to our immediate discussion of 1 Timothy.

60. Fee aptly states that "in Ephesus as seen in 1 Timothy, there is not a hint that the false teachers came from the outside. To the contrary, not only do they appear to be insiders, but the whole letter makes sense if the prophecy spoken to the elders-overseers of this church recorded in Acts 20:30 had actually been realized . . . If one takes this seriously, then the difficulty—and urgency—of the situation in Ephesus comes into clear focus. The problem is that *the church is being led astray by some of its own elders*" (*1 & 2 Timothy*, 7–8).

61. That Paul was addressing a situation in which "someone" was already leading as an overseer, see discussion in volume 2, chapter 2 regarding 1 Timothy 3:1.

they were certainly influencing the men and women in the Ephesian church and thus not sparing the flock (Acts 20:29–30).[62]

Altogether, the prompting for Paul to send the 1 Timothy letter was the presence and persuasion of "some" men who were overseers within the mid-sixties Ephesian church, who became overseers at a certain point after Paul's departure in the mid-fifties, and who were teaching something different than Paul. Such is the historic situation by which the 1 Timothy letter is to be understood by a modern audience in the twenty-first century.[63]

The relative maturity of the Ephesian church, which was at least ten years old at the time of the 1 Timothy letter, calls into question how the unqualified men—"some"—were allowed to be overseers in the first place. Moreover, the precise nature of their different teaching is not clearly defined in the letter; various statements throughout 1 Timothy, however, paint an overall picture. In 1 Timothy 1, Paul suggests that "some" who teach-different have a preoccupation with "myths and genealogies without-limit" (1:4) and are marked by a misunderstanding of the law (1:7); plainly, what is evident is that these false teachers had deviated from "the sound teaching," namely that which Paul indicates is synonymous with "the gospel" (1:10–11). In 1 Timothy 2, the false teachers appear to have influenced the women in the church to reject "what is proper for women who profess godliness"

---

62. It is worth noting several other of Paul's words to the Ephesian overseers in Acts 20 that may have resonated with them while hearing the 1 Timothy letter. Where the false-teaching overseers whom Paul predicts are described as "pulling-away the disciples after (ὀπίσω) themselves" (Acts 20:30), it seems relevant—and extremely polemical—for Paul to describe the influence of the false teachers upon the women in Ephesus who "have already turned-aside after (ὀπίσω) Satan (5:15), that is, are following the false teachers. See volume 3, chapter 2.

Moreover, Paul's use of the plural pronoun "you-all" (ὑμᾶς) in Acts 20:28–30 may be relevant to Paul's final words to the Ephesian church in view of the false teachers: "Grace with you-all (ὑμῶν, 1 Tim 6:21)." See volume 3, chapter 3.

Also, given Paul's specification in Acts that "men" (ἄνδρες)—not women—would arise as false teachers from among the male overseers in Ephesus (20:30), Paul's specification in 1 Timothy that a qualified overseer is a "man" (ἄνδρα) of one woman (3:2) seems to be a remedial address toward the false-teaching men. See volume 2, chapter 2.

Still, Paul's specification of the involvement of "the . . . Spirit (τὸ πνεῦμα)" in the appointment of the original overseers in Acts 20:28 may be relevant to Paul's discussion in 1 Timothy 4 regarding "the Spirit" (τὸ πνεῦμα, 4:1) and Timothy's divine appointment to lead the church in 4:14. See volume 2, chapter 3.

63. See discussion in Barcley, "1 Timothy," 359. Paul's rhetorical allusions that the false teachers in Ephesus are overseers in the church are particularly evident in 3:1–7 and 5:17–20, but become especially apparent by 6:9–10.

A similar picture of Ephesus is given in Revelation 2:1–7, particularly verse 2:2 (*ESV*): "I know your works, your toil and your patient endurance, and how you cannot bear with those who are evil, but have tested those who call themselves apostles and are not, and found them to be false."

(2:10). In 1 Timothy 3, Paul's outline of the qualifications of overseers and deacons suggests that the false teachers may have tried to implement different criteria for selecting leaders and—more significantly—that they did not meet the real qualifications required to lead the church. In 1 Timothy 4, Paul indicates that the false teachers advocated ascetic practices, forbidding marriage and certain foods (4:3). Throughout 1 Timothy 5, the ungodly lifestyle of the younger widows reiterates the false teachers's impact upon the women in 1 Timothy 2.[64] Finally, in the last chapter of the letter, 1 Timothy 6, Paul consistently highlights how the false teachers viewed "godliness to be a means-of-gain" (6:5); in short, the content of their different teaching was motivitated by "the affection-of-money" (6:10) rather than by an affection for Christ and the church. Beyond these comments, it is difficult—if not impossible—to state with certainty the precise content of the false teaching other than that it was markedly "different" (1:3, 10: 6:3) from "the teaching" of the church that the apostle Paul had proclaimed and established roughly ten years prior (1:10; 4:6, 13, 16; 6:1, 3). It is worth noting that the apostle Paul seemed more concerned with providing his (negative) assessment of the "false-named knowledge" (6:20) rather than outlining and responding to its content. What is clear, however, is that Paul (positively) assesses the final, disastrous result of the false teaching: "some—professing [false-named knowledge]—regarding the faith have swerved" (6:21).

Approach to 1 Timothy: Text-Centered, Literary-Rhetorical, and Audience-Oriented

Various scholars have argued that 1 Timothy is a composite letter, possessing little—if any—literary unity and integrity.[65] Recent studies, however, have challenged this position.[66] Following this latter trend, I treat 1 Timothy as a single, unified letter. Indeed, the chiastic structures that I propose for the letter (see chapter 2) strengthen the position for literary integrity, unity,

---

64. See esp. volume 3, chapter 2 regarding 1 Timothy 5:3–16.

65. See Miller, *Pastoral Letters as Composite Documents*; Guthrie, *PE*; Hanson, *PE*; Easton, *PE*.

66. Marshall, "Christology of Luke-Acts and the PE," 171: "There is a growing body of evidence that the Pastoral Epistles are not a conglomerate of miscellaneous ideas roughly thrown together with no clear plan, purpose, or structure. On the contrary, they demonstrate signs of coherent structure and of theological competence." See Donelson, "The Structure of Ethical Argument in the Pastorals," 108; Jeon, *To Exhort and Reprove*, 6–7; Towner, "Pauline Theology or Pauline Tradition," 288; Van Neste, *Cohesion and Structure*, 234–82.

and an integrated rhetorical strategy.⁶⁷ The 1 Timothy letter, then, is to be understood as single and coherent document written to be performed in a communal setting (most likely in a liturgical assembly) as a substitute for Paul's actual presence.⁶⁸

Throughout this commentary, the 1 Timothy letter will be analyzed according to a text-centered, literary-rhetorical, and audience-oriented method.⁶⁹ "Text-centered" means paying attention to what is actually contained and expressed in the language of the text versus speculations concerning what the author intended to say or include. "Literary-rhetorical" means that 1 Timothy falls under the literary genre of a "letter" with the rhetorical purpose of persuading the implied audience to the perspective of Paul, who is the author indicated in the text.⁷⁰ "Audience-oriented" indicates an interpretive approach that seeks to determine how the implied audience members are required to respond to Paul's instructions and exhortations as they are strategically revealed and audibly heard throughout the progression of the letter.⁷¹

---

67. Horsley aptly describes the integrated rhetorical purpose of the NT letters, which is most applicable to my analysis of 1 Timothy: "Biblical studies based in print culture has usually focused on text-fragments 'cut out' of longer texts. To interpret texts-in-performance it is first necessary to discern the contours of whole texts. The text-in-performance as communication, moreover, were interactive with groups of hearers in their respective contexts. To take a particular 'paragraph' out of the longer argument in 1 Corinthians 1–4, for example, will almost certainly miss how in one 'paragraph' (step in the argument) Paul is 'setting up' (some of) the hearers for his disagreement or disapproval in a subsequent 'paragraph.' Sensitivity to the oral performance of the argument can lead to hearing the 'tone of voice' that might be sarcastic in one step and authoritarian in another" (*Text and Tradition*, 20–21).

68. Ward, "Pauline Voice and Presence, 95–96: "Oral performance . . . is a way in which the author-in-the-work becomes an audible presence by means of the speech and movement of the presenter." See Holland, "Delivery, Delivery, Delivery," 136; Strange, "'His letters are weighty,'" 115.

69. Similarly, Horsley, *Text and Tradition*, 20: "Of greatest importance for understanding texts in oral performance is giving careful attention to three key interrelated facets of a text-in-performance. In order to hear and interpret New Testament texts, it is necessary to discern the contours of the *text*, to determine the historical *context* of the community of the responsive/interactive hearers, and to know as much as possible the cultural *tradition* out of which the voiced texts resonate with the hearers."

70. With regard to the literary genre of 1 Timothy, a few commentators—comparing it to Titus—have proposed that it is akin to a "church order letter" (e.g., Dibelius and Conzelmann, *PE*, 5–7; see Vegge, "Deuteropauline Epistles," 537 n. 148). While church order is a key theme, this designation fails to capture the overarching theme and tone of the letter, which I have summarized as "A Charge to Preserve the Teaching and Promote Godliness as God's Missional Household"; see above.

71. For more on the audience-oriented method in recent biblical studies, see Heil, *The Gospel of John*; Heil, *1–3 John*; Heil, *The Book of Revelation*; Heil, *Worship in the*

The Composition and Performance of the Letter

Specific to the text-centered, literary-rhetorical, and audience-oriented methodology of this study, recent scholarship has uncovered key insight into the function of the NT letters for a first-century Christian audience.[72] Particularly, the performance aspect of the text itself was essential for communicating the meaning therein.[73] The letters of Paul were "composed mentally and orally and then dictated to a scribe" with the intended purpose of being heard by the audience.[74] Once written, the letter was given to a letter carrier who, likely being present during the dictation of the letter, was trained by the author to perform—verbatim—the author's original dication to the intended audience.[75] The purpose of the actual written letter, then, was to aid the letter carrier as he performed a replica dication of what the author

---

Letter to the Hebrews.

72. Porter and Adams, "Pauline Epistolography," 2–3: "One of the main approaches in recent scholarship to understanding the form and purpose of the Pauline letter—and one that vies for preeminence in analyzing his letters—is the utilization of ancient rhetorical practice and categories . . . It is the perspective of these scholars that Paul had access to and used rhetorical methodology to shape his letters in order to have the greatest impact on his recipients."

73. Horsley, *Text and Tradition*, 18: "Increased recent attention to the dominance of oral communication in antiquity leads to the consideration of New Testament texts as *communication* in the course and context of their composition and cultivation."

74. Rhoads, "Translating for Oral Performance," 27. Rhoads and Dewey, "Performance Criticism," 16: "Oral dictation was the primary means to get something transcribed into writing." Thompson, *Preaching Like Paul*, 28: "[Paul,] *like other writers of antiquity, dictated his letters to an amanuensis* [scribe]. Therefore, the letters were the results of an oral event, and Paul's communication was meant for the ear, not the eye." Barcley, "Introduction to the PE," 352: "We know that Paul used a scribe when he wrote his letters (cf. Rom. 16:22)." Dewey, *Oral Ethos*, 16: "Paul himself was literate . . . however, we may overestimate the degree of Paul's literacy and his reliance on writing. Like other literates, he often dictated rather than wrote himself." See Harvey, *Listening to the Text*, 54.

75. Sampley, "Ruminations," ix–x: "we may readily suppose that this person, with insider cachet, would not only read the letter in its entirety to the assembly of believers in the appointed town but would also be there to lend authoritative interpretation."

Not just anyone could perform the letter to the audience. Nässelqvist, *Public Reading in Early Christianity*, 26: "Few people—even among trained lectors—were able to read a text aloud impromptu, without extensive preparation." Witherington with Hyatt, *Paul's Letter to the Romans*, 23: "It must be kept steadily in view that Paul's letter was meant to be read aloud, indeed meant to be orally delivered by a Pauline co-worker, not merely handed over to a congregation." Timothy would not have been the first to perform the letter for the Ephesian audience; yet, perhaps due to his close relationship with Paul, he likely would have been capable of repeating the performance for the Ephesian audience in a similar manner that Paul intended. See Kuruvilla, *Text to Praxis*, 23; Botha, "Verbal Art of the Pauline Letters," 417.

himself had dictated to the scribe.[76] By this procedure, not only would the content of the letter be communicated, but also the author's gestures, facial expressions, demeanor, and tone of voice would be performed to the audience exactly as the author had intended.[77] The performative function of 1 Timothy was meant to be a total experience of the presence of the author.[78]

For this reason, a text-centered, literary-rhetorical, and audience-oriented examination of 1 Timothy benefits a modern audience by not only "listening" to the letter's performance but also by considering how the performance of the letter's content was an exactment of the apostle Paul's own speech and performance directly to his audience in their first-century context.[79] Approaching the text of 1 Timothy in this way, a modern audience

---

76. Rhoads, "Translating for Oral Performance," 27: "The scrolls served mainly to assist a performer's memory." Rhoads and Dewey, "Performance Criticism," 15, 16: "Here, what was important was not that Paul *wrote* a letter but that the performer of the letter conveyed what Paul was *saying* in his letter . . . when writing occurred, it mostly served the needs of performance of prepared readings or oral performances from memory . . . For all intent and purpose, one needed to have studied the content and known it virtually by memory in order to enact a public reading with facility and in such a way as to make the content lively and meaningful."

The poor condition and nearly unreadable appearance of the letter would certainly have been a determining factor in the need for memorization over and above reading; see Nässelqvist, *Public Reading in Early Christianity*, 18–62; Dart, *Decoding Mark*, 50; Iersel, *Mark*, 71.

77. Thompson, *Preaching Like Paul*, 30–31: "The role of the letter carrier or public reader was decisive for the communication of the Pauline letter . . . in order that the emissary might present his intentions and symbols verbally and bodily to others." Rhoads, "Translating for Oral Performance," 27: "Everything we know about storytellers and orators in the ancient world suggests that storytelling and public reading alike would have been animated, emotional, and engaging . . . In fact, they likely visualized their whole embodied performance—gestures, movements, and facial expressions—as they composed ahead of actually performing." See Rhoads, "Performance Events in Early Christianity," 180.

78. Ward, "Pauline Voice and Presence," 105: "The performer of Paul's letter became an icon for the apostolic presence of Paul." See ibid., 103–4.

79. Horsley, *Text and Tradition*, 20: "Adequate appreciation and interpretation would require not just a sense of the rhetorical tone and rhythm of the respective speech, but a sense of the hearers' life circumstances and their historical situation and cultural tradition in which they hear and respond to the speeches." Thompson, *Preaching Like Paul*, 28: "As he dictated his letters, he undoubtedly envisioned the community of listeners before him. Like preachers who prepare their sermons as they envision concrete situations and personalities, Paul prepared his letters with specific listeners and situations in mind. The process of dicatation allowed Paul to speak to the gathered community at a distance. One may assume that the arrangement of his thoughts approximated his normal mode of presentation." Sampley, "Ruminations," ix–x: "Because Paul (and his scribe[s]) knew at their destination, the letters were to be read aloud, that is, performed, it is a necessity for us to treat them as letters *and as* speeches, because they were both from their beginning, and intentionally so."

can get closer to the authoritative presence of Paul in the preserved manuscripts that we have today.[80] The remainder of this commentary will focus on Paul's rhetorical and structuring use of *chiasm* as the essential tool for hearing and experiencing both the performative message of Paul in the 1 Timothy letter and his authoritative, apostolic presence from nearly two thousand years ago.[81]

---

80. Thompson, *Preaching Like Paul*, 28–29: "In the epistles of Paul, we come close to the actual voice of Paul as he addresses his communities . . . Paul clearly communicates his power through his letters, which function as the surrogates for his personal presence. The letter, therefore, partakes of his apostolic authority"; such authority "provided the occasion for *hearing*" (ibid., 35). Rhoads, "Performance Events in Early Christianity," 180: "In a sense, the letter bore the 'apostolic presence.' However, it is not the letter on a handwritten scroll that people experienced, but the embodied letter—the performer being Paul in the official act of presenting the letter. So it was the *letter-performer* who bore the apostolic presence." See Ito, "Paul the 'Herald,'" 351–70.

81. Mournet, *Oral Tradition and Literary Dependency*, 129: "Performance is at the very center of oral cultures . . . oral performance is often related to the production of written texts. This provides us with additional evidence that the processes of oral communication had a profound impact on both the content and structure of ancient texts."

2

The Chiastic Structures of 1 Timothy

Chiasm in 1 Timothy[1]

A CHIASM IS A PARALLEL structure in language that intentionally leads the audience through introductory themes toward a central point (or points); at the central point, the chiasm pivots and moves the audience's attention toward a cumulative conclusion that recalls and develops aspects of the introductory themes. In this way, the structure of a chiasm in language is organized by an introductory element, a pivot, and a concluding element; the introductory and concluding elements parallel each other and frame the language as a coherent unit that gravitates around the pivot point. The following provides a visual representation of a standard chiastic arrangement in language:

    A. *Introductory Theme*

        B. *Introductory Theme*

            C. *Pivot Point*

        B'. *Concluding Theme*

    A'. *Concluding Theme*

Such chiastic structures not only provide organization to the language of a text and the performance thereof but also—and perhaps more—foster aural comprehension and convey rhetorical meaning.[2] In the case of ancient

---

1. The first section of this chapter follows in large part the work of Heil (e.g., *Philippians*, 10–13; *Colossians*, 13–37; *Letter of James*, 6–28).

2. Dart, *Decoding Mark*, 45: "Some chiastic schemas stretch over many chapters. Whole books of the Bible, in some instances, are said to be written in chiastic patterns."

This commentary frequently employs the terms "rhetoric" and "rhetorical" in reference to Paul's deliberate and strategic use of the Greek language to convey meaning and to persuade his audience.

letters, which were performed aloud and in front of an intended audience, the chiastic patterns were pertinent for a letter's verbal recitation by the performer *and* for comprehension by the audience: chiasms functioned as mnemonic devices to help the performer communicate the letter in a memorable way, and then enabled the audience to follow, interpret, and recall the content of the performance, thus the content of the text and meaning of the letter itself.[3] Because linguistic chiasms were fairly common in ancient oral-auricular and rhetorical cultures such as Paul's first-century Greco-Roman audience in the Ephesian church, the original audience may not have been as intentional about noting and pondering over chiasms in the 1 Timothy letter to the same degree as this present study.[4] Rather, due to familiarity, the first-century audience of 1 Timothy would likely experience these chiastic patterns with a subtle but intentional impact on the way they heard and responded to the letter's content and performance.[5] For this reason, the identification, delineation, and articulation of such chiastic structures in ancient documents like the 1 Timothy letter are necessary aids for modern interpreters of the text who are unaccustomed to and unaware of such literary and performative devices.[6] In short, my analysis of 1

---

3. Rhoads and Dewey, "Performance Criticism," 15: "Compositions were structured and styled to facilitate the memory of the performer and the audience." Iersel, *Mark*, 71: "It is . . . probable that the concentric structures [chiasms] found in much ancient literature were originally a structuring and mnemonic device, which had the function of helping reciters structure the text for their listeners." Shively, *Apocalyptic Imagination*, 50: "this concentric structure [chiasm] is also a device of the implied author to aid the process of interpretation."

4. Chiasms in the Greco-Roman world were prevalent. Kuruvilla, *Mark*, 3 n. 19: students learned the Greek alphabet "in chiastic pairs beginning with the first and last letters (Α–Ω), the second and penultimate letters (Β–Ψ), the third and prepenultimate letters (Γ–Χ), and so on." See Thomson, *Chiasmus in the Pauline Letters*, 22–24; Brouwer, *Literary Development of John 13–17*, 23–27; White, "Apostolic Mission and Apostolic Message," 157; Herrick, *History and Theory of Rhetoric*, 40; Vena, *Jesus, Disciple of the Kingdom*, 55.

Chiasms were not only a Greco-Roman rhetorical strategy. Paul's use of chiasms would also have been an application of OT Jewish literary patterns; see Bailey, *Paul Through Mediterranean Eyes*, 22. Paul's letters, then, would have appealed broadly to both Greco-Roman and Jewish audience members.

Against the view that chiasms were common in ancient letters, see Smit, *Paradigms*, 160.

5. See Dewey, "Mark as Aural Narrative," 50–52; Hearon, "Implications," 4–17; Gray, *Opening Paul's Letters*, 51–52.

6. Iersel, *Mark*, 71–72: "the efficiency of such a structuring device [chiasm] is proportionate to the recognizability of the concentric structures concerned . . . This is, of course, even more true of present-day readers who are not used to this phenomenon and whose ability to appropriate a text aurally has decreased and in some respects even disappeared."

Timothy and the oral delivery thereof as a deliberately structured chiasm allows a modern audience to hear and experience the rhetorical method by which Paul communicated to his first-century Ephesian audience nearly two thousand years ago.[7]

In order to be credible, any proposal of an extended chiastic structure within an ancient document must be based on a meticulous and exacting methodology.[8] The methodology must demonstrate that the chiasm exists and operates objectively within the language of the text. My investigation of chiasm in the 1 Timothy letter follows seven criteria:[9]

1. There must be problems in recognizing the structure of the text in consideration, which traditional outlines have not been able to resolve.

2. There must be indications of parallelism and pendulum movements in the text that commentaries and specialized studies have already observed.

On the interpretive significance of chiastic structures, see Breck, "Biblical Chiasmus," 70–74; Breck, "Chiasmus as a Key to Biblical Interpretation," 251–67; Breck, *Scripture in Tradition*, 89–104, esp. 103–4; Longenecker, *Rhetoric at the Boundaries*, 16–17, 22–23. Man, "The Value of Chiasm for New Testament Interpretation," 146–57; Stock, "Chiastic Awareness and Education in Antiquity," 23–27; Assis, "Chiasmus in Biblical Narrative"; Engel, *Chiastic Design*, 2; Davidson, *Toward a Theology of Beauty*, 37, 79; Deppe, *All Roads Lead to the Text*, 25, 27. For a critique of chiastic interpretations in biblical studies, see deSilva, "X Marks the Spot?," 343–71; Long, "Roman Imperial Rule," 119, esp. n. 29.

7. Rhoads, "Performance Events in Early Christianity," 183: "Of course we cannot recover any of these myriad live performances among early Christians. Nevertheless, we have the 'scripts' to analyze. In this regard, the contents of the New Testament scrolls contain 'stage directions' for performers. There are . . . clues in the texts that help us to infer . . . some features of performances. One is *oral arts* of communication embedded in the texts that convey various storytelling patterns and memorable language and sound effects and rhetorical sequences, all of which give us some clues as to the style of the performance. Many of these same features served to facilitate memory on the part of the performer as well as the audience." Harvey, *Listening to the Text*, 56: "Oral composition was the rule, not the exception . . . an investigation of oral patterning must focus on 'acoustic resonances' *heard* by the original audience rather than on conceptual parallels found by silently rereading the texts." My analysis of 1 Timothy examines *chiasm* as both the main "script" of the letter and the "'acoustic resonances' *heard* by the original audience."

8. See Heil, "Chiastic Structure," 179, esp. n. 4.

9. See also Deppe, *Theological Intentions*, 97–98; Blomberg, "The Structure of 2 Corinthians 1–7," 4–8; Jeremias, "Chiasms in den Paulusbriefen," 145–56; Welch, "Chiasmus in the New Testament," 211–49; Welch, "Criteria for Identifying and Evaluating the Presence of Chiasmus," 157–74; Thomson, *Chiasmus in the Pauline Letters*, 13–45; Siew, *War Between*, 49–53.

3. Chiasms must be demonstrated to exist in the received text and do not require unsupported and excessive textual emendations for substantiation.

4. Precise verbal parallelism—supported by conceptual and syntactical parallels—should link the corresponding pairs in the chiasm.

5. Such verbal parallelism should involve significant terminology versus peripheral language and should be unique to the parallel units.

6. The pivot, that is, the center of the chiasm, should function as the turning point in the linguistic arrangement.

7. A corollary to the fourth and sixth observations is that chiasms must always be "framed," that is, parallel units must gravitate around the pivot.

The key feature of this study on 1 Timothy is that all chiasms in the letter are based on precise linguistic parallels in the original Greek text, which include cognates, synonyms, antonyms, alliterative terms, and, on occasion, identical grammatical forms of a word. In cases where linguistic parallels involve seemingly ordinary words to a modern audience, it will be demonstrated that such parallel words were significant to the rhetorical strategy of the author and to the situation of the original audience.[10] In short, the chiastic structures of the 1 Timothy letter will be made apparent by noting parallel words of the text, which function to identify the corresponding linguistic pairs of any given chiasm in the letter.

Furthermore, the linguistic parallels that organize the entirety of 1 Timothy into a chiastic structure also function to organize the letter into discernible sections of language, which in this study are called chiastic *units* or *elements*.[11] Thus the entirety of 1 Timothy is arranged by parallel sections of language, which are denoted in this study by corresponding pairs of alphabetic letters, for example: *A* is parallel to *A'*, *B* is parallel to *B'*, *C* is parallel *C'*.

Since the proposed chiasms in this study are based on linguistic parallels, the overall length and amount of language within any of the parallel units or elements may or may not be the same; for example, the introductory element of a chiasm (A) may be longer or shorter than its corresponding, parallel concluding element (A'). While this may seem unusual to a contemporary audience, Paul's first-century Ephesian audience would have

---

10. See e.g., volume 3, chapter 3 regarding the significance of "with" (μεθ') in 1 Timothy 6:21 in relation to "with" (μετά) in 6:6.

11. The distinction in terminology between *units* and *elements* is discussed in the next section below.

been attuned to the key linguistic parallels that organize sections of language—announced and perhaps emphasized by the performer of 1 Timothy—rather than to a balance in the length of the parallel sections. The main presupposition of this study is that a chiasm is operative—irrespective of a balance in length—wherever linguistic parallels and a pivotal section between them are evident.

Because this study of 1 Timothy concerns the specific language dictated in the letter, each of the proposed chiasms might not have the same number of parallel units or elements. For example (see *italics*), some chiasms in the letter are arranged with a single, central pivot element, A-B-*C*-B'-A', while others are arranged by dual, parallel pivotal elements, A-B-*C-C'*-B'-A'. Both arrangements operate as chiasms since they involve a movement from the introductory elements, to the pivot, and then to the concluding parallel elements. Given this rhetorical movement, and because chiasms are not merely circular or repetitive arguments, it is fitting to hear the central element or elements not only as the pivot of the chiasm but also as a hinging movement from the introducty A element toward a rhetorical climax in the final, concluding A' element. Such is the rhetorical function of the chiasm and thus the way that Paul's audience would have heard the performance of the 1 Timothy letter. Furthermore, listening for the climactic effect of the chiasm reinforces its rhetorical nature as a dynamic literary pattern that progresses and develops the meaning and impact of the linguistic parallels.

Terminology and Types of Chiasms in 1 Timothy

Throughout the 1 Timothy letter, three types of chiasms are operative. Listed in descending order from the most broad-reaching in scope to the narrowest in scope, they are: *macro*chiasm, *micro*chiasm, and *mini*chiasm.

Macrochiasm

The *macrochiasm* encompasses the arrangement of the entire 1 Timothy letter. It is composed carefully of six parallel *units*: A-B-C-C'-B'-A'. Each of the six *units* within the overall macrochiasm is synonymously known as a *microchiasm*. The following provides a visual representation of the macrochiastic units—the six microchiasms—of the 1 Timothy letter:

A unit: first microchiasm

B unit: second microchiasm

C unit: third microchiasm

C' unit: fourth microchiasm

B' unit: fifth microchiasm

A' unit: sixth microchiasm

As seen here, the macrochiasm is arranged and comprised of six parallel *units*, which are called microchiasms. The *A unit* of the macrochiasm refers to the *first microchiasm*, and the parallel *A' unit* of the macrochiasm refers to the *sixth microchiasm*. The *B unit* refers to the *second microchiasm*, and the parallel *B' unit* to the *fifth microchiasm*. The *C unit* refers to the *third microchiasm*, and the parallel *C' unit* to the *fourth microchiasm*. Throughout my commentary, references to *units* of the macrochiasm are used interchangeably with references to individual microchiasms, for example: "the A unit of the macrochiasm" is used synonymously with "the first microchiasm"; "the A' unit of the macrochiasm" is used synonymously with "the sixth microchiasm."

As noted above, the rhetorical function of a chiasm is to progress toward the pivot and then build to a cumulative climax. Given the A-B-C-C'-B'-A' macrochiastic arrangement of the 1 Timothy letter, it can be expected that the introductory A and B units progress the audience toward a significant pivot point occurring at the transition between the central C and C' units; the audience would then be moved across the B' unit toward a notable climax in the concluding A' unit, which would express the cumulative impact of the entire letter. The linguistic arrangement and structure of the 1 Timothy letter as a *macrochiasm* will be further discussed below; see "The Macrochiastic Structure of the 1 Timothy Letter."

Microchiasms

A *microchiasm* is one *unit* of the overall macrochiasm. There are *six microchiasms* in 1 Timothy, thus there are six macrochiastic *units* in 1 Timothy.[12] Given that the macrochiasm encompasses all six microchiasms, the rhetorical function of each microchiasm conveys and advances concentrated portions of Paul's overall intention to the audience.[13] For example, the

---

12. As noted above, references to the macrochiastic *units* as *microchiasms* will be used interchangeably throughout this commentary. For this reason, it is important to reiterate their synonymy: the *A unit* of the macrochiasm refers to the *first microchiasm*, etc.

13. Kim, *Sourcebook of the Structures*, 17, helps to explain the distinction and

concluding A' unit of the macrochiasm—the sixth microchiasm—progresses and develops the audience's understanding of the specific content of the parallel introductory A unit—the first microchiasm. In this way, each of the six microchiasms collectively augment the audience's understanding of the one overall macrochiasm—the 1 Timothy letter itself. In short, each of the six microchiasms derive their significance only as a unified part of the whole macrochiasm, yet each microchiasm collectively builds and conveys the unified structure and message of the whole macrochiasm.

Each microchiasm is composed carefully of parallel *elements*. Each of the six microchiasms may have a different number of parallel elements. The first and second microchiasms of the 1 Timothy letter are arranged by five elements, A-B-C-B'-A'. The third and fourth microchiasms are arranged by four elements, A-B-B'-A'. The fifth and sixth microchiasms are arranged by six elements, A-B-C-D-C'-B'-A'.[14]

As noted above, the rhetorical function of a chiasm is to progress toward the pivot and build to a cumulative climax. Thus a significant hinge point would be expected at the pivot element of each of the six microchiasms, and a significant climax would be expected in the concluding A' element, which would express the cumulative impact of each microchiasm. The linguistic arrangements of each of the *six microchiasms* that comprise the 1 Timothy letter as one *macrochiasm* will be further discussed below; see "The Six Microchiasms of the 1 Timothy Letter." Chapter 3 through the remaining chapters of this commentary will analyze and "hear" each microchiasm from the historic perspective of Paul's first-century Ephesian audience.

Transitional Words Between Microchiasms

A *transitional word* occurs at the very end of a microchiasm and at the immediate beginning of the next. These transitional words indicate that each macrochiastic unit is linked to its predecessor; thus, the six microchiasms are heard as a cohesive sequence within the unified purpose and progression of the one macrochiasm.[15] Given that 1 Timothy was heard aurally as a

---

interplay between the one *macro*chiasm and the six *micro*chiasms of 1 Timothy: "macro structure and micro style . . . are treated together and interactively. The macro understanding in structure becomes the solid ground of observing micro relations, among phrasal-sentential components, that also support the larger frame of units."

14. Visual representations of the chiastic structure for each microchiasm are included below along with my translations of the 1 Timothy text; see "The Six Microchiasms of the 1 Timothy Letter."

15. Van Neste's discussion ("Cohesion and Structure in the PE," 96) regarding "transitional devices" is helpful: "it is common in a new unit (or sentence) to repeat, or in some way to link back to, information from a previous unit (or sentence) . . . It is important that words that serve as 'hooks' are not common elsewhere in the units

performance, the transitional words would be identifiable not only by word cognates but also by sound. For example, the Greek transitional words between the first and second microchiasms, that is, between the A and B units of the macrochiasm—παρέδωκα and παρακαλῶ—are not cognates but would be easily recognized and paired according to the παρά prefix.[16] The same applies to the transitional words between the fourth and fifth microchiasms, the C' and B' units of the macrochiasm—ἐπίμενε and ἐπιπλήξῃς—which share the ἐπί prefix.[17] Furthermore, where transitional words are accompanied by another similar word or cognate, the rhetorical link between the microchiasms would be noticeably strengthened. For example, the transitional words between the third and fourth microchiasms, the C and C' units of the macrochiasm—πνεύματι and πνεῦμα—would be apparent and also strengthened by the immediate accompaniment of πνεύμασιν in the C' unit. The same applies to the transitional words between the C' and B' units of the macrochiasm—ἐπίμενε and ἐπιπλήξῃς—which would be strengthened by the ἐπί prefix in the verb ἔπεχε in the C' unit. Still, transitional words would also be heard with more rhetorical complexity. For example, between the fifth and sixth microchiasms—the B' and A' units—the combination of both δίδασκε and παρακάλει (B' unit) in relation to ἑτεροδιδασκαλεῖ (A' unit) would be apparent and also heard as an intensification;[18] in addition, the occurrence of δίδασκε (B' unit) and διδασκαλίᾳ (A' unit) would further emphasize the interconnectivity of the microchiasms. The following table lists each of the *transitional words* between each of the six microchiasms:

End of microchiasm ...	... beginning of next microchiasm
A unit: *first microchiasm* "I have given-over" (παρέδωκα) in 1:20	B unit: *second microchiasm* "I exhort" (παρακαλῶ) in 2:1
B unit: *second microchiasm* "faith" (πίστει) in 2:15	C unit: *third microchiasm* "faithful" (πιστός) in 3:1

---

connected. This suggests the author has intentionally placed them at the end of one unit to prepare for the next one."

16. Greek prefixes often function as significant rhetorical indicators. See discussion below regarding translation methodology.

17. It may be worth noting (see *italics*) that the terms "teaching" (διδασκαλίᾳ) in 4:16 and "exhort" (παρακάλει) in 5:1 would likely also be heard with aural similarities; such would also strengthen the unified movement from the C' to the B' unit.

18. Aurally (see *italics*), both verbs δίδασκε and παρακάλει in the B' unit are heard within the verb ἑτεροδιδασκαλεῖ in the A' unit.

End of microchiasm...	...beginning of next microchiasm
C unit: third microchiasm "Spirit" (πνεύματι) in 3:16	C' unit: fourth microchiasm "Spirit" (πνεῦμα) in 4:1; and "spirits" (πνεύμασιν) in 4:1
C' unit: fourth microchiasm "strongly-remain" (ἐπίμενε) in 4:16; and "Strongly-hold" (ἔπεχε) in 4:16	B' unit: fifth microchiasm "rebuke-violently" (ἐπιπλήξῃς) in 5:1
B' unit: fifth microchiasm "teach" (δίδασκε) and "exhort" (παρακάλει) in 6:2	A' unit: sixth microchiasm "teaches-different" (ἑτεροδιδασκαλεῖ) in 6:3; and "teaching" (διδασκαλίᾳ) in 6:3

Minichiasms

A *minichiasm* is encompassed within one element of a microchiasm and derives its significance therein. For example, the A element of the third microchiasm is itself composed of a minichiasm. However, not every element of a microchiasm is composed of a minichiasm; for example, in the second microchiasm, while there is no minichiasm within the A element, there is a minichiasm within the parallel A' element. Furthermore, it is possible for one element of a microchiasm to have one or more minichiasms; for example, in the first microchiasm, there are two minichiasms within the A element. Still, where a minichiasm is present, it does not necessarily comprise the entirety of a microchiastic element; for example, in the first microchiasm, the A element (1:1–7) has two minichiasms (1:1; 1:3–7), yet notably verse 1:2 is part of neither minichiasm; such would not impact the effect or recognizability of the minichiasms.

Within the various elements of each microchiasm in the 1 Timothy letter, seventeen minichiasms are heard in total. Each minichiasm is composed carefully of parallel *sub-elements*. Similar to each of the six microchiasms, each of the seventeen minichiasms may have a different number of parallel sub-elements. For example, within the A element of the first microchiasm (1:1–7), the first minichiasm (1:1) is arranged by three sub-elements, "a"-"b"-"a'", whereas the second minichiasm (1:3–7) is arranged by four sub-elements, "a"-"b"-"b'"-"a'".

Significantly, rather than being distracting or demanding intense focus by the audience, the rhetorical function of each minichiasm would be evident and important. That is, each minichiasm would convey and advance concentrated portions of Paul's overall intention of the microchiasm (or elements therein) to the audience. For example, in the fifth microchiasm, the minichiasm within the concluding B' element (5:11–16) progresses and develops the audience's understanding of the specific content in the parallel introductory B element (5:3–9); in this way, the *minichiasm* within the concluding B' element enhances the audience's understanding of the previously heard parallel B element, which, in turn, augments their understanding of the entire fifth *microchiasm*, and thus of the whole *macrochiasm*—the 1 Timothy letter itself. Such is an example of how the one *macrochiasm*, the six *microchiasms*, and the seventeen *minichiasms* are integrated and designed to enhance the rhetorical impact of the letter.

Notably, given that the rhetorical function of a chiasm is to progress toward the pivot and build to a cumulative climax, a significant hinge point would be expected at the pivot element of each minichiasm, and a significant climax would be expected in the concluding "a'" sub-element of each minichiasm. Where applicable, the following chapters of this commentary will identify, discuss, and analyze each minichiasm in tandem with the microchiastic element in which it occurs.

Translation of 1 Timothy

All translations of the 1 Timothy letter in this commentary are my own. Every effort has been made to be as literal as possible, both for the purpose of clarifying the exegesis of the Greek text and for replicating the performative effect that the Greek language would have upon the original first-century audience.[19] Namely, my translations of the Greek text into English have sought to preserve the rhetorical—and in many cases polemical—flare of the language that Paul uses to communicate to the Ephesian church in 1 Timothy. To that end, many of the Greek cognate terms—words that stem from and share a common root-word—have been conveyed in very wooden English translations, notably represented throughout my commentary as hyphenated words. The intended effect of such wooden English translations is to enable us, a modern audience, to hear the purposeful, integrated, and unified rhetorical strategy that is part of Paul's communication in Greek throughout 1 Timothy.

To summarize, the basis of my translation methodology seeks to maintain *both*: 1) the dynamic sense of the original Greek words, and 2) the

---

19. One benefit of adhering to a literal, wooden translation methodology—to be sure, a slightly awkward sounding translation—is to enable English readers to reflect upon the words and "hear" their rhetorical implication within the surrounding literary context that would otherwise be lost in a more dynamic, looser English translation.

cognate relationships among the original Greek words, which would have been aurally apparent *and* instrumental to the performance and rhetorical strategy of the letter. The following provides a more detailed explanation of my translation of 1 Timothy, which will be important for understanding my analysis of the letter throughout this commentary.

Many of the English translations that are hyphenated in this commentary signify their derivation from one Greek word, which itself is a combination of two Greek words, for example:

- "to teach-different" (ἑτεροδιδασκαλεῖν, 1:3); "household-law" (οἰκονομίαν, 1:4); "affection-of-stranger" (φιλόξενον, 3:2); "young-plant" (νεόφυτον, 3:6).

In this way, words that are hyphenated in the English translations draw attention to the rhetorical use of Greek cognate terms, for example (see *italics*):

- "to teach-*different*" (ἑτεροδιδασκαλεῖν, 1:3), "*different*" (ἕτερον, 1:10), "teaches-*different*" (ἑτεροδιδασκαλεῖ, 6:3);

- "to *teach*-different" (ἑτεροδιδασκαλεῖν, 1:3), "*teaching*" (διδασκαλίᾳ, 1:10), "*teacher*" (διδάσκαλος, 2:7), "to *teach*" (διδάσκειν, 2:12), "able-to-*teach*" (διδακτικόν, 3:2), "*teachings*" (διδασκαλίαις, 4:1), "*teach*" (δίδασκε, 4:11), "*teaches*-different" (ἑτεροδιδασκαλεῖ, 6:3);

- "useless-*words*" (ματαιολογίαν, 1:6), "*word*" (λόγος, 1:15), "*word*-quarreling (διαλογισμοῦ, 2:8), "double-*worded*" (διλόγους, 3:8), "false-*worders*" (ψευδολόγων, 4:2), "*words*" (λόγοις, 6:3), "*word*-fights" (λογομαχίας, 6:4);[20]

- "*falsifiers*" (ψεύσταις, 1:10), "*falsifying*" (ψεύδομαι, 2:7), "*false*-worders" (ψευδολόγων, 4:2), "*false*-named" (ψευδωνύμου, 6:20)

Furthermore, many words that are hyphenated in the English translations are intended to preserve their derivation from a single Greek word that is best conveyed with multiple English words or is gender specific, for example:

- "I-myself" (ἐγώ, 1:11); "was counted-faithful" (ἐπιστεύθην, 1:11), "able-to-teach" (διδακτικόν, 3:2); "a knowing-embrace" (ἐπίγνωσιν, 2:4);

- "younger-women" (νεωτέρας, 5:3), "faithful-woman" (πιστή, 5:16).

---

20. See also "confessedly" (ὁμολογουμένως, 3:16), "confessed" (ὡμολόγησας, 6:12), and "confession" (ὁμολογίαν, 6:12, 13). Literally, "same-*wordedly* (ὁμολογουμένως, 3:16), "same-*worded*" (ὡμολόγησας, 6:12a), and "same-*word*" (ὁμολογίαν, 6:12a, 13b). These literal translations would be too wooden to convey the natural meaning of the Greek words. As such, while I have translated these terms as "confessedly" (3:16), "confessed" (6:12a), and "confession" (6:12a, 13b), their use of the cognate term "word" (λόγος) is notated throughout my analysis.

In this way, the English translations preserve the original Greek words while drawing attention to the rhetorical use of cognate terms, for example:

- "faith" (πίστει, 1:2), "was counted-faithful" (ἐπιστεύθην, 1:11), "faithful" (πιστόν, 1:12), "to have-faith" (πιστεύειν, 1:16), "the faithful" (πιστῶν, 4:10), "faithful-woman" (πιστή, 5:16);
- "young-plant" (νεόφυτον, 3:6), "youth" (νεότητος, 4:12), "younger-men" (νεωτέρους, 5:3), "younger-women" (νεωτέρας, 5:3);
- "holiness" (ἁγιασμῷ, 2:15), "made-holy" (ἁγιάζεται, 4:6), "the holy-ones" (ἁγίων, 5:10).
- "child" (τέκνον, 1:18), "child-parenting" (τεκνογονίας, 2:15), "those-from-parents" (ἔκγονα, 5:4), "parents" (προγόνοις, 5:4), "to child-parent" (τεκνογονεῖν, 5:14);
- "violent" (πλήκτην, 3:3), "rebuke-violently" (ἐπιπλήξῃς, 5:1);
- "without-knowing" (ἀγνοῶν, 1:13), "a knowing-embrace" (ἐπίγνωσιν, 2:4), "those who have knowingly-embraced" (ἐπεγνωκόσιν, 4:3), "knowledge" (γνώσεως, 6:20).

Similarly, the hyphenated English translations draw attention to the juxtaposition of Greek words, often conveyed by prefixes—the absence, presence, or contrast thereof—which the original audience would have heard as part of Paul's rhetoric during the performance of the letter, for example (see *italics*):

- "godliness" (εὐσεβείᾳ, 2:2) versus "the *without*-godly" (ἀσεβέσιν, 1:9);
- "the faithful" (πιστοῖς, 4:3) versus "the *without*-faith" (ἀπίστου, 5:8);
- "I hold" (ἔχων, 1:11) versus "to hold-*toward*" (προσέχειν, 1:4);[21]
- "*without*-affection-of-money" (ἀφιλάργυρον, 3:2) versus "affection-of-money" (φιλαργυρία, 6:10).[22]

---

21. The comparative sense of "hold" versus "hold-toward" would be apparent, in effect: "holding onto" versus "giving oneself over to." This is a notable rhetorical theme throughout the letter; see discussions in the following chapters. See also discussion below regarding the decision to translate ἔχω as "I hold" instead of "I have."

22. Another example of Paul's rhetorical juxtaposition of prefixes would be heard between the comparative use of the term "same" (ὅμοιος) and "different" (ἕτερος) in the following words (see *italics*): "confessedly" (ὁμολογουμένως, 3:16), "confessed" (ὡμολόγησας, 6:12), and "confession" (ὁμολογίαν, 6:12, 13) versus "to teach-*different*" (ἑτεροδιδασκαλεῖν, 1:3) and "teaches-*different*" (ἑτεροδιδασκαλεῖ, 6:3). A literal translation in English would convey the comparative impact in Greek—"*same*-wordedly (ὁμολογουμένως, 3:16), "*same*-worded" (ὡμολόγησας, 6:12a), and "*same*-word" (ὁμολογίαν, 6:12a, 13b)—however, these literal translations would be too wooden to convey the natural meaning of the Greek words. As such, while I have translated these terms as "confessedly" (3:16), "confessed" (6:12a), and "confession" (6:12a, 13b), their

Also, in order to preserve consistent word associations throughout 1 Timothy and the rhetorical implications thereof, the English translations in this commentary also seek to maintain the linguistic uniformity that the audience would have heard in the performance of the letter in Greek, for example:

- "some" (τισίν, 1:3), "some-things" (τίνων, 1:7), "some-thing" (τι, 1:10), "some" (τινες, 1:19), "some" (τινῶν, 5:24), "some" (τις, 6:3);[23]
- "not" (μή, 1:3), "nor" (μηδέ, 1:4), "None" (μηδείς, 4:12), "nothing" (μηδέν, 5:21), "none" (μηδενί, 5:22), "No-longer" (μηκέτι, 5:23).[24]

Where possible, words that are not included in the Greek text but would make the English translation sound more natural are omitted. In several instances, however, English words that are not included but implied in the Greek text are added (see *italics*) to make the English translation intelligible, for example:

- 1:9: "knowing this, that *for* the just the law is not laid but *for* the without-law"; the term "*for*" was added because it is implied by the dative form of the Greek text.
- 1:11: "according to the gospel of the glory of the blessed God, *with* which I-myself was counted-faithful"; for intelligibility, the term "*with*" was added, likely implied by the Greek text.
- 1:15: "faithful *is* the word" (πιστὸς ὁ λόγος); the term "*is*" was added because it is implied by the Greek text.
- 2:5: "For *there is* one God, and *there is* one mediator" (εἷς γὰρ θεός, εἷς καὶ μεσίτης); the phrase "*there is*" was added because it is implied by the Greek text.

---

use of the cognate term "same" (ὅμοιος) is notated throughout my analysis.

23. Most translations do not preserve the rhetorical consistency of the term "some" and, therefore, lose the deliberate connotation that Paul intends to convey. For example, *ESV*: "certain persons" (τισίν, 1:3); "one" (τις, 1:8); "some" (τινες, 1:19); "anyone" (τις, 3:1); "someone" (τις, 3:5); etc.
It is worth noting that although the term "which" (αἵτινες, 1:4; ἥτις, 3:15; αἵτινες, 6:9) might consistently be translated as "which-some" in order to maintain its cognate similarity, English readability would be hindered. See explanation below.

24. For readability purposes in this commentary, terms that would preferably be translated "neither" (μήτε) and "nor" (μήτε) in 1:7 were translated "either" and "or," respectively. Most translations do not preserve the rhetorical consistency of the term "not" and its cognates; in this way, the deliberate rhetorical nuance is not adequately conveyed. For example, *ESV*: "not" (μή, 1:3), "nor" (μηδέ, 1:4), "without" (μή, 1:7), "either" (μήτε, 1:7), "or" (μήτε, 1:7), "No one" (Μηδείς, 4:12), "without" (μηδέν, 5:21), "not" (μηδενί, 5:22), "nor" (μηδέ, 5:22), "No longer" (Μηκέτι, 5:23).

Furthermore, as much as possible, the English translations of the Greek text in this commentary seek to avoid any artificial impression that words are cognates in Greek when in fact they are not, for example:

- The Greek verb ἔχω synonymously conveys "I have" and "I hold."[25] The choice to translate ἔχω as "I hold" avoids cognate confusion with English translations of Greek words that require the use of "have," such as perfect tense verbs—"have become-shipwrecked" (ἐναυάγησαν, 1:19); "we have hoped" (ἠλπίκαμεν, 4:10)—and participles—"who-have-become-seared" (κεκαυστηριασμένων, 4:2); "having-an-unhealthy-craving" (νοσῶν, 6:4). Arguably, this English translation of ἔχω and its cognates—"I hold" (ἔχω, 1:12), "holding" (ἔχων, 1:18)—accurately (and in many instances, more accurately) maintains the contextual and dynamic sense of the Greek word.

Occasionally, however, an English translation that avoids cognate confusion would be unduly awkward or unhelpful to convey the meaning of the sentence; in these specific instances, a looser or less literal translation was required.[26] Consequently, these occasions of less literal translations potentially introduce the unwanted implication in English that words are cognates in Greek when in fact they are not, for example:[27]

- The compound verb παρέχουσιν in 1:4 would preferably be translated as "hold-about" in order to preserve its juxtaposition with "holds-about" (παρέχοντι) in 6:17.[28] This literal, wooden translation "hold-about" in 1:4 would also draw attention to Paul's consistent rhetorical use and juxtaposition of other cognates throughout the 1 Timothy letter—"hold-toward" (παρέχουσιν, 1:4) versus "I hold" (ἔχω, 1:12); "holding" (ἔχων, 1:18) versus "holding-toward" (προσέχοντες, 4:2). However, given that the readability of 1:4 would be significantly hindered by the literal translation—"... which *hold-about* controversial-speculations rather than the household-law of God in faith"—a more flexible English translation was required for this specific instance,

---

25. See BDAG, s.v.

26. Anyone who has done translations from one language to another understands the difficulty to maintain all aspects of meaning, rhetoric, and the aural component that is heard in the original language. As much as possible, I have sought to allow the Greek language to be presented accurately in the English language.

27. Throughout my analysis of 1 Timothy, each of these instances is accompanied by an explanatory footnote.

28. The juxtaposition conveys a rhetorical contrast between the divisive activities of the false teachers (1:4) over and against the generous activity of God (6:17). See volume 3, chapter 3 regarding 1 Timothy 6:17.

hence: "bring-about"—". . . which *bring-about* controversial-speculations rather than the household-law of God in faith." Consequently, the looser translation "bring-about" incorrectly gives the impression that it shares a cognate relation to the verbs "we brought-in" (εἰσηνέγκαμεν) and "to bring-out" (ἐξενεγκεῖν) in 6:7. Yet, for the sake of English readability in this commentary, the looser translation "bring-about" (παρέχουσιν) in 1:4 was utilized. The same applies to the occurrence of the verb in 6:17, "brings-about" (παρέχοντι). All looser translations are footnoted with an explanation.

- The specific occurrences of the Greek terms ἔχει (5:4, 16), ἔχοντα (5:25), and ἔχοντες (6:2) were translated as "has," "having," and "who have," respectively. Although other occurrences of the verb ἔχω were translated as "I hold" rather than "I have" (see explanation above), the sense of the verbs in 5:4, 5:16, 5:25, and 6:2 would be less helpful to convey the meaning of the sentence if translated as "I hold." For this reason, such instances were translated as "I have"; subsequently, they are footnoted to avoid the impression of cognate confusion with verbs and participles that are translated with the word "have"—"has denied" (ἤρνηται, 5:8), "has shown-hospitality" (ἐξενοδόχησεν, 5:10), "have turned-aside" (ἐξετράπησαν, 5:15).

- The cognate words ἦλθεν ("came," 1:15), ἐλθεῖν ("to come," 2:4), ἐλθεῖν ("to come," 3:14), ἔρχομαι ("I come," 4:13) derive from the root verb ἔρχομαι, which means "I come." At the same time, the cognate words μελλόντων ("those who would-inevitably-come," 1:16), τῆς μελλούσης ("the inevitable-coming," 4:8), and τὸ μέλλον ("the inevitable-coming," 6:19) all derive from the root word μέλλω, which refers to an intended or inevitable future occurrence, "I intend to," "I am about to," "I inevitably will"; thus to adequately convey the future implication of the Greek word, the English word "come" or "coming" was included. This may give the artificial impression that "came" (ἦλθεν, 1:15) and "those who would-inevitably-come" (μελλόντων, 1:16) are cognates when in fact they are not.

- The English translations (see *italics*) of ἐναυάγησαν ("have *become-shipwrecked*," 1:19) and κεκαυστηριασμένων ("who have *become-seared*," 4:2) are not cognates of the verb γίνομαι ("I become"), which occurs throughout the letter—γέγονεν ("became," 2:15), γίνου ("be," 4:12), γεγονυῖα ("being," 5:9). However, the English word "become" was included to best convey the sense of the Greek word in English; for example, the translation "have become-shipwrecked" (1:19) highlights the intransitive nature of the Greek verb.

Similarly, in several instances it was not possible to maintain *both* the rhetorical consistency that the audience would have heard in the performance of the Greek text and simultaneously convey it in English with any intelligibility. Such instances necessitated a more flexible English translation (see *italics* and Greek text in parentheses), which unfortunately is unable to convey the original nuances of the Greek, for example:

- 1:4: Literal translation: "nor to hold-toward myths and genealogies without-end, *which-some* (αἵτινες) *hold-about* (παρέχουσιν) controversial-speculations rather than the household-law of God in faith." Adjusted translation of 1:4: ". . . *which bring-about* controversial-speculations . . ." In the adjusted translation, the rhetorical and comparative consistency of the Greek cognates for "some" and "hold" is not conveyed.

- 1:13: Literal translation: ". . . rather I was granted-mercy, because without-knowing I did in *without-faith* (ἀπιστίᾳ)." Adjusted translation of 1:13: ". . . because without-knowing I did in *unfaithfulness*." In the adjusted translation of 1:13, the rhetorical and comparative consistency of the Greek prefix "without" (ἀ-) is not conveyed, but in the literal translation, it is conveyed—"*without*-knowing" (ἀγνοῶν); "*without*-faith" (ἀπιστίᾳ).

Still, there were a few instances where the meaning of non-cognate Greek words were identical and had to be translated accordingly, for example:

- The cognate Greek words οἴδαμεν ("we know," 1:8), εἰδώς ("knowing," 1:9), οἶδεν ("know," 3:5), and εἰδῇς ("you may know," 3:15) derive from the root word οἶδα, which means "I know." At the same time, the cognate Greek words ἀγνοῶν ("without-knowing," 1:13), ἐπίγνωσιν ("a knowing-embrace," 2:4), ἐπεγνωκόσιν ("those who have knowingly-embraced," 4:3), and γνώσεως ("knowledge," 6:20) all derive from the root word γινώσκω, which also means "I know." Thus even though there is no cognate connection, the English translations could not avoid the artificial impression of cognate relations. Conceptually, the audience would recognize the similar implications of these words.

- The Greek words ἀπωσάμενοι ("rejecting," 1:19), παραιτοῦ ("reject," 4:7; 5:11), and ἠθέτησαν ("they rejected," 5:14) are not cognate terms; however, to adjust their English translations to convey different meanings would lose the dynamic sense of the Greek words, which are conceptually similar.

As noted, many words are hyphenated in the English translations in order to convey their derivation from a single Greek word; however, my intention is also to avoid unnecessary distraction that may result from an overuse of—albeit, accurate to the Greek text—hyphenated English words. As such, hyphenated English translations are only applied in a manner that would benefit the analysis of the Greek, for example:

- In 1:1, the Greek word κατά would literally be translated as the hyphenated term "according-to." Yet, while such a literal English translation maintains its derivation from a single Greek word, its presentation as a hyphenated term is not significant to the rhetoric or performance of 1 Timothy and would be distracting in English, hence: "according to" (κατ', 1:1). Similarly, "on behalf of" (ὑπέρ, 2:1) rather than "on-behalf-of"; "in the sight of" (ἐνώπιον, 2:3) rather than "in-the-sight-of"; "his own" (ἰδίοις, 2:6) rather than "his-own"; "it is necessary" (δεῖ, 3:2) rather than "it-is-necessary."

- In 1:13 and 1:16, the verb ἠλεήθην would literally be translated "I-was-granted-mercy." Yet, to avoid unnecessary distraction in English, the hyphens are only applied to the main part of the verb, hence: "I was granted-mercy" (ἠλεήθην). In this way, the limited application of hyphens also avoids distraction from its main cognate term "mercy" (ἔλεος, 1:2).

- In 3:11 the verb διακονείτωσαν would literally be translated "they-must-serve-as-deacons"; in 3:13 the participle διακονήσαντες would literally be translated "those-who-serve-as-deacons." However, because the main focus is to highlight the cognate relation and aural connection between the two terms (see *italics*), the English translations omit hyphens that would draw attention away from the cognate terms, hence: "they must *serve-as-deacons*" (διακονείτωσαν, 3:11); "those who *serve-as-deacons*" (διακονήσαντες, 3:13).

- Notably in 1:7, the literal translation of the verbs λέγουσιν—"they-are-saying"—and διαβεβαιοῦνται—"they-are-insisting"—applies hyphens to each English component of the translation. Here, the generous application of hyphens improved intelligibility and comprehension of the entire verse in English. Subsequently, although "they-are-saying" (λέγουσιν) has another cognate occurrence in the letter for which hyphens were not applied to each English component of the translation—"I am saying" (λέγω, 2:7)—it was determined that the hyphens in "they-are-saying" did not unnecessarily distract from the cognate terms; thus hyphens were applied. Moreover, given that "they-are-insisting" (διαβεβαιοῦνται) is unique and does not have another cognate occurrence in the letter, there was no need to omit hyphens that would otherwise draw attention away from its root term.

It is also worth noting that throughout this commentary, my English translations of the Greek text are often used without direct quotations; the purpose of such is to consistently utilize the 1 Timothy text as much as possible without signifying that a specific linguistic or rhetorical analysis is intended. Thus wherever my English translations are marked with direct quotations (often accompanied by the Greek text in parentheses), I am explicitly signifying that a specific analysis of a word or phrase is intended. For example, from volume 3, chapter 3 regarding 1 Timothy 6:4:

> By itself, the term "suspicions" (ὑπόνοιαι) conveys a neutral idea—"supposition, guess, true intent." Yet, heard together with the qualifier "wicked" (πονηραί)—connoting "evil" or even "guilty" or "unsound"—the phrase highlights the pathological mindset of Paul's opposition: the "wicked suspicions" of the false teachers are unfounded or—more strongly put—are evil precisely because such young-plant, unqualified overseers are grasping nothing while they are puffed-up (3:6; 6:4), both having turned-aside from love—a pure heart, a good conscience, and a without-hypocrisy faith (1:5–6) and having influenced others who themselves already have turned-aside after Satan (5:15).

In this example, the words and phrases "young-plant," "grasping nothing," "puffed-up," "turned-aside," "from love," "a pure heart," "a good conscience," "a without-hypocrisy faith," and "have turned-aside after Satan" are my English translations of the Greek text, which were previously analyzed in the commentary; here, they are used without quotations to draw attention to the linguistic analysis of "wicked suspicions" *and* to integrate the cumulative impact of what the audience have already heard in the letter. In instances where my English translations of the 1 Timothy text are used without direct quotations, verse references are included in parentheses; this signifies that the 1 Timothy text—not my own words—is being utilized.

In the rest of this chapter, I will demonstrate how the Greek text of 1 Timothy organizes itself into six distinct literary units—six *microchiasms* (A-B-C-C'-B'-A')—which are apparent through the linguistic parallels that occur objectively in the text and would be heard as such. Furthermore, I will demonstrate how these six microchiasms form one overall literary *macrochiasm*, which is also determined by the linguistic parallels that occur objectively in the text and would be heard accordingly.[29]

---

29. Contra Marshall, *PE*, 33: "No chiastic structure so far proposed appears to be cogent."

Outline of the Chiastic Structures of 1 Timothy

The following outline provides the structure of the 1 Timothy *macrochiasm* and a summary of the content presented within each of the *six microchiasms*:

> A. 1:1–20: Paul's Charge for Timothy to Preserve the Teaching
>
> > B. 2:1–15: Salvation for All through Prayer and Godly Conduct
> >
> > > C. 3:1–16: Godly Leadership in God's Household
> > >
> > > C'. 4:1–16: Preserving the Teaching and Promoting Godliness Amidst Apostasy
> >
> > B'. 5:1—6:2: Godly Conduct from All Members of God's Household
>
> A'. 6:3–21: The Teaching that is According to Godliness Is Great Gain for Eternal Life

The Six Microchiasms of the 1 Timothy Letter

This section analyzes how the Greek text of 1 Timothy organizes itself into six distinct literary units—six *microchiasms* (A-B-C-C'-B'-A').

A Unit. Paul's Charge for Timothy to Preserve the Teaching (1:1–20)

The first of six microchiasms within the 1 Timothy macrochiasm is composed carefully of five elements (A-B-C-B'-A'). Linguistic parallels identifying chiastic arrangements are indicated by the Greek text; this excludes the *transitional word* (see *italics*) in 1:20.[30]

> A. ¹:¹ Paul, apostle of Christ Jesus (Χριστοῦ Ἰησοῦ) according to (κατ') the command of God (θεοῦ) our Savior and Christ Jesus (Χριστοῦ Ἰησοῦ) our hope: ² To Timothy (Τιμοθέῳ), genuine child (τέκνῳ) in faith (πίστει): grace (χάρις), mercy (ἔλεος), peace from God (θεοῦ) the Father and Christ Jesus our Lord (Χριστοῦ Ἰησοῦ κυρίου ἡμῶν). ³ As I exhorted you to remain in Ephesus while-journeying for Macedonia, that you might charge (παραγγείλῃς) some not to teach-different (ἑτεροδιδασκαλεῖν) ⁴ nor to hold-toward myths and genealogies without-limit, which

---

30. The transitional word "*I have given-over*" (παρέδωκα, 1:20) is not part of the linguistic parallels.

bring-about (παρέχουσιν) controversial-speculations rather than the household-law of God (θεοῦ) in faith (πίστει). ⁵ But the end of the charge (παραγγελίας) is (ἐστίν) love (ἀγάπη) from a pure heart and a good conscience (συνειδήσεως ἀγαθῆς) and a without-hypocrisy faith (πίστεως), ⁶ which (ὧν) some (τινες)—swerving-from—have turned-aside for useless-words, ⁷ desiring to be law-teachers, not understanding either what they-are-saying or regarding some-things they-are-insisting.

> B. ⁸ᵃ But we know (οἴδαμεν) that the law (νόμος) is commendable,
>
>> C. ⁸ᵇ if someone uses it lawfully,
>
> B'. ⁹ knowing (εἰδώς) this, that for the just the law (νόμος) is not laid but for the without-law (ἀνόμοις) and without-obedience, the without-godly and sinners, the without-reverence and vile, patricides and matricides, murderers, ¹⁰ᵃ fornicators, sodomites, kidnappers, falsifiers, perjurers,

A'. ¹⁰ᵇ and if some-thing different (ἕτερον) lies-opposed to the sound teaching (διδασκαλίᾳ), ¹¹ according to (κατά) the gospel of the glory of the blessed God (θεοῦ), with which I-myself was counted-faithful (ἐπιστεύθην). ¹² I hold grace (χάριν) to him who empowered me, Christ Jesus our Lord (Χριστῷ Ἰησοῦ τῷ κυρίῳ ἡμῶν), because faithful (πιστόν) he considered me appointing for service, ¹³ though firstly being a blasphemer and a persecutor and a hubristic-person; rather I was granted-mercy (ἠλεήθην), because without-knowing I did in unfaithfulness (ἀπιστίᾳ); ¹⁴ but the grace (χάρις) of our Lord (κυρίου ἡμῶν) beyond-abounded with the faith (πίστεως) and love (ἀγάπης) that are in Christ Jesus (Χριστῷ Ἰησοῦ). ¹⁵ Faithful (πιστός) is the word and worthy of all acceptance, that Christ Jesus (Χριστὸς Ἰησοῦς) came into the world to save sinners, of whom (ὧν) I-myself am the first. ¹⁶ Rather consistent-with this I was granted-mercy (ἠλεήθην), that in me the first Christ Jesus (Χριστὸς Ἰησοῦς) might display all patience as an example to those who would-inevitably-come to have-faith (πιστεύειν) upon him for life eternal. ¹⁷ But to the King of the eternities, without-perishability, without-visibility, only God (θεῷ), honor and glory for the eternities of the eternities, amen. ¹⁸ This charge (παραγγελίαν) I entrust to you, child Timothy (τέκνον Τιμόθεε), according to (κατά) the prophecies preceding upon you, that you might war in them the commendable war, ¹⁹ holding faith (πίστιν) and a good conscience (ἀγαθὴν συνείδησιν), which some (τινες)—rejecting—regarding the faith (πίστιν) have become-shipwrecked, [20] of whom (ὧν) are (ἐστίν) Hymenaeus and Alexander, whom *I have given-over* (παρέδωκα) to Satan, that they might be-disciplined not to blaspheme.

Chiastic Analysis of the A Unit: the First Microchiasm (1:1–20)

The overarching concern of Paul's charge for Timothy to stop the false-teaching "some" brackets the entire unit (1:3, 18), thus establishing its literary and thematic cohesiveness. Also, the integrity of the first microchiasm as a literary unit (1:1–20) is further established by the A-B-C-B'-A' chiastic arrangement, as follows.

The A element (1:1–7) and A' element (1:10b–20) are established by parallel language. The sevenfold occurrences of "Christ Jesus" (Χριστοῦ Ἰησοῦ, 1:1a, 1b, 2; Χριστῷ Ἰησοῦ, 1:12, 14; Χριστὸς Ἰησοῦς, 1:15, 16),[31] the fivefold occurrences of "God" (θεοῦ, 1:1, 2, 4, 11; θεῷ, 1:17), the triple occurrences of "according to" (κατ', 1:1; κατά, 1:11, 18), of the noun "faith" (πίστει, 1:2, 4; πίστεως, 1:5, 14; πίστιν, 1:19a, b),[32] of "grace" (χάρις, 1:2, 14; χάριν, 1:12), of "our Lord" (κυρίου ἡμῶν, 1:2, 14; κυρίῳ ἡμῶν, 1:12), of the indefinite plural pronoun "some" (τισίν, 1:3; τινες, 1:6, 19),[33] and of the relative pronoun "which" (ὧν, 1:6, 15, 19), and the double occurrences of "Timothy" (Τιμοθέῳ, 1:2; Τιμόθεε, 1:18), of "child" (τέκνῳ, 1:2; τέκνον, 1:18), of "charge" (παραγγελίας, 1:5; παραγγελίαν, 1:18),[34] of "love" (ἀγάπη,

---

31. The precise parallelism of the A Element (1:1–7) and A' Element (1:10b–20) includes:
1:1a: "Christ Jesus" (Χριστοῦ Ἰησοῦ);
1:1b: "Christ Jesus" (Χριστοῦ Ἰησοῦ);
1:2: "Christ Jesus our Lord" (Χριστοῦ Ἰησοῦ τοῦ κυρίου ἡμῶν);
1:12: "Christ Jesus our Lord" (Χριστῷ Ἰησοῦ τῷ κυρίῳ ἡμῶν);
1:14: "Christ Jesus" (Χριστῷ Ἰησοῦ);
1:15–16: "Christ Jesus" (Χριστὸς Ἰησοῦς) . . . "Christ Jesus" (Χριστὸς Ἰησοῦς).

32. The cognate occurrences of the verbs "was counted-faithful" (ἐπιστεύθην) in 1:11 and "to have-faith" (πιστεύειν) in 1:16, of the adjectives "faithful" (πιστόν) in 1:12 and "faithful" (πιστός) in 1:15, and of the noun "unfaithfulness" (ἀπιστίᾳ) in 1:13 further strengthen the parallelism of the A and A' elements.

33. The plural form of the indefinite pronoun is unique to the A and A' elements. The form τι occurs in 1:10a of the A' element and clearly refers to an object instead of a person. The pronoun also occurs in 1:8b of the C element but is distinct from its occurrences in the A and A' elements because it occurs in the nominative singular (τις). It could be argued that the plural pronoun "some-things" (τίνων) in 1:7 of the A element refers to persons versus objects, in which case the parallelism of the A and A' elements is further strengthened; in this commentary, however, "some-things" (τίνων) in 1:7 is interpreted in reference to objects.

34. The occurrence of the verb "you might charge" (παραγγείλῃς) in 1:3 strengthens the parallelism of the A and A' elements.

1:5; ἀγάπης, 1:14), of "good conscience" (συνειδήσεως ἀγαθῆς, 1:5; ἀγαθὴν συνείδησιν, 1:19), and of "is" (ἐστίν, 1:5; ἐστιν, 1:20) all function to organize the language of the first microchiasm into two parallel sections, thus establishing the parallelism of the A element (1:1–7) and A' element (1:10b–20) within the first microchiasm.[35]

The B element (1:8a) and B' element (1:9–10a) are also established by parallel linguistic connections. The double occurrences of "know" (οἴδαμεν, 1:8a; εἰδώς, 1:9) and of "law" (νόμος, 1:8a, 9)[36] organize the language of the B and B' elements into a linguistic parallel.

The unique occurrence, both in this unit and in the entire letter, of the adverb "lawfully" (νομίμως) in 1:8b distinguishes the C element (1:8b) as the unparalleled pivot of the first microchiasm, thus forming the hinge between the two occurrences of "law" in the B and B' elements. All of the aforementioned parallel words are unique to their respective elements and do not appear elsewhere in the unit.

Chart of Linguistic Parallels in the A Unit (1:1–20)

Visually representing this chiastic analysis, we observe that the first microchiasm is arranged by the following linguistic parallels:

---

35. The occurrence of "teach-different"(ἑτεροδιδασκαλεῖν) in 1:3 of the A element and the occurrences of terms "different" (ἕτερον) and "teaching" (διδασκαλία) in 1:10a of the A' element strengthen the parallelism between the A and A' elements; as do the occurrence of "mercy" (ἔλεος) in 1:2 of the A element and double occurrences of "I was granted-mercy" (ἠλεήθην) in 1:13 and 1:16 of the A' element.

36. The occurrence of the adjective "without-law" (ἀνόμοις) in 1:9 strengthens the parallelism of the B and B' elements.

A Element (1:1-7)	A' Element (1:10b-20)
Χριστοῦ Ἰησοῦ in 1:1a, 1b, 2	Χριστῷ Ἰησοῦ in 1:12, 14; Χριστὸς Ἰησοῦς in 1:15, 16
κατ' in 1:1	κατά in 1:11; κατά in 1:18
θεοῦ in 1:1, 2, 4	θεοῦ in 1:11; θεῷ in 1:17
Τιμοθέῳ in 1:2	Τιμόθεε in 1:18
τέκνῳ in 1:2	τέκνον in 1:18
πίστει in 1:2, 4; πίστεως, 1:5	πίστεως in 1:14; πίστιν in 1:19
χάρις in 1:2	χάριν in 1:12; χάρις in 1:14
κυρίου ἡμῶν in 1:2	κυρίῳ ἡμῶν in 1:12; κυρίου ἡμῶν in 1:14
παραγγελίας in 1:5	παραγγελίαν in 1:18
ἐστίν in 1:5	ἐστιν in 1:20
ἀγάπη in 1:5	ἀγάπης in 1:14
συνειδήσεως ἀγαθῆς in 1:5	ἀγαθὴν συνείδησιν in 1:19
ὧν in 1:6	ὧν in 1:15, 20
τισίν, 1:3; τινες in 1:6	τινες in 1:19

B Element (1:8a)	B' Element (1:9-10a)
οἴδαμεν in 1:8a	εἰδώς in 1:9
νόμος in 1:8a	νόμος in 1:9

B Unit. Salvation for All through Prayer and Godly Conduct (2:1-15)

The second of six microchiasms within the 1 Timothy macrochiasm is composed carefully of six elements (A-B-C-C'-B'-A'). Linguistic parallels identifying chiastic arrangements are indicated by the Greek text; this excludes the *transitional words* (see *italics*) in 2:1 and 2:15.[37]

> A. [2:1] *I exhort* (παρακαλῶ), therefore (οὖν), first (πρῶτον) of all to-be-done supplications, prayers (προσευχάς), intercessions, thanksgivings on behalf of all humans, [2] on behalf of kings and all those being in authority, that a peaceful and quiet (ἡσύχιον) life we might lead-through in all (πάσῃ) godliness (εὐσεβείᾳ) and respectability. [3] This is commendable and acceptable in the sight of our Savior God, [4a] who desires all humans to-be-saved (σωθῆναι)

---

37. The transitional words "*I exhort*" (παρακαλῶ, 2:1) and "*faith*" (πίστει, 2:15) are not part of the linguistic parallels.

B. ⁴ᵇ and to come to a knowing-embrace of truth (ἀληθείας).

C. ⁵ᵃ For there is one (εἷς) God,

C'. ⁵ᵇ and there is one (εἷς) mediator of God and humans, the human Christ Jesus, ⁶ who gave himself as a ransom on behalf of all, the testimony at his own times.

B'. ⁷ To this I-myself was appointed proclaimer and apostle—the truth (ἀλήθειαν) I am saying, I am not falsifying—teacher of the Gentiles in faith and truth (ἀληθείᾳ).

A'. ⁸ I want, therefore (οὖν), men to pray (προσεύχεσθαι) in all place lifting reverent hands without anger and word-quarreling; ⁹ likewise also women to cosmetic themselves in cosmopolitan apparel with modesty and self-control, not in braids and gold or pearls or rich attire; ¹⁰ rather what is proper for women who profess godliness (θεοσέβειαν), consistent-with good works. ¹¹ A woman in quietness (ἡσυχίᾳ) must learn in all (πάσῃ) submissiveness; ¹² but I do not permit a woman to teach nor to govern a man; rather to be in quietness (ἡσυχίᾳ). ¹³ For Adam was formed first (πρῶτος), then Eve. ¹⁴ And Adam was not deceived, but the woman being-deceived in transgression became; ¹⁵ but she will be-saved (σωθήσεται) consistent-with child-parenting, if they remain in *faith* (πίστει) and love and holiness with self-control.

Chiastic Analysis of the B Unit: the Second Microchiasm (2:1–15)

The verb "I exhort (παρακαλῶ) in 2:1 of the introductory A element recalls the verb "I have given-over" (παρέδωκα) in the concluding statement (1:20) of the A' element of the preceding microchiasm. These terms function as the transitional words linking the A unit (1:1–20) to the B unit (2:1–15).

The repeated emphasis on prayer (2:1, 8) and salvation (2:4a, 15) in the A and A' elements brackets the pivotal declarations in the C and C' elements that there is one God (2:5a) and one mediator of God and humans (2:5b); the thematic focus identifies the literary cohesion of the microchiasm. Moreover, the A-B-C-C'-B'-A' chiastic arrangement further secures its integrity and distinctiveness as a linguistic unit (2:1–15), as follows.

The double occurrences of the conjunction "therefore" (οὖν, 2:1, 8) initiate the parallelism between the A element (2:1–4a) and A' element (2:8–15) of the second microchiasm. The double occurrences of "first" (πρῶτον, 2:1; πρῶτος, 2:13), of the cognates "prayers" and "to pray" (προσευχάς, 2:1; προσεύχεσθαι, 2:8), of the precise term "all" (πάσῃ, 2:2, 11), of the cognates "quiet" and "quietness" (ἡσύχιον, 2:2; ἡσυχίᾳ, 2:12), and of the verbs "to be-saved" and "will be-saved" (σωθῆναι, 2:4a; σωθήσεται, 2:14) further strengthen the parallelism. In addition, the terms "godliness" and "godliness" (εὐσεβεία, 2:2; θεοσέβειαν, 2:10), distinguished only by their prefixes, also strengthen the parallelism.

The triple occurrences of "truth" (ἀληθείας, 2:4; ἀλήθειαν, 2:7; ἀληθείᾳ, 2:7) organize the language and establish the parallelism between the B element (2:4b) and B' element (2:7).

The repetition of "one" (εἷς, 2:5a, 5b) determines the parallelism between the C element (2:5a) and C' element (2:5b). The parallelism between the C and C' elements forms the pivot of the second microchiasm. All of the aforementioned parallel words are unique to their respective elements and do not appear elsewhere in the unit.

Chart of Linguistic Parallels in the B Unit (2:1–15)

Visually representing this chiastic analysis, we observe that the second microchiasm is arranged by the following linguistic parallels:

A Element (2:1–4a)	A' Element (2:8–15)
οὖν in 2:1	οὖν in 2:8
πρῶτον in 2:1	πρῶτος in 2:13
προσευχάς in 2:1	προσεύχεσθαι in 2:8
ἡσύχιον in 2:2	ἡσυχίᾳ in 2:11, 12
πάσῃ in 2:2	πάσῃ in 2:11
εὐσεβείᾳ in 2:2	θεοσέβειαν in 2:10
σωθῆναι in 2:4a	σωθήσεται in 2:15

B Element (2:4b)	B' Element (2:7)
ἀληθείας in 2:4b	ἀλήθειαν, ἀληθείᾳ in 2:7

C Element (2:5a)	C' Element (2:5b)
εἷς in 2:5a	εἷς in 2:5b

C Unit. Godly Leadership in God's Household (3:1–16)

The third of six microchiasms within the 1 Timothy macrochiasm is composed carefully of four elements (A-B-B'-A'). Linguistic parallels identifying chiastic arrangements are indicated by the Greek text; this excludes only the *transitional word* (see *italics*) in 3:16.³⁸

> A. ³:¹ *Faithful* (πιστός) is the word: If someone aspires to overseer, a commendable work he longs-for. ² It is necessary, therefore, for the overseer to be irreproachable, man of one woman (μιᾶς γυναικὸς ἄνδρα), temperate (νηφάλιον), self-controlled, cosmopolitan, affectionate-of-stranger, able-to-teach, ³ not addicted-to-wine, not violent; rather kind, without-fighting, without-affection-of-money, ⁴ leading (προϊστάμενον) his own household (οἴκου) commendably, holding children (τέκνα) in submissiveness with all respectability, ⁵ but if someone does not know (οἶδεν) how (πῶς) to lead (προστῆναι) his own household (οἴκου), how will he care-for the church of God (ἐκκλησίας θεοῦ)?
>
>> B. ⁶ Not a young-plant, that he might not (ἵνα μή)—being-puffed-up—fall (ἐμπέσῃ) into the condemnation of the devil (διαβόλου).
>>
>> B'. ⁷ But it is necessary to hold a commendable testimony from those-outside, that he might not (ἵνα μή) fall (ἐμπέσῃ) into disgrace and the snare of the devil (διαβόλου).
>
> A'. ⁸ Likewise it is necessary for deacons to be respectable, not double-worded, not holding-toward much wine, not avaricious, ⁹ holding the mystery of the faith (πίστεως) in a pure conscience. ¹⁰ But they also must be-tested first; then they must serve-as-deacons, being blameless. ¹¹ Likewise it is necessary for women to be respectable, not devilishly-slanderous, temperate (νηφαλίους), faithful (πιστάς) in all. ¹² Deacons must be the man of one woman (μιᾶς γυναικὸς ἄνδρες), leading (προϊστάμενοι) children (τέκνων) commendably and their own households (οἴκων). ¹³ For those who serve-as-deacons commendably acquire for themselves a commendable standing and much confidence in faith that is in Christ Jesus. ¹⁴ These-things to you I write, hoping to come to you in quickness; ¹⁵ but if I am delayed, that you might know (εἰδῇς) how (πῶς) it is necessary to behave in the household (οἴκῳ) of God, which is the church of the living God (ἐκκλησία θεοῦ), a pillar and foundation of the truth. ¹⁶ And confessedly great is the mystery of godliness: he was manifested in flesh, was declared-just in *Spirit* (πνεύματι), was seen by angels, was proclaimed in the Gentiles, was counted-faithful in the world, was taken-up in glory.

---

38. The transitional word "*Spirit*" (πνεύματι, 3:16) is not part of the linguistic parallels.

Chiastic Analysis of the C Unit: the Third Microchiasm (3:1–16)

The adjective "faithful" (πιστός, 3:1) in the introductory A element recalls the noun "faith" (πίστει, 2:15) in the concluding statement of the A' element of the preceding microchiasm. These cognates function as the transitional words linking the B unit (2:1–15) to the C unit (3:1–16).

The explicit concern to establish qualified leadership and godliness within the household of God pervades this entire unit of the macrochiasm, thus establishing its thematic cohesiveness. Furthermore, the A-B-B'-A' chiastic arrangement of the third microchiasm bolsters its integrity and distinctness as a linguistic unit (3:1–16), as follows.

The A element (3:1–5) and A' element (3:8–16) are established by parallel language. The double occurrences of "faithful" (πιστός, 3:1; πιστάς, 3:11),[39] of "man of one woman" (μιᾶς γυναικὸς ἄνδρα, 3:2; μιᾶς γυναικὸς ἄνδρες, 3:12), of "temperate" (νηφάλιον, 3:2; νηφαλίους, 3:11), of "leading" (προϊστάμενον, 3:4; προϊστάμενοι, 3:12),[40] of "children" (τέκνα, 3:4; τέκνων, 3:12), of "know" (οἶδεν, 3:5; εἰδῇς, 3:15), of "how" (πῶς, 3:5, 15), and of "church of God" (ἐκκλησίας θεοῦ, 3:5; ἐκκλησία θεοῦ, 3:15) organize the language of the microchiasm into two parallel sections, thus establishing the A and A' elements and the parallelism thereof. Moreover, the fourfold occurrences of "household" (οἴκου, 3:4, 5; οἴκων, 3:12; οἴκῳ, 3:15) further support the parallelism. Finally, the cognate repetition of "wine" (see *italics*) in the leadership qualifications "not addicted-to-*wine*" (μὴ πάροινον, 3:3) and "not holding-toward much *wine*" (μὴ οἴνῳ πολλῷ προσέχοντες, 3:8) strengthens the parallelism between that A and A' elements.

The B element (2:6) and its parallel B' element (2:7) share two linguistic connections. The double occurrences of "that . . . not" (ἵνα μή), "fall" (ἐμπέσῃ), and "devil" (διαβόλου) in 3:6 and 3:7 organize the language into two parallel sections, thus establishing the B and B' elements and the parallelism between them.[41] The parallelism of the B and B' elements forms the pivot of the third microchiasm. All of the aforementioned parallel words are unique to their respective elements and do not appear elsewhere in the unit.

---

39. The occurrence of the cognate "faith" (πίστεως) in 3:9 strengthens this parallelism.

40. The occurrence of the infinitive "to lead" (προστῆναι) in 3:5 strengthens this parallelism.

41. The genitive masculine form of the adjective "devil" (διαβόλου) is unique to the B and B' elements. The accusative feminine form "devilishly-slanderous" (διαβόλους) occurs in 3:11 of the A' element and is therefore to be distinguished from the previous two occurrences.

Also, although the term "that" (ἵνα) occurs in 3:15, the uniqueness of the phrase "that . . . not" (ἵνα μή, 3:6, 7) in the B and B' elements is unaffected.

Chart of Linguistic Parallels in the C Unit (3:1–16)

Visually representing this chiastic analysis, we observe that the third microchiasm is arranged by the following linguistic parallels:

A Element (3:1–5)	A' Element (3:8–16)
πιστός in 3:1	πιστάς in 3:11
μιᾶς γυναικὸς ἄνδρα in 3:2	μιᾶς γυναικὸς ἄνδρες in 3:12
νηφάλιον in 3:2	νηφαλίους in 3:11
πάροινον in 3:3	οἴνῳ in 3:8
προϊστάμενον in 3:4	προϊστάμενοι in 3:12
οἴκου in 3:4, 5	οἴκων in 3:12; οἴκῳ in 3:15
τέκνα in 3:4	τέκνων in 3:12
οἶδεν in 3:5	εἰδῇς in 3:15
πῶς in 3:5	πῶς in 3:15
ἐκκλησίας θεοῦ in 3:5	ἐκκλησία θεοῦ in 3:15

B Element (3:6)	B' Element (3:7)
ἵνα μή in 3:6	ἵνα μή in 3:7
ἐμπέσῃ in 3:6	ἐμπέσῃ in 3:7
διαβόλου in 3:6	διαβόλου in 3:7

C' Unit. Preserving the Teaching and Promoting Godliness Amidst Apostasy (4:1–16)

The fourth of six microchiasms within the 1 Timothy macrochiasm is composed carefully of four elements (A-B-B'-A'). Linguistic parallels identifying chiastic arrangements are indicated by the Greek text; this excludes the *transitional words* (see *italics*) in 4:1 and 4:16.[42]

> A: ⁴:¹ But the *Spirit* (πνεῦμα) explicitly says that in later times some will apostasy from the faith (πίστεως), holding-toward (προσέχοντες) deceitful *spirits* (πνεύμασιν) and teachings (διδασκαλίαις) of demons, ² in the hypocrisy of false-worders, who have become-seared in their own conscience, ³ forbidding to marry, to avoid foods, which God created for reception with thanksgiving by the

---

42. The transitional words "*Spirit*" (πνεῦμα, 4:1), "*spirits*" (πνεύμασιν, 4:1), and "*Strongly-hold*" (ἔπεχε, 4:16), "*strongly-remain*" (ἐπίμενε, 4:16) are not part of the linguistic parallels.

faithful (πιστοῖς) and those who have knowingly-embraced the truth. ⁴ Because all creation of God is commendable and nothing is to be-rejected, being-received with thanksgiving; ⁵ for it is made-holy consistent-with the word of God and intercession. ⁶ Instructing these-things to the brothers you will be a commendable deacon of Christ Jesus, being-nourished in the words (λόγοις) of the faith (πίστεως) and of the commendable teaching (διδασκαλίας) that you have followed;

> B: ⁷ but the vile and silly myths reject. But train yourself toward (πρός) godliness (εὐσέβειαν); ⁸ᵃ for bodily training is toward (πρός) little profitability (ὠφέλιμος),
>
> B': ⁸ᵇ but godliness (εὐσέβεια) is toward (πρός) all profitability (ὠφέλιμός), holding the promise of life for the present and for the inevitable-coming.

A': ⁹ Faithful (πιστός) is the word (λόγος) and worthy of all acceptance; ¹⁰ for to this we toil and agonize, because we have hoped upon the living God, who is the Savior of all humans, especially of the faithful (πιστῶν). ¹¹ Charge these-things and teach (δίδασκε). ¹² None must look-down-on your youth; rather be an example of those of the faithful (πιστῶν) in word, in behavior, in love, in faith (πίστει), in purity. ¹³ Until I come hold-toward (πρόσεχε) to the reading, to the exhorting, to the teaching (διδασκαλίᾳ). ¹⁴ Do not be without-concern with the gift in you, which was given to you consistent-with prophecy with the-laying of hands of the presbytery. ¹⁵ These-things be concerned with; be in them, that your progress might be manifested to all. ¹⁶ *Strongly-hold* (ἔπεχε) yourself and the teaching (διδασκαλίᾳ), *strongly-remain* (ἐπίμενε) in them; for doing this you will save yourself and those who hear you.

Chiastic Analysis of the C' Unit: the Fourth Microchiasm (4:1–16)

The terms "Spirit" (πνεῦμα) and "spirits" (πνεύμασιν) in 4:1 of the introductory A element recall the term "Spirit" (πνεύματι) in the concluding statement (3:16) of the A' element of the previous unit. These terms function as the transitional words linking the C unit (3:1–16) to the C' unit (4:1–16).

The sustained contrast between the apostate false teachers who lead others in the teachings of demons (4:1–3) against Timothy whose commitment to the teaching of the church (4:6, 11, 13, 16) and to godliness (4:7, 8) pervades this entire unit of the macrochiasm, thus establishing its thematic cohesiveness. In addition, the A-B-B'-A' chiastic arrangement secures its integrity and distinctness as a linguistic unit of the letter (4:1–16), as follows.

The triple occurrences of the noun "faith" (πίστεως, 4:1, 6; πίστει, 4:12) initiate the parallelism of the A element (4:1–6) and A' element (4:9–16). The fourfold occurrences of the noun "teaching" (διδασκαλίαις, 4:1; διδασκαλίας, 4:6; διδασκαλίᾳ, 4:13, 16) and of the adjective "faithful" (πιστοῖς, 4:3; πιστός, 4:9; πιστῶν, 4:10, 12) further support the parallelism.[43] Finally, the double occurrences of the noun "word" (λόγοις, 4:6; λόγος, 4:9) and of the terms "holding-toward" and "hold-toward" (προσέχοντες, 4:1; πρόσεχε, 4:13) solidify the parallelism of the A and A' elements of the fourth microchiasm.

The B element (4:7–8a) and its parallel B' element (4:8b) of the fourth microchiasm are established by parallel linguistic connections. The double occurrence of "godliness" (εὐσέβειαν, 4:7; εὐσέβεια, 4:8b) and "profitability" (ὠφέλιμος, 4:8a, 4:8b) organize the language into the parallel B and B' elements. This parallelism is strengthened by the unique occurrences of the preposition "toward" (πρός, 4:7, 8a, 8b) in each of the B and B' elements. The parallelism of the B and B' elements forms the pivot of the fourth microchiasm. All of the aforementioned parallel words are unique to their respective elements and do not appear elsewhere in the unit.

Chart of Linguistic Parallels in the C' Unit (4:1–16)

Visually representing this chiastic analysis, we observe that the fourth microchiasm is arranged by the following linguistic parallels:

A Element (4:1–6)	A' Element (4:9–16)
πίστεως in 4:1, 6	πίστει in 4:12
πιστοῖς in 4:3	πιστός in 4:9; πιστῶν in 4:10, 12
προσέχοντες in 4:1	πρόσεχε in 4:13
διδασκαλίας in 4:1, 6	διδασκαλία in 4:13, 16
λόγοις in 4:6	λόγος in 4:9

B Element (4:7–8a)	B' Element (3:8b)
πρός in 4:7, 8a	πρός in 4:8b
εὐσέβειαν in 4:7	εὐσέβειαν in 4:8b
ὠφέλιμος in 4:8a	ὠφέλιμος in 4:8b

43. The occurrence of the cognate "teach" (δίδασκε) in 4:11 strengthens this parallelism.

B' Unit. Godly Conduct from All Members of God's Household (5:1—6:2)

The fifth of six microchiasms within the 1 Timothy macrochiasm is composed carefully of seven elements (A-B-C-D-C'-B'-A'). Linguistic parallels identifying chiastic arrangements are indicated by the Greek text; this excludes the *transitional words* (see *italics*) in 5:1 and 6:2.[44]

> A: ¹ An elderly-man (πρεσβυτέρῳ) do not *rebuke-violently* (ἐπιπλήξῃς); rather exhort (παρακάλει) as a father, younger-men as brothers (ἀδελφούς), ² elderly-women (πρεσβυτέρας) as mothers, younger-women as sisters (ἀδελφάς), in all purity.
>
>> B: ³ Honor widows—those truly widows (ὄντως χήρας). ⁴ But if some widow has (ἔχει) children or those-from-parents, they must learn (μανθανέτωσαν) first (πρῶτον) to be-godly to their own household (οἶκον) and to give-return repayments to their parents; for this is acceptable in the sight of God. ⁵ But she who is truly a widow (ὄντως χήρα) and who is left-remaining has hoped upon God and remains in the supplications and the prayers night and day, ⁶ but she who is self-indulgent—living—is dead. ⁷ And these charge, that they might be irreproachable. ⁸ But if someone does not provide-for those of his own and especially for household-members (οἰκείων), he has denied the faith (πίστιν) and is worse-than the without-faith (ἀπίστου). ⁹ A widow must be-enrolled not being less than sixty years, woman of one man,
>
>>> C: ¹⁰ᵃ in commendable works (ἔργοις) testified:
>
>>>> D: ¹⁰ᵇ if she raised-children, if she has shown-hospitality, if the feet of the holy-ones she washed, if the afflicted she assisted,
>
>>> C': ¹⁰ᶜ if she followed in all good work (ἔργῳ).
>
>> B': ¹¹ But younger widows reject; for when they are impassioned from Christ, they desire to marry ¹² holding condemnation because the first (πρώτην) faith (πίστιν) they rejected; ¹³ but simultaneously also they learn (μανθάνουσιν) to be idlers, going-about the houses (οἰκίας), but not only idlers; rather also gossips and busybodies, speaking what is not necessary. ¹⁴ I want, therefore, younger-women to marry,

---

44. The transitional words "*rebuke-violently*" (ἐπιπλήξῃς, 5:1) and "*teach*" (δίδασκε, 6:2) are not part of a linguistic parallel. However, the transitional word "*exhort*" (παρακάλει, 6:2) is part of a linguistic parallel to its occurrence in 5:1.

to child-parent, to master-households, to give no occasion to the opponent for maligning. ¹⁵ For already some have turned-aside after Satan. ¹⁶ If some faithful-woman has (ἔχει) widows, she must assist them and the church must not be-burdened, that it might assist those who are truly widows (ὄντως χήραις).

A': ¹⁷ The elders (πρεσβύτεροι) who lead commendably must be considered-worthy of double honor, especially those who toil in word and teaching. ¹⁸ For the writing says, "A threshing ox you shall not muzzle," and, "Worthy is the laborer of his pay." ¹⁹ Do not accept an accusation against an elder (πρεσβυτέρου), except upon two or three testifiers. ²⁰ Those who sin in the sight of all reprove, that also the rest might hold fear. ²¹ I testify in the sight of God and of Christ Jesus and of the elect angels, that these-things you might guard without prejudice, doing nothing according to favoritism. ²² Lay hands quickly on none, nor share in others's sins; keep yourself pure. ²³ No-longer drink water; rather a little wine use because of your stomach and frequent illnesses. ²⁴ The sins of some humans are conspicuous, preceding them for judgment, but for some they also follow. ²⁵ Likewise also the commendable works are conspicuous, and those having otherwise do-not have-the-power to be-hidden. ⁶:¹ Those who are under the yoke as slaves must consider their own masters worthy of all honor, that the name of God and the teaching might not be-blasphemed. ² But those who have faithful masters must not look-down because they are brothers (ἀδελφοί); rather all-the-more they must serve-as-slaves, because faithful and beloved are those who receive the beneficial-work. These-things *teach* (δίδασκε) and *exhort* (παρακάλει).

Chiastic Analysis of the B' Unit: the Fifth Microchiasm (5:1—6:2)

The verb "rebuke-violently" (ἐπιπλήξῃς) in 5:1 of the introductory A element recalls "strongly-remain" (ἐπίμενε) and "Strongly-hold" (ἔπεχε) in the concluding statement (4:16) of the A' element of the preceding unit.[45] These terms function as the transitional words linking the C' unit (4:1–16) to the B' unit (5:1—6:2).

---

45. The aural similarities between the terms (see *italics*) "teaching" (διδασκαλίᾳ) in 4:16 and "exhort" (παρακάλει) in 5:1 would also strengthen the unified movement from the C' to the B' unit.

The pervasive concern for godly conduct by all members of the household of God establishes the thematic cohesion of the microchiasm. Furthermore, the A-B-C-D-C'-B'-A' chiastic arrangement of the language secures the integrity and distinctness of the fifth microchiasm as a linguistic unit of the letter (5:1—6:2), as follows.

The cognate terms "elderly-man" and "elderly-woman" (πρεσβυτέρῳ, 5:1; πρεσβυτέρας, 5:2) and "elders" and "elder" (πρεσβύτεροι, 5:17; πρεσβυτέρου, 5:19) initiate the parallelism between the A element (5:1–2) and A' element (5:17—6:2). Similarly, the cognate terms "brothers" and "sisters" (ἀδελφούς, 5:1; ἀδελφάς, 5:2) and "brothers" (ἀδελφοί, 6:2) strengthen the parallelism. Finally, the double occurrences of the verb "exhort" (παρακάλει, 5:1; 6:2) in the first and last verses of the literary unit establish the linguistic framework and parallelism of the A and A' elements of the fifth microchiasm.

The B element (5:3–9) and its parallel B' element (5:11–16) are established by parallel linguistic connections. The only occurrences in the letter of the phrase "truly widow" (ὄντως χήρας, 5:3; ὄντως χήρα, 5:5; ὄντως χήραις, 5:16) function to organize the language into the parallel B and B' elements. The double occurrences of the verb "learn" (μανθανέτωσαν, 5:4; μανθάνουσιν, 5:13) and "has" (ἔχει, 5:4, 16) further supports the parallelism.[46] Finally, the double occurrences of the adjective "first" (πρῶτον, 5:4; πρώτην, 5:12) and the noun "faith" (πίστιν, 5:8, 12) establish the parallelism of the B and B' elements.[47]

The C element (5:10a) and C' element (5:10c) also form a parallel linguistic connection. The repetition of "works" and "work" (ἔργοις, 5:10a; ἔργῳ, 5:10c) establishes the parallelism of the C and C' elements.

The unparalleled, central, pivotal D element (5:10b) hinges the microchiasm upon the godly conduct of the true widow in God's household. All of the aforementioned parallel words are unique to their respective elements and do not appear elsewhere in the unit.

Chart of Linguistic Parallels in the B' Unit (5:1—6:2)

Visually representing this chiastic analysis, we observe that the fifth microchiasm is arranged by the following linguistic parallels:

---

46. The present active indicative third person singular "has" (ἔχει) is unique to the B and B' elements and is therefore to be distinguished from the variants of the verb that occur elsewhere in the unit—"holding" (ἔχουσαι) in 5:12, "might hold" (ἔχωσιν) in 5:20, and "holding" (ἔχοντα) in 5:25.

47. The occurrence of the adjective "without-faith" (ἀπίστου) in 4:11 strengthens this parallelism.

A Element (5:1–2)	**A' Element (5:17—6:2)**
πρεσβυτέρῳ in 5:1; πρεσβυτέρας in 5:2	πρεσβύτεροι in 5:17; πρεσβυτέρου in 5:19
παρακάλει in 5:1	παρακάλει in 6:2
ἀδελφούς in 4:1; ἀδελφάς in 4:1	ἀδελφοί in 6:2
B Element (5:3–9)	**B' Element (5:11–16)**
ὄντως χήρας in 5:3; ὄντως χήρα in 5:5	ὄντως χήραις in 5:16
ἔχει in 5:4	ἔχει in 5:16
μανθανέτωσαν in 5:4	μανθάνουσιν in 5:13
πρῶτον in 5:4	πρώτην in 5:12
οἶκον in 5:4; οἰκείων in 5:8	οἰκίας in 5:13
πίστιν in 5:8; ἀπίστου in 5:8	πίστιν in 5:12
C Element (5:10a)	**C' Element (5:10c)**
ἔργοις in 5:10a	ἔργῳ in 5:10c

A' Unit. The Teaching that is According to Godliness Is Great Gain for Eternal Life (6:3–21)

The sixth and final microchiasm within the 1 Timothy macrochiasm is composed carefully of seven elements (A-B-C-D-C'-B'-A'). Linguistic parallels identifying chiastic arrangements are indicated by the Greek text; this excludes the *transitional words* in 6:3.[48]

> A: ³ If someone (τις) *teaches-different* (ἑτεροδιδασκαλεῖ) and does not come-toward the sound words of our Lord Jesus Christ and to the *teaching* (διδασκαλίᾳ) that is according to godliness, ⁴ he is puffed-up, grasping nothing; rather having-an-unhealthy-craving regarding (περί) controversies and word-fights, from which become envy, rivalry, blasphemy, wicked suspicions, ⁵ friction of humans who are depraved in the mind and who are deprived of the truth, supposing godliness to be a means-of-gain. ⁶ But godliness with (μετά) contentment is great gain; ⁷ for we brought-in nothing into the world, that to bring-out some-thing we do-not have-the-power; ⁸ but holding food and clothing, these we will be-content with.
>
> B: ⁹ But those wanting to be-rich (πλουτεῖν) fall into temptation and snare and many senseless and harmful longings, which

---

48. The transitional word *"teaches-different"* (ἑτεροδιδασκαλεῖ, 6:3) and *"teaching"* (διδασκαλίᾳ, 6:3) are not part of a linguistic parallel.

plunge humans into ruin and destruction. ¹⁰ For the root of all evils is the affection-of-money, which some—aspiring—have wandered from the faith and have pierced themselves with many pains. ¹¹ But you, O (ὦ) human of God, flee these; but pursue justice, godliness, faith, love, steadfastness, gentleness. ¹² Agonize the commendable agony of the faith, take-possession (ἐπιλαβοῦ) of the eternal life (ζωῆς) to which you were called and to which you confessed the commendable confession in the sight of many testifiers. ¹³ I charge (παραγγέλλω), in the sight of God who provides-life to all-things and of Christ Jesus who testified before Pontius Pilate the commendable confession, ¹⁴ you to keep the commandment spotless, irreproachable until the manifesting of our Lord Jesus Christ,

> C: ¹⁵ᵃ which in his own times the blessed and only (μόνος) Power (δυνάστης) will display,
>
>> D. ¹⁵ᵇ the King of those who-are-kings and Lord of those who-are-lords,
>
> C': ¹⁶ who only (μόνος) holding without-death, housing-in without-approachable light, which no human has seen nor has power (δύναται) to see; to him honor and eternal strength, amen.

B': ¹⁷ As for the rich (πλουσίοις) in this present age, charge (παράγγελλε) them not to be-haughty, nor to hope upon the without-certainty of riches (πλούτου); rather upon God, the one who brings-about to us all-things richly (πλουσίως) for enjoyment; ¹⁸ to do-good-work, to be-rich (πλουτεῖν) in commendable works, to be generous, liberal, ¹⁹ storing-up for themselves a commendable basis for the inevitable-coming, that they might take-possession (ἐπιλάβωνται) of that which is truly life (ζωῆς). ²⁰ O (Ὦ) Timothy, the entrustment guard, turning-aside from the vile empty-talk and contradictions of false-named knowledge,

A': ²¹ which some (τινες)—professing—regarding (περί) the faith have swerved. Grace with (μεθ') you-all.

Chiastic Analysis of the A' Unit: the Sixth Microchiasm (6:3–21)

The terms "teaches-different" (ἑτεροδιδασκαλεῖ) and "teaching" (διδασκαλίᾳ) in 6:3 of the introductory A element recall the verbs "teach" (δίδασκε) and "exhort" (παρακάλει) in the concluding statement (6:2) in the A' element of the preceding unit.[49] These terms function as the transitional words linking the B' unit (5:1—6:2) to the A' unit (6:3–21).

The explicit attention toward those who do not agree with the words of Jesus Christ or the teaching that is according to godliness *and* the unprecedented way in which Paul discusses their affection-of-money establish the thematic cohesiveness of the sixth microchiasm as a literary unit. The A-B-C-D-C'-B'-A' chiastic arrangement establishes the integrity of the final linguistic unit of the letter (6:3–21), as follows.

The double occurrences of the pronouns "someone" and "some" (τις, 6:3; τινες, 6:21)[50] and the prepositions "regarding" (περί, 6:4, 21) and "with" (μετά, 6:6; μεθ', 6:21) establish the parallelism between the A element (6:3–8) and the A' element (6:21) of the sixth microchiasm.

The double occurrences of the verb "to be-rich" (πλουτεῖν, 6:9, 18),[51] the emphatic vocative "O" (ὦ, 6:11; Ὦ, 6:20), the verb "take-possession" (ἐπιλαβοῦ, 6:12; ἐπιλάβωνται, 6:19), the term "life" (ζωῆς, 6:12, 19), and the verb "charge" (παραγγέλλω, 6:13; παράγγελλε, 6:17) establish the parallelism between the B element (6:9–14) and the B' element (6:17–20).

The double occurrences of the adjective "only" (μόνος, 6:15a, 16) initiate the parallelism of the C element (6:15a) and C' element (6:16).

The unparalleled, central, and pivotal D element (6:15b) hinges the microchiasm upon the identification of God as the sole "King of those

---

49. Aurally in Greek (see *italics*), both verbs "teach" (δίδασκε) and "exhort" (παρακάλει) in 6:2 of the B' unit are heard within the verb "teaches-different" (ἑτεροδιδασκαλεῖ) in 6:3 of the A' unit.

50. The argument could be made that the pronoun "someone" (τις) at the beginning of the introductory A element in 6:3 and the pronoun "some" (τινες) at the beginning of the concluding A' element in 6:21 are deliberately arranged as part of the parallel microchiastic structure. Both pronouns (τις, 6:3; τινες, 6:21) are clearly referring to the same group who teach-different and do not come-toward the sound words of the Lord Jesus Christ and the teaching that is according to godliness (6:3). In this way, it is likely that Paul's use of the indefinite pronoun intends to strengthen the parallelism between the A and A' elements. Yet, if we are to strictly observe the rules for establishing parallels based on linguistic evidence, given that the pronoun "some" (τινες) also occurs in 6:10 of the B element, the pronouns "someone" (τις, 6:3) and "some" (τινες, 6:21) cannot be included as unique verbal parallels between the A and A' elements. At the same time, however, the strategic placement of the pronoun at the beginning and end of the microchiasm and the clear reference to the same group of false teachers would not go unnoticed by the audience and, therefore, cannot be disregarded completely in our analysis; see volume 3, chapter 3.

51. The triple occurrence of the cognates "to be-rich" (λουσίοις), "riches" (λούτου), and "richly" (λουσίως) in 6:17 strengthens this specific connection.

who-are-kings and Lord of those who-are-lords." All of the aforementioned parallel words are unique to their respective elements and do not appear elsewhere in the unit.

Chart of Linguistic Parallels in the A' Unit (6:3–21)

Visually representing this chiastic analysis, we observe that the sixth microchiasm is arranged by the following linguistic parallels:

A Element (6:3–8)	A' Element (6:21)
τις in 6:3	τινες in 6:21
περί in 6:4	περί in 6:21
μετά in 6:6	μεθ' in 6:21

B Element (6:9–14)	B' Element (6:17–20)
πλουτεῖν in 6:9	πλουτεῖν in 6:18
ὦ in 6:11	Ὦ in 6:20
ἐπιλαβοῦ in 6:12	ἐπιλάβωνται in 6:19
ζωῆς in 6:12	ζωῆς in 6:19
παραγγέλλω in 6:13	παράγγελλε in 6:17

C Element (6:15a)	C' Element (6:16)
μόνος in 5:15a	μόνος in 6:16

The Macrochiastic Structures of the 1 Timothy Letter

Having demonstrated that there are six distinct literary units—six microchiasms—that organize, structure, and arrange the language within the 1 Timothy letter, the following section will show how these six microchiasms form an A-B-C-C'-B'-A' structure that organizes and arranges the language of the entire letter into one unified literary unit—one macrochiasm.

The Parallel Arrangement of the A and A' Units

A. 1:1–20: Paul's Charge for Timothy to Preserve the Teaching

A'. 6:3–21: The Teaching that is According to Godliness Is Great Gain for Eternal Life

The A and A' units of the macrochiasm are connected by multiple sets of parallel terms and phrases.[52]

A (1:1-20)	A' (6:3-21)
Τιμοθέῳ in 1:2; Τιμόθεε in 1:18	Τιμόθεε in 6:20
χάρις in 1:2; χάριν in 1:12; χάρις in 1:14	χάρις in 6:21
κυρίου ἡμῶν in 1:2; κυρίῳ ἡμῶν in 1:12; κυρίου ἡμῶν in 1:14	κυρίου ἡμῶν in 6:3; κυρίου ἡμῶν in 6:14
ἑτεροδιδασκαλεῖν in 1:3; ἕτερον in 1:10b	ἑτεροδιδασκαλεῖ in 6:3
παρέχουσιν in 1:4	παρέχοντι in 6:17
ἐκζητήσεις in 1:4	ζητήσεις in 6:4
ἀστοχήσαντες in 1:6	ἠστόχησαν in 6:21
ὑγιαινούσῃ in 1:10	ὑγιαίνουσιν in 6:10
μακαρίου in 1:11	μακάριος in 6:15
δείξηται in 1:16	δείξει in 6:15
αἰώνων, αἰῶνας, and αἰώνων in 1:17	αἰώνιον, 6:16; αἰῶνι in 6:17
ἀμήν in 1:17	ἀμήν in 6:16

All of the aforementioned parallel terms and phrases are unique to the A and A' units of the macrochiasm and do not appear elsewhere in the letter.

The Parallel Arrangement of the B and B' Units

B. 2:1-15: Salvation for All through Prayer and Godly Conduct

B'. 5:1—6:2: Godly Conduct from All Members of God's Household

The B and B' units of the macrochiasm are connected by multiple sets of parallel terms and phrases.

B (2:1-15)	B' (5:1—6:2)
δεήσεις in 2:1	δεήσεσιν in 5:5
προσευχάς in 2:1; προσεύχεσθαι in 2:8	προσευχαῖς in 5:5
ἡσύχιον in 2:2	ἡσυχία in 2:11, 12
ἀπόδεκτον in 2:3	ἀπόδεκτον in 5:4
χωρίς in 2:8	χωρίς in 5:21
μανθανέτω in 2:1	μανθανέτωσαν in 5:4; μανθάνουσιν in 5:13

---

52. The first four terms listed in the A unit ("Timothy"; "grace"; "our Lord"; "teach-different"/"different") are worth noting. Within the A unit, they each occur in a parallel arrangement in the A and A' elements; see above regarding the analysis of the first microchiasm. Such would strengthen the rhetorical force and deliberate arrangement of the 1 Timothy letter.

All of the aforementioned parallel terms and phrases are unique to the B and B' units of the macrochiasm and do not appear elsewhere in the letter.

The Parallel Arrangement of the C and C' Units

C. 3:1–16: Godly Leadership in God's Household

C'. 4:1–16: Preserving the Teaching and Promoting Godliness Amidst Apostasy

The C and C' units of the macrochiasm are connected by multiple sets of parallel terms and phrases.

C (3:1–16)	C' (4:1–16)
διακόνους in 3:8; διακονείτωσαν in 3:10; διάκονοι in 3:12; διακονήσαντες in 3:13	διάκονος in 4:6
προσέχοντας in 3:8	προσέχοντες in 4:1
ἀναστρέφεσθαι in 3:15	ἀναστροφῇ in 4:12
θεοῦ ζῶντος in 3:15	θεῷ ζῶντι in 4:10
πνεύματι in 3:16	πνεῦμα and πνεύμασιν in 4:1

All of the aforementioned parallel terms and phrases are unique to the C and C' units of the macrochiasm and do not appear elsewhere in the letter.[53]

---

53. There are two exceptions. One involves the verb προσέχω. The participle forms "holding-toward" (προσέχοντας) in 3:8 and "holding-toward" (προσέχοντες) in 4:1 are unique to the C and C' units and are to be distinguished from the infinitive and imperative variants of the verb that occur elsewhere in the letter—"to hold-toward" (προσέχειν) in 1:4 and "hold-toward" (πρόσεχε) in 4:13.

The other exception involves the noun and verbal forms of διάκονος. Although the cognate term "service" (διακονίαν) occurs in 1:12 of the A unit, it is an entirely different word and does not disrupt the unique occurrence of the noun and verbal forms of "deacon" in the C and C' units.

3

1 Timothy 1:1–20: Paul's Charge for Timothy to Preserve the Teaching

(A Unit)

THIS CHAPTER EXAMINES THE A unit of the macrochiasm—the first of six microchiasms within the 1 Timothy letter.[1] Within this first microchiasm (1:1–20), three minichiasms are heard (1:1; 1:3–7; 1:11–17).

The First Microchiasm

The 1:1–20 microchiasm is composed carefully of five elements (A-B-C-B'-A'); linguistic parallels identifying chiastic arrangements are indicated by the Greek text:

> A. ¹:¹ Paul, apostle of Christ Jesus (Χριστοῦ Ἰησοῦ) according to (κατ') the command of God (θεοῦ) our Savior and Christ Jesus (Χριστοῦ Ἰησοῦ) our hope: ² To Timothy (Τιμοθέῳ), genuine child (τέκνῳ) in faith (πίστει): grace (χάρις), mercy (ἔλεος), peace from God (θεοῦ) and Christ Jesus our Lord (Χριστοῦ Ἰησοῦ κυρίου ἡμῶν). ³ As I exhorted you to remain in Ephesus while-journeying for Macedonia, that you might charge (παραγγείλῃς) some not to teach-different (ἑτεροδιδασκαλεῖν) ⁴ nor to hold-toward myths and genealogies without-limit, which bring-about (παρέχουσιν) controversial-speculations rather than the household-law of God (θεοῦ) in faith (πίστει). ⁵ But the end of the charge (παραγγελίας) is (ἐστίν) love (ἀγάπη) from a pure heart and a good conscience

---

1. For the establishment of 1 Timothy as a macrochiasm, clarifications of terminology, and an explanation of my translation methodology, see chapter 2.

(συνειδήσεως ἀγαθῆς) and a without-hypocrisy faith (πίστεως), ⁶ which (ὧν) some (τινες)—swerving-from—have turned-aside for useless-words, ⁷ desiring to be law-teachers, not understanding either what they-are-saying or regarding some-things they-are-insisting.

    B. ⁸ᵃ But we know (οἴδαμεν) that the law (νόμος) is commendable,

        C. ⁸ᵇ if someone uses it lawfully,

    B'. ⁹ knowing (εἰδώς) this, that for the just the law (νόμος) is not laid but for the without-law (ἀνόμοις) and without-obedience, the without-godly and sinners, the without-reverence and vile, patricides and matricides, murderers, 10a fornicators, sodomites, kidnappers, falsifiers, perjurers,

A'. ¹⁰ᵇ and if some-thing different (ἕτερον) lies-opposed to the sound teaching (διδασκαλίᾳ), ¹¹ according to (κατά) the gospel of the glory of the blessed God (θεοῦ), with which I-myself was counted-faithful (ἐπιστεύθην). ¹² I hold grace (χάριν) to him who empowered me, Christ Jesus our Lord (Χριστῷ Ἰησοῦ τῷ κυρίῳ ἡμῶν), because faithful (πιστόν) he considered me appointing for service, ¹³ though firstly being a blasphemer and persecutor and hubristic-person; rather I was granted-mercy (ἠλεήθην), because without-knowing I did in unfaithfulness (ἀπιστίᾳ); ¹⁴ but the grace (χάρις) of our Lord (κυρίου ἡμῶν) beyond-abounded with the faith (πίστεως) and love (ἀγάπης) that are in Christ Jesus (Χριστῷ Ἰησοῦ). ¹⁵ Faithful (πιστός) is the word and worthy of all acceptance, that Christ Jesus (Χριστὸς Ἰησοῦς) came into the world to save sinners, of whom (ὧν) I-myself am the first. ¹⁶ Rather consistent-with this I was granted-mercy (ἠλεήθην), that in me the first Christ Jesus (Χριστὸς Ἰησοῦς) might display all patience as an example to those who would-inevitably-come to have-faith (πιστεύειν) upon him for life eternal. ¹⁷ But to the King of the eternities, without-perishability, without-visibility, only God (θεῷ), honor and glory for the eternities of the eternities, amen. ¹⁸ This charge (παραγγελίαν) I entrust to you, child Timothy (τέκνον Τιμόθεε), according to (κατά) the prophecies preceding upon you, that you might war in them the commendable war, ¹⁹ holding faith (πίστιν) and a good conscience (ἀγαθὴν συνείδησιν), which some (τινες)—by rejecting—regarding the faith (πίστιν) have become-shipwrecked, ²⁰ of whom (ὧν) are (ἐστιν) Hymenaeus and Alexander, whom I have given-over (παρέδωκα) to Satan, that they might be-disciplined not to blaspheme.

1 Timothy 1:1–7: Charge Some Not to Teach-Different

(A Element)

Within the introductory A element of the microchiasm (1:1–7), the audience hear two minichiasms (1:1; 1:3–7). In this section, each of the two minichiasms will be examined.

1 Timothy 1:1: A Minichiastic Unit

The Ephesian audience hear the first verse of the letter as a minichiasm in itself. Verse 1:1 is composed carefully of three sub-elements ("a"-"b"-"a'"); linguistic parallels identifying chiastic arrangements are indicated by the Greek text:

"a". [1:1a] Paul, apostle of Christ Jesus (Χριστοῦ Ἰησοῦ)

"b". [1b] according to the command of God (θεοῦ) our Savior

"a'". [1c] and Christ Jesus (Χριστοῦ Ἰησοῦ) our hope

The first minichiasm of the 1:1–20 microchiasm is framed by the person of "Christ Jesus," who is both the introduction and conclusion of Paul's discussion in the "a" and "a'" sub-elements. The minichiasm gravitates around the activity and personal description of "God our Savior" in the pivot "b" sub-element. Thematically and rhetorically, where "Christ Jesus" centers and hinges upon "God our Savior," a close personal association between them is highlighted.[2]

---

2. This is most likely intentional, communicating to the audience a high Christology. For more regarding the christological intention of 1 Timothy, see Belleville, "Christology, the PE," 317–38.

1 Timothy 1:1a: Paul, Apostle of Christ Jesus

("a" sub-element)

In the introductory "a" sub-element (1:1a), the letter begins with the author's self-identification as "Paul, apostle of Christ Jesus."[3] That Paul is an "apostle" (ἀπόστολος) communicates that he has been "sent out" with authority to deliver a message on behalf of the sender.[4] That he is specifically an apostle of "Christ Jesus" (Χριστοῦ Ἰησοῦ) expresses both the source of his authority and his commitment to the one who has sent him.[5] The audience, therefore, understand that they are about to hear and experience not only what "Paul" (Παῦλος) intends to say but also—and far more significantly—what "Christ Jesus" (Χριστοῦ Ἰησοῦ) himself will communicate through his very own

---

3. Belleville comments on the word order of "Christ Jesus," suggesting a specific emphasis on the connection between Jesus and salvation: "The word order Χριστὸς Ἰησοῦς is significant. Ἰησοῦς is descriptive—'Christ the Saving One,' rather than the usual Ἰησοῦς Χριστός—Jesus the 'Anointed One' or 'Messiah'" ("Christology," 322).

4 Swinson, *Letters to Timothy*, 47–48: "The idea of being dispatched or commissioned so as to represent another person lies chiefly in the use of ἀπόστολος. Lexically, the word typically expresses the sense of 'envoy,' 'messenger,' delegate,' or 'one sent by another.'" See Heil, *Ephesians*, 47 n. 3; Knight, *PE*, 58.

Much has been written on the subject of apostleship. Some introductory works include Barrett, *Signs of an Apostle*, 49–60; Gaffin, *By Faith*, 14–15; Ridderbos, *Redemptive History*, 1–52; Agnew, "Origin of the NT Apostle-Concept," 75–96; Pfitzner, "Office and Charism," 28–38.

5. Towner, *Letters*, 95: ". . . he signals primarily that the letter with its teaching falls under the category of apostolic authority . . . His status is therefore that of an authoritative leader, one to whom a divine commission has been given . . . This history conferred on Paul the obligation and right to adjudicate, as Christ's sent one,' in all matters of church life." Swinson, *Letters to Timothy*, 48: "Syntactically, this impression [authority] is reinforced by the genitival Χριστοῦ Ἰησοῦ, likely expressing origin, source, or possession. Together with the subsequent prepositional phrase, it serves to indicate whom the apostolic agent represents and under whose auspices he carries out his appointed tasks." Becker, "The Person of Paul," 126: "Paul's apostolicity goes back to a calling . . . of the Son of God, Jesus Christ . . . From that time on Paul considers himself directly dependent on Jesus Christ—the term 'apostle' is more precisely qualified by a *genitives qualitatis* (Iēsou Christou) . . . This 'professional qualification' which distinguishes Paul from other, competing or even hostile, apostles is linked to Paul's whole person and existence . . . This subordination to Christ, however, at the same time becomes for Paul a co-ordination with Christ . . . Hence with regard to the person of Jesus Christ Paul sees himself in an extremely close relationship." See Heil, *Ephesians*, 48 n. 4. For more on apostolic authority, see Ridderbos, *Paul*, 448–50; Phillips, *Paul, His Letters, and Acts*, 157 n. 2; Belleville, "1 Timothy," 26. That apostleship does not connote an authoritative office but rather a function, see Wills, *What Paul Meant*, 189–90.

representative messenger—his "apostle" (ἀπόστολος)—in the entirety of the letter and its performance.⁶

1 Timothy 1:1b: According to the Command of God Our Savior

("b" sub-element)

In the pivot "b" sub-element of the minichiasm (1:1b), Paul underscores that he is an apostle of Christ Jesus "according to the command of God our Savior." With this, Paul communicates three significant points to the audience. First, Paul is an apostle of Christ Jesus not according to his own decision or doing but "according to (κατ') the command (ἐπιταγήν) of God (θεοῦ)" (1:1b).⁷ That is, at the beginning of the letter, Paul immediately invites the audience to interpret his apostolic calling—his legitimacy to represent Christ Jesus—as the direct action of "God" himself. Indeed, the authoritative connotation of the word "command" (ἐπιταγήν) would not only convey God's authority over Paul's life but also—and subsequently—Paul's authoritative status as an apostle. In short, the audience understand that "Paul, apostle" is both an expression of divine will and carries the direct authority of "God" himself.⁸

Second, that Paul is an apostle by the command of God "our Savior" (σωτῆρος ἡμῶν) both identifies God as the personal orchestrator of salvation and conveys the unique, vital role that Paul has in God's orchestration thereof.⁹ In other words, that the "Savior" himself has commanded Paul, the audience understand that anything and everything Paul says in the letter

---

6. Gaffin aptly captures the intended posture that the Ephesian audience are to have toward Paul: "Rather, our deepest concern with him is as he is an apostle—that is, as he is an instrument of God's revelation, authorized by the exalted Christ to attest and interpret the salvation manifested in Christ" (*By Faith*, 8). For the performative aspect of the 1 Timothy letter, see chapter 1.

7. Towner notes the appearance of this term to refer to commands issued by the apostle and his coworkers. In this particular instance, he asserts that the term is to be understood specially "in relation to Paul's calling to preacher" (*Letters*, 96 n. 11). For further discussion on the phrase "according to the command" (κατ' ἐπιταγήν), see Couser, "Sovereign Savior," 109–10.

8. Barcley, *1 & 2 Timothy*, 34: "1 Timothy is unique in that Paul stresses that his apostleship is by God's command. This phrase ... strengthens Paul's (and, consequently, Timothy's) authority." Knight, *PE*, 61: "ἐπιταγή ... which means 'command,' 'order,' or 'injunction' ... should probably be explained by Paul's desire to relate his being under orders ..." See Fairbairn, *Commentary*, 70; Belleville, "1 Timothy," 25.

9. See Saarinen, *PE*, 32.

will have salvific implications.¹⁰ Thus at the outset of the letter, Paul highlights that salvation is at stake; such would be a summons for the audience's full attention and response.

Third, the audience would likely hear a subversive note suggested by Paul's immediate use of the term "Savior." During this period of history in the first-century Greco-Roman world, "Savior" was used to describe Hellenistic kings, gods, heroes, and emperors.¹¹ Moreover, specific to the historic context of Ephesus, "Savior" was associated with the Ephesian goddess Artemis.¹² For those in the Ephesian church, therefore, the rhetorical declaration that God is "our (ἡμῶν) Savior" would not go unnoticed. In full, the phrase "God our Savior" would be understood as a mutual, shared, and significant assertion by Paul and the Ephesian audience that their God alone is the true Savior of all mankind.¹³

1 Timothy 1:1c: And According to the Command of Christ Jesus Our Hope

("a'" sub-element)

In the concluding "a'" sub-element of the minichiasm (1:1c), Paul conveys that he is an apostle *both* by the command of God our Savior "and Christ Jesus our hope."¹⁴ The immediate repetition of "our" (ἡμῶν) in the phrase

---

10. Barcley, *1 & 2 Timothy*, 35: "Thus Paul's reference to God as 'Saviour' here in the salutation gives us a hint that God's purposes and activities with regard to the work of salvation are going to be at the very heart and soul of the letter."

11. See Wendland, "Σωτήρ," 335–53; Towner, *Letters*, 97; Caulley, "*Christianos* and Roman Imperial Cult," 199, 201; Belleville, "Christology, the PE," 335.

12. See discussion in chapter 1 esp. regarding the events that transpired during the founding of the church in Ephesus, which are recorded in Acts 19.

13. Wall with Steele, *1 & 2 Timothy*, 55: "the congregation's accommodation of Greco-Roman culture" may have been part of the "theological crisis that occasions 1 Timothy." Marshall, *PE*, 355: "The use of ἡμῶν emphasises the reality of the purpose of God as it is experienced by his people and is not meant in any kind of exclusive manner . . . There may even be a polemical note against any opponents who denied the universality of God's saving purposes." Similarly, see Barcley, *1 & 2 Timothy*, 35.

Given the widespread worship of Artemis in Ephesus, it is likely that many of the Ephesian converts had once been devotees of Artemis. Paul's collective statement here in 1:1b—"God *our* Savior"—would likely be a reminder of their former lives—without God as their Savior—thus spurring them to gratitude and sober reflection.

14. Marshall, *PE*, 35: "The collocation of God and Christ in phrases such as this (and in the actual greeting formula) indicates how natural it was for early Christians to place the two persons alongside one another without any sense of incongruity and demonstrates the way in which Christ was seen to belong on the divine side of reality."

"Christ Jesus our hope" strengthens the bond between Paul and his audience.[15] That is, although Paul has been uniquely commissioned as an apostle of Christ Jesus (1:1a) and has divine authority in relation to the audience (1:1b), Paul makes equally clear that he is not superior to the audience: Christ Jesus is both his hope and the audience's hope (1:1c).[16] The description of Christ Jesus as Paul and the audience's common "hope" (ἐλπίδος) conveys a certainty that awaits them.[17] Significantly, the certainty of their future is grounded in a person, "Christ Jesus." What is more, the acutely personal, rhetorical emphasis that Paul is an apostle of "Christ Jesus" (Χριστοῦ Ἰησοῦ, 1:1a) according to the command of "Christ Jesus" (Χριστοῦ Ἰησοῦ,, 1:1c) not only highlights Paul's legitimacy to fully represent Christ Jesus but also underscores that Paul's representational authority is fully derived from Christ Jesus himself. In effect, then, the significance of "Paul, apostle of Christ Jesus" (1:1a) in the "a" sub-element reaches its full implication with the pivotal movement of the minichiasm across the "b" sub-element and into the "a'" sub-element: as an apostle (1:1a), Paul communicates with the authority of "God" (1:1b), delivers a message of salvation by "our Savior" (1:1b), and rightfully carries the direct, personal message of "Christ Jesus" who is "our hope" (1:1c).

As the minichiasm concludes, the linguistic arrangement and thematic unity asserts a clear introduction to Paul's audience of the 1 Timothy letter. Paul's message to the audience is to be understood as authoritative because it hinges upon "the command of God" in the "b" sub-element (1:1b), and his parallel representational status as an "apostle of Christ Jesus . . . Christ Jesus our hope" (1:1a, 1c) in the "a" and "a'" sub-elements frames the scope of Paul's message. In sum, Paul's communication in the 1 Timothy letter as an apostle of Christ Jesus represents the collaborative orchestration of God and Christ Jesus to effect salvation in history toward a definitive, certain hope. The audience are thus prepared to hear and respond to what God and

---

Wall with Steele, *1 & 2 Timothy*, 59: "The grammatical parallel between . . . God and Jesus implies that the divine command that legitimizes Pauline apostleship is given by both in unison and with mutual support."

15. See Knight, *PE*, 62.

16. A looser translation would read: "Christ Jesus who is our common hope." In passing perhaps it is worth noting how this form of the pronoun "our" (ἡμῶν) occurs disproportionately more in the first microchiasm (five occurrences: 1:1, 2, 12, 14) in comparison to the rest of the letter (three occurrences: 2:3; 6:3, 14). It would appear that from the outset Paul is seeking to deepen his bond with the audience.

17. Knight, *PE*, 62: ". . . the sure expectation Paul has for himself and those who respond to the gospel embodied in Christ as our hope. In the NT, because ἐλπίς is based on the person and work of Christ Jesus, the word takes on a note of confident expectation, even if that expectation is not yet fully realized and is still in the future."

Christ Jesus, their common Savior and hope (1:b, c), will uniquely communicate through the full, representational authority of Paul, an apostle of Christ Jesus (1:1a).

1 Timothy 1:2: To Timothy, Genuine Child
In Faith, Grace, Mercy, Peace

(A Element, continued)

Having communicated not only that his authority is from God but also that his allegiance is strictly to Christ Jesus, the apostle now extends his authority to Timothy, whom Paul addresses as "genuine child." The adjective "genuine" (γνησίῳ) implies "legitimate," a descriptor of children born in wedlock.[18] In effect, the figurative application to Timothy calls the audience to recognize Timothy as Paul's "apostle," that is, as Paul's true emissary—sent and vested with Paul's authority—even as Paul is Christ's genuine representative.[19] Significantly, then, from the outset of the letter Paul establishes an unbreakable link: to receive Timothy is to receive Paul, which is to receive Christ Jesus.[20] Moreover, the use of familial language—"child" (τέκνῳ)—conveys a twofold nuance. On the one hand, "child" introduces the predominant theme of the letter, namely viewing other believers in light of Christ Jesus as family—fellow household members. On the other hand, Paul's specification of Timothy as "child" carries the sense that Timothy must properly represent his "father"—Paul—in the same way that the authorized apostle Paul must properly represent Christ Jesus in accordance with the command of God.

---

18. BDAG, s.v. Barcley, *1 & 2 Timothy*, 36: "The Greek word *gnēsios* has the sense of 'genuine' or 'legitimate,' and was often used to contrast legitimate from illegitimate children." See Schlatter, *Die Kirche der Griechen*; Fairbairn, *Commentary*, 72. See also Knight, *PE*, 64.

19. Towner, *Letters*, 99: "Extended figuratively to the fictive relationship (cf. Phil 2:20), the authenticity implied by the term guarantees Timothy's faith and right to represent Paul in Ephesus, as it also underlines his obligation to serve the father with authentic commitment (Phil 2:22)." Belleville, "1 Timothy," 26: "The Ephesian church must understand that whatever Timothy did, he did so with the full force of apostolic authority." For more on Timothy's representational status, see Wall with Steele, *1 & 2 Timothy*, 55, 59; Knight, *PE*, 25, 58.

20. Barcley, *1 & 2 Timothy*, 34: "Paul sets up . . . a chain of command. All the orders that come from Paul to Timothy, and through Timothy to the church, ultimately originate in God himself." Mitchell, "New Testament Envoys," 645, 647: "proper reception of the envoy necessarily entails proper reception of the one who sent him . . . The principle that the envoy should be received according to the status of the one by whom he was sent is abundantly attested in Greco-Roman writings."

(1:1a–b).²¹ Still, the additional qualifier "in faith" (ἐν πίστει) defines the relationship between Paul and Timothy even more precisely. The preposition "in" (ἐν) suggests the two share a common sphere of existence with respect to both the act and object of "faith" (πίστει).²² No doubt marked by the double-repetition of Christ Jesus's name in 1:1 (Χριστοῦ Ἰησοῦ, 1:1a, 1c), such a sphere is not only entered through "faith" "in" Christ Jesus but also has as its object Christ Jesus. In short, Paul underscores that his personal, familial relationship with Timothy is wholly defined by their common relation to Christ Jesus. It is because of Christ Jesus that Paul and Timothy's shared existence "in faith" unites them as family (1:2).

Verse 1:2 continues with the apostle's note of blessing for Timothy and the audience: "grace, mercy, peace from God the Father and Christ Jesus our Lord."²³ This blessing is clearly derived "from" (ἀπό) God, the source whom Paul identified as "our Savior" in 1:1b. Therefore, as blessings directed to the audience from God our Savior, the terms "grace," "mercy," and "peace" are to be understood in a soteriological manner, that is, as blessings associated with God's plan of salvation. The term "grace" (χάρις) refers not just to "kindness" or "favor," but rather a gift of kindness and favor that has "God our Savior" and "Christ Jesus our hope" as the point of reference (1:1b–c).²⁴

---

21. Wall with Steele, *1 & 2 Timothy*, 60: "'genuine son,' expresses... the expectation that one who is truly a son will imitate his father... the rhetorical relationship between author and audience may be understood as mimetic. Paul is Timothy's role model, whose character and sacred practices are learned firsthand." Keegan, *First and Second Timothy*, 9: "This expression illustrates an understanding of the church as a genuinely new family that needs to be nurtured and protected as it grows and matures, as well as designating Timothy as the legitimate representative authorized to minister in Paul's name." See Brookins, "'I Rather Appeal to *Auctoritas*,'" 315–17.

22. Knight, *PE*, 64: "ἐν πίστει demarcates the sonship as being in the realm of faith." Towner, *Letters*, 99: "The locus of their relationship was their shared belief in Christ. The prepositional phrase that describes this, 'in faith,' is Pauline shorthand for being a Christian; here it describes the sphere in which Timothy is Paul's child, the common bond that unites them as family... It is the equivalent of the reality described by the other Pauline phrase, 'in Christ,' with 'in faith' viewing that reality from the perspective of the activity (and content) of belief." For discussion on the equivalence of the phrases "in faith" and "in Christ Jesus," see 1:14 below; see also volume 2, chapter 2 regarding 1 Timothy 3:13. Cf. Belleville, "1 Timothy," 25: "the phrase should be translated as either (1) 'through faith' (i.e., Timothy became Paul's spiritual son through faith in Christ) or (2) 'in the sphere of faith' (i.e., Timothy is Paul's son in the household of faith)."

23. Towner, *Letters*, 101: "The terms were already linked in blessings, in non-epistolary contexts, in Judaism, and the form occurring in Paul's greetings approximates the benediction or blessing he might have pronounced orally in person to a church." For further discussion on Paul's greeting formula, see Jervis, *Comparative Letter Structure*, 83–85; Lieu, "'Grace to you and Peace,'" 161–78.

24. There may also be a subversive element. Barcley, "1 Timothy," 358: "Grace (χάρις) is a Pauline, Christianized adaptation of the standard greeting in Greco-Roman

Similarly, "mercy" (ἔλεος) does not merely express "steadfast love" or "compassion," but specifically has to do with the "grace" associated with Christ Jesus.[25] Finally, "peace" (εἰρήνη) refers to both inner and outer restfulness, yet only insofar as these realities have been realized through "God our Savior," whose blessings of "grace" and "mercy" become factitive in light of "Christ Jesus our hope" (1:1).[26] Evidently, Paul's concern is that Timothy specifically, but also the audience generally, would have a continual and deeper experience of these blessings, that is, a richer experience of the salvation that is from God.

Paul further specifies that the source of these blessings is "God the Father and Christ Jesus our Lord" (1:2).[27] By referencing God as "Father" (πατρός), Paul expounds several aspects of the letter thus far. First, Paul progresses the audience's view that God is both "our Savior" (1:1) and "Father" (1:2). Second, that "God the Father" is also "God our Savior" indicates that the three blessings from God the Father are salvific in nature. Third and finally, God's identification as "Father" also highlights again the explicit familial emphasis of the letter, as introduced by Timothy's identification as "genuine child."[28] The clear implication is that Paul wants his audience to appreciate the blessings of salvation within the framework of "family." Moreover, that God is the "Father" means that the household members live according to his provisions and under his rule; in this way, the audience are to respond to "God the Father" with both love and reverent fear.[29]

---

letters (χαίρειν)." See Köstenberger and Patterson, *Biblical Interpretation*, 456; Schreiner, *Interpreting the Pauline Epistles*, 15.

25. Heil, *Letters of Paul*, 161: "Distinctive to this prayer-greeting is the inclusion of 'mercy' (*eleos*) to provide a specific focus for the grace." See Knight, *PE*, 66; Barcley, *1 & 2 Timothy*, 38–39.

26. See Knight, *PE*, 67. The term "peace" (εἰρήνη) would also refer to a Jewish greeting, particularly the OT theme of *shalom*; see Barcley, "1 Timothy," 358. Köstenberger and Patterson, *Biblical Interpretation*, 456: Paul's "inclusion of a Greek and Hebrew type of greeting may indicate the fact that Paul was writing to a mixed audience including both Jews and Gentiles." See Schreiner, *Interpreting the Pauline Epistles*, 15.

27. Knight, *PE*, 67: "These three gifts have one common source: God and Jesus; ἀπό occurs once and therefore includes both persons." Barcley, *1 & 2 Timothy*, 39: "Father and Son together are the single source of divine blessing."

28. See Belleville, "1 Timothy," 28.

29. For Paul's Greco-Roman audience, the use of "Father" would likely identify God as the ruling of a household. Plessis, *Roman Law*, 113: "Roman family law was based on the fundamental concept that each family had a *paterfamilias*—the head of the household. He was the eldest living male ancestor of a specific family. He had in his power (*potestas*) all *descendents* traced through the male line (and also exercised forms of control over other members of the household). The *paterfamilias* was *sui iuris*, i.e., legally independent—he could not be in anyone else's power."

Still, where "Christ Jesus" (Χριστοῦ Ἰησοῦ) is equally named as the source of the three salvific blessing, it is clear that salvation involves the mutual participation of "Christ Jesus" with "God the Father" (1:2). Notably, at this point in the letter the audience have heard the name "Christ Jesus" repeated three times, suggesting that Paul wants to remove any possible misunderstanding: Christ Jesus is the foundation of everything that Paul will say in the letter. By referencing Christ as "our Lord" (κυρίου ἡμῶν), Paul progresses the audience's view of Christ in several important ways. First, the audience have a fuller understanding of who Christ Jesus is, namely both "our hope" (1:1) and "our Lord" (1:2). Second, by ascribing the title "Lord" (κυρίου) to Christ Jesus in direct view of God the Father, Paul effectively identifies that Christ Jesus is equally the very God of the OT.[30] Thus Paul makes clear that Christ Jesus is the "Lord" who shares in God the Father's position as ruler of the same household.[31] Third, Paul's use of the term "Lord" (κυρίου)—a title widely used for the Roman emperor—may carry a subversive connotation, calling upon his audience to affirm and agree about the superior lordship of Christ Jesus.[32] Fourth and finally, through the

---

30. In the Hebrew Bible (the OT), God's personal name (commonly referred to as the Tetragrammaton) consists of four Hebrew letters: YHWH. However, because God's name was considered too sacred for anyone to speak, Hebrew vowels for the word "Lord" were superimposed on the Hebrew letters YHWH, which indicated that each time God's name appeared in the OT, the title "Lord" was to be read aloud. For this reason, each time God's personal name appears in the Greek translation of the Hebrew Bible—the Septuagint (LXX)—the Greek word "Lord" (κύριος) is used to refer to the sacred name of God. To be sure, Paul's application of "Lord" (κυρίου) to Christ Jesus in 1 Timothy 1:2 would not go unnoticed. For further discussion see Bowman and Komoszewski, *Putting Jesus in His Place*, 157–58. Collins, *1 & 2 Timothy*, 39: "This usage of the Greek Bible, in which 'Lord' regularly renders the Hebrew 'Yahweh,' is indicative of the practice of Hellenistic Judaism to identify the God of Abraham, Isaac, and Jacob as 'Lord.'" Akin, "Mystery of Godliness is Great," 151: "Paul was comfortable in ascribing divine attributes, titles, and prerogatives to Jesus. He is the Lord (κύριος = Yahweh)." See Schreiner, *Paul*, 168.

Belleville provides a helpful nuance for understanding the term: "The title κύριος prior to resurrection, can be understood as equivalent to our 'Sir' (a title of respect) . . . But beyond the resurrection-ascension, κύριος becomes the title of divinity" ("'Son' Christology," 74). That post-resurrection-ascension divinity is intended, see volume 2, chapter 2 regarding 1 Timothy 3:16.

31. Knight, *PE*, 68: "Christ Jesus (see v. 1) is joined to God the Father . . . by the use of καί and is called κύριος." Belleville, "Christology, the PE," 322: "Christology in the Pastorals is expressed primarily by means of titles, particularly the titles κύριος and σωτήρ . . . κύριος and σωτήρ are not independent titles. In each instance they are descriptive of the primary title Χριστὸς Ἰησοῦς." Harris indicates that Paul places "ἡμῶν after the reference to Christ and thus make it imperative to coordinate κυρίου Ἰησοῦ Χριστοῦ with θεοῦ πατρός" (*Second Epistle to the Corinthians*, 136).

32. Collins, *1 & 2 Timothy*, 161: "The title 'Lord' was readily applied to the gods and

repetition of the pronoun "our" (ἡμῶν), Paul further highlights the bond between himself and the audience. At this point in the letter, the audience have heard "our" for the third time; as with the name of Christ Jesus, then, Paul leaves no room for ambiguity: for those who accept *both* Paul as Christ Jesus's apostle (1:1a) and Christ Jesus as their common hope (1:1c), they are united together in a common allegiance to Christ Jesus "our Lord" (1:2). In this way, Paul's cumulative movement in the beginning of the letter is clear: as an apostle according to the command of God and Christ Jesus, Paul serves and lives according to the direct lordship of Christ and fatherhood of God (1:1–2); as a genuine child who represents his father Paul "in faith," Timothy serves and lives by Paul's authority within the direct lordship of Christ and fatherhood of God (1:2); and as recipients of Paul's letter and God's saving blessings, the audience serve and live under the direct lordship of Christ and fatherhood of God, specifically within the immediate representational authority of Paul and thus Timothy (1:1–2). Having been reminded of their common experience of grace, mercy, and peace as members of God's family, the audience are freshly prepared to hear what Christ Jesus, their common hope and Lord, will communicate with authority through his very own personal messenger, the apostle Paul.

1 Timothy 1:3–7: A Minichiastic Unit

Within the A element of the microchiasm (1:1–7), the audience hear 1:3–7 as a minichiasm in itself. Verses 1:3–7 are composed carefully of four sub-elements ("a"-"b"-"b'"-"a'"); linguistic parallels identifying chiastic arrangements are indicated by the Greek text:

> "a". ³ As I exhorted you to remain in Ephesus while-journeying for Macedonia, that you might charge (παραγγείλῃς) some (τισίν) not to teach-different (ἑτεροδιδασκαλεῖν)
>
>> "b". ⁴ᵃ nor to hold-toward (προσέχειν) myths and genealogies without-limit,
>>
>> "b'". ⁴ᵇ which bring-about (παρέχουσιν) controversial-speculations rather than the household-law of God in faith.
>
> "a'". ⁵ But the end of the charge (παραγγελίας) is love from a pure heart and a good conscience and a without-hypocrisy faith, ⁶ which some (τινες)—swerving-from—have turned-aside for useless-words, ⁷ desiring to be law-teachers (νομοδιδάσκαλοι),

---

to the emperor." See Seo, *Luke's Jesus*, 16–17.

not understanding either what they-are-saying or regarding some-things they-are-insisting.

The second minichiasm of the 1:1–20 microchiasm is framed by the "charge" that Timothy must carry out toward "some" who "teach-different" and "some" who are desiring to be "law-teachers" in the "a" and "a'" sub-elements. The minichiasm gravitates around Paul's rhetorical use of the cognate terms "hold-toward" and "bring-about" in the "b" and "b'" sub-elements

1 Timothy 1:3: I Exhorted You to Remain in Ephesus, that You Might Charge Some

("a" sub-element)

The introductory "a" sub-element of the minichiasm (1:3) abruptly begins the body of the letter: "As I exhorted you to remain in Ephesus while-journeying for Macedonia, that you might charge some not to teach-different."[33] The conjunction "As" (καθώς) draws attention to the fact that it is Paul, apostle of Christ Jesus, who has "exhorted" (παρεκάλεσά) Timothy to remain in Ephesus.[34] The combination of the conjunction "as" and verb "exhorted" functions to explain that Timothy is in Ephesus not only in obedience to Paul but also with the authority of the apostle. The infinitive verb "to remain" (προσμεῖναι) carries the sense of persistence, suggesting Timothy is already engaged in some conflict in Ephesus—the sense being that Timothy is to "persevere."[35] The urgency of the situation in Ephesus is reiterated by the fact that it was prominent in Paul's mind even

---

33. This abrupt sentence remains incomplete, lacking an independent clause to complete it (e.g., "so now finish the task I have given you"). Scholars speculate this was the case either because Timothy already knew what was to follow or because Paul became so impassioned and lost in thought. Cf. Lock, *PE*. 7; Marshall, *PE*, 362–63.

The abruptness of Paul's clause in 1:3 also draws attention to the condensed greeting of the letter. Barcley, "1 Timothy," 358: "The other unusual feature of the opening verses of 1 Timothy is that Paul skips the thanksgiving section that we normally find in his letters and that was a standard feature of Greco-Roman letters in general. Instead, he gets right down to business and addresses the false teachers and false teaching."

34. Some translations read "urged" for παρεκάλεσά to highlight Paul's collegial tone. "Exhorted" is a better translation because the opening two verses of the letter highlight the difference between Paul and Timothy despite their partnership in ministry. Paul is uniquely an apostle of Christ Jesus. Moreover, in relation to Timothy he stands as a father "in faith" (1:2). As such, he expects full compliance both from Timothy, his genuine child, and from the audience.

35. See Schlarb, *Die gesunde Lehre*, 17.

"while-journeying for Macedonia" (πορευόμενος εἰς Μακεδονίαν).³⁶ What is more, given that Timothy is "to remain" in Ephesus, the audience would certainly not be unaware of the situation into which Paul was speaking. In other words, because Paul has established camaraderie with his audience, has identified their common allegiance to Christ Jesus, and has established a chain of command that extends to Timothy, it would be unmistakably clear that Paul is calling upon the Ephesian audience to support Timothy in whatever Paul has exhorted him to do.

The first purpose—"that" (ἵνα)—for which Timothy has been exhorted to remain in Ephesus is to "charge some not to teach-different." The verb "charge" (παραγγείλῃς) carries the sense of "command" or "order," making clear that Timothy is one with authority among the church in Ephesus.³⁷ As such, he not only merits the audience's full compliance but also—and specifically—the full adherence of "some." Given that the charge is directly geared toward "some" (τισίν), Paul's rhetorical and connotative use of the indefinite pronoun would be clear. In effect, Paul is distinguishing among the entire audience a sub-set who are anonymously identified as "some" (τισίν).³⁸ Moreover, it would be apparent to the audience that Paul and Timothy's definitive, familial relationship "in faith" (1:2) shares no commonalities with the indefinite "some" (1:3). That is, the notable contrast between "Timothy, genuine child" (1:2) over and against "some" (1:3) would clearly introduce the polemical nature of the letter.³⁹ Indeed, "some" are the reason why Paul exhorted Timothy to remain in Ephesus.

36. The precise historical backdrop is impossible to reproduce. Did Paul leave Timothy in Ephesus as the apostle made his way to Macedonia or was Timothy sent on his own? Towner, while noting the provisional nature of any proposal, suggests that Acts 20:1–3 forms the likely background to 1 Timothy, given its "close connection with the Ephesian and ongoing Corinthian stages of Paul's work" (*Letters*, 107). In passing, it should be noted that such historical references seem to weigh against interpreting 1 Timothy as a pseudonymous letter; see Knight, *PE*, 6; Kostenberger, "Hermeneutical and Exegetical Challenges," 6–8.

37. Barcley, "1 Timothy," 359: "The verb translated here 'charge' also means 'command' and has the sense of an army commander commanding his troops." Witherington, *Letters*, 172–73: "The verb *parangello* ('command, instruct') occurs more frequently here than in any other Pauline letter . . . What makes this particularly striking is that in the earlier Paulines, Paul is on record as saying that he would rather persuade than command (see, e.g., Philem 8–9; cf. 2 Cor 5:13; 8:8)." Cf. Wall with Steele, *1 & 2 Timothy*, 63: "The meaning of παραγγέλλω (*parangellō*, 'instruct') was quite elastic, and its use here has been variously translated." For more on the use of the verb παραγγέλλω, see Smith, *Timothy's Task*, 27–29.

38. See Towner's comments (*Letters*, 108 and n. 18).

39. Towner, *Letters*, 105: "As we will observe throughout the letter, Paul relies heavily on the persuasive power of contrast—the technique, which compares closely with the polemics found in the philosophical writings of that day, intended to expose

Paul's use of the indefinite pronoun "some" in direct connection with the terms "not" and "teach-different" further establishes the rhetorical and connotative force that Paul intends. The negative particle "not" (μή) clearly draws attention to the indecent activity of "some" and why they must be stopped. The verb "to teach-different" (ἑτεροδιδασκαλεῖν) is a compound term, taken from the adjective "different" (ἕτερος) and the verb "teach" (διδάσκω). The former has the sense of being "qualitatively another of a different kind."[40] Significantly, then, Paul's rhetorical use of the verb "teach-different" emphatically communicates that the teaching of "some" is qualitatively different than the teaching he received as an apostle according to the command of God and Christ Jesus (1:1); indeed, it is different than the teaching that Paul's "genuine child" Timothy (1:2) heard during their nearly twenty years of missionary work together; to be sure, it is different than the teaching that Paul's audience heard when he established the Ephesian church roughly ten to fifteen years prior.[41] In this way, given that Paul's teaching derives directly from the divine, personal authority of God and Christ Jesus (1:1), "to teach-different" than what the apostle Paul teaches does not merely represent a propositional error but a personal rejection of Paul and—more ultimately—of Christ Jesus whom Paul represents (1:1a) and God who commanded him (1:1b). Here at the outset of the letter, then, Paul has firmly connected "some" (τισίν) who "teach-different" (ἑτεροδιδασκαλεῖν) with an explicitly negative activity ("not"; μή) that must be stopped by Timothy's authoritative "charge" (παραγγείλῃς). In other words, the rhetorical contrast and linguistic connotations of letter are clearly established: the audience understand that the activity of "some" directly opposes God our Savior, God the Father, Christ Jesus our hope, and Christ Jesus our Lord; it is for this reason, therefore, that Paul, in full obedience to his apostolic duty as Christ's very own personal representative, has exhorted Timothy to remain in Ephesus (1:1–3).[42] In no uncertain terms, Paul is sum-

---

and denounce the dangers of the opposing group and its teaching. The technique was designed to leave no doubt about the matter of the superiority and authority of the apostolic teaching and its representatives."

40. Friberg, s.v. For further analysis of the connotative nuance of ἕτερος, see Sandiyagu, "῎ΕΤΕΡΟΣ and ῎ΑΛΛΟΣ in Luke," 105–7. Smith, *Pauline Communities*, 75: "As the combination with ἕτερος suggests, it denotes teaching activity 'other' or 'different' from orthodox Christian instruction, which consistently in the Pastorals is referred to with the simplex verb."

41. Marshall, *PE*, 365: "The verb ['to teach-different'] presupposes the existence of an accepted standard of teaching." See Swinson, *Letters to Timothy*, 49.

For discussion on Paul and Timothy's collaborative work and Paul's establishment of the Ephesian church, see chapter 1.

42. To be sure, the indefinite pronoun "some" (τισίν) occurs regularly throughout

moning the audience to align themselves with Christ's true teaching and with Christ's genuine teachers Paul and Timothy over and against "some" in Ephesus who "teach-different."

1 Timothy 1:4a: Myths and Genealogies Without-End

("b" sub-element)

In the "b" sub-element (1:4a), Paul continues to state the purpose of his exhortation for Timothy to remain in Ephesus: to charge some not to teach-different, "nor to hold-toward myths and genealogies without-limit." The negative conjunction "nor" (μηδέ) in 1:4a recalls the cognate term "not" (μή) in 1:3, which underscored the negative activity of "some" who teach-different. The immediate repetition of the back-to-back terms "not" and "nor" would strengthen the force of Paul's exhortation—Timothy *must* stop the activities of "some"—and would also further establish the connotative association of "some" with regard to the negative terms "not" and "nor." The verb "to hold-toward" (προσέχειν) means to pay close attention to in a devotional manner—more succinctly and negatively, to be addicted. The specific content and nature of these "myths and genealogies without-limit" (μύθοις καὶ γενεαλογίαις ἀπεράντοις) are not specified aside from their obvious association with the different teaching.[43] That is, while Paul does not appear to be concerned with the details of the myths and genealogies, his concern is most definitely about the false content of their teachings.[44]

---

the NT with a neutral connotation. However, clearly within the context of 1 Timothy, Paul immediately associates "some" with a negative connotation (1:3). As heard throughout the remainder of the letter, Paul consistently employs the indefinite pronoun "some" in this overtly negative context.

43. Ancient sources (e.g., Polybius, *Histories* 9.2.1) indicate that the coupling of these terms was not uncommon. Still, the precise meaning of the phrase is difficult to determine despite a long history of tenuous interpretation. See, e.g., Viviano, *Matthew and His World*, 24–44; Quinn, *Letter*, 245–46; Haufe, "Gnostische Irrlehre und ihre Abwehr in den Pastoralbriefen." For further discussion on the history of the phrase's interpretation, see Towner, *Goal*, 28.

44. Presumably, Timothy and the audience understood what Paul had in mind; hence, there was no need to clarify. Marshall, *PE*, 42: "The writer is endeavoring to combat the heresy not by engaging in refutation of its views but by simply dismissing it as trivial and unimportant . . . He did not want to enter into what he saw as endless argument that could never come to a conclusion and [thus] prevent people from coming to terms with what he regarded as central to the gospel." Witherington, *Letters*, 190: "The main function of this material is exhortation not apologetics, for Paul does not really pause to refute the errors of the false teachers in detail." Towner, *Letters*, 110: "rather than identifying the content of the teaching, the term 'myths' evaluates it as

The term "myths" (μύθοις) functions in the "b" sub-element to convey the false and deceptive nature of that which "some" hold-toward.[45] The term "genealogies" (γενεαλογίαις)—literally, "gene-words"—likely refers to a common ancient practice of establishing a person's identity and all related benefits by associating him to a certain family or tribe. It may have been the case that the false teachers were engaged in surmising the genealogies of biblical characters or in tinkering with the genealogical lists in non-canonical Jewish writings.[46] Whatever the specific practices was of the false teachers, Paul's assessment of it is clear: "without-end" (ἀπεράντοις), connoting "meaningless" or possibly "inconclusive,"[47] though likely the former.[48] The force of the "b" sub-element is to progress Paul's low assessment of the false teachers whom he introduced in the "a" sub-element: "some" not only teach-different (1:3) but also hold-toward—devote themselves—to useless enterprises that effect no good for the community.

1 Timothy 1:4b: Controversial-Speculations rather than the Household-Law of God

("b'" sub-element)

In the "b'" sub-element, Paul communicates the result of some who teach-different and hold-toward myths and genealogies without-end: "which bring-about controversial-speculations rather than the household-law of God in faith."[49] Here in 1:4b of the "b'" sub-element, the verb "bring-about" (παρέχουσιν)—literally, "hold-about"—recalls its cognate verb "to hold-toward" (προσέχειν) in 1:4a of the parallel "b" sub-element.[50] Heard together,

---

false and pernicious." See Muddiman and Barton, "PE," 247. Paul may also have been employing a common rhetorical strategy. Bassler, *1 & 2 Timothy*, 39: "[Myths were] a standard feature of the attacks leveled by philosophers against their rivals, the sophists, to discredit their ideas as 'mere myths' (see, e.g., Lucian *Lover of Lies* 9)."

45. See Dibelius and Conzelmann, *PE*, 16–17; Bruce, *NIDNTT* 2:643–47; Quinn, *Letter*, 245. Towner, *Letters*, 109: "the term is in the plural, as throughout the NT, which contains a negative evaluative assessment in itself (namely, spurious, contradictory, human) in contrast to the divinely imbued singularity and unity of the gospel"; see also ibid. n. 27.

46. Ibid., 110. For further detail on the term, see Marshall, *PE*, 335–36; Schlarb, *Die gesunde Lehre*, 86–93; Kittel, "Genealogia des Pastoralbriefe," 49–69.

47. See Fee, *1 & 2 Timothy*, 42.

48. Cf. Spencer, *1 Timothy*, 26, who suggests the latter.

49. Witherington, *Letters*, 192: "In other words, it went beyond the divine plan or household rules of God that Paul had preached or offered."

50. For an explanation for the English translation of "bring-about" rather than

they convey a cause and effect relation: the things that "some" "hold-toward" (1:4a) actually "bring-about" (1:4b) a result. More specifically, it is the personal devotion of "some"—their holding-toward—that effects a result.[51] Moreover, heard within the arrangement of the minichiasm, the parallel cognate verbs "hold-toward" (1:4a) in the "b" sub-element and "bring-about" in the "b'" sub-element form a pivot and hinge the theme of the literary unit forward, thus moving the audience's attention from the devotion of "some" (1:4a) to the direct result thereof: "controversial-speculations" (1:4b). Particularly in view of the negative connotations within the current minichiastic literary unit, the term "controversial-speculations" (ἐκζητήσεις) would most likely contain a divisive and polemical quality to it.[52] Namely, as the product of deep devotion by the false teachers, such "controversial-speculations" are resulting in division among the audience rather than unity. By highlighting the impact that these activities are having, Paul is seeking to further discredit "some," to strengthen the camaraderie between himself and the audience, and thus to call to action those "in faith" who, alongside Paul and Timothy, declare that God is "our" Savior and Christ Jesus is "our" Lord (1:1–2).

Furthermore, Paul's use of the phrase "rather than" (μᾶλλον ἤ) in 1:4b highlights an explicit contrast. That is, antithetical to the "controversial-speculations" caused by "some" who teach-different (1:3–1:4b), there is evidently proper and good teaching that will unify, foster, and bring-about "the household-law of God in faith" (1:4b).[53] The term "household-law" (οἰκονομίαν) reminds the audience of the familial language heard in 1:2—"Timothy, genuine child"; "God the Father"—and is a composite of the nouns "house" (οἶκος) and "law" (νόμος), giving the sense of

---

"hold-about," see chapter 2.

51. Given Paul's immediately prior use of "some" (τισίν) in 1:3 to describe the negative activity "to teach-different, it is worth noting the term "which" (αἵτινες)—to be very literal and observe its similarity, "which-some." The implication is not merely that inanimate "myths and genealogies without-limit" actually "bring-about controversial-speculations"; much rather, it is the personal activities of "some" (τισίν) whom Timothy must charge (1:3). The linguistic connection between "some" (τισίν) and "which-some" (αἵτινες) would not go unnoticed.

For an explanation regarding the translation of αἵτινες as "which" instead of "which-some," see chapter 2.

52. The majority of the MSS contain the variant ζητήσεις ("disputes"); see Metzger, TCGNT, 571. The accepted reading is extremely rare and represents the more difficult reading. Nevertheless, the connotation of "dispute" seems included in ἐκζητήσεις; see Marshall, PE, 362.

53. See Swinson, Letters to Timothy, 49.

"house-law," "house-rule," or "house-order."[54] Understood in contrast to "controversial-speculations," the term refers not only to order but to the healthy functioning that occurs when the various parts of the house work in proper relationship to one another.[55] Heard with the verb "bring-about" (παρέχουσιν), the audience understand that Paul's concern is for the continual order and progress of the household that has "God" (θεοῦ) as its head, namely the same "God" (θεοῦ) who is Savior (1:1b) and the "God" (θεοῦ) who is Father (1:2). The clear implication is that anyone living in God's household will adhere to God's household rules—the household of their Savior and Father (1:1-2). Significantly, then, the audience's adherence to "the rules of the house" will not only bring-about "the household-law of God (θεοῦ)" (1:4b) but will also tangibly demonstrate the result of their gratitude to "God (θεοῦ) our Savior" (1:1b) and their personal admiration for "God (θεοῦ) the Father" (1:2). Undoubtedly, the rhetorical juxtaposition would resound in the letter's performance: "some" in the audience who teach-different (1:3) bring-about "controversial-speculations" (1:4b) whereas those in the audience who declare with Paul that God is "our" Savior (1:1b) bring-about "the household-law of God" (1:4b). The former are chaotic and disruptive; the latter are steady and constant.

Any ordering of life that stems from "the household-law of God," then, must be done according to the will of God, a reality that Paul expresses through the phrase "in faith" (ἐν πίστει).[56] Hearing this phrase for the second time, the audience no doubt understand its importance. The exact same phrase occurred in 1:2 to capture the sphere in which Timothy relates to Paul as a "genuine child" and where God is "Father"; it was understood as the locus of existence that a person enters through faith in Christ Jesus, a

---

54. The literature on the phrase is massive, with various scholars offering different interpretations. For a sample of interpretations, see Dibelius and Conzelmann, *PE*, 17–18; Kelly, *PE*, 45; Brox, *Die Pastoralbriefe*, 103; Reumann, "*Oikonomia* = 'Covenant'"; Coiner, "Secret"; Robinson and Wall, *Called to Lead*, 26–27; Belleville, "1 Timothy," 31. For similar interpretations offered in this analysis, see Marshall, *PE*, 367; Towner, *Letters*, 112–13; Knight, *PE*, 75–76. For more regarding the phrase and its Greco-Roman connotations, see Westgate, "Greek House," 235–36.

55. Towner, *Letters*, 113: "That is, the first thought is not of administration as ministry and responsibility, but of the shape of things and the ordering of life to be achieved through the various activities of ministry and service."

56. The definitive article τήν ("the") which clearly has in view the anarthrous noun οἰκονομίαν ("household-law"), precedes the phrase ἐν πίστει ("in faith"). Thus, it is "the household-law" that must be done "in faith." Marshall suggests that such a syntax accentuates the qualification that the household-law must be done *in faith* (*PE*, 368); see also BDF §269.3. Johnson interprets the entire phrase to mean "'God's way of ordering reality as it is apprehended by faith'" (*Contested Issues*, 371). See Wall with Steele, *1 & 2 Timothy*, 65.

realm where Christ himself is the central object of faith—a realm of existing, as it were, "in Christ Jesus." Thus, where "the household-law of God" is qualified by "in faith," it is apparent to the audience that Paul and Timothy are able to view each other in familial categories because they share in a common sphere of existence in God's household, "in faith," that is, in Christ. In like manner, the phrase's occurrence in 1:4 refers to the proper ordering of God's household that is possible only by abiding in this sphere, namely— as the preceding emphasis on false teaching highlights—by accepting Paul's apostolic status and teaching.[57] Moreover, the qualifying phrase "in faith" (1:4b) is also telling of a profound reality in the Ephesian church. Given that "some" bring-about controversial-speculations while others bring-about "the household-law of God" (1:4b), it is clear that the latter exist in the realm "in faith" where "the household-law of God" exists—the former do not. In short, the apprehension and application of God's proper arrangement and function of all things cannot happen apart from abiding in the realm "in faith"—the realm of Christ—which has been revealed through Paul according to the command of God (1:1). Such a qualification is significant because it both highlights the authoritative superiority of Paul's teaching over and against the different teaching propagated by "some," and it subtly suggests that the false teachers themselves are not actually abiding in the sphere "in faith." That is, while "some" are standing among the audience in Ephesus, "some" might not be standing in the realm of Christ.

1 Timothy 1:5–7: The End of The Charge is Love, Some are Not Understanding

("a'" sub-element)

The concluding "a'" sub-element of the minichiasm (1:5–7) begins by summarizing the purpose of the charge given to Timothy in the parallel "a" sub-element: "But the end of the charge is love from a pure heart and a good conscience and a without-hypocrisy faith" (1:5). The term "charge" (παραγγελίας) in 1:5 of the "a'" sub-element recalls its verbal cognate "charge" (παραγγείλῃς) in 1:3 of the parallel "a" sub-element. Given the parallel connection, the audience understand that the "charge" in 1:5 is undoubtedly the same as in 1:3.[58] In effect, then, Paul's statement in 1:5 carries

---

57. Towner, *Letters*, 113: "Paul's point is then that 'by faith,' that is, through acceptance of the correct apostolic preaching and teaching, this divine arrangement can be apprehended and implemented."

58. Cf. Knight, *PE*, 76; Roloff, *Der Erste Brief an Timotheus*, 66; Tomlinson, "Purpose

the combined sense of, "But the end of the charge, that is, the charge for some not to teach-different, is love . . ." Although the connotation of the term "charge" is commanding and authoritative, Paul makes clear that the "end" (τέλος)—the goal—of the charge is nothing other than "love" (ἀγάπη). To be sure, the deliberate and conclusive "end" of the charge (1:5) presents a stark contrast to the false teachers's devotion to that which is "without-limit" (1:4a).[59] Moreover, where the end of the charge against the false teachers is intended to result in "love" (1:5), such is reminiscent of the salvific blessings of "grace, mercy, peace from God the Father and Christ Jesus our Lord" (1:2). However, the "love" in view is not that which God the Father gives to believers; rather, it is the opposite, namely the response of "love" by God's people for receiving his grace, mercy, and peace. In short, "love" here in 1:5 is a response of salvation. Thus where "love" is the goal of Timothy's charge for "some" not to teach-different, the clear implication is that "the end of the charge" is salvation for "some" (1:3, 5).[60] Indeed, the audience are to understand that Paul's polemic against "some" who teach-different is not merely an agenda to defend a proposition but is an outworking of his personal "love" and relationship with God the Father and Christ Jesus his Lord, from whom he has received blessings of salvation (1:2) and for whom he obediently strives to bring-about the household-law of God "in faith" (1:4). That is, being "in faith" and expressing "love" for God as the result of receiving salvation—grace, mercy, and peace (1:2)—are tangibly shown by bringing about "the household-law of God" (1:4)—the household wherein God is the Father and Christ Jesus is the Lord (1:2). Notably, where "the charge" against "some" will bring-about the household-law of God "in faith" (1:4-5), Paul's motivation and goal is for "some" to also express tangible "love" for God—not only as their Savior but also as their Father (1:2, 4, 5). The audience understand that concerately expressing "love" for "God the Father" is abiding by "the household-law of God"; it is living out one's existence "in faith" (1:4-5)—the outworking of salvation. Unmistakably, such is Paul's intention for "some" who currently teach-different in the Ephesian church and bring-about controversial-speculations instead (1:3-4).

Reiterating the reflexive nature of the love in view, Paul goes on in 1:5 to identify the source of this love. It issues "from a pure heart and a

---

and Stewardship Theme," 58.

59. Although the terms "end" (τέλος, 1:5) and "without-limit" (ἀπεράντοις, 1:4) are not cognates, their conceptual similarity and comparison thereof would be apparent.

60. Cf. Keegan, *First and Second Timothy*, 10: "The purpose of the instruction . . . is not simply to negate the false teaching but to 'love from a pure heart, a good conscience, and a sincere faith.'" See Barcley, *1 & 2 Timothy*, 46.

good conscience and a without-hypocrisy faith."[61] This tripartite description succinctly expresses Paul's description of those who exist "in faith" (1:2, 4) and mirrors the tripartite salvific blessings—"grace, mercy, peace"—that have God the Father and Christ Jesus as their source (1:2). Thus, the "love" in view here is substantiated as a response to what God given to those "in faith," namely salvation; it is "love" from the heart of a person who has been purified, whose conscience has been renewed, and whose faith is genuine.

Both in Paul's teaching and in the OT the "heart" (καρδία) represents a person's inner being by which he relates to God either in worship or rebellion.[62] The accompanying adjective "pure" (καθαρᾶς) highlights an activity that has already been carried out by God; hence, a person whose heart is now clean.[63] The "conscience" (συνείδησις) is the faculty through which a person applies truth to actual life.[64] That such a conscience is "good" (ἀγαθῆς) connotes that it is operating correctively, having rooted itself in Paul's teaching that itself is rooted in the command of "God our Savior and Christ Jesus" (1:1).[65] Finally, "faith" (πίστεως), which echoes its occurrences in 1:2 and 1:4, refers to a sphere of existence that is entered by receiving Paul's teaching concerning Christ Jesus. In this context, the related adjective "without-hypocrisy" (ἀνυποκρίτου) conveys the sense of "sincere" and refers to actual subsistence in the realm "in faith" (1:2, 4), which can be quantified by actions and their results. The implication is that the false teachers are not in "a without-hypocrisy faith" but in a hypocritical faith, as attested by their different teaching (1:3) and the results of their devotion, namely controversial-speculations rather than the household-law of God "in faith" (1:4). In sum, in tandem with the three salvific blessing (1:2), these three intangible gifts from God in 1:5 result in an expression of tangible "love" to-

---

61. See Knight, *PE*, 77.

62. See Jewett, *Paul's Anthropological Terms*, 448; Marshall, *PE*, 370; LXX Deut 30:6; Ps 50:12; etc. Wall with Steele, *1 & 2 Timothy*, 66: "the integration of inward affections and outward practices is central to a Pauline definition of the Christian life."

63. This reference to God's activity on the heart likely pertains to the covenantal blessing of Deuteronomy 30:1–11, wherein God enables his people's hearts to love and obey him (see also Jer 31:31–34). The result of this blessing is that the people may now love God as he commanded of them (Deut 6:4).

64. Towner, *Letters*, 116: "The focus in 'good conscience,' however, is on the organ of decision that facilitates the process by which a person may move from some norm (in this case that existing in the gospel, the faith, the sound teaching, etc.) to appropriate behavior." For further discussion on the term, see Stelzenberger, *Syneidesis im Neuen Testament*, 51–95; Jewett, *Paul's Anthropological Terms*, 421–26; Towner, *Letters*, 117–19; Towner, *Goal*, 154–58.

65. Combined with the OT implications of "a pure heart," "a good conscience" likely implies that regeneration by the Holy Spirit is in view.

ward him. Quite dramatically, then, the audience are challenged to examine themselves. On the one hand, to side with Timothy's "charge" against the false teachers would be an expression of "love" for God, that is, of having received his salvific blessings—grace, mercy, peace, a pure heart, a good conscience, and a without-hypocrisy faith (1:2, 5). On the other hand, to not side with Timothy would demonstrate an absence of love for God and a rejection of his blessings.

In regard to these three qualities that produce love, Paul continues the "a'" sub-element by identifying the contrasting activity of the false teachers: "which some—swerving-from—have turned-aside for useless-words" (1:5). The indefinite pronoun "some" (τινες) in 1:6 of the "a'" sub-element recalls for the audience its parallel occurrence in 1:3 of the "a" sub-element regarding "some" (τισίν) who teach-different.[66] Here, then, Paul's overarching concern is both substantiated and advanced: not only do "some . . . teach-different" as a demonstration of their lack of love for God (1:3), but "some" are "swerving-from" and "have turned-aside" from the very qualities that produce love for God (1:5–6). Thus where the end of the charge is love (1:5), Paul intends for Timothy to restore "some" to what they are "swerving-from" and "have turned-aside" (1:5–6), namely an expression of love for God as the response of salvation. At the same time, Paul further highlights the distance between himself and the false teachers by noting that the very qualities that produce his motivation for the charge—love—are altogether absent among "some."

The juxtaposition of the participle "swerving-from" (ἀστοχήσαντες) and the verb "have turned-aside" (ἐξετράπησαν) indicates a cause and effect relationship, the sense being that "some" have "missed" or "abandoned" a pure heart, a good conscience, and a without-hypocrisy faith, and have subsequently "strayed" or "become lost."[67] Likely, the more fundamental point of the juxtaposition is that "some" do not have "a without-hypocrisy faith," that is, they are not "in faith"—hence why they bring-about controversial-speculations rather than the household-law of God "in faith" (1:4b). Paul is certainly underscoring that "some" are unworthy spiritual guides for the audience, for "some" are not existing in the realm where Christ Jesus is Lord. Indeed, where "some" in 1:6 of the "a'" sub-element have turned-aside for "useless-words" (ματαιολογίαν)—a pejorative compound term emphasizing the "emptiness" or "futility" (μάταιος) of their "word" (λόγος)—it is clear that the indecent activity of "some" who "teach-different" in 1:3 of the

---

66. See Collins, *1 & 2 Timothy*, 28.
67. See Knight, *PE*, 79.

parallel "a" sub-element is profoundly inadequate for any degree of leadership or instruction in the Ephesian church.

Verse 1:7 brings the "a'" sub-element and the 1:3–7 minichiasm to a conclusion by highlighting the full irony of "some" who teach-different with useless-words: they are "desiring to be law-teachers, not understanding either what they-are-saying or regarding some-things they-are-insisting." The participle "desiring" (θέλοντες) in itself is somewhat neutral, noting a strong eagerness or will.[68] The compound term "law-teachers" (νομοδιδάσκαλοι), derived from "law" (νόμος) and "teacher" (διδάσκαλος), is intended to highlight the central place the OT law has in their teaching. The use of the term may be a subtle allusion to the desire of "some" to establish for themselves an authoritative place among the audience comparable to that formerly enjoyed by Jewish teachers.[69] Yet, the precise rhetorical implication that Paul intends by the term "law-teachers" is conveyed by the linguistic arrangement of the minichiasm. The term "law-teachers" (νομοδιδάσκαλοι) in 1:7 of the "a'" sub-element recalls the cognate verb "teach-different" (ἑτεροδιδασκαλεῖν) in 1:3 of the parallel "a" sub-element. In other words, Paul's point to the audience is that "some" (τισίν) who "teach-different" in 1:3 of the "a" sub-element are the same group of "some" (τινες) who are desiring to be "law-teachers" in 1:6–7 of the parallel "a'" sub-element. Moreover, Paul's ironic cognate juxtaposition (see *italics*) of "some" who bring-about controversial-speculations rather than the "household-*law*" (οἰκο*νομ*ίαν) of God in faith (1:4) and "some" who are desiring to be "*law*-teachers" (*νομ*οδιδάσκαλοι, 1:7) would not go unnoticed. Heard within the linguistic scope of the 1:3–7 minichiasm, the cumulative rhetorical irony is clear: "some" teach-different (1:3) and are desiring to be law-teachers (1:7) yet do not bring-about the household-law of God in faith (1:4b) precisely because—swerving-from a without-hypocrisy faith—they have turned-aside for useless-words (1:6–7) and thus bring-about controversial-speculations instead (1:4b).

Further still, despite the desire of "some" to be law-teachers (1:7), they not only teach-different (1:3) but are also "not understanding either what they-are-saying or regarding some-things they-are-insisting" (1:7). Indeed, such would be characteristic of their "useless-words" (1:6). The rhetorical rapid-fire use of the negative particles "not ... either ... or" (μὴ ... μήτε ... μήτε) in 1:7 of the "a'" sub-element recalls their prior occurrence in regard to "some" whom Timothy must charge "not (μή) to teach-different, nor (μηδέ)

---

68. See discussion in Marshall, *PE*, 427.

69. For this interpretation of the term "law-teachers," see Rengstorf, *TDNT* 2:159; Spencer, *1 Timothy*, 30–31.

to hold-toward myths and genealogies without-limit (1:3–4).⁷⁰ Here in 1:7, then, the audience not only understand that Paul is clearly referencing the false teachers but also—and significantly—that Paul is rhetorically strengthening, emphasizing, and confirming to the audience that these negative terms—"not (μή) . . . nor (μηδέ)" (1:3–4); "not (μή) . . . either (μήτε) . . . or (μήτε)" (1:7)—are Paul's definitive way of referencing the negative activities of "some."⁷¹ To be sure, Paul is not critiquing the fact that "some" are "desiring to be law-teachers" but rather the ignorance of their desiring. Such is indicated by the use of the participle "understanding" (νοοῦντες), which carries the sense "to discern, perceive." Clearly, the issue is that "some" are "not understanding" (1:7). Indeed, the negative descriptors "not . . . either . . . or" intensify Paul's implication, conveying that a comprehensive ignorance is in view.⁷² Given that "some" have turned-aside (see *italics*) for "useless-*words*" (ματαιολογίαν, 1:6), it is clear why they do not understand what "they-are-*saying*" (λέγουσιν, 1:7). Moreover, Paul goes on to underscore that "some" (τινες, 1:6) are not regarding "some-things" (τίνων, 1:7), namely the very things that "they-are-insisting" (διαβεβαιοῦνται). That is, although "they-are-saying" much, such are merely useless-words despite how much confidence that "some" have about "some-things they-are-insisting."⁷³ In this way, the audience understand that the most loving thing that Paul and Timothy can do for "some" is to stop them not only from causing controversial-speculations (1:4) but also from existing in a comprehensive state of "not understanding" (1:7) as the direct result of swerving-from a pure heart, a good conscience, and a without-hypocrisy faith for useless-words (1:5–6)—such is the purpose of the charge (1:3, 5).

In sum, the comprehensive ignorance and futile activities by "some" who teach-different in the Ephesian church stem from their refusal to exist and remain "in faith" (1:2, 4); they are actively swerving-from a

---

70. The double occurrence of the term μήτε in 1:7 would preferably be translated "neither" and "nor"; however, for readability purposes, they were translated as "either" and "or." See explanation of translation methodology in chapter 2.

71. This is a significant theme throughout the 1 Timothy letter and has important rhetorical implications; see e.g., volume 2, chapter 2 regarding 1 Timothy 3:1–7.

72. Towner succinctly notes: "the development from 'what they say' to 'what they so confidently affirm' places all of their teaching activities under the category of ignorance. The effect in Paul's argument is to render all of their speaking activities null and void" (*Letters*, 121).

For the use of correlative conjunctions as emphasis, see Wallace, *Greek Grammar*, 672.

73. The combination of the term "useless-words" (ματαιολογίαν) and its similar verbal cognate "they-are-saying" (λέγουσιν) likely emphasizes the degree of their ignorance.

without-hypocrisy faith (1:5–6); they have turned-aside for useless words (1:6). Subsequently, Paul actively intends for "some" to join him, Timothy, and those among the audience "in faith" as those who delight in salvation, thereby expressing "love" for God the Father and Christ Jesus (1:5), and thus participating in activities that bring-about the household-law of God "in faith" (1:4). Indeed, Paul's exhortation for Timothy to "charge some not to teach-different" (1:3) is a "charge" that intends for "some" to "love" God the Father and Christ Jesus (1:5). It is a charge that has salvation as the end.

1 Timothy 1:8a: Paul and Timothy, True Teachers of the Commendable Law

(B Element)

In the B element of the microchiasm (1:8a), Paul states: "But we know that the law is commendable." The disjunctive "But" (δέ) initiates a stark contrast. In effect, whereas "some" are "desiring to be law-teachers, not understanding either what-they-are-saying or regarding some-things they-are-insisting" (1:7), "we"—certainlyPaul and Timothy but likely also those in the audience who agree—"know that the law is commendable" (1:8a). Significantly, the audience understand that "some" have a completely different view of the law than Paul and Timothy. Indeed, given that "some" are ignorantly desiring to be "law-teachers" (νομοδιδάσκαλοι, 1:7), they clearly do not know that "the law (νόμος) is commendable" (1:8a). In this way, the rhetorical force of Paul's statement "we know" (οἴδαμεν) communicates that he and Timothy are the true and reliable interpreters and teachers of Jewish "law" as it appears throughout the OT.[74] Specifically, it is Paul and Timothy who understand that "the law is commendable" (καλός)—inherently good—since it is from God.[75] Thus the polemical and rhetorical force of the B element in 1:8a carries forward and builds upon the implicit suggestion of the A element: over and against "some" who teach-different in the Ephesian

---

74. Towner indicates that the phrase "we know" is "a formulaic appeal to accepted tradition . . . By opening the appeal in this way, Paul places himself on the side of authoritative tradition and the false teachers outside the mainstream" (*Letters*, 122). If this is the case, Paul is advancing his polemical goal of persuading the audience to disregard the false-teaching "some" who have a low estimation of the church's tradition. See also Yarbrough, *Preformed Traditions*, 63.

It has been suggested that "law" here refers to Roman law (e.g., Hasler, *Die Briefe an Timotheus*, 14), but the immediate context and the letter's overall content do not support this position; see Belleville, "1 Timothy," 30.

75. See Rom 7:7–25 for a more extensive treatment by Paul on the intrinsic goodness of the law.

church (1:3), the audience must listen and respond not only to the apostle Paul—Christ Jesus's very own personal messenger who was divinely authorized according to the command of God (1:1)—but also to Timothy—the apostle Paul's "genuine child in faith" (1:2).[76]

1 Timothy 1:8b: The Lawful Use of the Law

(C Element)

In the pivot C element (1:8b) of the 1:1–20 microchiasm, the audience hear a critical comparison to Paul and Timothy's view of the law: "if someone uses it lawfully." The indefinite pronoun "someone" (τις) recalls its consistent use throughout the microchiasm in reference to "some" (τισίν) who teach-different (1:3), that is, "some" (τινες) who—swerving-from a without-hypocrisy faith—have turned-aside for useless-words (1:5–6). Undoubtedly, the audience understand that the same group of "some" (τισίν, 1:3; τινες, 1:6) are the subject of the statement "if someone (τις) uses it lawfully" (1:8b). As such, the rhetorical strategy of Paul's language is clear (see *italics*): if "some" who are desiring to be "*law*-teachers" (νομοδιδάσκαλοι, 1:7) knew the "*law*" (νόμος, 1:8a) in the commendable way that Paul and Timothy know it, then "someone" from this group would be able to use it "*lawfully*" (νομίμως). That is, if "someone" actually "uses" (χρῆται) the law of which that they are desiring to be teachers—the sense being, "appropriately applies" the law—then they would actually understand what they-are-saying and would be able to regard some-things they-are-insisting (1:7).[77] Still, Paul is emphatic about the reality of the situation: "someone" in 1:8b does not understand how to use the law in a commendable way; they are unable to apply the law lawfully (1:8a–b). For sure, Paul intends the audience to understand that "some" in the Ephesian church are unqualified for the very things that they-are-insisting; "someone" does not know the proper application of the law (1:8b), nor that the law is commendable (1:8a), and thus has no grounds to be a law-teacher (1:7). As the pivot C element of the microchiasm concludes, therefore, the momentum of Paul's language hinges upon an assertion of the false teachers's ignorance. It is from this central pivot

---

76. See Mappes, "Heresy Paul Opposed," 454.

77. Towner, *Letters*, 123 n. 5: "The combination of the adv. νομίμως . . . and the verb χρῆται . . . expresses appropriate use or application, and not something like 'observance of the law.'" See Marshall, *PE*, 376.

1 Timothy 1:9-10a: The Right Use of the Law

(B' Element)

In the B' element of the microchiasm (1:9–10a), Paul goes on to delineate that the proper use and application of the law derives from "knowing this, that for the just the law is not laid" (1:9a). The participle "knowing" (εἰδώς) here in 1:9a of the B' element recalls its cognate verb "we know" (οἴδαμεν) in 1:8a of the parallel B element. Furthermore, the term "law" (νόμος) here in the B' element recalls "law" (νόμος) in the parallel B' element. In other words, where Paul and Timothy are the subjects who "know . . . the law" in the B element, the audience understand that Paul and Timothy are also the subjects who are "knowing . . . the law" in the parallel B' element. Significantly, then, given the parallel arrangement of Paul's language and the implication thereof, it would be clear to the audience that he and Timothy, who "know . . . the law" in the B element (1:8a), are not merely "knowing . . . the law" in the parallel B' element (1:9a); more more, Paul and Timothy are also "the just" for whom "the law is not laid" in the B' element (1:9a). In short, Paul and Timothy know that the law is commendable (1:8a), know how to use the law lawfully (1:8b), and know that the law is not laid for them (1:9a).

The disjunctive "but" (δέ) in 1:9b of the B' element continues Paul and Timothy's contrast against "someone" who does not use the law lawfully in the C element (1:8b). In effect, unlike Paul and Timothy for whom the law is not laid, the term "but" introduces those for whom the law *is* laid: "the without-law" (1:9a). To be sure, where the sustained contrast throughout the microchiasm has pitted Paul and Timothy against "some" and "someone," the clear implication is that the latter are those for whom the law is laid. Paul's rhetorical use of "law" and its cognates is thus heard with a cumulative impact (see *italics*): "some" who are desiring to be "*law*-teachers" (νομοδιδάσκαλοι, 1:7) are comprised of "someone" who does not use it "*lawfully*" (νομίμως, 1:8b) because they are "the without-*law*" (ἀνόμοις, 1:9b) for whom the "*law*" (νόμος) is laid (1:9a) and are antithetical to Paul and Timothy who know the "*law*" (νόμος, 1:8a) and thus bring-about the "household-*law*" (οἰκονομίαν) of God "in faith" (1:4b). In other words, Paul's point is that it is impossible to use the law lawfully (1:8b), that is, to

---

78. For the performative intention of the letter, see chapter 1. For the rhetorical effect of the letter's chiastic arrangements, see chapter 2.

know that the law is commendable (1:8a) unless a person adheres to Paul and Timothy's teaching. For those in the audience who are allied with Paul and Timothy, therefore, Paul's description of the law's proper use would come as no surprise; however, for "some" who teach-different and do not use the law lawfully (1:3, 8b), Paul's statements here in the B' element would be a public reproval, not merely for their ignorance but for not listening to Paul's teaching. By their own doing—by swerving-from a without-hypocrisy faith—"some" have turned-aside for useless-words (1:5–6); in response, Paul sends a letter for their own good: Timothy is exhorted to charge "some" not to teach-different (1:3) so that "some" woud understand what they-are-saying (1:7), know that the law is commendable (1:8a), know how to use the law lawfully (1:8b), and thus realize for whom the law is actually laid (1:9a).

The force of the verb "laid" (κεῖται) relates to existence, that is, the reason why the law was established. In this way, Paul specifies that the mistake of the false teachers is their failure to perceive the reason why the law was enacted, namely for whom it was "laid."[79] Thus where the sustained contrast of the microchiasm—particularly in the B-C-B' arrangement—implied that the law is laid for "someone," the resounding irony is upheld in full force: the false teachers do not know that the law is laid for them. Here, then, it is undeniably clear why Paul describes "some" as desiring to be law-teachers yet not understanding either what they-are-saying or regarding some-things they-are-insisting (1:7). Indeed, if "someone" actually used the law lawfully (1:8b), then they would use it on themselves as those who are "without-law" (1:9a). In stark contrast, the "just" (δικαίῳ) for whom the law is not laid—Paul and Timothy—is a reference to genuine Christians who exist "in faith" (1:2, 4), namely those who evidence their love from a purified heart, a good conscience, and a without-hypocrisy faith (1:5) through their their common commitment to bring-about the household-law of God (1:4). In clear rhetorical fashion, Paul makes clear that it is "the just" over and against "the without-law" (1:9a)—the latter are most certainly inept to be "law-teachers" (1:7).

Continuing the B element, Paul further describes the people for whom the law is laid through the use of a vice-list, including the one vice already mentioned: ". . . the without-law and without-obedience, the without-godly and sinners, the without-reverence and vile, patricides and matricides, murderers, fornicators, sodomites, kidnappers, falsifiers, perjurers" (1:9b–10a).[80] The audience hear a list that describes immoral persons along with

---

79. See Knight, *PE*, 82.

80. Gray, *Opening Paul's Letters*, 50: Paul's "use of the virtue-and-vice list [was] a literary form common among philosophers in the Hellenistic era." For vice-lists in general, see the multiple references in Towner, *Goal*, 160–61. For vice-lists specifically in

particular vices; the language paints a picture that is altogether antithetical to "the just for whom the law is not laid" (1:9a), that is, those who exist "in faith" (1:2) and bring-about "the household-law of God in faith" (1:4b). In short, Paul is contrasting non-Christians—"the without-law . . ."—versus Christians—"the just" (1:9).[81] Moreover, particularly in view of Paul's repeated use of "law" and its cognates, the audience likely hear the vice-list in 1:9b–10a as an allusion to the Decalogue (Exod 20:1–17; Deut 5:6–21), which delineates sin against God and other people.[82]

Although the vice-list is initiated by directly juxtaposing "the law" (νόμος, 1:9a) with "the without-law" (ἀνόμοις, 1:9b), the latter term would certainly be heard as the beginning of and in connection with the vice-list's corresponding pairs.[83] In this way, the audience hear the organizational flow of the vice-list from a general application—"the without-law and without-obedience, the without-godly and sinners, the without-reverence and vile, patricides and matricides" (1:9b)—to a specific application of individual law-breakers—"murderers, fornicators, sodomites, kidnappers, falsifiers, perjurers" (1:9b–10a). The initial pairing of "the without-law and without-obedience" is synecdochical, clarifying the meaning and relation of each ensuing pair in the vice-list. That is, "the without-law" (ἀνόμοις) is not merely a person without the law—for example, a Gentile without the OT—but rather is a person who is "without-obedience" (ἀνυποτάκτοις). The pairing

---

the Pastorals, see McEleney, "The Vice-Lists of the Pastoral Epistles," 203–19.

81. For further discussion on the identification of Christians as "the just" in 1:9a, see volume 2, chapter 2 regarding 1 Timothy 3:16; see also volume 3, chapter 3 regarding 1 Timothy 6:11.

82. The allusion is evident from the obvious vertical-horizontal division that is heard in the Decalogue. The first several pairs in 1 Timothy 1:9b–10a, Exodus 20:2–17, and Deuteronomy 5:6–21 focus on "vertical" sins—the sins of idolatry and irreverent worship. The consequent pairs and descriptors are exaggerated expressions of "horizontal" sins—sins committed against people. The degree of the correspondence, however, is unclear. Compare discussions in Knight, *PE*, 82–88; Marshall, *PE*, 379; Dibelius and Conzelmann, *PE*, 23; Barclay, *1 & 2 Timothy*, 55–56. Towner rightly asserts: "The list echoes the Decalogue in such a way that the relationship is close enough not to be missed and broad enough to appeal to the Hellenistic ear of the church that would have overheard this letter."

It may be worth noting that Paul's Ephesian audience certainly had non-Jewish converts who did not grow up knowing the Decalogue; however, given that the Ephesian church was roughly ten to fifteen years old (see chapter 1), it is unlikely that converts would be unaware of the Decalogue. Presumably, along with Jewish converts, they would be familiar with the OT foundation of Paul's vice-list.

83. The sustained alliterative pattern of α- prefixes would not go unnoticed, signifying a connected linguistic chain (see *italics*): ἀνόμοις . . . ἀνυποτάκτοις . . . ἀσεβέσιν . . . ἁμαρτωλοῖς . . . ἀνοσίοις ("*without*-law . . . *without*-obedience . . . *without*-godly . . . sinners . . . *without*-reverence," 1:9b).

of terms in the 1:9b–10a vice-list are thus to be understood as complementary: "the without-law" is a person who lives lawlessly, as if they were not under any law at all and is, therefore, "without-obedience."[84] Indeed, given Paul's sustained polemic against the false teachers in the Ephesian church, the audience would likely understand that Paul is alluding to "some" who teach-different and bring-about controversial-speculations rather than the household-law of God (1:3–4).

The second pair in the vice-list—"the without-godly and sinners"—can be found in various places of the LXX (e.g., Ps 1:1, 5) and describes persons who live as if there is no God and thus are wicked.[85] Specifically in view of the paired terms, "without-godly" (ἀσεβέσιν) describes a life given over to something else more than to God—in a word, idolatry—which the OT regularly indentifies as the definitive trademark of "sinners" (ἁμαρτωλοῖς).[86] The third pair in the vice-list—"the without-reverence and vile"—also describe a mutual relation, "without-reverence" (ἀνοσίοις) referring to profane acitivities with respect to the worship of God and devout living (e.g., LXX Ezek 22:9), and "vile" (βεβήλοις) referring to sacrilegious forms of defilement (e.g., LXX Lev 21:9).[87] The last pairing of terms in the vice-list—"patricides and matricides"—shifts attention from sins of rebellion, idolatry, and irreverence—all of which are directed toward God—to sins that are committed against other people.[88] The paired terms "patricides . . . matricides" (πατρολῴαις . . . μητρολῴαις) are found in Greek literature;[89] yet, their correspondence to the fifth commandment would be apparent—"Honor your father (πατέρα) and mother (μητέρα)" (LXX Exod 20:12). To be sure, the particular heinousness of dishonoring one's parents to the point of killing them highlights the certain antithesis between

---

84. Wall with Steele, *1 & 2 Timothy*, 69: the "proper use of Torah . . . targets the 'lawless and rebellious.'"

85. Compare the Greek texts:
1 Tim 1:9b: "ἀσεβέσιν καὶ ἁμαρτωλοῖς";
LXX Ps 1:1: "ἀσεβῶν καὶ ἐν ὁδῷ ἁμαρτωλῶν";
LXX Ps 1:5: "ἀσεβεῖς ἐν κρίσει οὐδὲ ἁμαρτωλοί."

86. Cf. Philo, *Special Laws* 1.102, uses "without-godly" to describe the work of a prostitute.

87. Towner, *Letters*, 126.

88. Both terms are biblical *hapaxes*; see BDF §26; 35.2; 119.2; Marshall, *PE*, 380 n. 58. For more on the occurrence of *hapaxes* in the 1 Timothy 1:9–10 vice-list, see Yarbrough, *Preformed Traditions*, 65.

89. E.g., Plato, *Phaedo* 114a. Here the pair also occurs with the term ἀνδροφόνοις. Paul, then, appears to be noting a combination that would have been familiar with the audience.

those for whom the law is laid—those in the vice-list (1:9b)—and those for whom it is not—"the just" (1:9a).

Transitioning from paired terms in the vice-list, the reference to "murderers" (ἀνδροφόνοις) corresponds directly to the sixth commandment—"Do not murder (φονεύσεις)" (LXX Exod 20:13). Although the term "murderers" in 1:10a is a NT *hapax legomenon* and occurs rarely in the LXX, it has an association with blasphemy (e.g., 2 Macc 9:28); hence, it aptly describes the representative enemy of God.[90] The next two terms in the vice-list—"fornicators" (πόρνοις) and "sodomites" (ἀρσενοκοίταις)—both correspond to the seventh commandment (Exod 20:14) in regard to adultery, that is, sexual sin;[91] "fornicators" refers generally to all sexual activity outside of marriage, and "sodomites" refers specifically to all same-sex activity (see LXX Lev 18:22; 20:13).[92] The term "kidnappers" (ἀνδραποδισταῖς) corresponds to the eighth commandment in regard to stealing (Exod 20:15), referring to the business of literally stealing people and selling them into slavery, a practice found in Greek literature (e.g., Xenophon, *Memorabilia*, 4.2.15).[93] The final terms "falsifiers" (ψεύσταις) and "perjurers" (ἐπιόρκοις) correspond to the ninth commandment—"Do not false-testify (ψευδομαρτυρήσεις) against your neighbor a false (ψευδῆ) testimony" (LXX Exod 20:16). Like the coupling of "fornicators" and "sodomites," the pairing here begins with the general description of duplicity—"falsifiers"—and then moves to a specific example of it—"perjurers," those who falsify under oath. Also like the prior two terms in the vice-list, the two activities of "falsifiers" and "perjurers" are paired in both Jewish (e.g., Wis 14:28) and Greek literature (e.g., Phil, *On the Special Laws* 1.235) in reference to immoral and deplorable persons.

As the vice-list in 1:9b–10a concludes the B' element of the microchiasm, the overall effect of describing those for whom the law is laid within

---

90. It may be worth noting (see *italics*) that a cognate term for "*murderers*" (ἀνδροφόνοις, 1 Tim 1:9b) was used to describe Paul in Acts 9:1, who was "still breathing threats and *murder* (φόνου) upon the disciples of the Lord" (*ESV*). In this way, Paul's own suggestion may be that prior to his conversion and subsequent existence "in faith" (1 Tim 1:2, 4), the law was laid specifically for people like himself. See below regarding Paul's self-description in 1:13.

91. The expansion of the seventh commandment in Leviticus 18:22 and 20:13 is likely in view.

92. See the exchange in Wright, "Homosexuals or Prostitutes?," 125–53; Petersen, "Can ΑΡΣΕΝΟΚΟΙΤΑΙ Be Translated by 'Homosexuals'?," 187–91; Wright, "Translating ARSENOKOITAI," 396–98; De Young, "Source and NT Meaning of ARSENOKOITAI," 191–215; Robinson and Wall, *Called to Lead*, 22 n. 1.

93. For more on this aspect of the eighth commandment, see Douma, *Ten Commandments*, 285–89.

the backdrop of the Decalogue highlights Paul's original point, namely that the law is not laid for the just—those who exist "in faith" (1:2) and thus bring-about the household-law of God "in faith" (1:4). Indeed, where Paul's rhetoric implies that "some" who are desiring to be law-teachers (1:7) do not actually know the lawful use of the law (1:8b) and that they show themselves to be "the without-law" (1:9b) by bringing about controversial-speculations rather than the household-law of God (1:4b), it is clear that Paul, the authorized representative of Christ Jesus, intends for the false teachers to see themselves for who they truly are—sinners (1:9b) in need of grace, mercy, and peace from God the Father and Christ Jesus (1:2).

1 Timothy 1:10b–20: Coming to Have-Faith Versus Shipwrecked Faith

(A' Element)

The concluding A' element of the 1:1–20 microchiasm begins with an abrupt summary clause of why the law is laid: "and if some-thing different lies-opposed to the sound teaching" (1:10b). Having heard sequential allusions to the latter half of the Decalogue in 1:9b–10a of the preceding B' element, the audience might have expected Paul to conclude the vice-list with a reference to the tenth commandment in regard to coveting.[94] Instead, Paul explicitly declares that "if some-thing different lies-opposed to the sound teaching," then the lawful use of the law applies in full force. Notably, the phrase occurs in the immediate context of the extended vice-list; the connotation, therefore, is unmistakable: "if some-thing different lies-opposed to the sound teaching" (1:10b), then it is within the same category as "the without-law and without-obedience, the without-godly and sinners, the without-reverence and vile, patricides and matricides, murderers, fornicators, sodomites, kidnappers, falsifiers, perjurers" (1:9b–10a). Moreover, given that the conjuction "and" (καί) most certainly connects Paul's statement in 1:10b with the preceding vice-list in 1:9b–10a, the former would be heard as an aggregate summary of the latter. That is, the rhetorical force

---

94. A few commentators suggest that coveting, being a comprehensive and general sin, is implied in this comprehensive and general description of "some-thing different"; see Marshall, *PE*, 380–81; Towner, *Letters*, 129.

In passing, the specific term in LXX Exodus 20:17 in reference to coveting is "long-for" (ἐπιθυμήσεις): "Do not long-for (ἐπιθυμήσεις) the wife of your neighbor. Do not long-for (ἐπιθυμήσεις) the house of your neighbor . . ." Paul uses this term twice in 1 Timothy (ἐπιθυμεῖ, 3:2; ἐπιθυμίας, 6:9); see discussions in volume 2, chapter 2 and volume 3, chapter 3.

of the phrase "if some-thing different lies-opposed to the sound teaching" would delineate the cumulative apex of sin.

The indefinite pronoun "some-thing" (τι) in 1:10b recalls its prior cognates in reference to "some" (τισίν) who teach-different (1:3), "some" (τινες) who have turned-aside for useless-words (1:6), and "someone" (τις) who does not know how to use the law lawfully (1:8b). Here, then, while there is a shift from persons (1:3, 6, 8b) to a concept (1:10b), the implication is that they are connected: "some," "some," and "someone" all play a part in "some-thing." Furthermore, given that "some-thing" is explicitly defined as that which is "different" and "lies-opposed to the sound teaching," Paul is not only conveying a contrast but also that "some-thing different" intends a deliberate hostility—it "lies-opposed to the sound teaching." Still, where the term "some-thing" (1:10b) has in view "some" (1:3, 6) and "someone" (1:8a), its rhetorical combination with the term "different" (ἕτερον) would most certainly be intended to orient the audience to "some" who "teach-different" (ἑτεροδιδασκαλεῖν, 1:3).[95] To be sure, the phrase "some-thing (τι) different (ἕτερον)" in 1:10b of the A' element recalls that "some (τισίν) ... teach-different (ἑτεροδιδασκαλεῖν)" in 1:3 of the parallel A element. What is more, where some-thing "different" (ἕτερον) is placed in the immediate context of "the sound teaching (διδασκαλίᾳ)" in 1:10b, the audience understand that Paul's rhetoric clearly intends a connection to the fact that "some ... teach-different (ἑτεροδιδασκαλεῖν)" in 1:3.[96] In short, Paul's point is that "some-thing different" (1:10b) is directly associated with "some" who "teach-different" (1:3). Here, Paul's linguistic organization of the first microchiasm would be apparent as the audience hear the same three terms repeated within the parallel A and A' elements:

A element: "charge some (τισίν) not to teach-different (ἑτεροδιδασκαλεῖν)" (1:3);

A' element: "if some-thing (τι) different (ἕτερον) lies-opposed to the sound teaching (διδασκαλίᾳ)" (1:10b).

The rhetorical framing effect of the first microchiasm makes Paul's point memorable to the audience, signifies the boundaries of the linguistic unit, and solidifies the main thrust thereof. Paul's audience are thus prepared to interpret Paul's statements according to the overarching concern of the

---

95. The term "different" (ἕτερον) in 1:10b is included (see *italics*) within the verb "teach-*different*" (ἑτεροδιδασκαλεῖν) in 1:3.

96. The terms "different" (ἕτερον) and "teaching" (διδασκαλίᾳ) in 1:10b of the A' element are combined within the verb "teach-different" (ἑτεροδιδασκαλεῖν) in 1:3 of the parallel A element.

microchiasm, namely that there are "some" who "teach-different" in the Ephesian church (1:3; A element), which is not only "some-thing different" than "the sound teaching" but also "lies-opposed" to it (1:10b; A' element). Significantly, given the interconnected implications of the A and A' elements, Paul's awareness and certainty that there are "some" in the mid-sixties Ephesian church who teach-different (1:3) clearly conveys to the audience that his use of the term "if" (εἴ) in 1:10b is not conditional or hypothetical but rather is rhetorically emphatic to describe a real situation. In other words, "some-thing different" *in fact* "lies-opposed to the sound teaching" (1:10b) in the same way that "some" *in fact* "teach-different" in the Ephesian church (1:3).

Paul's framing concern about "some" who teach "some-thing" different (1:3, 10b) is specifically expressed by the verb "lies-opposed"—there is a definitive situation of opposition and hostility in the Ephesian church. Such is not surprising, given that "some" bring-about controversial-speculations (1:4b).[97] Moreover, where the verb "lies-opposed" (ἀντίκειται) recalls the cognate verb "laid" (κεῖται), the rhetorical implication of Paul's statement is clear to the audience (see *italics*): the law is "*laid*" (*κεῖται*, 1:9a) for that which "*lies*-opposed" (ἀντίκειται) to the sound teaching (1:10b). Significantly, therefore, given Paul's implication that the law is laid for "some" (1:6) and "someone" (1:8b)—namely, the without-law (1:9b) who do not know how to use the law lawfully (1:8a–b) but are desiring to be law-teachers (1:7)—it is clear that the law is laid *both* for "some-thing different" that "lies-opposed" to the sound teaching (1:10b) and "some" who "teach-different" (1:3). Furthermore, a twofold implication is conveyed to the audience. Negatively, "someone" demonstrates that they do not know how to use the law lawfully (1:8b) by teaching "some-thing different" that "lies-opposed" to the sound teaching (1:10b). Positively, it is "the sound teaching" that demonstrates a proper understanding and use of the law, namely that it is commendable (1:8a). In sum, then, given the sustained focus toward the false teachers throughout the first microchiasm, the audience have been prepared for the cumulative conclusion of Paul's rhetorical and polemical strategy: "some" who teach-different and who are desiring to be law-teachers (1:3, 6) are "the without-law and without-obedience" for whom the law is laid (1:9a–b); such is plainly evidenced by "some-thing" different that they teach, which "lies-opposed" to the sound teaching (1:10b).

---

97. See discussion above regarding 1:4b, namely the rhetorical use of αἵτινες—literally, "which-some"—to connect "controversial-speculations" with the personal activity of "some" (τισίν) rather than the suggestion that the inanimate concepts of "myths and genealogies without-limit" are that which produce such results.

Particularly in view of the sustained polemical context against the false teachers, it is clear that the phrase "the sound teaching" underscores a stark contrast to "some-thing" different that "some" are teaching. To be sure, "the sound teaching" (τῇ ὑγιανούσῃ διδασκαλίᾳ) in 1:10b is Paul's reference to his apostolic teaching that brings about the household-law of God (1:4b).[98] As such, it is most evident why "some-thing different lies-opposed to the sound-teaching" (1:10b): the former brings about controversial-speculations—in a word, chaos (1:4b). Indeed, in contrast to "the . . . teaching" (τῇ . . . διδασκαλίᾳ, 1:10b), the audience understand that "some" who are desiring to be "law-teachers" (νομοδιδάσκαλοι, 1:7) actively work against the very purpose of the law and against the familial relationships that are ordered and arranged by the household-law of God that belong to the sphere "in faith" (1:2, 4). That is, the very nature of "some-thing different" demonstrates that "some" who teach-different are not "in faith."

The phrase "the sound teaching" is itself polemical.[99] Notably, "the . . . teaching" (τῇ . . . διδασκαλίᾳ) occurs in the singular, likely signifying its unique authority in contrast to "some-thing different" (1:10b) and certainly to the "myths and genealogies without-limit" that "some" hold-toward (1:4a). The adjective "sound" (ὑγιαινούσῃ) is medical terminology, connoting that which is "healthy."[100] In effect, where "the . . . teaching" is "healthy," it is evident that "if some-thing different lies-opposed to the sound teaching," then "some-thing different" is most certainly unhealthy, particularly for the household-law of God in faith (1:4b). In other words, Paul's point is graphic and forceful: the impact of the false teaching is like a deadly virus spreading from person to person, undermining the health of God's entire household. Consequently, any willingness on the part of the audience to adhere to "some-thing different" (1:10b)—and thus adhere to "some" who teach-different (1:3)—is tantamount to voluntarily harming themselves. It is only by adhering to "the sound teaching"—that which results in health—that the Ephesian church and those within it will survive. With their attention piqued, the audience are now prepared to hear Paul's definition of "the sound teaching."

---

98. Towner, *Letters*, 130–31.

99. Johnson, *Contested Issues*, 390–91: Paul's rhetorical construction "bears marks of the stereotypical slander found in fights among ancient philosophers."

100. Wall with Steele, *1 & 2 Timothy*, 68, summarize the term ὑγιανούσῃ as "a Greek medical term that provides an apt metaphor of a functional sense of Christian instruction developed in the Pastoral Epistles." See also Robinson and Wall, *Called to Lead*, 29.

1 Timothy 1:11–17: A Minichiastic Unit

Within the concluding A' element of the microchiasm, the audience hear 1:11–17 as a minichiasm in itself. Verses 1:11–17 are composed carefully of six sub-elements ("a"-"b"-"c"-"d"-"c'"-"b'"-"a'"); linguistic parallels identifying chiastic arrangements are indicated by the Greek text:

> "a". ¹¹ᵃ according to the gospel of the glory (δόξης) of the blessed God (θεοῦ),
>
>> "b". ¹¹ᵇ with which I-myself was counted-faithful (ἐπιστεύθην). ¹² I hold grace to him who empowered me, Christ Jesus our Lord, because faithful (πιστόν) he considered me appointing for service,
>>
>>> "c". ¹³ though firstly (πρότερον) being a blasphemer and a persecutor and a hubristic-person; rather I was granted-mercy (ἠλεήθην), because without-knowing I did in unfaithfulness; ¹⁴ but the grace of our Lord beyond-abounded with the faith and love that are in Christ Jesus.
>>>
>>>> "d". ¹⁵ᵃ Faithful is the word and worthy of all acceptance, that Christ Jesus came into the world to save sinners,
>>>
>>> "c'". ¹⁵ᵇ of whom I-myself am the first (πρῶτός). 16a Rather consistent-with this I was granted-mercy (ἠλεήθην), that in me the first (πρώτῳ) Christ Jesus might display all patience
>>
>> "b'". ¹⁶ᵇ as an example to those who would-inevitably-come to have-faith (πιστεύειν) upon him for life eternal.
>
> "a'". ¹⁷ But to the King of the eternities, without-perishability, without-visibility, only God (θεῷ), honor and glory (δόξα) for the eternities of the eternities, amen.

The third and final minichiasm of the 1:1–20 microchiasm is framed by Paul's focus on "God" and the "glory" that is associated with him in the "a" and "a'" sub-elements. The "b" and "b'" sub-elements are arranged by cognate language pertaining to "faith." The "c" and "c'" sub-elements convey the theme of being "granted-mercy" despite a former life of being a prominent sinner. Significantly, the minichiasm gravitates around the entrance of Christ Jesus into the world to save sinners in the pivot "d" sub-element.

1 Timothy 1:11a: According to the Gospel of the Glory of the Blessed God

("a" sub-element)

In the introductory "a" sub-element (1:11a), Paul begins by specifying that "the sound teaching" (1:10b) is "according to the gospel of the glory of the blessed God." In other words, "the sound teaching" is defined by "the gospel."[101] The preposition "according to" (κατά) here in 1:11a of the microchiasm's A element recalls the opening statement of the letter in 1:1 of the parallel A element: Paul is an apostle of Christ Jesus "according to" (κατ') the command of God our Savior and Christ Jesus our hope (1:1). Significantly, then, in the same way that Paul's authoritative status to fully represent Christ Jesus as an apostle was divinely commanded by and "according to . . . God" (κατ' . . . θεοῦ, 1:1) so also is "the sound teaching" (1:10b) not the choice or product of Paul's decision or doing but is the direct expression of the divine will "according to . . . God" (κατὰ . . . θεοῦ, 1:11a).[102] Furthermore, where both Paul's apostleship (1:1) and the sound teaching (1:10b) stem from the direct activity of God (1:1, 11a), the parallel application of "according to" (1:1, 11a) suggests a deliberate connection: Paul is an "apostle of Christ Jesus" for the purpose of "the sound teaching."[103] Furthermore, where "the sound teaching" (1:10b) is "according to the gospel . . . of God" (1:11a), it is equally apparent that "the gospel" is rooted in and stems from God's divine authority and expression thereof.[104] The audience thus hear an articulation of synonymy: "the sound teaching" (1:10b) is simultaneously "the gospel . . . of God" (1:11a).

The noun "the gospel" (τὸ εὐαγγέλιον)—literally, "the good-message"—is a compound term from the adverb "well" (εὖ) and the noun

---

101. Knight, *PE*, 90: "κατὰ τὸ εὐαγγέλιον by its connection with ὑγιαιούσῃ διδασκαλίᾳ provides the norm for that teaching and for its soundness." Swinson, *Letters to Timothy*, 52: "he explicitly associates this 'sound teaching' with 'the gospel of the glory of the blessed God.'"

102. The interconnected sequence of genitives in 1:11a concludes with "God."

103. Here, it may be helpful to visualize (see *italics*) the parallel relation of "Paul, apostle" (1:1) and "the sound teaching":
A element: "*Paul, apostle of Christ Jesus* according to (κατ') the command of God our Savior and Christ Jesus our hope" (1:1);
A' element: "*the sound teaching*, according to (κατά) the gospel of the glory of the blessed God" (1:10b–11a).

104. Dodd, "The Gospel," 6: "the Gospel . . . comes to us *from* God. It is not something that wise or holy men made up out of their own heads, for that would bring glory to men who invented it." Swinson, *Letters to Timothy*, 52: Paul is "anchoring its origin in God himself; it is God's gospel message."

"message" (ἀγγελία).¹⁰⁵ In one sense, Paul's use of the term "gospel" (εὐαγγέλιον) is likely subversive; its contemporary use to describe the political and military victories of the emperor would have been familiar to Paul's first-century Ephesian audience.¹⁰⁶ Here, however, specifically in connection with "the sound teaching" (1:10b) by Paul who is the "apostle of Christ Jesus" (1:1), "the gospel" would be understood as a summary term, in effect: "the sound teaching concerning the authoritative representation of Christ Jesus." That is, Christ Jesus would be understood as the content of "the gospel" and, therefore, of "the sound teaching" by "Paul, apostle of Christ Jesus" (1:1, 10b, 11a).¹⁰⁷

In view of Christ Jesus, Paul's explicit reference to "the gospel" reminds the Ephesian audience to shift all their allegiance away from anything that "lies-opposed to the sound teaching, according to the gospel" (1:10b–11a)—to be sure, to shift their allegiance away from "some-thing different" (1:10b), and thus from "some" who "teach-different" (1:3). Certainly, anyone listening in the audience would hear Paul's point loud and clear: a decision to agree with "some" who teach-different (1:3) and thus adhere to

---

105. It may be worth noting how the Greek word εὐαγγέλιον is translated into the English word "gospel." Bird, *The Gospel of the Lord*, 5: "our English word 'gospel' comes from the old English word 'godspel,' which means something akin to 'good tale' . . . The English is a translation of the Latin *evangelium* and the Greek εὐαγγέλιον . . . The lexical root of these words signifies notions of glad tidings and joyous news that is declared to others."

106. Reasoner, *Roman Imperial Texts*, 9: "the word 'gospel' . . . was used to describe what actions or events associated with various Roman emperors had occurred for the welfare of the world." Dunn, *Jesus, Paul, and the Gospels*, 45: "The noun 'gospel, good news' (*euangelion*) is one of several terms which Christianity owes to Paul . . . A strong body of New Testament scholarship believes that Paul borrowed the term 'gospel' from its political use in relation to Caesar. And it is certainly true that the word *euangelion* (usually in the plural) was used for the good news of Caesar Augustus's achievements." Bird, *The Gospel of the Lord*, 6, 8: "In the Greco-Roman world, the noun εὐαγγέλιον was primarily associated with positive news in general and news of military victory in particular . . . Importantly, when the good news is associated with the news of military victory, it is sometimes invested with religious connotations like divine favor and a gift of providence . . . There are occasions where 'good news' simply means a favorable report, but the technical usage of the language applies to settings that have social, religious, and political connotations."

For more on the Greco-Roman context of "gospel," see Elliot and Reasoner, *Documents*, 63; Caulley, "*Christinos* and Roman Imperial Cult," 198–202; Humphries, *Early Christianity*, 137; Wright, *What Saint Paul Really Said*, 41–44. For more on Paul's subversive use of the Greek language, see Ehrensperger, "Speaking Greek Under Rome," 9–28, esp. 24–25.

107. Elliot and Reasoner, *Documents and Images*, 63: "Paul's letters are all written to communities of people who have already accepted his 'gospel.' In them, he reminds his hearers of his initial proclamation."

"some-thing different" (1:10b), rather than "the sound teaching" (1:10b), would not only be the same as rejecting "the gospel" (1:11a) but also Christ Jesus's very own representative messenger, Paul (1:1) and thus Christ Jesus himself—the person whom "the gospel" concerns.

Paul goes on to connect a genitive phrase to the gospel: "of the glory of the blessed God" (1:11a).[108] The noun "glory" (δόξης) typically expresses splendor and value; yet, with reference to the God of the OT, it refers to the visible, radiant display of God, namely the tangible expression of his invisible qualities—the indescribable revealing of himself (e.g., LXX Ezek 1:28; 10:4).[109] With this connotation, the first part of Paul's statement regarding "the gospel of the glory of . . . God" is to be understood as a description of the content of the glory, namely that "the gospel" showcases, expresses, and exhibits the divine radiance of God. Here, then, "the gospel" is not merely a message but a personal revealing of God himself—the radiant "glory of . . . God." Moreover, where "the gospel" defines "the sound teaching" (1:10b–11a), it is clear that the revealing of God's radiance both has informed and is the content thereof.[110] In this sense, "the gospel" is simultaneously both "the sound teaching" of the apostle Paul *and* God's very own self-disclosure: "the gospel" is God's exhibition of his radiant "glory" through "the sound teaching" of which God himself commanded Paul to be an authorized messenger (1:1). This is precisely what makes the action of "some" who "teach-different" (1:3) so particularly heinous: it showcases, expresses, and exhibits themselves rather than and in contradiction to God.

The adjective "blessed" (μακαρίου) would have held several connotations. On the one hand, it was commonly used to describe people who had experienced God's blessing, as is the case with Paul, Timothy, and those among the audience who have received the salvific blessings of grace, mercy, peace, a pure heart, a good conscience, and a without-hypocrisy faith (1:2,

---

108. The genitive phrase "of the gospel of the glory of God" has led to some interpretive challenges. Compare various translations (e.g., *NRSV, NASB, KJV*, "the glorious gospel of the blessed God"; *REB*, "the Good News from the glorious and blessed God").

109. Forster, "Meaning of Δόξα," 316: "δόξα acquires a meaning 'radiance' which it has not in Greek literature . . . [it] was Ezekiel's word to translate the fiery glow of the vision of God." De Vries, "Glory of YHWH," 54: God's glory "highlights the dual and paradoxical nature . . . as both defying verbal description and being potentially visible." Knight, *PE*, 106: "δόξα reflects the OT Hebrew k̲ā̲b̲ô̲d̲ (which it renders in the LXX), which indicates the luminous manifestation of God's person, his glorious revelation of himself." See also my comments on Titus 2:13 in *To Exhort and Reprove*, 83. For discussion regarding the Greco-Roman application of "glory" to emperors, see Harrison, "Paul's *Doxa* Terminology," 174–87.

110. It may be worth noting that where "the sound teaching" signifies the proper understanding of the law (see above), so too does "the gospel." That is, "the sound teaching . . . according to the gospel" is what informs a sound, healthy teaching of the law.

5).¹¹¹ On the other hand, Greek literature often referenced gods as "blessed" (e.g., see Homer, *Odyssey* 10.299), and such language was also found in the Imperial cult referring to the emperor.¹¹² Thus, it may be that here Paul is including a subversive edge, asserting his God alone is the truly blessed one. Either way, "the blessed God" (θεοῦ) recalls the two prior occurrences of "God (θεοῦ) our Savior" (1:1) and "God (θεοῦ) the Father" (1:2). Thus connotations of salvation and family are in view. Moreover, "the blessed God" (θεοῦ) seems to also have in mind "the household-law of God (θεοῦ) in faith" (1:4)—"in faith" referring to the sphere of existence pertaining to Christ Jesus that makes the letter's familial language possible (1:2). The "gospel . . . of the blessed God" is therefore not only a summons for the audience to recall God's salvific blessings but also—and much more—to respond by blessing God, namely by calling upon him as "Father" and submitting to his "household-law." Such blessing is contrasted by the stark opposition of "some" in the audience whose teachings "bring-about controversial-speculations rather than the household-law of God" (1:4). The false teachers do not bless God, likely because they know him neither as "Savior" nor as "Father"; they have no concept of being in a family or a household where God is its head.

From all this, the audience understand the overall meaning of Paul's qualifying statement in the "a" sub-element. In full, "the gospel of the glory of the blessed God" defines "the sound teaching" both as God's very own self-disclosure of and about himself—given to Paul by God's very own command—and as that which, in turn, commands only one appropriate response—to bless God through reverent adherence to what God has disclosed through "the sound teaching," that is, "the gospel." Negatively, against "some" who "teach-different" (1:3), it is clear that "some-thing different" (1:10) not only lies-opposed to "the sound teaching" but also, therefore, to

---

111. See Collins, *1 & 2 Timothy*, 34–35; Marshall, *PE*, 273.

112. Neyrey, "Rhetoric," 68, 80, 81: "The deities are often called 'blessed' (μάκαρ, μακάριος) which distinguishes their blissful lot from the turmoil of mortals . . . since we saw in the Greek Orphic hymns that most of the gods there were acclaimed 'blessed', we find considerable evidence which indicates that μακάριος was a common attribute of Greco-Roman gods . . . It represents, then, a quality unique to a deity." See Collins, *1 & 2 Timothy*, 34–35. Towner, *Letters*, 132: "The gods were 'happy' [blessed] in that they, in contrast to mere humans, were immortal. Such epithets were known in the Imperial cult, which suggests the possibility that the emergence of the term in reference to God here and in Titus reflects a new degree of polemical dialogue with the political powers on the part of Paul." Cf. Marshall, *PE*, 383, who is hesitant to accept a polemical note against the Imperial cult.

In passing, one might observe the apparent similarity between the struggle taking place between God and the Imperial cult and Paul and the false teachers. It may be that Paul's struggle to assert his authority and message represents a larger effort to assert God's glory over the gods and emperors of Greco-Roman culture.

"the gospel." The different teaching of "some" does not reveal God's radiance nor does it result in blessing to him. For the Ephesian audience—and particularly "some" among them—Paul is encouraging and inviting an allegiance to "the gospel," to "the sound teaching," and thus to actively bless God.

1 Timothy 1:11b–12: Counted-Faithful, I Hold Grace to Christ Jesus

("b" sub-element)

In the "b" sub-element of the minichiasm (1:11b–12), Paul highlights his direct connection to the gospel: "with which I-myself was counted-faithful" (1:11b). The rhetorical use of the personal pronoun "I-myself" (ἐγώ) is emphatic; where "I-myself was counted-faithful" with the gospel, Paul's implication is that he has been uniquely assigned with it (1:11b).[113] Paul, who has already identified himself as a uniquely appointed apostle of Christ Jesus by the command of God our Savior and Christ Jesus our hope (1:1), now makes explicit what message God and Christ Jesus have assigned to him, namely "the gospel" (1:11a), that is, "the sound teaching" (1:10a). In other words, the audience understand that while "the sound teaching" and "the gospel" effectively belong and originate from God and Christ Jesus, the fact that Paul "was counted-faithful" with both "the sound teaching" and "the gospel" by both God and Christ Jesus conveys Paul's personal and inseparable connection to his assignment: it is simultaneously Paul's sound teaching and Paul's gospel.[114] Undoubtedly, then, it is for this reason that Paul exhorted Timothy to remain in Ephesus to "charge some not to teach-different" (1:3)—Paul intends to preserve "the . . . teaching"—the gospel—with which he was counted-faithful (1:10b–11a). The verb "was counted-faithful" (ἐπιστεύθην) here in 1:11b of the A' element recalls the three parallel cognate phrases in the A element—"in faith (πίστει)" in 1:2 and 1:4 and "a without-hypocrisy faith (πίστεως)" in 1:5. The passive voice of the verb "was counted-faithful" suggests that Paul is "in faith" and possesses "a without-hypocrisy faith" by God's doing. Moreover, where Paul has been vocationally "counted-faithful," it is no wonder to the audience why he employs a rather direct and polemical disposition toward "some" who oppose the purpose of his vocation.

---

113. Paul's inclusion of the pronoun ἐγώ is grammatically unnecessary and, therefore, intentional. The translation "I-myself" captures the nuance.

114. Such is directly conveyed in other letters by Paul (Rom 2:16; 16:25; 2 Tim 2:8).

Paul immediately declares his gratitude for being counted-faithful with the gospel: "I hold grace to him who empowered me, Christ Jesus our Lord, because faithful he considered me appointing for service" (1:12). The audience would certainly hear an echo of the letter's beginning: such "grace" (χάριν) from Paul to "Christ Jesus our Lord" (Χριστῷ Ἰησοῦ τῷ κυρίῳ ἡμῶν, 1:12) here in the A' element represents a response to the "grace" (χάρις) that came from God the Father and "Christ Jesus our Lord" (Χριδ τοῦ Ἰησοῦ τοῦ κυρίου ἡμῶν, 1:2) in the parallel A element.[115] Again, the linguistic arrangement of the microchiasm would be apparent:

A element: "grace (χάρις), mercy, peace from . . . Christ Jesus our Lord (Χριστοῦ Ἰησοῦ κυρίου ἡμῶν)" (1:2);

A' element: "I hold grace" (χάριν) to . . . Christ Jesus our Lord (Χριστῷ Ἰησοῦ τῷ κυρίῳ ἡμῶν)" (1:12).

By extending the blessing of "grace" back to Christ Jesus, that is, back to God,[116] Paul demonstrates that he is living according to the gospel that reveals God's radiance and results in a response of blessing to God. That is, immediately after defining the gospel in 1:11, Paul lives it in 1:12. In this way, Paul reminds his audience that the Christian life flows primarily from Christ's initiating grace. Such an emphasis was implied at the beginning of the letter in the A element—the name "Christ Jesus" was stated three times (1:1-2)—and here again is made explicit in the A' element by the reference to "Christ Jesus our Lord" (1:12). Moreover, Paul's declaration in 1:12 of the A' element reiterates that his ministry and calling is the divine empowerment and appointment from the same Christ Jesus in 1:1 of the A element. Thus, while highlighting his marvelous appointment with the gospel that reveals God's radiant glory, Paul is careful to make clear to his audience that it is Christ Jesus alone who deserves all blessing and gratitude. For Paul, "the blessed God" (1:11) is the one who "empowered me, Christ Jesus" (1:12).

In addition, the aorist tense of the participle "empowered" (ἐνδυναμώσαντί) suggests that Paul has in mind his experience after his Damascus Road conversion where he "all-the-more increased-in-power

---

115. In Paul's other letters, he prefers to express thanks through the verb εὐχαριστέω (e.g., 1 Cor 1:4; Phil 1:3); for comments on the nuances, see Spicq, *Les Épîtres Pastorales*, 340. Paul's choice of language here may have been to highlight the reciprocal nature of the Christian life, that gratitude to God is an overflow of the grace that God has revealed particularly in Christ Jesus, as the proceeding verses will highlight.

116. In 1:11, "the gospel" taught by Paul results in giving blessing specifically to "God." For Paul to give blessing of "grace" specifically to "Christ Jesus" is likely not insignificant. As a parallel to the A element, Paul's blessing to Christ Jesus makes explicit that what he received was from God (1:1-2).

(ἐνεδυναμοῦτο)" (Acts 9:22).[117] It is Paul's direct calling and empowerment from Christ Jesus that would have placed Paul squarely in the tradition of the OT prophets who were uniquely called and empowered by God with a specific task.[118] This point is not insignificant, adding to the polemical nature of this letter. Unlike "some," Paul's calling is divine and in line with the prophetic tradition.[119] Moreover, where the audience receive Paul's teaching, they are able to receive God's revelation and blessing. Thus, in the same way that "Christ Jesus our Lord" (Χριστῷ Ἰησοῦ τῷ κυρίῳ ἡμῶν) has uniquely blessed Paul according to 1:12 of the A' element, so too does "Christ Jesus our Lord" (Χριστοῦ Ἰησοῦ τοῦ κυρίου ἡμῶν) bless the audience through Paul's message with grace, mercy, and peace according to 1:2 of the A element. That is, both Paul and the audience together share a unique affinity with one another as recipients of God's blessings from Christ "our" (ἡμῶν) Lord. This stands in stark contrast to the false teachers who do not receive Paul's teaching.

The statement in 1:12b "faithful he considered me appointing for service" further highlights Christ's unique empowerment in Paul's life. The statement would not be understood as a suggestion that Christ foreknew that Paul would be faithful. Rather, where the adjective "faithful" (πιστόν) here in 1:12b of the A' element recalls its cognate terms in the parallel A element (1:2, 4, 5), it would be clear that Paul is referring to the sphere of existence "in faith" (ἐν πίστει, 1:2, 4) that is marked by "a without-hypocrisy faith (πίστεως)" (1:5). In other words, the audience understands that Paul was considered "faithful" as a salvific action by Christ Jesus toward Paul. Moreover, where Paul was "considered" (ἡγήσατο) faithful, as demonstrated by his "appointing" (θέμενος) for "service" (διακονίαν), the implication is that Paul's appointment was for the purpose of revealing the existential realm "in faith" as part of the sound teaching with which he "was counted-faithful" (1:10b). Notably, Paul's vocation by Christ's empowering, salvific activity

---

117. The likely reference to Acts 9:22 would also draw attention to Acts 9:5-6, where it is specifically Jesus who issues the imperative command to Paul that inaugurates Paul's Christian life and ministry. In the same way, then, the explicit statement "I hold grace to him who empowered me, Christ Jesus" (1:12) would draw attention to the fact that he is an "apostle of Christ Jesus according to *the command* of God our Savior and Christ Jesus our hope" (1:1).

118. It may be worth noting that in 2 Corinthians 12:2-3, that Paul was caught up into the third heaven to receive visions and revelations articulates his place among the true OT prophets who, likewise, were summoned to the throne-room of God (e.g., 1 Kgs 22:19; Isa 6:1-8; Jer 23:18, 22; Ezek 1:26).

119. In the OT prophetic books, there is generally an explicit contrast between true and false prophets (e.g., Jer 2-29). Paul's polemic against the false teachers seems to therefore place Paul even more in line with the OT prophetic tradition.

stands in stark contrast to "some" who actively work against the household-law of God "in faith" (1:4b). That is, whereas "some" teach-different (1:3), bring-about controversial-speculations (1:4b), and thereby demonstrate that they are neither from nor reveal the contents of the realm "in faith" (1:2, 4), Paul "was counted-faithful" with the sound teaching (1:10b) by the direct activity of Christ Jesus, who personally considered Paul "faithful" for service (1:12). Paul's status is defined by Christ; the status of "some" is not.

1 Timothy 1:13–14: A Blasphemer, Granted-Mercy, Grace Beyond-Abounded

("c" sub-element)

To further highlight that his existence in the realm "in faith" is solely by divine activity, in the "c" sub-element Paul adds that Christ appointed him for service "though firstly being a blasphemer and a persecutor and a hubristic-person" (1:13a). It is unlikely that Paul is revealing anything new about himself to his audience.[120] The rhetorical purpose here is to accentuate that it was indeed Christ Jesus who empowered and qualified him for service, although "firstly" (πρότερον)—the moment in time before Christ empowered him—he was a blasphemer, persecutor, and hubristic-person. Such an individual, Paul communicates, should not have been appointed for service; yet, he was. In this way, the phrase "though firstly being" (τὸ πρότερον ὄντα) in 1:13 further accentuates the supremacy of Christ's grace on Paul's life (1:12) and thus the greatness of "the sound teaching" (1:10b), "the gospel" (1:11a) that has Christ Jesus as its content.[121] It was despite Paul—specifically his past, which he describes in terms of being "a blasphemer and a persecutor and a hubristic-person"—that Christ Jesus appointed him for service. As noted, the adverbial phrase "firstly" (πρότερον) is meant to highlight that, at some point in actual history prior to his encounter with Christ Jesus, Paul was not "in faith." To emphasize this fact, he makes use of another vice-list—albeit much briefer than the one found in the B' element—to describe this former life as a "blasphemer and a persecutor and a hubristic-person" (6:13). The term "blasphemer" (βλάσφημον) is also found in LXX Isaiah 66:3

---

120. Paul's prior conduct as a non-Christian would have been known by the Ephesians. Acts 9:13 indicates that Paul's tirades against Christians were well-known, and Paul regularly rehearses this fact to his audiences (Acts 22:6–8; 26:9–11, 14–15).

121. Knight, *PE*, 95: "τὸ πρότερον is used here as an adverb of time in a concessive sense, 'even though.'" However, as Marshall indicates, the concessive participle is ὄντα (*PE*, 391). The translation here "though firstly being" therefore accurately captures the nuance.

to describe one who pays superficial homage to God while being otherwise insulting. Such a term aptly describes Paul's former life, given his apparent dedication to God while persecuting Christ and the first disciples.[122] Given the sustained polemic against "some," Paul may be suggesting here that the false teachers are committing a similar error, considering themselves devout while doing a disservice to God through their misunderstanding of the law (1:7) and their different teaching (1:3, 10b).[123] The term "persecutor" (διώκτην) is a *hapax legomenon* in the NT, but descriptions of Paul's previous life make clear that he is referring to his persecution of the early believers. In particular, Paul is likely recalling Jesus's very own summary of him in Acts: "Saul, Saul, why are you persecuting (διώκεις) me? . . . I-myself am Jesus whom you are persecuting (διώκεις)" (Acts 9:4, 6). Where Paul is associating "some" with his prior life, the implication is jarring: in effect, by teaching some-thing different that lies-opposed to the sound teaching, "some" are persecuting the church—and Jesus—from within the church itself. Finally, the term "hubristic-person" (ὑβριστήν), which is also rare in the NT (see Rom 1:30), is found in LXX Isaiah 2:12 (and elsewhere throughout the OT) to describe a person who proudly sets himself opposed to God.[124] Its occurrence immediately after "persecutor" may function to explain the hostile nature of Paul's persecution.[125] In sum, the force of this vice-list is to make clear that Paul fully viewed himself as a sinner—indeed, of the worst degree.[126] Such a self-description undoubtedly functions to balance out

122. Acts 26:11 may be worth noting. Paul's speech uses the cognate verb "blaspheme" (βλασφημεῖν) to describe his attempt to make Christians renounce their faith in Christ. Thus his acts as a "blasphemer" against the church are likely in view.

123. Johnson, "First Timothy," 30–31: "It is difficult to avoid the impression that Paul is deliberately identifying himself in his former life with those who, in their faithlessness and ignorance, now wish to be teachers of law."

124 Towner suggests that the term "describes the seething attitude of insolent anger and boastful pride that often fills the void caused by fear and insecurity and produces the worst acts of behavior" (*Letters*, 139). See ibid. n. 25. See also Johnson, "First Timothy," 30 n. 43.

125. Collins, *1 & 2 Timothy*, 37: "'Persecutor' is the central element in the triad, with 'blasphemer' and 'violent person' the interpretive elements. Paul's persecution of the church was blasphemy against God and violence against God's people."

126. See Marshall, *PE*, 391. A few commentators suggest that such a self-description appears to be at odds with his self-description in Philippians 3:4–6, especially his closing declaration of being "blameless" with respect to the law (e.g., Roloff, *Der Erste Brief an Timotheus*, 93). In Philippians, however, Paul is simply referring to his innocence with respect to the Torah and Jewish purity laws. Conversely in the passage above, he is describing his moral guilt for zealously persecuting Christ and his followers. In 1 Corinthians 15:9 Paul himself provides an explicit assessment of this former life: "For I am the least of the apostles, unworthy to be called an apostle, because I persecuted the church of God." Thus, there is no contradiction between what Paul says here and

any misunderstanding that Paul possessed an unduly high self-estimation of himself on account being an apostle of Christ Jesus.[127] To be sure, the rhetorical effect would highlight God's sovereignty in the matter: Paul is a divinely chosen vessel—an apostle according to the command of God and Christ Jesus (1:1)—and had absolutely no involvement in his appointment thereof (1:12).

In the second half of verse 1:13, Paul highlights Christ's response to his deplorable life: "rather I was granted-mercy, because without-knowing I did in unfaithfulness" (1:13b). The disjunction "rather" (ἀλλ') highlights that instead of receiving the just judgment for his actions, he "was granted-mercy" (ἠλεήθην). Certainly, such articulates the contrast between Paul's prior actions toward God (1:13a) and God's action toward Paul (1:13b). The passive voice of the verb "I was granted-mercy" further accentuates God's sovereign mercy in his life; it was Christ's initiating and gracious response to Paul that alone accounts for his status as an apostle.[128] Furthermore, the verb "I was granted-mercy" (ἠλεήθην) here in 1:13 of the A' element recalls the blessings of "grace, mercy (ἔλεος), and peace" from God the Father and Christ Jesus our Lord in 1:2 of the parallel A element.[129] Beyond any doubt, then, it is clear that such salvific "mercy" (1:2) has been concretely experienced by Paul who "was granted-mercy" (1:13)—indeed, the reception of such "grace" (1:2) has led Paul to hold "grace" back to Christ (1:12). Paul's sound teaching, then—"the gospel"—both at the beginning of the letter and now intends the same rich experience of God's sovereign grace—as well as the resulting impact—for his audience. In short, as Paul's own life demonstrates, it is a blessing from God (1:2, A element) to be able to bless God (1:12, A' element). Moreover, here in the A' element, in the same way that Paul "was counted-faithful" (ἐπιστεύθην, 1:11) and considered "faithful" (πιστόν, 1:12) by Christ Jesus, he "was granted-mercy" (ἠλεήθην) by Christ Jesus (1:13). Notably, the same was heard in the parallel A element wherein Paul and Timothy's existence "in faith (πίστει)" was the result of "mercy" (ἔλεος) from Christ Jesus (1:2). Thus the audience's entire understanding of the letter so far has been rhetorically framed in the A and A' elements by a

---

elsewhere in his letters, including his statements in Philippians 3:4-6.

127. Collins, *1 & 2 Timothy*, 37: "Paul's persecution of the church was blasphemy against God and violence against God's people. Paul is, in fact, a prime example of a blasphemer, persecutor of the church, and violent person . . . Paul had effectively spoken against God. Through his action he had denied what God had done (through Christ Jesus) for his people."

128. See Marshall, *PE*, 392.

129. Barcley, "1 Timothy," 358: "Paul anticipates this discussion [in 1:13] by inserting this atypical word [ἔλεος] into his greeting [1:2]."

singular theme: the sphere "in faith"—the realm of Christ—is entered only by being granted-mercy—to be sure, undeservedly.

In the context of Paul's discussion, the phrase "because without-knowing I did in unfaithfulness" in 1:13b is particularly significant. To be sure, "because without-knowing I did" (ὅτι ἀγνοῶν ἐποίησα) does not exonerate him of guilt; the clear purpose of Paul's statement has been to highlight that he undeservedly "was granted-mercy" for the things that he did as a blasphemer, persecutor, and hubristic-person (1:13). Instead, the rhetorical focus of Paul's statement (see *italics*) would be heard in the relationship between "*without*-knowing" (ἀγνοῶν) and "*un*faithfulness" (ἀπιστίᾳ)—literally, "*without*-faith."[130] The former explains that his errors were unintentional; he was acting out of ignorance. The latter explains the state of his existence; Paul committed these grievous errors *before* entering into the sphere "in faith" (ἐν πίστει, 1:2, 4), that is, as a non-Christian living in the sphere "in unfaithfulness" (ἐν ἀπιστίᾳ, 1:13). Heard together, the collective sense of the phrase is that "I did these things before I was enlightened by the grace of God concerning the truth of Christ Jesus as articulated in the sound teaching—the gospel." Precisely here, given the sustained polemical context in which Paul is addressing the Ephesian audience, his point would not go unheard.

Paul's reference to his own ignorance—"without-knowing" (1:13)—conceptually echoes the mindset of "some" who are desiring to be law-teachers but "not understanding" either what they-are-saying or some-things they-are-insisting (1:7).[131] Thus, the initial impact on the audience is that "some" are acting, living, and doing as Paul did when he was not a Christian and existing in the sphere "in unfaithfulness" (1:13). However, Paul's far more jarring implication is that "some" within the Ephesian church are "not understanding" even *after* having experienced the revelation of God's grace in Christ Jesus as expressed, exhibited, and articulated by the sound teaching—the gospel—taught by Paul to the Ephesian church at least ten years prior.[132] That is, unlike Paul, "some" who teach-different are not "without-knowing"; instead, "some" in the mid-sixties Ephesian church are acting "in

---

130. The two terms would be heard by Paul's audience as alliterative due to the negative α- prefixes—literally, "without-knowing (ἀγνοῶν) . . . without-faith (ἀπιστίᾳ)." For readability purposes in English, the translation "unfaithfulness" was necessary; see chapter 2 for further explanation.

131. Although the term "without-knowing" (ἀγνοῶν, 1:13) and the phrase "not understanding" (μὴ νοοῦντες, 1:7) do not share a direct cognate root, their conceptual similarity would be apparent.

132. Paul established the Ephesian church in the early to mid-fifties; the 1 Timothy letter was composed in the mid-sixties; see chapter 1.

unfaithfulness" but as people who had once been "in faith." In other words, the guilt of "some" is categorically different—and worse—than Paul's.[133] Such is the resounding rhetorical force and polemical purpose of Paul's statement "but without-knowing I did in unfaithfulness" (1:13).

Yet, Paul immediately continues the "c" sub-element of the minichiasm by presenting the prevailing reality of the gospel: "but the grace of our Lord beyond-abounded" (1:14a). Given Paul's preceding statement, the disjunctive "but" (δέ) in 1:14 would convey the force of, "but not only so—all the more." To be sure, such would be indicated by the compound verb "beyond-abounded" (ὑπερεπλεόνασεν) that Paul uses to initiate the statement—the sense being, "overflowed."[134] The phrase "our Lord" (τοῦ κυρίου ἡμῶν) in 1:14 recalls Paul's prior references to Christ Jesus "our Lord" (τῷ κυρίῳ ἡμῶν) in 1:12 of the current A' element and Christ Jesus "our Lord" (τοῦ κυρίου ἡμῶν) in 1:2 of the parallel A element. Moreover, where the term "grace" (χάρις) in 1:14 equally recalls "grace" (χάριν) in 1:12 of the current A' element and "grace" (χάρις) in 1:2 of the parallel A element, the the overwhelming linguistic arrangement of Paul's rhetoric is apparent:

> A element: "grace (χάρις), mercy (ἔλεος), peace from God the Father and Christ Jesus our Lord (Χριστοῦ Ἰησοῦ τοῦ κυρίου ἡμῶν)" (1:2);
>
> A' element: "I hold grace (χάριν) to . . . Christ Jesus our Lord (Χριδ τῷ Ἰησοῦ τῷ κυρίῳ ἡμῶν) . . . I was granted-mercy (ἠλεήθην) . . . the grace (χάρις) of our Lord (τοῦ κυρίου) beyond-abounded . . ." (1:12–14).

Here, the performative impact of the letter is clearly conducive for memory, comprehension, meaning, and effect. Unmistakably, Paul's

---

133. Towner writes something similar (*Letters*, 141): "What is the intention of the admission? For this the controlling feature of the whole discourse is the contrast between Paul/Timothy/sound teaching/gospel and false teachers/false teaching. In contrast to Paul, who sinned before coming to faith in Christ, the false teachers are portrayed as believers (or those who profess to believe) who by their sin have rejected their faith . . . Paul's preconversion sin and that of the opponents, though remarkably similar in the preference for Torah evident in both cases, belong to different categories: Paul's sin predates the enlightenment provided by the risen Lord, while the false teachers' sin postdates their enlightenment by the gospel. The consequences for the latter are much to be feared . . ." Barclay, *1 & 2 Timothy*, 64: "there is good biblical evidence to support understanding the 'unpardonable sin' as knowing who Christ is, yet blaspheming or rejecting him. Paul . . . was still in a state of unbelief."

134. The connotative force of the verb πλεονάζω already conveys an abundance or more than a person needs. The addition of the prefix ὑπέρ elevates the force of Paul's statement to new heights.

intention is to communicate the inseparable relation not only between "grace" and "Christ Jesus" but also of "Christ Jesus" as "Lord." In other words, exactly unlike a ruthless tyrant, "Christ Jesus" is the "Lord" who is marked by "grace"—indeed, granting-mercy to people like Paul who directly persecuted him (1:13; Acts 9:4, 6). Thus as much as Paul is describing the kind of person he was, he is at once describing the kind of person Christ Jesus is. The salvific blessing of "grace" that Paul continually receives from God the Father and Christ Jesus (1:2) accounts for the "grace" that Paul continually holds towards Christ Jesus (1:12); it is the "grace" of the Lord Christ Jesus that beyond-abounded into Paul's life, drawing him out of his former existence of living and doing "in unfaithfulness" (1:13), into a new mode of existing, thinking, living, and doing "in faith" (1:2, 4). The overall phrase "the grace of our Lord beyond-abounded," then, is to be understood as the merciful activity of Christ Jesus pouring his saving blessings upon those who deserve the opposite. Indeed, Paul's passivity in the matter of his salvation is demonstrated by the fact that he "was granted-mercy" despite his destructive activities "in unfaithfulness" (1:13). Paul "was counted-faithful" (ἐπιστεύθην, 1:11b) and considered "faithful" (πιστόν, 1:12) even though he was "in unfaithfulness" (ἐν ἀπιστίᾳ, 1:14). Paul was "firstly" in a condition that was the antithesis of being "in faith" (ἐν πίστει, 1:2, 4); he was operating in a sphere of existence that was clearly opposed to Christ Jesus. Yet, in view of all of this, Paul "was granted-mercy" with "grace" that beyond-abounded (1:13–14); that is, Paul received the salvific blessings of "grace" and "mercy" from Christ Jesus (1:2) despite his abject opposition.

What is more, given Paul's preceding statement regarding the far greater guilt of "some" who teach-different in the Ephesian church (1:3) despite having already received the sound teaching concerning Christ Jesus, the gospel (1:10b–11a), Paul's implication is clear: where Christ's grace "beyond-abounded" for Paul, there is more than enough grace for anyone—even for "some" who functionally act as blasphemers, persecutors, and hubristic-persons within the Ephesian church. In this way, as much as Paul is announcing the heinous offense of "some," he is simultaneously inviting "some" to receive the beyond-abounding grace that Christ Jesus offers, to humbly submit themselves—along with Paul, Timothy, and the faithful in the audience—to Christ as "our Lord" (1:2, 12, 14), and thus to adhere to "the sound teaching" that concerns him, the gospel—*not* "some-thing different" that lies-opposed to it (1:10b–11a).

Paul goes on to state that the grace of the Lord beyond-abounded "with the faith and love that are in Christ Jesus" (1:14b). The coupling of the terms "faith" (πίστεως) and "love" (ἀγάπης) here in 1:14b of the A' element is not insignificant, recalling the prior occurrences of "faith" (πίστει) in 1:2 and 1:4 and "love . . . faith" (ἀγάπη . . . πίστεως) in 1:5 of the parallel A element.[135] As heard in the introductory A element, "faith and love" here in the concluding A' element would most likely be understood in reference to the sphere "in faith," namely an existence that is concretely expressed in "love" for God and for others (1:5), particularly those in God's household (1:4b). Such is the reason why Timothy must remain in Ephesus to "charge some not to teach-different" (1:3): the end goal of Paul's charge—"love" (ἀγάπη, 1:5)—is possible because he and Timothy exist "in faith" (ἐν πίστει, 1:2), and thus they have the "faith (πίστεως) and love (ἀγάπης)" that are in Christ Jesus (1:14)—to be sure, "a without-hypocrisy faith (πίστεως)" (1:5). Indeed, given that it is from these qualities that "some" have turned-aside (1:6), Paul is highlighting that "some" who teach-different in the church are not actually "in faith" (1:2, 4) but are living "in unfaithfulness" (1:13). Subsequently, the performative intention of the letter is not only for "some" to recognize their dire situation but also to be persuaded of it.

As the "c" sub-element of the minichiasm concludes, Paul has connected and solidified key rhetorical themes within the overall arrangement of the microchiasm. The contrast between an existence "in faith" versus "in unfaithfulness" is underscored—particularly in view of "some" who demonstrate that they belong to the latter. Furthermore, where the same values of "grace," "faith," and "love" equally belong "in Christ Jesus" and to the sphere of existence "in faith," it precisely because both speak to the same reality: an existence "in faith" (ἐν πίστει, 1:2, 4) is synonymously an existence "in Christ Jesus" (ἐν Χριστῷ Ἰησοῦ, 1:14b). Significantly, then, as conveyed with the strategic placement of linguistic parallels in the A and A' elements, the audience understand that "grace," "faith," and "love" find their source and power in the person of Christ Jesus—an existence "in faith" (1:2, 4) and thus "in Christ Jesus" (1:14b).[136] Moreover, given this connection, it is equally apparent that the unifying activities in the Ephesian church that bring-about the household-law of God "in faith" (1:4b) derive from one's existence "in Christ Jesus" (1:14b). Conversely, where the activities of "some" bring-about controversial-speculations instead (1:4b), it is clear that they do not exist "in Christ Jesus" (1:14b); thus, the missional urgency of Paul's letter to reach "some" within the Ephesian church is made known through its oral delivery in front of the entire church. Paul intends for "some" to recognize their current state and subsequent need to abandon their different teaching (1:3, 10b) and to accept the sound teaching, that is, the gospel (1:10b, 11a).

135. The terms are used elsewhere in Paul's letters as marks of genuine faith (e.g., Gal 5:6).

136. Knight, *PE*, 99: "By saying that ἀγάπη and πίστις are ἐν Χριστῷ Ἰησοῦ, Paul indicates that their sources are in Christ because of his being in Christ."

1 Timothy 1:15a: Faithful is the Word, Christ Jesus Came For Sinners

("d" sub-element)

Up to this point in the 1:1–20 microchiasm, Paul has led his audience through a chiastic progression, gradually building a contrast between the sound teaching according to the gospel (1:10b–11) over and against the false teaching of "some" (1:3, 10b). In addition, the movement of the language has been escalating the contrast between Paul, Timothy, and those among the audience for whom Christ Jesus is "our Lord" (1:2, 12, 14)—those "in faith" (1:2, 4), that is, "in Christ Jesus" (1:14b)—over and against "some" who are evidently "in unfaithfulness" (cf. 1:13). Still, within the immediate context of the 1:11–17 minichiasm, Paul has underscored that he was granted-mercy solely by the beyond-abounding grace of the Lord Christ Jesus. It is in this context that the pivot "d" sub-element of the 1:11–17 minichiasm begins with Paul's declaration: "Faithful is the word and worthy of all acceptance" (1:15a).[137] Given the sustained connotation of the term "faith" and its cognates in the minichiasm and within the broader microchiasm, the audience would undoubtedly hear "Faithful" (πιστός) as pertaining to the realm of existing "in faith" (πίστει, 1:2, 4), that is, "in Christ Jesus" (1:14b) wherein "faith" (πίστεως, 1:5, 14b) is found. Thus where "the word" (ὁ λόγος) is qualitatively described as "Faithful," the implication is that it most certainly is connected to the same realm. That is, "the word" corresponds to "the sound teaching"—"the gospel"—that characterizes the common adherence of Paul, Timothy, and those who are "in faith" (1:2, 4) and "in Christ Jesus" (1:14b). In this way also, in tandem with "the sound teaching, according to the gospel," the audience understand that "the word" exhibits God's radiance and results in blessing toward him (1:10b–11a). Certainly for this reason Paul indicates that "the word" is "worthy of . . . acceptance" (ἀποδοχῆς ἄξιος); still Paul's insistence that the word is worthy of "all" (πάσης) acceptance would be particularly emphatic.[138]

Furthermore, where the qualifying description of "the word" as "Faithful" (πιστός) recalls the description of Paul who "was counted-faithful" (ἐπιστεύθην) with the gospel (1:11) and was considered "faithful" (πιστός) by Christ Jesus for service (1:12), the clear implication is that both the message and the messenger are "worthy of all acceptance" (1:15a). Such would

---

137. Much has been written on the "faithful sayings." See esp. Knight, *Faithful Sayings*; Towner, *Letters*, 143–45; Marshall, *PE*, 326–30; cf. Campbell, "Identifying the Faithful Sayings."

138. See Knight, *Faithful Sayings*, 25–29.

once again be a summons to "some" in the Ephesian church who teach "some-thing different" that "lies-opposed to the sound teaching . . . the gospel" (1:10b–11a). In effect, Paul is imploring "some" to recognize that he was authoritatively sent by the divine command of God to represent Christ Jesus (1:1)—indeed, was directly appointed by Christ Jesus (1:12)—and, therefore, everything that he is communicating in the letter is in fact "worthy of all acceptance" (1:15a). Consequently, to not view "the word" that the apostle Paul is presenting as "worthy of all acceptance" (1:15a) designates a full rejection of "the word" of Christ Jesus whom Paul represents. Heard within the polemical rhetoric of the letter, such is undoubtedly Paul's point. The phrase "Faithful is the word" (λόγος) stands in stark contrast to the "useless-words" (ματαιολογίαν) for which "some" have turned-aside (1:6). It is the deliberate movement of "some" to accept "useless-words" over and against "the word"—the sound teaching, the gospel—that demonstrates their existence "in unfaithfulness" (cf. 1:13).[139] In sum, the adjective "Faithful" is undoubtedly polemical: over and against any objection that the false teachers in Ephesus may cast upon Paul's teaching, and certainly against the different teaching that "some" pose (1:3, 10b), the audience are to unreservedly accept the faithful word—the sound teaching, according to the gospel of the glory of the blessed God (1:10b–11a)—that God and Christ Jesus have chosen to communicate through the apostle Paul, a fully authorized representative of Christ Jesus (1:1, 11b, 12).[140] Simultaneously, the invitation is for "some" to join the faithful in the audience. The impetus of Paul's letter clearly intends to reach those within the church—particularly "some."

Continuing in the "d" pivot sub-element, Paul declares the content of "the word" that is worthy of all acceptance: "that Christ Jesus came into the world to save sinners" (1:15a). The statement emphasizes two aspects of Christ's work. First, "that Christ Jesus came into the world" highlights the historicity undergirding this event, which is accentuated by the aorist tense of "came" (ἦλθεν). At a single point in history, "Christ Jesus came" (1:15).

---

139. The singular form of "the word" (λόγος, 1:15a) would likely be heard in contrast (see *italics*) to the plural form of "useless-*words*" (ματαιολογίαν, 1:6)—perhaps even in contrast to the plural "myths and genealogies (γενεαλογίαις) without-limit" (1:4).

140. Towner, *Letters*, 144–45: "While the trustworthiness of the 'saying' in each context surely owes to its divine origin, that factor would seem to be somewhat farther back in Paul's thinking and the desire to continue to draw the line between the sound teaching encapsulated by the sayings and the false teaching by means of the πίστις word group more to the fore . . . The 'trustworthy saying' formula is a technique by which Paul, in one motion, rearticulates his gospel (and corresponding aspects of teaching), asserts its authenticity and apostolic authority, and alienates the opposing teaching that, by implication (and this is the polemical significance of the πίστις word group), does not belong to the category denoted by the term πίστις ('trustworthy')."

Significantly also, where "Christ Jesus" in 1:1 of the parallel A element was identified as a divine collaborator alongside God the Father, the clear implication in 1:15b of the A' element is that this divine, eternal person came "into the world" (εἰς τὸν κόσμον), namely the world that he himself created.[141] In this sense, the suggestion may be that Christ's divine entrance into the world—and the sound teaching concerning him—is that which exhibits the radiant "glory" of God in the gospel (1:10b–11).[142]

Second, Paul makes clear that the purpose of Christ's entrance into history—the incarnation—is salvation: Christ Jesus came into the world "to save sinners."[143] The term "sinners" (ἁμαρτωλούς, 1:15b) recalls Paul's extensive attention to the Decalogue in the B' element of the microchiasm, namely that the law is laid for "sinners" (ἁμαρτωλοῖς, 1:9). That is, by the lawful use of the law (1:8b), "sinners" (1:9) would see that they are "sinners" (1:15a). Yet, far more strikingly, then, "sinners" would also see that Chris Jesus came "to save" them (1:15a). The verb "to save" (σῶσαι) here in 1:15a of the A' element recalls the cognate description of "God our Savior (σωτῆρος)" in the opening statement of the letter (1:1). Thus where the immediate identification of God as "Savior" at the outset of the letter was rhetorically deliberate, establishing that the theme of salvation is significant for understanding the letter (1:1), here in 1:15a Paul connects the theme of the letter directly to Christ Jesus who came "to save." Moreover, given that "God our Savior" was understood as a mutual assertion by Paul and the Ephesian audience that their God alone is the true Savior of all mankind (1:1), Paul is reminding his audience that their God demonstrated that he is the "Savior" through to activity of Christ Jesus who came "to save" sinners (1:15a).

---

141. See Knight, *PE*, 101; Fairbairn, *Commentary*, 96. See also discussion in Marshall, *PE*, 398–99.

142. See Couser, "Sovereign Savior," 112.

143. The similarity of Paul's statement in 1:15 to Jesus's statement in Mark 2:17 is worth noting:
1 Tim 1:15: "Christ Jesus came (ἦλθεν) into the world to save sinners (ἁμαρτωλούς)"
Mark 2:17: "I came (ἦλθον) not to call the just but sinners (ἁμαρτωλούς)"
Where the allusion is deliberate, it would be clear that Paul is not only rooting the validity of his statement in Jesus's own words—hence, that it is "worthy of all acceptance (1:15)—but also directing the audience's attention to the source of all that Paul is saying, Christ Jesus himself.
Such an allusion presupposes that his Ephesian audience were familiar with Jesus's statement therein. Proposed dates for manuscript compositions of Mark leave the possibility open that the Ephesian church were exposed to the written narratives, which were likely composed in the late fifties or in the sixties (see e.g., Carson and Moo, *Introduction*, 180–82). However, presumably the oral tradition—which preceded any written composition of Mark's Gospel—was at least made known to them by Paul.

Here, the rhetorical, thematic arrangement of the microchiasm would be apparent:

> A element: "God our Savior (σωτῆρος) and Christ Jesus (Χριστοῦ Ἰησοῦ) our hope" (1:1);
>
> A' element: "Christ Jesus (Χριστὸς Ἰησοῦς) came into the world to save (σῶσαι) sinners" (1:15a).

The theme of salvation in the introductory A element is advanced and articulated in the concluding A' element of the microchiasm. It is the activity of "God our Savior" (1:1) in tandem with "Christ Jesus" who came "to save" sinners (1:15a) by which Christ Jesus is "our hope" (1:1). Here, then, Paul's chiastic arrangement of the language not only fosters memory and comprehension for the performer and the audience; much more, the linguistic arrangement also conveys meaning and its importance thereof. The fact that "God our Savior" (1:1) in the A element is tangibly articulated as "Christ Jesus came to save sinners" (1:15a) in the parallel A' element is highly suggestive.[144] Moreover, given that "some" in the Ephesian church are not accepting the sound teaching—the gospel—that both concerns Christ Jesus and exhibits God's radiant glory (1:10b–11a), they are not accepting that Christ came "to save" them (1:15a) and thus cannot partake in the church's opening assertion that God is *our* "Savior" (1:1). It is for this reason that Paul intends for "someone" to know the lawful use of the law (1:8b) and thus their dire need to accept Christ's action to save them.

In sum, as the pivot "d" sub-element of the minichiasm concludes, the crux of Paul's languages hinges upon the fact that salvation from the lawful use of the law that justly judges sinners (1:9b, 1:15a) is found in the God who came into the world to save them.[145] Furthermore, the parallelism of the A and A' elements solidifies Paul's overall teaching regarding salvation: in one sense, the "word" that is "worthy of all acceptance"—the gospel—is not for "the just" (1:9a) but for "sinners" (1:9b), that is, specifically for those who live contrary to the sound teaching—indeed, specifically for "some" (1:3, 6; cf. 1:8b).[146] The sustained use of "faith" and its cognates

---

144. Similar to Paul's statements in 1:2 regarding the divine collaboration of "God the Father and Christ Jesus," the chiastic parallelism between "God our Savior" (1:1) in the A element and "Christ Jesus came to save" (1:15a) in the A' element would likely communicate and reiterate a high Christology to the audience.

145. Belleville, "Christology, the PE," 325: "v. 15 echoes the central point of the kerygma: salvation is the result of Christ's entrance into history. This makes Christology and soteriology inseparable both here in 1:15 and throughout the Pastorals." For an overview of scholastic treatments regarding this phrase, see ibid., 324–25.

146. Here, Paul's overall allusion to Mark 2:17 in the A' element of 1 Timothy 1 is

in this minichiasm (1:11, 12, 13, 14, 15), combined with the overall force in both A and A' elements of the microchiasm, communicates that "the gospel"—God's way of exhibiting his radiance—is the faithful "word" that is directed to faithless people. Here, then, in 1:15, the theme of salvation is missional, specifically oriented toward and intending the salvation of "some" who refuse the sound teaching (the gospel), the messenger who teaches it (Paul), and thus the source of the message (Christ Jesus). Strikingly, the missional impetus here is directed within the Ephesian church itself—"some" must accept "the word," the gospel for salvation. For those "in unfaithfulness," it is only the gospel, the word concerning Christ Jesus—the sound teaching—that can bring them into a new realm "in faith," that is, "in Christ Jesus."

1 Timothy 1:15b–16a: Consistent-with This, I was Granted-Mercy

("c'" sub-element)

Lest the audience suppose that Paul is excluding himself from the category of "sinners," in the "c'" sub-element of the 1:11–17 minichiasm Paul quickly asserts: "of whom I-myself am the first" (1:15b). To be sure, Paul goes beyond mere inclusion. Among such sinners—"of whom" (ὧν)—Paul emphatically declares that "I-myself am (εἰμι ἐγώ) the first."[147] The personal pronoun "I-myself" (ἐγώ) reminds the audience of Paul's earlier statement, "I-myself" (ἐγώ) was counted-faithful" with the gospel (1:11b)—indeed, the same Paul who was a blasphemer, persecutor, and hubristic-person (1:13), who was without-knowing and acting in the realm "in unfaithfulness" (1:13). Beyond any doubt, Paul is clear that he is a sinner in constant need of grace—the same grace that "some" need. Moreover, Paul's use of the adjective "first" to describe his status as a sinner is significant. The term "first" (πρῶτός) here in 1:16 of the "c'" sub-element recalls the cognate adverb "firstly" (πρότερον) in 1:13 of the parallel "c" sub-element. However, unlike Paul's earlier reference that he was "firstly" (πρότερον, 1:13)—*sequentially* and historically—a blasphemer "in unfaithfulness" before the specific point in time that Christ

---

particularly notable:

1 Tim 1:9, 15: "... for the just (δικαίῳ) the law is not laid but for ... sinners (ἁμαρτωλοῖς) ... Christ Jesus came into the world to save sinners (ἁμαρτωλούς)";

Mark 2:17: "I came (ἦλθον) not to call the just (δικαίους) but sinners (ἁμαρτωλούς)."

147. As in 1:11, Paul's inclusion of the pronoun "I-myself" (ἐγώ) with the verb "I am" (εἰμι) is grammatically unnecessary and, therefore, intentional. The translation "I-myself am" captures the nuance.

Jesus granted-mercy to him (1:13; see Acts 9:6, 15–16), here in 1:15b Paul's use of the term "first" (πρῶτός) underscores the *status* and degree to which he is a sinner—the clear sense being "foremost, lead, prominent."[148] In other words, as a man who directly persecuted Christ, the audience understand that Paul is identifying himself as the "first"—foremost, lead, prominent—of sinners. Indeed, the phrase "of whom I-myself *am* the first" communicates that Paul *still is* the lead, prominent sinner.[149]

Remarkably, immediately following this jarring statement, Paul declares: "Rather consistent-with this, I was granted-mercy" (1:16a). The disjunction "rather" (ἀλλά) dramatically reorients the expectation that the "first"—foremost, lead, prominent—of sinners deserved the full force of Christ Jesus's wrath. Indeed, it is not only striking that the "first" of sinners "was granted-mercy" (1:16a); much more, it is entirely shockingly that "consistent-with this" Paul was granted-mercy (1:16a). In other words, where the sense of the preposition "consistent-with" (διά) connotes "in keeping with," and the referent of "this" (τοῦτο) refers both to Christ's activity "to save sinners" (1:15a) and to Paul's status as the "first," lead, prominent of sinners (1:15b, 16a), Paul is underscoring that he himself is living proof—and the most extreme example—of Christ's saving activity. Still, the shocking fashion of Paul's statement not only highlights himself but also Christ Jesus—Paul's statement focuses on the entirely shocking fact that Christ Jesus would actually save the first, lead of sinners! The rhetorical intent is clearly to magnify the beyond-abounding grace of Christ Jesus (1:14) in comparison to the unmatched degree of Paul as a sinner (1:16a).

Moreover, the parallel repetition of the verb "I was granted-mercy" in 1:13 of the "c" sub-element and here in 1:16 of the "c'" sub-element conveys a progression from the personal import of Paul's experience of mercy to its fuller application, namely "that in me the first Christ Jesus might display all patience" (1:16a)."[150] Here again, while the language clearly draws attention to Paul—"in me the first" (ἐν ἐμοὶ πρώτῳ, 1:16a)—and immediately

---

148. Knight, *PE*, 102: "Paul does not mean the "first" in a sequence, since he was not the first one saved by Christ. He means, rather, that he (notice emphatic) is first in the sense of 'foremost' (see BAGD) in the category of sinners." For further discussion, see Marshall, *PE*, 400–401.

149. The connection of the present active verb "I am" (εἰμι) with Paul being the "first" (πρῶτός) of sinners indicates that his status as a sinner has not changed; even though he no longer persecutes the church, the reality that he is a sinner is ongoing. See Knight, *PE*, 102; Marshall, *PE*, 399–401.

150. Towner, *Letters*, 148 n. 52: "The TNIV and NRSV translate the causal prepositional phrase διὰ τοῦτο as if the preceding statement were the reason. But the following ἵνα-clause suggests that it supplies the reason for the mercy shown to Paul; i.e., 'but I received mercy for this reason, namely, that in me Christ might display . . .'"

reiterates that he is the "first" (πρῶτός), lead, prominent of sinners (1:15b), the rhetorical, double emphasis that Paul is the "first" (1:15b, 16) of sinners actually directs the audience's attention toward the profound activity and intent of Christ Jesus. Paul's point in 1:16 is to highlight Christ; that is, fully consistent-with the faithful word that Christ Jesus came to save sinners (1:15), Paul himself was granted-mercy to display that no sinner is beyond the scope of Christ's saving purpose. In view of Paul's history as a blasphemer, persecutor, and hubristic-person (1:13), the verb describing Christ Jesus's action to "display" (ἐνδείξηται) is telling—likely alluding to Jesus's very own statement about Paul in Acts: "he is to me a chosen vessel to bear my name in the sight of the Gentiles and kings and the sons of Israel. For I-myself will display (ὑποδείξω) to him how much it is necessary for him to suffer on behalf of my name" (Acts 9:15–16). Notably, then, the purpose for which Paul was granted-mercy conforms to Christ's orchestrating activity. Indeed, where the impact of Paul's statement "consistent-with this I was granted-mercy" highlighted the magnitude of Christ's grace, here Paul upholds the corresponding magnitude of Christ's "all patience" (1:16). The term "patience" (μακροθυμίαν)—literally, "far-from-wrath"—would certainly be heard in juxtaposition with Paul's status as the "first"—lead, prominent—of sinners.[151] Of all sinners, Paul deserves wrath; the fact that he was granted-mercy by Christ Jesus (1:13, 16) puts all the attention on Christ as the Lord who has "patience"—even for a persecutor like Paul who was actively involved in killing and imprisoning Christians.[152] Emphasizing this point, in the same way that "all" (πάσης) was heard in 1:15a regarding the faithful word, the term "all" (ἅπασαν) here in 1:16a uhpolds the complete and far-reaching extent of the "patience" in view. In other words, Paul was not granted-mercy only for himself; Christ Jesus was merciful to Paul in order that Christ "might display" himself—particularly, his "all patience" (1:16). This recalls the purpose of "the gospel," which is to exhibit God's radiance in a way that results in blessing him (1:11a). It comes as no surprise, then, that Paul "was counted-faithful" with the gospel (1:11b) for the express purpose that God the "Savior" (1:1) in tandem with Christ Jesus who came "to save" sinners (1:15a) would display himself through Paul by granting him mercy. Such a display of "all patience" not only highlights the gospel but also has its underpinning in the OT, wherein God's patience was meant to lead people to repentance (e.g., LXX Jonah 4:2).[153]

---

151. The term "patience" (μακροθυμίαν) is a compound term of "far" (μακράν) and "wrath" (θυμός).

152. See chapter 1 regarding Paul's activities in Acts.

153. Compare the Greek texts:
1 Tim 1:16: ". . . I was granted-mercy (ἠλεήθην), that in me the first Christ Jesus

As the "c'" sub-element concludes, the audience understand that Christ Jesus's "all patience" counterbalances and surpasses Paul's ongoing status as the "first" (1:15b, 16a), lead of sinners. That is, where the faithful "word"—the gospel—is "worthy of all (πάσης) acceptance" and has in view the historic event that "Christ Jesus came into the world" *and* the factitive purpose thereof "to save sinners" (1:15), so too is Christ's "all (ἅπασαν) patience" part and parcel of the gospel. Christ's "all patience" is for those living "in unfaithfulness" (1:13) so that they would eventually be living "in Christ Jesus" (1:14), that is, "in faith" (1:2, 4). Indeed, such is definitely displayed in Paul's own life—the persecutor who did everything without-knowing that he was living "in unfaithfulness" (1:13), but now is an apostle "in faith" (1:2, 4). Paul, then, is who he is solely by the grace, mercy, and all patience of Christ Jesus, the one who came into the world to save even the "first" of sinners. Such is the faithful word, the gospel, the sound teaching.

1 Timothy 1:16b: An Example to Those Who Would-Inevitably-Come to Have-Faith

("b'" sub-element)

In the "b'" sub-element (1:16b), Paul continues by stating that he was granted-mercy "as an example to those who would-inevitably-come to have-faith upon him for life eternal." That the "first," lead of sinners (1:15b, 16a) was granted-mercy "as" (πρός) an "example" (ὑποτύπωσιν)—a "pattern"—not only conveys and reiterates the far-reaching scope of the gospel but also provides tangible evidence of the gospel in reality: given that none are worse sinners than Paul, every single sinner may view Paul as a tangible "example" that Christ Jesus came into the world to save them (1:15a). Furthermore, the movement of the minichiasm has highlighted for the audience the passive aspect of salvation: in the "a" sub-element, Paul "was counted-faithful"; in the "b" sub-element, Christ Jesus "empowered" Paul (1:12); in the "c" and "c'" sub-elements, Paul "was granted-mercy" (1:13, 16). Nevertheless, here in the "b'" sub-element, Paul underscores the proactive aspect of salvation by identifying "those who would-inevitably-come to have-faith upon him for life eternal" (1:16b).

---

might display all patience (μακροθυμίαν)";
    LXX Jonah 4:2: "... for I knew you, who is merciful (ἐλέημων)... patient (μακρόθυμος)..."
    See Muddiman and Barton, "PE," 248.

In connection with Paul's tangible "example," the participle phrase "those who would-inevitably-come" (τῶν μελλόντων) in 1:16b suggests a correlation. In effect, by observing the reality of salvation with Paul "as an example," Christ's intent to grant-mercy to Paul (1:16a) was that people "would-inevitably-come" (μελλόντων) to proactively participate in their own salvation, namely "to have-faith upon him [Christ]" (1:16b).[154] The infinitive verb "to have-faith" (πιστεύειν) highlights in full force the activity of "those who would-inevitably-come." That is, although Paul passively "was counted-faithful" (ἐπιστεύθην, 1:12), such was "an example" for those who would actively "have-faith" (πιστεύειν, 1:16b). In other words, the audience are reminded of their need to proactively "have-faith" (πιστεύειν) upon Christ Jesus, the person who makes even the faithless faithful. Thus, while the "example" in view undoubtedly underscores the immensity of Christ's patience, it also represents a normative pattern of what it means "to have-faith": salvation is not only Christ Jesus coming to sinners—his entrance into the world (1:15)—but also sinners coming to Christ Jesus—their faith upon him and his coming for them (1:16). The passive and active aspects of the sound teaching (1:10b), the gospel (1:11a), the word (1:15a) concerning Christ Jesus and the salvation he offers are thus both emphasized: the mode of existence "in faith," that is, "in Christ," is entered solely by "the grace of our Lord" (1:14); yet, for anyone who "would-inevitably-come to have-faith" they will be ushered in, the same as Paul. In short, Paul "as an example" is proof that Christ Jesus came to save the sinners, and all that a sinners needs to do is "to have-faith" upon him (1:16b). To be sure, the minichiastic progression centering on the pivot "d" sub-element makes clear that to have-faith "upon him" (ἐπ' αὐτῷ) is to believe specifically that Christ came into the world to save sinners (1:15a). This is not to suggest that "to have-faith upon him" is merely to accept a propositional truth. Rather, for all who are sinners, they are summoned "to have-faith upon *him*," a person named Christ Jesus who personally came for them—to save them, and thus enable them experience life in a new existence "in faith" (1:2, 4), that is, a personal existence "in Christ Jesus" (1:14). In effect, the phrase "those who would-inevitably-come to have-faith upon him" (1:16b) communicates a personal dynamic of trusting Christ's life rather than anything else—including one's own life—for salvation; such is to live "in faith" (1:2), "in Christ Jesus" (1:14). Notably also, the prepositional phrase "upon him" (ἐπ' αὐτῷ) not only focuses the audience on the person of Christ Jesus but also high-

---

154. The verb μελλόντων could be understood as "intended to" or "destined for" (UBS), thus suggesting predestination subtleties. While Paul is not concerned here with this particular doctrine, the doctrine itself may still be present here; contra Towner, *Letters*, 150.

lights that salvation comes from trusting "upon him"—not from trusting upon "some-thing different" (1:10b). In short, the audience understand that salvation came with Christ Jesus (1:15a), and it comes by depending entirely "upon him" (1:16b).

Paul concludes the "b'" sub-element by stating the inevitable outcome for those who have-faith upon Christ Jesus: "for life eternal" (1:16b). Here, salvation is stated in its positive consequence. Negatively, Paul reminded the audience—and particularly "some"—that Christ Jesus came to save sinners (1:15a), that is, those for whom the law is laid (1:9a–b) from the consequence of their sin as determined by the lawful use of the law (1:8b). However, Paul makes clear in 1:16b that salvation is not merely *salvation from* but also *salvation for*. By coming to have-faith upon Christ, salvation is "for" (εἰς) that which Paul describes as "life eternal" (ζωὴν αἰώνιον). Significantly, where the personal dynamic of salvation is "upon him," Paul intends to directly correlate the person of Christ Jesus with "life eternal." On the one hand, the phrase "life eternal" conceptually echoes Paul's prior assertion regarding the historic event when "Christ Jesus came into the world" (1:15a); such implied that Christ was living beyond the realm of "the world"—to be sure, as a divine collaborator with God the Father (1:2). On the other hand, given that Paul most certainly established the Ephesian church on the historic fact of Christ's resurrection from death, the phrase "life eternal" would convey the reality of salvation for "those who would-inevitably-come to have-faith upon him"—an existence "in faith" (1:2), thus "in Christ Jesus" (1:14)—"for life eternal" as Christ himself now lives (1:16).

1 Timothy 1:17: The King of Eternities, Honor and Glory for the Eternities, Amen

("a'" sub-element)

Given that "the gospel" in the "a" sub-element (1:11a) both exhibits God's radiant glory and results in blessing him, Paul appropriately concludes the minichiasm in the parallel "a'" sub-element (1:17) with a climactic doxology: "But to the King of the eternities, without-perishability, without-visibility, only God, honor and glory for the eternities of the eternities, amen."[155] Here, the disjunctive "but" (δέ) is not intended to convey a different line

---

155. It is worth noting the alliterative pattern of α- prefixes that would be aurally apparent in the performance of the letter to Paul's original audience (see *italics*): "But to the King of the *eternities* (αἰώνων), *without*-perishability (ἀφθάρτῳ), *without*-visibility (ἀοράτῳ), only God, honor and glory for the *eternities* (αἰῶνας) of the *eternities* (αἰώνων), *amen* (ἀμήν)."

of thought but to indicate a pause following the apostolic delineation of the gospel; in this sense, the disjunction could be translated "now."[156] The emphasis hitherto on Christ Jesus leaves Paul's reference to "the King of the eternities" (βασιλεῖ τῶν αἰώνων) somewhat ambiguous. On the one hand, the descriptors "without-perishability" (ἀφθάρτῳ) and "without-visibility" (ἀοράτῳ) do not seem to describe Christ Jesus—who died and was seen—and suggest that God the Father is in view;[157] in addition, where every preceding occurrence of "God" (θεοῦ, 1:1, 2, 4, 11a) seemed to refer to God the Father in distinction from Christ Jesus, the phrase "only God" (μόνῳ θεῷ) in 1:17 would most likely be understood by Paul's audience to the same effect.[158] On the other hand, the sustained focus specifically on Christ Jesus throughout the 1:11–17 minichiasm strongly suggests that Christ Jesus would be understood by the audience as "the King."[159] In this way, the ambiguity of the doxology in the concluding "a'" sub-element (1:17) may have been Paul's indirect way of expressing the personal dynamic of "the sound teaching"— "the gospel"—in the parallel "a" sub-element (1:11a). That is, where Christ Jesus is the content of the gospel and thus personally exhibits God's radiant glory in a way that results in blessing toward God, it seems that the first-century Ephesian church would hear that the immanent, divine person of Christ Jesus who "came into the world" is also the transcendent "only God" who is "without-perishability, without-visibility."[160]

---

156. See Knight, *PE*, 104.

157. That these terms function as an assertion of God's uniqueness and superiority over and against the Greco-Roman gods, see Neyrey, "Rhetoric," 65–66, 75; Collins, *1 & 2 Timothy*, 45. Compare to other scholarship suggesting that the phrase "the King of the eternities" is likely Jewish in origin and not directly subversive; see Knight, *PE*, 105; Nystrom, "We Have No King But Caesar," 31 n. 51: "It was not until the third century that the use of *basileus* became a usual designation for Caesar."

158. Hence, Towner's interpretation (*Letters*, 151–52): "Not only does the shift of focus to God establish a balance with the heavily Christocentric testimony just concluded, but it also reveals Paul's deeply theological presuppositions about salvation in Christ . . . The need Paul felt to emphasize the humanity of Christ in the salvation plan does not diminish his belief in God as the author of salvation (2:3–4; 4:10)." Marshall further suggests that the descriptor "only" (μόνῳ) may have God the Father in view, e.g., Romans 16:27 (*PE*, 405).

159. Keegan, *First and Second Timothy*, 13: "Interestingly, while the thanksgiving is addressed to Christ Jesus (1:12), the doxology is addressed to God."

160. Barcley, *1 & 2 Timothy*, 69: "Interestingly, at the end of a passage that tells of the immanence of God, Christ Jesus' coming into the world to save sinners, Paul reflects on God's transcendence. And perhaps herein lies the point of the whole passage. The transcendent God is the very God who came into the world to save sinners. God's immanence does not detract from his transcendence in any way." See Collins, *1 & 2 Timothy*, 46.

Paul's immediate use of the phrase "King of the eternities (αἰώνων)" (1:17) recalls the preceding statement regarding "life eternal" (αἰώνιον, 1:16b). The rhetorical connection conveys that it is the King of "eternities" (αἰώνων), in distinction to human kings, who bestows "life eternal (αἰώνιον)" to those who would-inevitably-come to have-faith upon Christ (1:16b), that is, to those who accept "the word" concerning Christ's entrance into the world to save sinners (1:15a), namely, the sound teaching (1:10b), the gospel (1:11a). Furthermore, where Paul's reference to the King of the eternities as the only "God" (θεῷ) here in 1:17 of the "a'" sub-element recalls Paul's reference to the blessed "God" (θεοῦ) in 1:11a of the parallel "a" sub-element, and where Paul's ascription of "honor and glory (δόξα)" (1:17) recalls "the gospel of the glory (δόξης) of the blessed God" (1:11a), the framing linguistic arrangement of the minichiasm is apparent:

"a" sub-element: "the gospel of the glory (δόξης) of the blessed God (θεοῦ)" (1:11a);

"a'" sub-element: "only God (θεῷ), honor and glory (δόξα)" (1:17).

That is, the minichiastic movement from the "a" to the "a'" sub-element highlights that the God who exhibits his radiant glory in the gospel not only bestows the blessing of life eternal to those who have-faith upon Christ but also receives blessing from from those who have-faith. Specifically, as the gospel of "the glory (δόξης) . . . of God" in the "a" sub-element makes visible the radiant splendor of God, so now "honor (τιμή) and glory (δόξα)" are given to God in the parallel "a'" sub-element.[161] Indeed, the progression of the minichiasm toward its concluding doxology (1:17) highlights the final intention of "the gospel of the glory of the blessed God" (1:11a): those who have-faith upon Christ Jesus are given "life eternal (αἰώνιον)" in order that they may give "honor and glory" back to the King for "the eternities of the eternities" (τοὺς αἰῶνας τῶν αἰώνων), that is, for their entire eternal life.[162] The concluding "amen" (ἀμήν) of the doxology is intended to evoke and invite an enthusiastic response of agreement and participation from the audience.[163] Thus in the performance of the letter, the audience hear the ex-

---

161. Neyrey, "Rhetoric," 59 n. 4: "It is well known that in the New Testament δόξα is used synonymously with τιμή, with the meaning esteem, honor." See ibid., 78; Marshall, PE, 405. Both words "honor and glory" together suggest a rhetorical emphasis: an abundance of blessing ought to be given to God. For more on Paul's understanding of this biblical pattern, see Rotenberry, "Blessing in the Old Testament," 34–36.

162. Towner notes that "the eternities of the eternities" is a Hebrew idiom that expresses "beyond all limits to eternity" (*Letters*, 154). See Yarbrough, *Preformed Traditions*, 74–75. For Greco-Roman connotations, see Neyrey, "Rhetoric," 79.

163. See Marshall, PE, 406; Collins, *1 & 2 Timothy*, 46–47; Heil, *Letters of Paul*, 161;

pansive progression of the minichiasm: the "a" sub-element began with only Paul blessing Christ Jesus (1:12), but the concluding "a'" sub-element ends with the audience—those who have-faith upon Christ—collectively blessing the King with the honor and glory that are due to him (1:17). Notably, then, as a dramatic point of contrast, such participation by the audience in Paul's doxology is diametrically contrary to what their collective response should be toward the false teaching of "some." In effect, Paul's rallying invitation for the Ephesian audience to participate in the outworking of the sound teaching would likely leave "some" sitting on the bench.

In sum, verse 1:17 not only provides a fitting doxological conclusion to the minichiasm but also provides insight into Paul's burden in the letter. The adjective "only" (μόνῳ), which is preceded by the descriptors "without-perishability" and "without-invisibility," brings to the fore that the God of the gospel is the true God who alone merits all honor and glory—not only for being "God our Savior" (1:1) but also for his divine activity of coming into the world "to save" sinners (1:15a). In short, 1:17 seems to provide both ontological and historical justifications for attributing worship to God alone, the King of eternities, for the eternities of eternities.[164] While the subversive quality of the doxology certainly speaks against the worship of any other god or figure in Greco-Roman culture that would make divine claims, it also clearly undermines all different teaching that suggests salvation does not depend exclusively "upon him," the person Christ Jesus.[165] Paul's charge (1:3, 5), therefore, to preserve "the sound teaching" against "some" who "teach-different" (1:3)—who specifically teach "some-thing different" that "lies-opposed to the sound teaching" (1:10b)—and against the influence of Greco-Roman beliefs in the first-century city of Ephesus is borne out of his apostolic appointment not only to represent Christ Jesus under the commanding authority of God (1:1) but to ensure that the glory of God continues to shine in the gospel (1:11a).

Neyrey, "Rhetoric," 73.

164 That this phrase "only God" is subversive against Greco-Roman religious thought, see Neyrey, "Rhetoric," 70.

165. Towner, *Letters*, 152: "Whether this [phrase "King of eternities"] intends a further explicit challenge to the claims of the emperor is harder to determine; but trumping such counterclaims of pagan rulers had become a common part of Hellenistic Jewish liturgical expression and was probably also a common function of the early church's doxological expression. That is to say, some degree of polemics is an inevitable part of the dialogue with the pagan world that the church sustained through its proclamation and expressions of worship. . . ." Robinson and Wall, *Called to Lead*, 32, suggest that the purpose of Paul's doxology in 1:17 is "to invite a conversation between these two worlds." See also Towner's note 68; Fay, "Greco-Roman Concepts of Diety," 70–72.

1 Timothy 1:18–20: This Charge I Entrust to You, Child Timothy

(A' Element, continued)

In verse 1:18 of the A' element, Paul abruptly transitions: "This charge I entrust to you, child Timothy." The phrase "This charge" (ταύτην τὴν παραγγελίαν) here in 1:18 of the A' element is specific and recalls "the charge" (τῆς παραγγελίας) that intends love as its outcome in 1:5 of the parallel A element. To be sure, this specific "charge" (παραγγελίαν, 1:18) in the A' element recalls the reason why Paul exhorted Timothy to remain in Ephesus, that he might "charge (παραγγείλῃς) some not to teach-different" (1:3) in the parallel A element. Significantly, along with the rhetorical framing effect of the A and A' element, the progression of the first microchiasm cumulatively qualifies the "charge." Where "charge" in the A element was primarily concerned with "some" who teach-different (1:3) and intended their restoration to a without-hypocrisy faith (1:15), it is now evident to the audience that the "charge" in the A' element (1:18) is derived from a concern for God's glory that is exhibited in the gospel, that is, the sound teaching (1:10b–11a).[166] In other words, while "the charge" is personally directed toward "some," Paul makes clear that the "charge" in his letter is to be understood as a defense against the personal attack of "some" toward God. Paul's point is that where "some" teach-different in the Ephesian church (1:3), that is, where "some-thing different lies-opposed to the sound teaching" (1:10b), it is not merely a propositional affront but a personal attempt to obstruct God's radiance. The importance of the "charge," therefore, is not only motivated by love to restore the false teachers to faith (1:5–6) but also by love for God and the proper worship of him (1:17).

The very personal dynamic of Paul's "charge" to preserve the sound teaching is articulated in the way that he personally transfers it to Timothy: "I entrust to you, child Timothy" (1:18). The verb "I entrust" (παρατίθεμαί) conveys that Paul is placing this specific charge under Timothy's responsibility, thereby reiterating the gravity of Paul's exhortation in 1:3 for Timothy to remain in Ephesus.[167] In effect, where the "charge" has the protection of God's glory in view, Paul's statement "I entrust to you, child

---

166. Similarly, Tomlinson, "Purpose and Stewardship," 58: "In 1 Timothy it [παραγγελία] appears to be primarily the apostolic message of the gospel with its obligation to mission and, secondarily, the apostolic charge to correct false teachers who teach contrary to apostolic teaching. This understanding is borne out in the parallel wording between the two occurrences of παραγγελία (1:5, 18) which frame the introductory section (1:3–20)."

167. See Knight, *PE*, 107–8.

Timothy" carries a definite solemnity: not only is the onus placed squarely on Timothy, but the clear expectation is that Timothy will complete his assigned duty to "charge some not to teach-different" in the mid-sixties church in Ephesus (1:3).[168] Furthermore, the conceptual similarity between the verb "I entrust" (παρατίθεμαί) in 1:18 and the participle "appointing" (θέμενος) in 1:12 suggests a similar articulation of allegiance. That is, just as Christ appointed Paul for service (1:12), so too is Paul entrusting Timothy with the charge (1:18).

The personal pronoun "you" (σοι) would have a twofold rhetorical significance. On the one hand, Paul is specifically highlighting that Timothy—"you"—among everyone in the entire audience is Paul's entrusted representative. On the other hand, Paul's specification of "you" (σοι) here in 1:18 of the A' element recalls the prior occurrence of "you" (σε) in 1:3 of the the parallel A element. Thus not only is Paul doubly emphasizing Timothy over and above anyone else in the audience as an authority, but he is also framing the arrangement of the first microchiasm in view of Timothy's role as Paul's appointed representative to carry out the charge. In effect, the audience are to view Timothy as their authoritative leader in Paul's absence. In the same way, the identification "child Timothy" (τέκνον Τιμόθεε) here in 1:18 of the concluding A' element recalls for the audience the introductory A element wherein Paul addresses Timothy directly as "Timothy (Τιμοθέῳ), genuine child (τέκνῳ) in faith" (1:2).[169] Paul's linguistic organization would be apparent:

A element: "To Timothy (Τιμοθέῳ), genuine child (τέκνῳ) in faith ... As I exhorted you (σε) ... charge (παραγγείλῃς) some not to teach-different" (1:2–3);

A' element: "This charge (παραγγελίαν) I entrust to you (σοι), child (τέκνον) Timothy (Τιμόθεε)" (1:18).

---

168. Marshall, *PE*, 408: "Thus the whole phrase, ταύτην τὴν παραγγελίαν παρατίθεμαί σοι, refers back to the instruction or charge passed on from Paul to Timothy to oppose and correct the heretics." Saarinen, *PE*, 46: "The instructions are not simply 'given,' since the verb *paratithēmi* here means that the recipient is endowed with responsibility and power over the instruction received. The apostle solemnly hands over his message as well as his authority and responsibility to Timothy."

169. Keegan, *First and Second Timothy*, 13: "The mention of Timothy's name in verse 18 is a departure from the style of the letter writing in the Hellenistic world. Names of recipients would normally appear only in the opening and closing of the letter. Mention of his name at this point serves the bracketing function of this passage and refocuses the letter on Timothy ..."

Notably, compared to "Timothy" (Τιμοθέῳ, 1:2) in the A element, Paul's rhetorical use of the vocative "Timothy" (Τιμόθεε, 1:18) in the A' element would not go unnoticed, certainly drawing attention to the personal weightiness of Paul's appeal and the gravity with which he is addressing Timothy. Such is fitting, given both the importance of the charge (1:3, 5, 18) and the importance of the apostle Paul—the authorized representative of Christ Jesus (1:1).

Throughout the progression of the microchiasm, Paul has circumscribed himself from "some" who have turned-aside from a pure heart, a good conscience, and a without-hypocrisy faith (1:5-6) and are desiring to be law-teachers but not understanding what they-are-saying (1:7). Here in the concluding A' element of the microchiasm, then, it is not insignificant that Timothy is again addressed as "child" (τέκνον). That is, over and against "some" who demonstrate their existence "in unfaithfulness" (cf. 1:13) by teaching some-thing different that lies-opposed to the sound teaching (1:10b), the reiteration that Timothy is Paul's "child" in 1:18 would effectively underscore that Timothy exists the familial realm "in faith" (1:2, 4)—"in Christ Jesus" (1:14). Not only, then, are those in the audience who have-faith upon Christ (1:16b) to follow Timothy's leadership "in faith" (1:2), but Timothy himself would be emphatically reminded that he must live and lead accordingly—he must remain in Ephesus (1:3) for the preservation of the sound teaching concerning Christ Jesus (1:10b) so that sinners may be-saved by Christ unto life eternal (1:15-16) and subsequently give honor and glory to God for the eternities of the eternities (1:17). In this way, while the A element outlines Timothy's duty and profound filial relation to the apostle Paul "in faith" (1:2-3), the A' element underscores and stirs Timothy's motivation to fulfill his duty.

For further motivation to carry out the charge, Paul describes the divine nature of Timothy's own calling: "according to the prophecies preceding upon you" (1:18). The preposition "according to" (κατά) here in 1:18 of the A' element not only recalls "the sound teaching, according to (κατά) the gospel of the glory of the blessed God" in 1:10b–11a of the current A' element but also that Paul is an "apostle of Christ Jesus according to (κατ') the command of God" in 1:1 of the parallel A element. In this sense, as much as Paul acknowledges both his divine appointment as an apostle (1:1) and the divine nature of the gospel (1:11a), he also affirms the divine quality of Timothy's calling that is specifically according to "the prophecies preceding upon you" (τὰς προαγούσας ἐπὶ σὲ προφητείας, 1:18). Paul does not specify the precise historical situation of "the prophecies" that were made about Timothy. Instead, the rhetorical purpose here is for both Timothy and the audience to appreciate fully the divine nature of Timothy's task to stop the false teachers.[170] Here, too, Paul's immediate repetition of the personal pronoun "you" (σέ) in 1:18b would not only underscore the connection of the prophecies to Paul's entrustment of the charge to "you" (σοι, 1:18a)—Timothy—but also to Paul's exhortation in 1:3 to "you" (σε)—Timothy—to remain in Ephesus. Timothy, over and against "some," is being upheld as the leader in the Ephesian church by the full authoritative endorsement of the apostle Paul, who has the full authoritative endorsement of God and Christ Jesus (1:1).

Continuing in verse 1:18, Paul makes clear that the main reason for his statement is to highlight to the audience and remind Timothy of the many (notice the plural form of) "prophecies" previously made about him for a specific purpose: "that you might war in them the commendable war" (1:18). Here, the explicit reason—"that" (ἵνα, 1:18)—and importance of recalling such prophecies is reflected by its occurrence between the verb "war" and the phrase "commendable war": "in them" (ἐν αὐταῖς)—the prophecies—Timothy can arise victorious.[171] The repetition of the verb "war" (στρατεύῃ) and its cognate noun "war" (στρατείαν) underscores the nature of the task—its urgency and difficulty. Moreover, the description of Timothy's charge in view of the false teachers (1:3, 5, 18) reiterates to the audience that neutrality is impossible—such is the reality of war. Paul is making clear that the audience are either aligned with Timothy, Paul, God and Christ Jesus, or they are for "some" who bring-about controversial-speculations rather than the household-law of God in faith (1:4b).[172] To be sure, where the rhetoric of Paul's letter intends a participatory response, a passive audience would function as an active answer.[173] The phrase "commendable war" (καλὴν στρατείαν) would have been familiar with the audience, given that such military imagery was found both in Jewish (e.g., 4 Macc 9:24) and Hel-

---

170. Knight, *PE*, 108: "Paul's charge to Timothy is . . . 'in accordance with' God's supernatural declaration communicated by the prophecies."

171. Concerning prophecies in this historical milieu, see Aune, *Prophecy in Early Christianity*.

172. Johnson, "First Timothy," 26: "The image of battle (στρατιά, 1,18) is appropriate, for Paul contrasts the rhetorical situation in terms of a stark contrast . . . between those certain people (τινες, 1,3.7.19) who 'teach other' (ἑτεροδιδασκαλεῖν, 1,3), among whom are Hymenaeus and Alexander (1,20), on one side, and, one the other side, 'the healthy teaching according to the good news' (ὑγιαινούσῃ διδασκαλίᾳ κατὰ τὸ εὐαγγέλιον, 1,10–11), to which both Paul (1,12) and his delegate Timothy (1,18) have been committed."

173. Wall with Steele, *1 & 2 Timothy*, 78, indicate that neutrality is equally impossible even when choosing not to war: "Failure to do so would be tantamount to excusing oneself from the battle and abandoning the faith."

lenistic literature (Plutarch, *Moralia* 204A). Here in 1:18 of the A′ element, the qualifier "commendable" (καλήν) recalls its occurrence in 1:8 of the parallel A element regarding Paul's assertion that "the law is commendable (καλός)." In this way, Paul is underscoring the fundamentally good quality of Timothy's struggle against "some" who teach-different. In short, "the commendable war" is a necessary battle—particularly given that the salvation of sinners and the honor and glory of God are at stake.

Specifically, Timothy is to go to war by "holding faith and a good conscience" (1:19a). Undoubtedly, the phrasing is intentional: "holding faith (πίστιν) and a good conscience (ἀγαθὴν συνείδησιν)" here in 1:19a of the A′ element recalls Paul's statement in 1:5 of the parallel A element that "the end of the charge is love from a pure heart and a good conscience (συνειδήσεως ἀγαθῆς) and a without-hypocrisy faith (πίστεως)." Given that such blessings are part and parcel of Timothy's existence "in Christ Jesus" (1:14), it is evident that Timothy himself has the responsibility of "holding" (ἔχων) them—tightly clinging to them—particularly while he in the midst of war. In short, Timothy is to "war" in a manner that accords with his existence in Christ. Furthermore, where "some" have turned-aside from love, a pure heart, a good conscience, and a without-hypocrisy faith (1:5–6), the suggestion is that Timothy's opponents—"some"—are waging war according to their existence "in unfaithfulness," namely, therefore, as blasphemers, persecutors, and hubristic-persons (1:13). In effect, Timothy and the audience are thus warned to do exactly the opposite of what the false teachers do. In stark contrast to "some" who "hold-toward" (προσέχειν) myths and genealogies without-limit (1:14a) in the A element, Timothy is "holding" (ἔχων) faith and a good conscience (1:19a) in the parallel A′ element. Specifically, it is by holding "faith" (πίστιν, 1:19a)—the "faith" (πίστεως) that is "in Christ Jesus" (1:14)—and thus by continuing "to have-faith" (πιστεύειν) upon Christ Jesus (1:16b)—to live and exist "in faith" (ἐν πίστει, 1:2, 4)—that Timothy must lead the audience to "war . . . the commendable war" (1:18), namely to preserve the sound teaching, the gospel (1:10b–11a), against the different teaching of "some" (1:3, 10b).

To make the polemical focus of Paul's statement even more explicit, almost to a redundant extreme, Paul declares: "some—rejecting—regarding the faith have become-shipwrecked" (1:19b). Immediately, Paul's fourfold combination of the relative pronoun "which," the indefinite pronoun "some," a participle, and a passive verb here in 1:19b of the A′ element recalls the same combination in 1:6 of the A element; Paul's deliberate organization of the language would be apparent:

A element: "which (ὧν) some (τινες)—swerving-from (ἀστοχήσαντες)—have turned-aside (ἐξετράπησαν) for useless-words" (1:6);

A' element: "which (ἥν) some (τινες)—rejecting (ἀπωσάμενοι)—regarding the faith have become-shipwrecked (ἐναυάγησαν)" (1:19b).

The arrangement of both phrases in the parallel A and A' elements would not only emphasize the purposeful structuring of the first literary unit of the letter—the first microchiasm—but would also highlight that "some"—the false teachers—frame Paul's entire concern in the first microchiasm. Moreover, the intentional arrangement between 1:6 and 1:19b would draw explicit attention to the net effect of the false teachers's activities: by "swerving-from" and "rejecting" (1:6, 19), it is clear that the same group of "some" (τινες, 1:6, 19) "have turned-aside" and "have become-shipwrecked" (1:6, 19). Here in 1:19b, the participle "rejecting" (ἀπωσάμενοι) implies a movement with regard to an object, the sense being "cast aside" or "driven away."[174] Thus where "some" are "rejecting" faith and a good conscience (1:19a–b), the audience further understand the contrast between the pre-converted Paul who "without-knowing did in unfaithfulness" (1:13) versus the false teachers who are knowingly and intentionally "rejecting," which has been implicit throughout the microchiasm.[175] Unmistakably, the "rejecting" activities of "some" is that they teach-different (1:3), hold-toward myths and genealogies without-limit (1:4a), and bring-about controversial-speculations (1:4b); consequently, they have misunderstood the law (1:7–9), possibly as a means of salvation rather than a revealer of sin.[176]

Significantly also, in the parallel phrases of 1:6 and 1:19b, Paul is clearly focused on the false teachers's relational position to "the faith." Where the passive verb "have turned-aside" (ἐξετράπησαν) in 1:6 of the A element conveyed a movement away from "faith" (πίστεως, 1:5), in 1:19b of the parallel A' element Paul indicates that such movement results is nothing but

---

174. Oropeza, *Opponents of Paul*, 266 n. 28: "Here the middle participle ἀπωσάμενοι conveys 'thrust away from oneself.'"

175. Cf. Knight, *PE*, 109, who suggests that the relative pronoun ἥν refers only to συνείδησιν and not to πίστιν: "It is a rejection of 'good conscience,' not rejection of faith." See also Marshall, *PE*, 411.

176. This tended to be common problem among other churches in Asia Minor of the first-century (see e.g., Galatians). It is certainly not beyond a possibly that the Ephesian church faced a similar threat, especially given Paul's sustained attention to "law" in first microchiasm of the letter (1:4, 7, 8, 9).

catastrophe—indeed, "regarding the faith" (τὴν πίστιν) they "have become-shipwrecked" (ἐναυάγησαν). The audience would hear the clause "regarding the faith have become-shipwrecked" to indicate an antithesis of living "in faith"; the loss of one's own personal faith seems to be in view—the sense being, "regarding their own faith, they have become-shipwrecked."[177] The intransitive nature of the verb "have become-shipwrecked" (ἐναυάγησαν) highlights the damage incurred by "some" upon themselves;[178] the imagery is graphic, emphasizing the disaster that the false teachers have experienced as a result of rejecting the sound teaching, the gospel, and thus their faith.[179] Timothy and the audience are thus alerted to the dire consequences of failing to "war" while "holding faith and a good conscience" (1:18–19a); they are "to have-faith" (1:16b) and live "in faith" (1:2, 4) while they are engaged in the commendable war to preserve the sound teaching. What Paul has in view of 1:19, then, is not only an encouragement toward faithfulness but a warning against faithlessness. Heard in parallel with 1:6, Paul intends the audience to understand the overtly negative and disastrous implications of aligning themselves with "some"—the false teachers in the Ephesian church

The indefinite pronoun "some" (τινες) here in 1:19b of the concluding A' element recalls its prior occurrences throughout the first microchiasm. Notably, where its prior occurrences were heard by the audience in the parallel introductory A element and in the pivot C element, the thematic arrangement and significance of the first microchiasm would be apparent:

> A element: "some (τισίν) . . . teach-different" (1:3); "some (τινες)—
> swerving-from—have turned-aside for useless-words"
> (1:6);

---

177. Oropeza, *Opponents of Paul*, 267–68: the loss of *"personal faith . . . appears to be the correct meaning . . .* Timothy is supposed to be 'holding faith and a good conscience' (1:19a), which almost certainly concerns personal faith here . . . in 1:19b it would seem awkward for us to read the nuance of 'faith' as suddenly changed to the content of faith (i.e., 'the Christian faith') . . . *they had personal faith comparable to Timothy's* (1:18–19a), *but that faith was destroyed.* What Timothy currently has, they have lost." See Witherington, *Letters*, 179. To be sure, "regarding the faith" is somewhat ambiguous, indicating either "from the perspective of faith" or "concerning their own faith." The latter, however, is more likely.

178. See Marshall, *PE*, 412; contra Mounce, *PE*, 67.

179. Barcley, *1 & 2 Timothy*, 74: "The imagery suggests total disaster, and thus apostasy." Oropeza, *Opponents of Paul*, 268: "being shipwrecked (ναυαγέω) . . . seems to convey utter ruin in ancient traditions."

A possible allusion may be worth noting. Wall with Steele, *1 & 2 Timothy*, 77: it "recalls the dramatic story of Paul's shipwreck, in which the forces of evil are pitted against the forces of good, with everyone who stands with Paul saved from the sea (Acts 27:27–44)." The same may be implied in 1 Timothy for everyone who stands with Paul against the forces of "some."

C element: "if someone (τις) uses it [the law] lawfully" (1:8b);

A' element: "some (τινες)—rejecting—regarding the faith have become-shipwrecked" (1:19).[180]

Where the chiasm functions to introduce a theme, progresses it to a central pivotal point, and then advances the theme toward a climactic conclusion, the audience understand that the false teachers—"some"—not only frame Paul's concern in the first microchiasm but also convey Paul's entire concern thereof. Indeed, "some" are the introduction, the pivot, and the conclusion. Thus here in the concluding A' element of the first microchiasm, the audience understand that Paul thoroughly intends to address the presence, influence, and danger of "some" in the Ephesian church.

The concluding verse of the A' element within the 1:1–20 microchiasm ends with Paul finally specifying the identity of two individuals within the group of "some": "of whom are Hymenaeus and Alexander" (ὧν ἐστιν Ὑμέναιος καὶ Ἀλέξανδρος).[181] Up to this point in the letter, Paul has pejoratively referenced these two men anonymously as "some" (1:3, 6, 8, 19); such was likely intended for rhetorical purposes, revealing now in dramatic fashion the names of those within the Ephesian church who are hindering the household-law of God in faith (1:4b). The use of the relative pronoun "of whom" (ὧν) here in the A' element of the microchiasm recalls its parallel occurrence in 1:6 of the A element; yet, whereas the earlier instance leaves the identity of the false teachers unknown, here the microchiasm has progressed to reveal their actual names.[182] Paul's willingness to expose their

---

180. It is worth noting the full use of the indefinite pronoun "some" and its cognates in relation to the activities of the false teachers (see *italics*):
A element: "some (τισίν) . . . teach-different" (1:3); "which (αἵτινες) bring-about controversial-speculations (1:4b); "some (τινες)—swerving-from—have turned-aside for useless-words" (1:6); "not understanding either what they-are-saying or "somethings" (τίνων) they-are-insisting" (1:7);
C element: "if someone (τις) uses it [the law] lawfully" (1:8b);
A' element: "and if some-thing (τι) lies-opposed to the sound teaching (1:10b); "some (τινες)—rejecting—regarding the faith have become-shipwrecked" (1:19).

181. For more on the possibility background of these individuals, see notes in Towner, *Letters*, 30–33; see Marshall, *PE*, 413. For the rhetorical purposes of this letter, it is sufficient to simply note that they were well known among the believers in Ephesus; otherwise, it would have made little sense for Paul to identify persons with whom the audience would have been unfamiliar. Oropeza, *Opponents of Paul*, 267: "Hymenaeus and Alexander would no doubt be included among this party of false teachers."

182. In passing it may be worth commenting on the phrase here, "of whom are" (ὧν ἐστιν). In the present microchiasm, the only other combination of the pronoun ὧν with the verb ἐστιν (εἰμι) occurs in 1:16 and is applied to Paul (ὧν . . . εἰμι) being the "first" of sinners. If any connection is intended, it may be for Hymenaeus and Alexander to see themselves as sinners, and thus accept the faithful word concerning Christ Jesus for

identity in front of the entire audience listening to the letter suggests the urgency of the situation and the gravity of their rebellion. Still, where Paul's use of the verb "are" (ἐστιν) here in 1:20 of the A' element recalls Paul's assertion that "the end of the charge is (ἐστίν) love" in 1:5 of the parallel A element, the audience are reminded that Paul's discussion pertaining to these two men among "some" is motivated by love and intends for their restoration to a pure heart, good conscience, and without-hypocrisy faith from which they have turned-aside (1:5–6).

That the sin of Hymenaeus and Alexander is grievous and warrants official censure is reflected in the apostle Paul's subsequent activity in 1:20: "whom I have given-over to Satan" (οὓς παρέδωκα τῷ Σατανᾷ). Notably, the act of being "given-over" (παρέδωκα) by Paul in 1:20 directly contrasts his act to "entrust" (παρατίθεμαί) Timothy with the charge in 1:18, likely underscoring the antithesis between "some" for whom the charge applies—namely Hymenaeus and Alexander (1:20)—and Timothy who is entrusted with authority to carry out the charge. Given the immediate context that both men "regarding the faith have become-shipwrecked" (1:19b), Paul's statement "whom I have given-over to Satan" (1:20) would likely be understood by the audience as Paul's definitive way of marking Hymenaeus and Alexander—two among "some"—as those who are not "in faith"; subsequently, Paul's statement clearly marks the two men as those who need to have-faith upon Christ (1:16).[183] The verb "I have given-over" (παρέδωκα) assumes authority on the part of the person doing the action.[184] Here,

---

salvation (1:15).

183. Towner, *Letters*, 161: "Several texts [from the NT] would seem to indicate that 'handing over to Satan' involved a last stage in which the unrepentant sinner was turned out of the church to be treated as an unbeliever . . . This was probably envisioned as removal from the sphere of God's protection into the world where Satan still held sway." Wall with Steele, *1 & 2 Timothy*, 78: "the severity of the practice, which carries life-death consequences, appears to be available only to the apostle."

The double reference in the A element to the phrase "in faith" (1:2, 4)—in addition to the repeated occurrences of the term "faith" and its cognates throughout the A' element—further suggests that Paul's particular activity toward Hymenaeus and Alexander has "faith" in view.

184. For this sort of use of the verb παραδίδωμι, see MM 432. A similar statement is found in LXX Job 2:6 (ἰδοὺ παραδίδωμί σοι αὐτόν), which states God gave-over Job to be tried by Satan. What is evident particularly in Job's narrative is the authority of God as the one overseeing the action.

It is also worth noting the use and connotation of the verb "I have given-over" (παρέδωκα, 1:20) in the Gospels. For example, in Mark, the chief priests, scribes, and Sanhedrin "gave-over" (παρέδωκαν) Jesus to Pilate (15:1), and Pilate "gave-over" (παρέδωκεν) Jesus to be crucified (15:15). Significantly in Mark 15, not only is authority implied in the use of verb, but the net result was salvation through Jesus's death. The restorative intention of Paul both connotes authority and intends salvation for

then, Paul is not only conveying his authority in relation to Hymenaeus and Alexander, but he is also clearly reiterating the fact of his authority to do so as an "apostle of Christ Jesus according to the command of God" (1:1). Thus here in the climactic, concluding statement in the A′ element of the first microchiasm, the audience hear a conceptual parallel of the introductory statement in the A element: Paul's authority as an apostle is underscored (1:1), and the necessity for him to exercise such authority on these two men highlights the severity of the situation in Ephesus. In short, Paul is responding with God's authority and by God's command (1:1) because "some" (1:19)—"of whom are Hymenaeus and Alexander" (1:20)—are acting against God. The consequent effect of Paul's statement is clear: Paul—not "some," and specifically not these two men Hymanaeus and Alexander—is Christ Jesus's fully authorized representative (1:1, 12); anyone among the audience who is "in faith" (1:2), thus "in Christ Jesus" (1:14), and thus along with Paul is able to say "Christ Jesus our Lord" (1:2, 12; cf. 1:14) must, therefore, agree and adhere to Paul's authoritative action to preserve the sound teaching, the gospel, that both exhibits God's radiant glory and results in blessing toward him (1:10b–11a). Indeed, for "some" among the audience, Paul's authoritative declaration is a summons to demonstrate their allegiance to Christ Jesus—to have-faith upon him (1:16) by agreeing with his very own personally appointed apostle (1:1, 12).

Paul immediately states his intended result for giving-over Hymenaeus and Alexander to Satan: "that they might be-disciplined not to blaspheme" (1:20). The purpose—"that" (ἵνα)—is clearly for Hymenaeus and Alexander to "be-disciplined" (παιδευθῶσιν), that is, with the intention of being brought back into the sphere "in faith."[185] In other words, the audience

---

Hymenaeus and Alexander; see discussion below.

185. Morgan-Wynne, "Attitudes Towards Erring Brothers," 247: "The purpose of this step is remedial—it is to induce a 'learning experience', which will lead to reformation and a return to sound attitudes and beliefs (here encapsulated in the phrase 'not to blaspheme')." Patterson and Kelley, "1 Timothy," 660: "The apostle's purpose in turning them over to Satan was redemptive: so that they may be taught not to blaspheme." Krause, *1 Timothy*, 44: "While the situation seems bleak, the notion that they might yet be taught (*paideuthosin*) does offer at least a glimmer of the possibility of their redemption and inclusion back into the church."

The translation "be-disciplined" does not carry a negative connotation; rather, it is the sort of discipline that reflects God's sovereign knowledge and ability to apply enough pressure to bring about a positive outcome. For further clarification, see its occurrences and explanation in Hebrews 12:1-13. Oropeza, *Opponents of Paul*, 269, suggests that they are "*banished to protect the congregation while at the same time providing those who are expelled a chance to repent*." Regarding God's use of Satan as an agent for the believer's spiritual restoration, see Wall with Steele, *1 & 2 Timothy*, 77; Marshall, *PE*, 415; Knight, *PE*, 111–12.

understand that the authoritative action that Paul was required to exercise toward these two men was motivated by love; such is the end goal of "the charge" against "some" (1:5). The passive sense of the verb "be-disciplined" (παιδευθῶσιν), consistent with the passive verbs throughout the 1:12–17 A' element—"was counted-faithful" (ἐπιστεύθην, 1:11a), "was granted-mercy" (ἠλεήθην, 1:13, 16)—is likely a divine passive, indicating that it is God who will ultimately carry out the discipline. That Paul would use the verb "to blaspheme" (βλασφημεῖν) to summarize their grievous activities recalls Paul's use of the cognate term "blasphemer" (βλάσφημον) to describe his own actions while being "in unfaithfulness" (1:13). Undoubtedly, that "some" of whom are Hymenaeus and Alexander are engaged in activities that "blaspheme" makes clear that they are conducting themselves as those who are not "in faith." Furthermore, Paul's use of the negative particle "not" (μή) here in 1:20 of the A' element would not go unnoticed, recalling its cognate occurrences throughout the parallel A element in direct reference to the activities of "some." That is, "some" are "not" (μή) to teach-different "nor" (μηδέ) to hold-toward myths and genealogies without-limit (1:3–4a); "some" are "not" (μή) understanding "either" (μήτε) what they-are-saying "or" (μήτε) regarding some-things they-are-insisting (1:7). To be sure, the linguistic and thematic juxtaposition between Paul's intention for Hymenaeus and Alexander and his intention for Timothy would be apparent:

> A element: "I exhorted (παρεκάλεσά) you to remain in Ephesus . . . that (ἵνα) you might charge (παραγγείλῃς) some (τισίν) not (μή) to teach-different (ἑτεροδιδασκαλεῖν)" (1:3);
>
> A' element: "some (τινες) . . . of whom are Hymenaeus and Alexander, whom I have given-over (παρέδωκα) to Satan, that (ἵνα) they might be-disciplined (παιδευθῶσιν) not (μή) to blaspheme (βλασθημεῖν)" (1:20).

In both parallel statements, Paul's use of authoritative language would clearly be heard by the audience—"I exhorted (παρεκάλεσά, 1:3), "I have given-over" (παρέδωκα, 1:20). Moreover, the explicit purpose—"that" (ἵνα, 1:3, 20)—of Paul's authoritative action is for the conduct of "some" (τισίν, 1:3; τινες, 1:20) to change. Still, Paul's indirect involvement in carrying out the required change—"you [Timothy] might charge" (παραγγείλῃς, 1:3); "they might be-disciplined [by God] (παιδευθῶσιν, 1:20)—combined with Paul's use of "not" (μή, 1:3, 20) and an infinitive verb—"to teach-different (ἑτεροδιδασκαλεῖν, 1:3); "to blaspheme" (βλασθημεῖν, 1:20)—would likely communicate an integrated rhetoric. In short, "to teach-different" is "to blaspheme," and for this reason "some" must "not" do so any longer. Indeed, where the term "blasphemer" in 1:13 conveyed speaking in an insulting manner against God, it is evident why Timothy must "charge some not to teach-different" (1:3) and thus "not to blaspheme" (1:20).[186]

In sum, given that "the gospel" is the presentation of God's radiant glory, the audience understand that "some-thing different" that "lies-opposed to the sound teaching, according to the gospel" (1:10b–11a) is not merely a deviation from truth but a personal attack against God, an attempt to obstruct his radiance from shining forth. Furthermore, the situation in the mid-sixties Ephesian church wherein "some . . . teach-different" (1:3) is not merely a difference of opinion but a direct hindrance to salvation, causing its adherents to swerve-from, turn-aside, reject, and become-shipwrecked regarding their faith in Christ Jesus, who specifically came to save them (1:6, 15a, 16b, 19). Paul has clearly conveyed the grave implications of adhering to the different teaching of "some," and as much as Paul's language engages the false teachers with polemical rhetoric, it is evident that his purpose is motivated by love and intends their restoration and salvation (1:5, 1:16, 1:20). At the conclusion of the first microchiasm, the A unit of the 1 Timothy letter, the audience reflect on their participation in the history of salvation: they are listening to and experiencing the performative presence of a man who was once a persecutor of Christ Jesus (1:13) but now is an apostle of Christ Jesus (1:1)—a man who was commanded by God our Savior (1:1) to fully represent Christ Jesus who came to save (1:15a). As the representative messenger of salvation, Paul's charge to preserve the sound teaching fully intends salvation for those who hear him. Thus sets the stage for the 1 Timothy letter and its audience.

---

186. Regarding 1 Tim 1:13, a possible allusion to Acts 26:11 was noted. Where the verb in Acts 26:11 seemed to imply a renunciation of faith, Paul may have the same in view here. More likely, "blaspheme" simply recalls Paul's reception of mercy and his yearning for "some"—particularly these two men Hymenaeus and Alexander—to receive likewise.

4

1 Timothy 2:1–15: Salvation for All through Prayer and Godly Conduct

(B Unit)

THIS CHAPTER EXAMINES THE B unit of the macrochiasm—the second of six microchiasms within the 1 Timothy letter.[1] Within this second microchiasm (2:1–15), one minichiasm is heard (2:9–15).

The Second Microchiasm

The 2:1–15 microchiasm is composed carefully of six elements (A-B-C-C'-B'-A'); linguistic parallels identifying chiastic arrangements are indicated by the Greek text:

> A. ²:¹ I exhort, therefore (οὖν), first (πρῶτον) of all to be-done supplications, prayers (προσευχάς), intercessions, thanksgivings on behalf of all humans, ² on behalf of kings and all those being in authority, that a peaceful and quiet (ἡσύχιον) life we might lead-through in all (πάσῃ) godliness (εὐσεβείᾳ) and respectability. ³ This is commendable and acceptable in the sight of our Savior God, ⁴ᵃ who desires all humans to be-saved (σωθῆναι)
>
> B. ⁴ᵇ and to come to a knowing-embrace of truth (ἀληθείας).
>
> C: ⁵ᵃ For there is one (εἷς) God,

---

1. For the establishment of 1 Timothy as a macrochiasm, clarifications of terminology, and an explanation of my translation methodology, see chapter 2.

C': ⁵ᵇ there is one (εἷς) mediator of God and humans, the human Christ Jesus, ⁶ who gave himself as a ransom on behalf of all, the testimony at his own times.

B'. ⁷ To this I-myself was appointed proclaimer and apostle—the truth (ἀλήθειαν) I am saying, I am not falsifying—teacher of the Gentiles in faith and truth (ἀληθείᾳ).

A'. ⁸ I want, therefore (οὖν), men to pray (προσεύχεσθαι) in all place lifting reverent hands without anger and word-quarreling; ⁹ likewise also women to cosmetic themselves in cosmopolitan apparel with modesty and self-control, not in braids and gold or pearls or rich attire; ¹⁰ rather what is proper for women who profess godliness (θεοσέβειαν), consistent-with good works. ¹¹ A woman in quietness (ἡσυχίᾳ) must learn in all (πάσῃ) submissiveness; ¹² but I do not permit a woman to teach nor to govern a man; rather to be in quietness (ἡσυχίᾳ). ¹³ For Adam was formed first (πρῶτος), then Eve. ¹⁴ And Adam was not deceived, but the woman being-deceived in transgression became; ¹⁵ but she will be-saved (σωθήσεται) consistent-with child-parenting, if they remain in faith and love and holiness with self-control.

1 Timothy 2:1–4a: Prayer, A Life in All Godliness, God Desires All Humans to Be-Saved

(A Element)

The A element (2:1–4a) begins with the verb "I exhort" (παρακαλῶ), thus yielding several effects upon the audience. First, similar to the beginning of the introductory A element in the first microchiasm—"I exhorted" (παρεκάλεσα, 1:3)—its occurrence here likewise indicates the beginning of a new section in the letter, the second microchiasm. Second, the use of the same verb for the introductory A element of the second microchiasm suggests that it is similar—if not identical—in importance to Timothy's charge in the A element of the first microchiasm to silence the false teachers. Third and finally, the audience hear a seamless movement—via transitional words—from "I have given-over" (παρέδωκα, 1:20) in the concluding A' element of the first microchiasm to "I exhort" (παρακαλῶ, 2:1) in the introductory A element of the second microchiasm; such enables the audience to hear the flow and sustained progression of the first two microchiasms within the overall 1 Timothy macrochiasm.² That is, given Paul's authoritative action toward Hymenaeus and Alexander at the end of the first microchiasm, the second microchiasm would continue to emphasize the full weight of Paul's apostolic authority. To be sure, the connection of the verb "I exhort" in the A element of the second microchiasm to both the introductory A element and concluding A' element of the first microchiasm would have a summarizing effect: Timothy must carry out these exhortations, and the audience must fully comply with them. Still, the importance of the verb "exhort" is signaled further by the use of "first of all." The term "first" (πρῶτον) in 2:1 recalls the first microchiasm wherein Paul described his lead, prominence—"first" (πρῶτός, 1:15b; πρώτῳ, 1:16a)—among sinners. This would not only further demonstrate the progression and connection of the first and second microchiasms but also would highlight the special significance of Paul's exhortation here in 2:1. That is, whatever he exhorts, it is to be given prominence, that is, a "first"—foremost, leading—importance.³

Careful thought should be given to the use of the conjunction "therefore" (οὖν). It is usually translated "therefore, then, thus, accordingly," and given what Paul has said in the first microchiasm of the letter—underscoring Timothy's authoritative duty to charge "some" not to teach-different—it seems appropriate to interpret "therefore" in light of Paul's entire polemic against the false teachers.⁴ Whereas their teaching likely promoted a spiri-

---

2. The aural emphasis on the verbal prefix (παρά) would be apparent. Regarding the function of *transitional words*, see chapter 2.

3. Significant attention has been given to use of the term πρῶτον. Towner, *Letters*, 165 n. 6: "Gk. πρῶτον . . . it is to be taken either as a superlative ('first' in importance) or simply as an indication of the 'first' in a series of items . . . There is no way to be sure which nuance Paul intends, but often the first mentioned is of greatest importance or urgency." Knight, *PE*, 113-14: "(πρῶτον) may mean either first in sequence or first in importance. The predominant useage of Paul elsewhere is that of sequence or time, although there are possible exceptions . . . we should probably understand the word in a sequential sense here, but with the qualification that what is placed first in sequence may be so placed because it is also considered first in importance." Marshall, *PE*, 418: "The superlative stresses either the priority (first in time or sequence) or the importance (first in degree) of the instruction. Here it may simply indicate that this is the first instruction to be given in the letter. Or the meaning might be 'above all', implying that this is the most important instruction and therefore the first thing that should happen in the church."

The chiastic structure of the letter—the progression and connection of the A' element in the first microchiasm to the A element in the second microchiasm—demonstrates that the use of of πρῶτον in 2:1 carries the same connotation as its occurrence (πρώτῳ) in 1:15, namely prominence. See chapter 3.

4 There are differing interpretations. Barcley, "1 Timothy," 364: "The word 'then' (or 'therefore') at the beginning of 2:1 shows that Paul's instructions on prayer in this chapter are directly tied to what he has just said about Timothy's 'charge' at the end

tual elitism based on a misunderstanding of the law's intended use, the gospel, as exemplified in Paul's own life (1:12–17), is available to sinners—"the without-law and without-obedience, the without-godly and sinners" (1:9). The gospel—Paul's teaching—is radically inclusive: it is proclaimed to all humans irrespective of their past. In this sense, contrary to false teaching, Paul's sound teaching of the gospel is inherently missional and outward oriented. Thus the audience are reminded to think of "the gospel of the glory of the blessed God" even as they hear the particulars of what Paul will exhort.[5]

The exhortation concerns four types of prayer: "to be-done supplications, prayers, intercessions, thanksgivings on behalf of all humans" (2:1b). The rhetorical force of the repetition of "all" in this single verse conveys the following impression, "First of *all*, prayers are to be-done on behalf of *all*." That is, praying on behalf of all people should be a leading activity among all activities of the church. The term "supplications" (δεήσεις) conveys the nuance of pleading urgently for a specific need; "prayers" (προσευχάς) broadly refers to communicating with God in general; "intercessions" (ἐντεύξεις) would likely carry the nuance of pleading to a superior in another person's stead; and "thanksgivings" (εὐχαριστίας) encompasses the disposition of all three, namely joy that it is even possible to communicate with, plead to, and urgently ask God for help.[6] Still, given Paul's non-specific, all-encompassing concern for "all humans," the audience would likely hear the overall emphasis of Paul's exhortation to be less on the precise meaning of each term and more that *any, every, and all* types of prayers should be-done on behalf of *any, every, and all* types of humans.[7] That the focus of Paul's exhortation is

---

of chapter 1." Similarly, Marshall suggests that "it picks up 1.18 after the digression in 1.19b–20" (*PE*, 418). However, given the above mentioned impact of "exhort," it is most likely that "therefore" (οὖν) encompasses the entire first microchiasm rather than certain parts of it. See Patterson and Kelley, "1 Timothy," 660.

5. Contra Towner, *Letters*, 165 n. 4: "This is the sense of the conjunction οὖν, namely, to make the turn to parenesis/exhortation after there has been a break... Otherwise, there is no sense in which 2:1–2 forms a logical conclusion to the preceding passage."

6. Regarding the nuance of each term, see Knight, *PE*, 114–15; Marshall, *PE*, 419–20; Barclay, *1 &2 Timothy*, 78. For an in-depth discussion of each kind of biblical prayer, see Neyrey, *Give God the Glory*, 5–30.

7. Towner, *Letters*, 166: "Rather than understand the four terms as descriptive of a systematic liturty of prayer, the thought is one of completeness—every dimension and action of prayer being focused on the need at hand... The variety evident in the English translations shows the range of meaning covered by the terms, and there is a good degree of overlap." See Towner's brief comments and notes on each of the terms (ibid., 166–67). See also Barclay, *1 & 2 Timothy*, 78.

The aural similarity between the last three terms would be apparent (see *italics*), perhaps emphasizing the comprehensive and integrated nature of all three: "prayers"

"all humans" (πάντων ἀνθρώπων), of course, is not accidental given Paul's pronouncement of the gospel in the immediately preceeding A' element of the first microchiasm, namely that it extends even to the foremost, lead sinner (1:15). The emphatic message for the audience is clear: the gospel applies to and includes "all humans"—none are precluded from the category of "those who would-inevitably-come to have-faith upon [Christ Jesus] for life eternal" (1:16); none are precluded from the category of sinners whom Christ came to save (1:15). The prayers in view, then, have a soteriological purpose. Paul's specification here of prayers being made on behalf of "all humans" certainly aligns with his own life's purpose to be a model of salvation for sinners in general (1:16); yet, it also possibly addresses an inward disposition developing in the church as a result of the false teachers. The double occurrence of "all" here in 2:1 is forceful, challenging the audience to pray not only for those "in faith," that is, those in the household of God (1:4) but also—and especially—for those who are "in unfaithfulness" (cf. 1:13).[8] In short, the audience are reminded that God's household is meant to be a missional household, characterized by prayer for the salvation of all humans.[9] Given the immediate connection to the concluding A' element of the first microchiasm, such prayer would no doubt have in mind "some" who "regarding the faith have become-shipwrecked" (1:19). Thus Paul's concern is not merely to war the commendable war (1:18) against the false teachers but also—and much more—to have a victory that results in their salvation.

Still, while prayers are to be-done "on behalf" (ὑπέρ) of all humans, Paul specifies in 2:2a that they should be made "on behalf (ὑπέρ) of kings and all those being in authority." The sustained exhortation on prayer is evident through the repetition of "on behalf" (ὑπέρ). To be sure, the mention of "kings" (βασιλέων) would likely cause the audience to pause; as the immediately preceeding A' element of the first microchiasm makes clear, both Paul and the audience view God as "King" (βασιλεῖ, 1:17).[10] This recognition, however, does not mean that they are to have a low view of earthly kings and "those being in authority" (ἐν ὑπεροχῇ ὄντων). Rather, believers are to regularly pray, intercede, and even give thanks on behalf of "all (πάντων) those being in authority."[11] In a time when the Roman emperor was particularly

---

(προσευχάς), "intercessions" (ἐντεύξεις), and "thanksgivings" (εὐχαριστίας).

8. Marshall, *PE*, 420: "This universalistic thrust is most probably a corrective response to an exclusive elitist understanding of salvation connected with the false teachers." Similarly, see Barcley, *1 & 2 Timothy*, 78.

9. See Barcley, "1 Timothy," 364.

10. See Wall, "Empire," 14.

11. Barcley notes, "Prayer for leaders is a recognition of their God-ordained authority and is one aspect of the Christian's submission" (*1 & 2 Timothy*, 79). This may be

hostile to Christianity, Paul's exhortation may have been heard with some degree of shock.[12] Yet, just as the gospel offers salvation to even the "first"—lead, prominent—of sinners (1:15b, 16), prayers for such authorities are clearly included as the "first"—lead, prominent—activity of church (2:1). In short, the saving purpose of prayers on behalf of "all (πάντων) humans" (2:1) applies to "all (πάντων) those being in authority" (2:2).[13]

In light of the soteriological purpose of prayer, Paul goes on to describe the intended result of such prayers: "that a peaceful and quiet life we might lead-through in all godliness and respectability" (2:2b). The audience have now heard a fourfold repetition of "all," leaving the following impression: "First of *all*, prayers are to be-done on behalf of *all*, but particularly on behalf of *all* in authority so that we may live in *all* godliness and respectability." In part, this is Paul being a realist, conveying to the audience that the attitude and actions of those in authority have some bearing on the audience's ability to pursue a "peaceful and quiet life." The burden of 2:2b, however, is much less on the actions and decisions of those in authority and more on the observable lifestyle that the audience, as members of God's household, are called to live. The term "peaceful" (ἤρεμον) conveys being calm and recalls the salvific blessing of inner and outer "peace" (εἰρήνη) from God the Father and Christ Jesus in 1:2 of the first microchiasm. The audience understand that the peace they have received is to be missionally exhibited to all.[14] The term "quiet" (ἡσύχιον) conveys a gentle disposition rather than mute silence, in effect emphasizing the character of a "peaceful" life.[15] At the same time, Paul's reference to "a peaceful and quiet life" would not convey a lack of presence in the city in of Ephesus.[16] Rather, by being

---

relevant when the discussion of authority arises in 2:12.

12. Nero, known for his cruelty against Christians, was most likely the emperor of the Greco-Roman world at the time when 1 Timothy was composed. Simply put, "Nero made belief in Christianity criminal" (Ermatinger, *Christians in Ancient Rome*, 69).

13. Mitchell, "Corrective Composition," 56: "The bottom line, for the author of 1 Tim 2, 1–8, is that Paul was not against prayer for emperors and rulers, but actually commanded it to be performed, both to ensure a peaceful life [1 Tim 2:2], and because it is consistent with his gospel—a universal soteriology that is far from suspicion of exclusive sectarian, and hence treasonable, religious separatism." Wall and Steel, *1 & 2 Timothy*, 81: "Prayers for the emperor's personal safety and political wisdom were ultimately offered to God in prospect of his salvation."

14. Towner helpfully notes: "Paul characterizes a 'life' that is observable, lived among people in society in a way that *registers*. The phrase 'peaceful and quiet life' may express the Hellenistic ideal (conveyed variously) of a tranquil life free from the hassles of a turbulent society" (*Letters*, 169, italics mine).

15. Belleville, "1 Timothy," 41: "*quiet* . . . has to do with a gentle, peaceful disposition, rather than an absence of speech or sound."

16. Barcley, *1 & 2 Timothy*, 81: "a quiet and peaceful life (2:2) does not mean a life of

both "peaceful" and "quiet"—calm and pleasant—Paul intends the audience to have an outward focus, discerning whether those outside the household of God find the Christian way of life appealing.[17] The verb "lead-through" (διάγωμεν) carries the nuance of overt conduct that is both observable and intelligible to others. Hence, what the audience perceive from these initial verses of the second microchiasm is not only a "first" concern for prayer but also—and perhaps much more—a "first" burden for the audience to live intentionally in order to promote the gospel.[18]

Paul characterizes such an observable life using the phrase "in all godliness and respectability." The adjective "all" (πάσῃ) points to the sense of being completely immersed in "godliness and respectability." Still, its prior occurrences in 2:1 and 2:2a also suggest that it means to pursue attractive—missional—lives in all situations with all humans. Furthermore, Paul appears to be using terms that would have resonated with his audience. In particular, the term "godliness" (εὐσεβείᾳ) was closely associated with the Artemis cult in Ephesus.[19] However, as is characteristic of the apostle's earlier language in the letter, Paul is using common Greco-Roman language in order to be both intelligible and subversive. That is, he is not simply endorsing a Hellenistic view of ethics but is redefining every aspect of life according to the entrance of Christ Jesus into the world.[20] The term "godliness" was Paul's summary way of encapsulating the Christian life as a dynamic interplay between having faith upon Christ (1:16) and the particular, observable life that ensues.[21] Whereas the audience may have previously defined the source and

---

solitude void of active involvement in the surrounding culture. There is an evangelistic and missionary thrust to Paul's words here."

17. Beattie, *Women and Marriage in Paul*, 92: "in other words, a life unlikely to attract censure from outside observers." Tellbe, *Christ-Believers in Ephesus*, 191: "there is thus a connection between social respectability and the desire to communicate belief in Christ to the surrounding society." Hughes and Chappell, *1–2 Timothy*, 61: "the best argument *for* and *against* Christianity is Christianity . . . Christianity lived out can make inroads where few other things can." See Keegan, *First and Second Timothy*, 15.

18. Pate, *Apostle of the Last Days*, 264: "The motive for ethical behavior is not a desire to avoid persecution and live peacefully, but it stems from the fact of salvation and a desire to proclaim the saving message."

19. See Harrison, "Priestess of Artemis," 35; Pate, *Apostle of the Last Days*, 263.

20. Note that Paul did the same with his use of the Hellenistic terms "Savior" (1:1), "Lord" (1:2, 12), and "the gospel" (1:11). For further comments, see Towner, *Letters*, 169–75, esp. his excursus comments on the terms "godliness" and "respectability." Cf. Ehrensperger, "Striving for Office," 105: "A significant number of scholars see in this the intention to accommodate the assemblies to the norms of the dominatin Graeco-Roman society, its values and patterns of life."

21. Patterson and Kelley, "1 Timothy," 673: "In the Pastoral Epistles, the term 'godliness' referred to the practical, godly living that is observable by others."

outworking of godliness from Artemis, now, as those who are "in faith" (1:2, 4) and thus "in Christ Jesus" as recipients of "grace . . . faith and love" (1:14), "godliness" is completely redefined in terms of the person Christ Jesus.[22] This observation is especially important because it articulates the essence of Christian life. On the one hand, Paul would have the audience pray for ideal circumstances in which to practice godliness, namely "a peaceful and quiet life"; yet, on the other hand, he recognizes that the source—and therefore possibility—of godliness in the audience's life transcends circumstances because it flows from their existence in an entirely different realm—a life "in faith," that is, "in Christ Jesus." The second term "respectability" (σεμνότητι) reinforces what has already been said regarding Paul's concern for the audience to pursue behavior that is both readily observable and admirable.[23] Heard together, verses 2:1–2 demonstrate the apostle Paul's strong desire for God's household to engage its surrounding society in a manner that positively honors God through honorable living. Moreover, the microchiastic progression from the A' element of the first microchiasm to the A element of the second microchiasm indicates that Paul's desire is to be shared by his audience: the doxological invitation—"amen"—to actively participate in giving "honor and glory" to God (1:17) is done through a life "in all godliness and respectability" (2:2). For the false teachers in the audience, Paul's call to godly living—the outworking of the sound teaching, the gospel with which he was counted-faithful (1:10b–11a)—would likely be polemical, not only suggesting that the false-teaching of "some" brings-about conduct that dishonors God—to be sure, controversial-speculations rather than the household-law of God (1:4)—but also that it is unappealing to others, especially the cultural milieu of the Greco-Roman world.

Paul continues the A element by saying, "This is commendable and acceptable in the sight of our Savior God" (2:3). The precise reference of "this" (τοῦτο) in 2:3 is unclear, perhaps referring to the exhortation to pray (2:1–2a) or perhaps to pursue godly and respectable lives (2:2b).[24] Both are likely in view,[25] or the two are to be viewed in totality: prayers facilitate the conditions for living a peaceable and quiet life—all this "is commendable and acceptable in the sight of our Savior God" (2:3). More significant is the terminology that Paul employs in this assessment: "This is commendable and acceptable in the sight of our Savior God" has clear echoes from

---

22. See Marshall's discussion, *PE*, 424.

23. Marshall, *PE*, 423: "εὐσέβεια and σεμνότης together describe a life that is completely acceptable both to God and people."

24. Barcley, *1 & 2 Timothy*, 80, suggests that prayer is in view.

25. Stout, *The "Man Christ Jesus,"* 14.

Deuteronomy.²⁶ The adjective "commendable" (καλόν), as in the formulaic expression in Deuteronomy, indicates what God defines as good according to his lawful standards.²⁷ Paul's use of the term here in the second microchiasm to describe the church's acitivies of prayer and the resultant godliness demonstrates a progression from its use in the first microchiasm: contrary to "some" who teach-different (1:3), those among the audience who are "in faith" (1:2, 4) and thus "in Christ Jesus" (1:14) not only "know that the law is commendable (καλός)" (1:8) but also strive to do what is "commendable" (καλόν) in the sight of God (2:3). Furthermore, Paul appears to replace the Deuteronomic adjective "pleasing" (ἀρεστόν) in the LXX expression with the adjective "acceptable" (ἀπόδεκτον), thus highlighting sacrificial language from Leviticus (δεκτός; see, e.g., LXX Lev 1:3). The net effect of combining OT legal and cultic language is to communicate that the "first," lead activities of the audience—those living in the realm "in Christ Jesus" as God's people "in faith"—are now to be seen as the lawful, cultic practices of the OT, a participatory act of worship toward God.²⁸

The entrance of Christ into the world, then, has resulted in radical changes with prayer and godliness doing what the law commands and replacing the old sacrificial system. As such, the first half of 2:3 in the second microchiasm is not merely a positive assessment of Paul's exhortation in 2:1-2 but is another—albeit subtle—attack against the false teachers who do not understand the law (1:8b) despite their desire to be law-teachers (1:7). As the apostle indicated in 1:8-10 of the first microchiasm, the lawful use of the commendable law exposes various forms of sin, thus rendering just judgment; yet, it cannot make sinners lawful or just, thus cannot save sinners from judgment. Rather, salvation from just judgment is not only through the coming of Christ Jesus into the world to save sinners but—quite equally—is through the coming of sinners to have-faith upon him (1:15-16), namely that he came to fully save them, a soteriological reality that Paul's opponents fail to perceive. In 2:3a of the second microchiasm, then, it is quite possible that their failure to correctly understand the law

---

26. Compare the Greek texts:
1 Tim 2:3: "τοῦτο καλὸν καὶ ἀπόδεκτον ἐνώπιον τοῦ σωτῆρος ἡμῶν θεοῦ";
LXX Deut 6:18a: "καὶ ποιήσεις τὸ ἀρεστὸν καὶ τὸ καλὸν ἐναντίον κυρίου τοῦ θεοῦ ὑμῶν."

27. Marshall, *PE*, 424: the Deuteronomic phrase "describes various kinds of behaviour as in keeping with the law and therefore as meeting God's standard."

28. Towner, *Letters*, 177, summarizes: "Thus Paul explains the prayer for the salvation of all people, and specific prayer for the effectiveness of the civic powers, conforms to the will of God. It is not simply an optional church practice that pleases God, but a practice as integral to the church's life with God as was sacrifice in the time before Christ."

includes a continual dependence on observing various aspects of the OT cultic practices, rather than depending upon and observing what Christ did. The implicit force of Paul's rhetoric on the audience is for them to not only move away from the false teaching of "some"—which has the law as its focus rather than Christ (1:7)—but also from their useless practices—which have myths and genealogies without-limit as its focus rather than Christ (1:4). To be sure, Paul's central focus on Christ distinguishes "the sound teaching" from the different teaching of "some" that lies-opposed to it (1:3, 10b). Thus the progression from the first microchiasm to the second microchiasm is evident: the audience are not only to know "the sound teaching" of Paul but are to do it—namely, to do activities that conform to a realm of existence "in faith" as a result of the coming of Christ Jesus (1:15) and of coming to have-faith upon him (1:16).

Still echoing the Deuteronomy formula, 2:3 concludes with the prepositional phrase, "in the sight of our Savior God." The phrase demonstrates a specific movement throughout the letter. At the outset of the A element of the first microchiasm, Paul highlighted that his apostolic calling is "according to the command of God our Savior (θεοῦ σωτῆρος ἡμῶν)" (1:1), thus initiating a soteriological thrust in the letter. The theme of salvation then continued in the parallel A' element of the first microchiasm where Christ Jesus was identified as the one who came "to save (σῶσαι) sinners" (1:15). Now in the A element of the second microchiasm, the letter's preoccupation with salvation is reiterated: "our Savior God (σωτῆρος ἡμῶν θεοῦ)" (2:3). What is more, Paul's replacement of "Lord" (κυρίου) in the LXX Deuteronomic formula with "Savior" (σωτῆρος) further accentuates the salvific concern of the letter. Here in the second microchiasm, then, one thing is certain: not only Paul but specifically God, who himself is Paul's "Savior," is fixated on saving. Thus even in the initial stages of the 1 Timothy macrochiasm, the progression and consistent heartbeat is audible: for those living "in faith" who call upon God as "Father" (1:2), "the household-law of God" (1:4) has a "first," lead concern with the salvation of all humans and particularly of sinners (1:16; 2:1). In sum, this sustained emphasis on God and Christ Jesus as the architect and accomplisher of salvation undoubtedly communicates to the audience that they are to pursue prayer and godliness within a soteriological framework: the salvation of "all (πάντων) humans" (2:1) is related to the united efforts—"our" (ἡμῶν, 2:3)—of Paul, Timothy, and the audience to pray and pursue godliness. Simply, the audience are to embrace their calling as constituents of God's missional household through which he is saving the world.[29]

---

29. Marshall, *PE*, 425: "As Saviour, he calls for the involvement of his people in and

As if the message were not clear enough, God's concern for and commitment to salvation is highlighted further in 2:4a. Paul declares that God "desires all humans to be-saved." The term "desires" (θέλει) recalls the false teachers in 1:7 of the first microchiasm who are "desiring" (θέλοντες) to be law-teachers. However, clearly the audience hear a stark contrast: whereas the false teachers are "desiring" to teach that which lawfully condemns sinful humans (1:9), God "desires all humans to be-saved" (2:4a). In effect, the audience understand that the content of that which God "desires" is markedly different from that which the false teachers are "desiring," that is, God "desires" all humans to be-saved from the consequences of the different teaching of "some." Furthermore, Paul's comparison between the "desires" of God (2:4a) and the "desiring" of the false teachers (1:7), that is, of humans, would undoubtedly also denote that the way God "desires" is qualitatively different from human desire. Yet, the comparison to human desire—particularly its intensity and profundity—would provide a helpful lens for the audience to grasp the depth of God's salvific desire.[30] In short, Paul in 2:4a conveys an explicit statement of God's will, thus affirming why prayer and godliness are commendable and acceptable in the sight of God (2:3)—they perfectly conform to God's missional will.[31] Such is corroborated for the audience by the immediate, redundant juxtaposition of the cognates "Savior" (σωτῆρος, 2:3) and "to be-saved" (σωθῆναι, 2:4a), which underscores God's salvific disposition. Still—and perhaps more significantly—the terms "Savior" (σωτῆρος, 2:3) and "to be-saved" (σωθῆναι, 2:4a) recall Christ Jesus's willful action in the first microchiasm "to save" (σῶσαι) sinners (1:15). In other words, the audience understand that God not only "desires" all humans to be-saved—a disposition—but also acts upon it. Emphatically, then, the audience hear the heartbeat of the macrochiasm even louder: Christ Jesus came into the world "to save" sinners (1:15) because the "Savior God" desires all humans "to be-saved" (2:4a).

The phrase "all humans" (πάντας ἀνθρώπους) is almost an exact repetition of the earlier occurrence in the microchiasm, "all humans" (πάντων ἀνθρώπων, 2:1), and is reminiscent of "all those being in authority" (πάντων τῶν ἐν ὑπεροχῇ ὄντων, 2:2). It is unlikely that the phrase should

---

through their prayer for all." Wall with Steele, *1 & 2 Timothy*, 81: "the congregation's public prayers reflect not a program of political domestication but a Christian mission that boldly evangelizes the surrounding pagan culture from top to bottom."

30. Wall, "Empire," 17: Paul "is pressing for the global scope of God's salvation as the principal theological motive why the congregation should pray for everyone, including their pagan rulers. Sharply put, Christians pray for everyone in agreement with God's chief desire."

31. See Mitchell, "Corrective Composition," 48–49.

be taken literally—that God's desire for all humans to be-saved means that all humans will be-saved; Paul's clear teaching is that only those who would-inevitably-come to have-faith upon Christ Jesus receive life eternal (1:16).³² Nor would it be the case that God desires (but somehow is unable) to save all humans—Christ Jesus in fact came to save them (1:15).³³ Rather, the context of the letter suggests that "all humans" expresses the inclusive nature of the gospel.³⁴ The phrase "all humans" in 2:4a would likely be polemical against the false teaching, which was based on a misunderstanding of the law and likely resulted in some form of spiritual elitism or exclusivism.³⁵ Moreover, the fact that all manner of sinners, as listed in 1:9–10 of the first microchiasm, have the same access to life eternal through Christ Jesus who came to save "sinners"—note, a broad, all-encompassing term (1:15–16)—indicates that inclusivity is clearly intended.

Such salvation, which includes all types of people, is not intended to be merely a future, final, eschatological reality, although it is certainly not less than that.³⁶ Instead, as indicated at the outset of the second microchiasm, God's desire to include all people—without partiality—is a salvific reality that the audience are to pursue and experience in their present lives

---

32. Stout, *The "Man Christ Jesus,"* 15: "This raises the question whether the desire of God is always determinative, so that He actually shall save 'all men' universally. Such a view, however, would force a contradiction in Paul's own theology . . . Thus, in this particular context, θέλει should should not be viewed as determinative but as desirative, as Paul may be echoing Ezek 18:23, where the same verb is found in God's question, 'Do I have any pleasure (μὴ θελήσει θελήσω) in the death of the wicked rather than that he should turn form his ways and live?'" Belleville, "1 Timothy," 46: "God desires that all be saved. However, it is human responsibility to reject or accept . . . 'all' must be understood in its broadest sense. Yet while Christ died for all of humanity, it is only believers who reap the benefits . . . The scope of Christ's redemptive work may be all-encompassing, but the application is particular." Marshall, *PE*, 427: "The condition of belief in the gospel, the human responsibility in the process, places limits on the results which will be achieved."

33. The notion that God wills to save all humans regardless of their acceptance of the gospel is not the sense of this text (contra. Hasler, "Epiphanie und Christolgie," 204–7). Such a notion is altogether foreign to Paul, as reflected both in 1 Timothy and his other letters, who never compromised the message that salvation comes through faith upon Christ Jesus.

34. Schreiner, *Paul, Apostle of God's Glory*, 185: "No people group is excluded from his [God's] saving intentions."

35. Marshall, *PE*, 425: "the emphasis on 'all' is presumably directed at the false teaching in some way. There were various types of exclusivism in the environment of early Christianity which may underlie the attitude implicitly criticized here."

36. Johnson helpfully observes Paul's concern here for present expression among the believers of future salvific realities, but perhaps errs on minimizing the import of eternal life ("The Social Dimensions of Sōtēria," 520–36).

through prayer and a life in all godliness. Furthermore, as indicated by the connection to the immediate A' element of the first microchiasm, Timothy and the audience are to participate in this saving reality by warring against divisive, false teaching of "some" (1:18–19) and by preserving the sound teaching, the inclusive gospel (1:11–17). In sum, along with the macrochiastic movement, the overall sense of the A element in the second microchiasm is that God is a saving God—indeed, he is "Savior"—who desires for all humans to be-saved, and the way God accomplishes his desire is through the prayers and missional godliness of those who live within his household—"in faith" (1:2, 4), "in Christ Jesus" (1:14)—and thus according to his household-law (1:4).

1 Timothy 2:4b: A Knowing-Embrace of Truth

(B Element)

As the second microchiasm moves to the B element (2:4b), the audience hear a specification of the concluding thought in the A element: "and to come to a knowing-embrace of truth." The "and" (καί) is epexegetical, indicating that "to be-saved" in 2:4a equals "to come to a knowing-embrace of truth" (2:4b).[37] The noun "a knowing-embrace" (ἐπίγνωσιν) does not connote merely "recognition" or "knowledge" but a full acceptance and commitment.[38] Such "a knowing-embrace" is certainly evidenced by a commitment to and participation in the "first," lead activity of the church, namely missional prayer and godliness that would attract others "to be-saved" in conformity to what God desires (2:4a). At the same time, "a knowing-embrace" also highlights the very personal, intimate response that Paul has clearly associated with receiving the grace, faith, and love that are in Christ Jesus (1:12–17). Such a personal aspect of salvation aligns with the personal tone of the polemic highlighted in the concluding A' element of the first microchiasm: acceptance (1:15) or rejection (1:19) of the gospel of the glory of the blessed God is, according to the apostle, an intensely personal matter—it concerns Paul's personal teaching and God's personal gospel. The "truth" (ἀληθείας) in view is undoubtedly a reference to "the sound teaching" as summarized in the 1:11–17 minichi-

---

37. Stout summarizes Paul's point: "A universal plan is not the same as a universal salvation, in that 'all men' need to 'come to the knowledge of the truth,' a description of actual conversion" (*The* "*Man Christ Jesus*," 15). Marshall, *PE*, 428: it "is a technical phrase in the PE for coming to faith in Christ . . . 'To come to a knowledge' views conversion from the standpoint of the rational decision about the divine message, 'truth,' which it entails."

38. See my comments in Jeon, *True Faith*, 8.

asm—the gospel—which hinges upon Christ's entrance into the world to save sinners and climaxes in the doxology to the King of eternities—the blessed God. Indeed, that the Savior desires all humans "to come" (ἐλθεῖν) recalls Christ Jesus who "came" (ἦλθεν) into the world to save sinners (1:15), thus strengthening the salvific connection between "a knowing-embrace of truth" (2:4b) and "to have-faith" upon Christ (1:16). Furthermore, such would also convey the reciprocal, relational dynamic between the humans whom the Savior God desires to be-saved (2:4) and those who actually will be-saved: Christ Jesus actively "came" into the world to save them; humans, then, are to actively "come" to be-saved, that is, to come to a knowing-embrace of Christ's action to save them (2:4). The "truth," then, stands in antithetical relationship to the different teaching of "some"—of whom are Hymenaeus and Alexander (1:20).[39] The term further reflects Paul's assessment of the gospel—that it is the truth of God, which God commanded Paul to preserve, and thus why Paul was counted-faithful with the sound teaching (1:1). This, in turn, challenges the audience to consider whether they align themselves with God's gospel—the truth—or whether they give themselves over to untruth—the false teaching. In sum, the microchiastic progression in the B element not only highlights that salvation is "a knowing-embrace of truth" but also that salvation is an embrace of a person, namely Christ Jesus (1:15), and thus his very own personally chosen representative Paul (1:1)—the apostle who initially taught the saving truth to the Ephesian church at least ten years prior when he established the church.[40]

1 Timothy 2:5a: For There Is One God

(C Element)

The C element (2:5a) forms the first half of the pivot in the second microchiasm: "For there is one God." Here, Paul broadly provides an explanation for the preceding verses, but particularly the conjuction "For" (γάρ) marks the basis for the immediately preceeding 2:4 verse. In effect, the audience understand that the reason for the Savior God's desire for all humans to be-saved and to come to a knowing-embrace of truth (2:4) is because "there is one God" (2:5a). Indeed, Paul's obvious shift in language from "all (πάντας) humans" (2:4) to "one (εἷς) God" (2:5a) rhetorically underscores the direct connection between the salvation of humans and the desire of the "one God

---

39. Marshall, *PE*, 428: "the phrase implies the need to commit oneself to the traditional gospel and reject competing messages."

40. See discussion in chapter 1.

(θεός)" (2:5a) who is the "Savior God (θεοῦ)" (2:3). At the same time, the audience hear a movement from Paul's universal, inclusive language—"all humans" (2:4)—to particular, exclusive language—"one God" (2:5a). In other words, the salvation of "all humans" (2:4) is only available through the "one God" (2:5a). The exclusive claim that "there is one (εἷς) God (θεός)" is likely Paul's abbreviation of the *Shema* found in LXX Deuteronomy 6:4: "the Lord, our God (θεὸς), the Lord is one (εἷς)."[41] In LXX Deuteronomy 6:4 and elsewhere in Jewish literature, the statement subverts the belief in many gods.[42] In its immediate context within the second microchiasm of the 1 Timothy letter, however, Paul's declaration would be understood specifically in regard to salvation, namely the inclusive scope thereof—"our Savior God . . . desires all humans to be-saved" (2:3–4a)—yet the exclusive means thereof—"there is one God" (2:5a). In sum, then, the audience hear the C element less as a response to polytheism and more as a direct explanation for Paul's insistence that humans must come to a knowing-embrace of the very basic truth: because there is one God, all humans can be-saved by him.[43]

1 Timothy 2:5b–6: There Is One Mediator, Christ Jesus

(C' Element)

In the C' element (2:5b–6), Paul continues his explanation of the truth that the Savior God desires all humans to be-saved: "and there is one mediator of God and humans, the human Christ Jesus" (2:5b). The immediate repetition of the exclusive term "one" (εἷς) here in 2:5b of the C' element recalls that "there is one (εἷς) God" in 2:5a of the parallel C element. The rhetorical effect of the parallelism conveys an inseparable connection, the sense being: "one God, one mediator." Moreover, the conjunction "and" (καί) furthers and intensifies the connection between Paul's statements in pivotal C and C' elements. In other words, where the conjunction "For" (γάρ, 2:5a) marked the basis for the preceeding 2:4 verse, the full, integrated reason for the Savior God's desire for all humans to be-saved and to come to a knowing-embrace of truth (2:4) is because "there is one God, and there is one mediator of God

---

41. See Wall, "Empire," 16; Belleville, "1 Timothy," 47.

42. See Dalbert, *Die Theologie der hellenistisch-jüdischen Missions-Literatur*, 124–30.

43. Hutson captures the logic of Paul's statement: "Such a blunt assertion of monotheism [the *Shema*] pushes in the direction of God's universal concern for all peoples, because if there is only one God, then that God is the creator of all peoples and interested in their welfare" ("Ecclesiology," 166). Ho, "Mission in the PE," 251: "God's will to save people is theologically rooted in the truth that 'there is one God . . .'"

and humans, the human Christ Jesus" (2:5a–b). Thus where the inclusive scope of salvation for "all humans" (2:4) was exclusively linked to the "one God" (2:5a), so too is salvation directly and only possible through the "one mediator of God and humans, the human Christ Jesus" (2:5b).[44] In short, the exclusive claim that there is one God becomes even more exclusive: instead of there being "one God" and many—or *all*—ways to for "humans to be-saved" by this God, the apostle asserts there is only *one* way for "all humans to be-saved" by this "one God," that is, through the "one mediator of God and humans."[45] To be sure, Paul's statement regarding the exclusive means of salvation is not merely propositional but personal—the "one mediator" is "human," and he has a name, "Christ Jesus" (2:5b).

Still, given the situation in the Ephesian church wherein "some . . . teach-different" (1:3), that is, "some-thing different" that lies-opposed to "the sound teaching" with which Paul was divinely counted-faithful (1:10b–11), it would be evident to the Ephesian audience, then, that the exclusive claims regarding the salvation of all humans in the C and C' elements—"one God (θεός) . . . and one mediator . . . Christ Jesus (Χριστὸς Ἰησοῦς)" (2:5a–b)—are exclusively linked to Paul, who is not only an apostle of the one mediator "Christ Jesus" (Χριστοῦ Ἰησοῦ, 1:1) but is an apostle "according to the command of God (θεοῦ) our Savior and Christ Jesus (Χριστοῦ Ἰησοῦ) our hope" (1:1). In short, "some" who teach-different than Paul (1:3, 10b)—the false teachers in the Ephesian church—are not legitimate venues for knowing the one mediator Christ Jesus whom Paul represents (1:1) and thus are not legitimate teachers regarding the one way that all humans can be-saved by the one God (2:4–5). Paul's assertion, therefore, would have been uniquely unsettling not only for "some" but also for anyone in the church who was aligned with "some"—their salvation was unmistakably in danger.

---

44. Given the widespread Greco-Roman belief both in many gods and many ways to intercede with these gods, such an assertion would certainly remind the Ephesian audience—who were likely once Artemis worshipers (see chapter 1)—that their salvation is secure only through "the mediator of God and humans . . . Christ Jesus" (2:5b).

45. Ho, "Mission in the PE," 251: "though salvation is universally accessible, it can only be appropriated by the one redemptive act of Christ Jesus, God's chosen mediator between him and sinful humanity." Belleville, "Christology, Greco-Roman," 234: "There is 'one God' and 'one mediator' who mediates between a singular divinity (εἷς θεός) and a plural humanity (ἀνθρώπων) . . . while the target audience is universal, the means is not. The route to redemption is wholly exclusive . . . the role of mediator between God and humans is uniquely Christ's." Long, *1 & 2 Timothy*, 66: "The bridge to God is Christ and Christ alone." See Witherington, *Letters*, 217; Belleville, "1 Timothy," 47; Marshall, *PE*, 429.

Within Greco-Roman culture, the term "mediator" (μεσίτης) referred to a broker between two legal or commercial parties;[46] non-Jewish Ephesian converts might have leaned toward this understanding, but Paul's use of it derives more likely from the OT.[47] The term appears only once in the LXX and is found in Job 9:33.[48] This is important for understanding the effect that Paul intended for his audience. The overall context of Job's cry for a mediator (9:1–35) is due to his inability to stand before God. Specifically for Job, he sees the unscalable partition between divinity and humanity: "For [God] is not a human (ἄνθρωπος) as I, that I might answer him, that we might come together for trial" (9:32). In other words, the audience are not only to be reminded of Job's situation but also to agree with his assessment: in order to interact with God, everyone—all humans—needs a mediator.[49] That is, without a mediator, all humans cannot naturally relate with the one God. What is more, the fact of this desperate condition reaches utter hopelessness when Job concludes, "There is no mediator (μεσίτης) between us, who might lay his hand on us both" (9:33 *ESV*).[50] Clearly, where a mediator is required yet none exists, the audience along with Job would have an indisputable reason to despair. Yet, as if in direct response to Job, Paul affirms the indisputable reason to rejoice: yes, "there is one mediator." The dire situation is no longer impossible; a mediator exists for all who need one. Thus for Paul's believing audience, there seems to be a movement in the second microchiasm to not only come to a knowing-embrace of truth through action—prayer and godliness—but also through active reflection—the profundity that they indeed have a mediator.

That the mediator is identified as "the *human* Christ Jesus" is intriguing. In the first microchiasm, the divinity of Christ Jesus was implied—if

---

46. Marshall, *PE*, 429–30: it "is a Hellenistic term . . . found in diplomatic, legal and commercial language . . . The basic sense is of a person who facilitates a transaction of some sort between two parties." See Belleville, "Christology, Greco-Roman," 233. For further discussion, see Gill, *Jesus as Mediator*, 112–20.

47. The relatively mature age of the church in Ephesus (see chapter 1) recommends that the non-Jewish converts in the audience were not unaware of the OT. Presumably, where Paul alludes to the OT, he expected his audience to be familiar with it.

48. Stout, *The "Man Christ Jesus,"* 20: "Actually, it seems quite likely that Paul does in fact have in mind here the only LXX appearance of *mesítes* (μεσίτης), found in Job's complaint about God." Not a few commentators disagree about the relationship between 1 Timothy 2:5 and LXX Job 9:33. For a sample of discussions, see Hanson, *Studies in the PE*, 57–58; Twomey, *PE Through the Centuries*, 37; Towner, *1-2 Timothy*, 66 n. 2:5; Wieland, *Signifance of Salvation*, 256–57.

49. Barclay, *1 & 2 Timothy*, 82: "they [all people] must recognize that this rupture exists, that they . . . need a mediator."

50. *ESV*: "There is no arbiter"; the term "mediator" is my translation according to the LXX.

not asserted—in the parallel A and A' elements (1:1–2, 11–17).⁵¹ Yet here in the second microchiasm, the apostle declares that this same Christ Jesus is a "human" (2:5b). Thus whereas the one God and all humans need a mediator to relate them, the progression of the macrochiasm articulates Christ Jesus's unique ability to stand as the one mediator: he is both God and a human.⁵² What is more, with the movement of the high Christology within the first microchiasm into the second microchiasm, the fact that "there is one God" in the C element takes on a christological nuance in the parallel C' element: in order for humans to relate with God, the one God came into the world to relate as a human, namely "the human Christ Jesus" (2:5b). In effect, Job's predicament—"For [God] is not a human (ἄνθρωπος) as I" (Job 9:32)—is perfectly resolved: with the coming of Christ Jesus into the world as the "one mediator," it is God taking for himself a human nature, removing the unscalable partition between divinity and humanity. For Paul's audience, an updated statement by Job may be heard to the effect of: "For Christ Jesus is God, and also a human, as I am. There is a mediator."

The progression of the overall macrochiasm not only enhances the audience's understanding of Christ but also of Paul. At the beginning of the letter (1:1–2) in A element of the first microchiasm, the rapid-fire triple repetition of "Christ Jesus" (Χριστοῦ Ἰησοῦ) established that this person was the foundation of everything that his apostle Paul was to say—such was clearly affirmed by the fourfold repetition of "Christ Jesus" in the parallel A' element. Here is the second microchiasm, Paul underscores exactly why "Christ Jesus" (Χριστὸς Ἰησοῦς) is the foundation not only for Paul but for all. That is, Paul is not merely concerned with the exclusive claim that there is "one mediator" but rather with a far more exclusive claim, effectively reducing all possibilies to only one person: "Christ Jesus." Thus Paul has channeled everything into the person of Christ Jesus: in order to get to the "one God," all humans are required to have-faith upon him (1:16) and thus go through him as their mediator (2:5b). There is no other way nor any other person. As a corollary, then, the macrochiastic polemic against the false teachers is further accentuated, and the charge to preserve Paul's true teaching is advanced. That is, where the second microchiasm declares that the reception of salvation by all humans from the one God specifically requires the mediator Christ Jesus, the significance of Paul's authority in the first microchiasm comes more clearly into view: he is the very apostle of this

---

51. See chapter 3.

52. Barcley, *1 & 2 Timothy*, 82: "the focus on Christ's humanity . . . indicates that Christ identifies with sinful humanity. As both God and man, he is the only effective mediator to bring reconciliation to these estranged parties."

one and only mediator (1:1). Only the sound teaching of Paul (1:10b)—not the different teaching of "some" (1:3, 10b)—has saving implications.

In 2:5b of the C' element, the audience hear Paul draw special attention to the humanity of Christ Jesus in relation to other humans. The rhetorical juxtaposition and word order of "humans, the human Christ Jesus (ἀνθρώπων, ἄνθρωπος Χριστὸς Ἰησοῦς)" would not go unnoticed. Without a doubt, Paul is emphasizing that Christ was in fact fully human.[53] Furthermore, this recalls the prior occurrences in the A element where the apostle exhorts prayers on behalf of all "humans" (ἀνθρώπων, 2:1) and also declares that God's desire is on behalf of all "humans" (ἀνθρώπων, 2:4a) to be-saved. Two things are to be heard by these connections. First, Paul appears to be underscoring the fact that humans can be-saved because their mediator became a human in complete solidarity with them.[54] To be sure, humanity's salvation was accomplished by a human.[55] At the same time, Paul in the flow of the macrochiasm seems to be underscoring that salvation was also accomplished by a human who was not always such, for "Christ Jesus *came into the world* to save sinners" (1:15). The audience are to understand the nuance: "the human, Christ Jesus" (2:5b) came to save sinners because

---

53. Long, *1 & 2 Timothy*, 66: "This emphasis on the humanity of Jesus is not a reflection of a low Christology but instead a trumpeting of the incarnation . . . Jesus was no spiritual gas, no mystical presence floating above time and circumstance; he was flesh and blood." Belleville, "Christology, Greco-Roman," 233: "the lack of an article with the noun ἄνθώπος places the stress not on a definite person ('the man') but on the humanity of Christ—'himself human' . . . It is as ἄνθώπος, however, that Christ fully identifies with all people; it is through a shared versus representative humanity that God seeks to save all people"

54. See discussions in Kelly, *PE*, 63; Towner, *Goal*, 55; Barcley, *1 & 2 Timothy*, 82. Not a few scholars suggest that Christ's humanity here is a representative function for all humanity. E.g., Stout, *The "Man Christ Jesus,"* 39: "The echo of Adam lingering in the context of 1 Timothy 2 [see verses 13–14] indicates that Paul relies on the OT to establish his understanding of Jesus as the 'Man' (in Hebrew, *adam* = 'man') in a singular, covenantal sense, especially since the designation in 1 Tim 2:5, ἄνθρωπος Χριστὸς Ἰησοῦς ('Man Christ Jesus'), is unique in biblical literature and quite unusual as a description of any individual." Conversely, Marshall (*PE*, 431) concludes that "the Christ-Adam analogy . . . is missing here." At the very least, the movement of the microchiasm from "all" to "one" may recommend that (inclusively) all humans have the opportunity to be represented to God (exclusively) by one mediator, the human Christ Jesus.

55. In passing it may be worth noting that the accent of Jesus's humanity—"the human (ἄνθρωπος) Christ Jesus"—here in the context of salvation seems to highlight LXX Isaiah 19:20b: "And the Lord shall send them a man (ἄνθρωπον) who shall save them; he shall judge and save them." In Isaiah 19:20b, the promise pertains not only to Israel but to all nations. Thus where the connection to 1 Timothy 2:6 is intentional, Paul is likely both implying that Christ is the fulfillment and corroborating the universal thrust of this microchiasm.

he is the "Savior God, who desires all human to be-saved" (2:3b–4a). Thus humanity's salvation was also accomplished by God.

From here, the C' element goes on in 2:6 to elaborate that Christ Jesus "gave (δούς) himself as a ransom (ἀντίλυτρον) on behalf of all." The audience would hear clear echoes of Jesus's own declaration: "For also the Son of Man came not to be-served but to serve and to give (δοῦναι) his life as a ransom (λύτρον ἀντί) of many" (Mark 10:45; see Matt 20:28).[56] The statement in 2:6 is full of meaning. That Christ "gave himself" (δοὺς ἑαυτόν) underscores his own willingness to do so: his self-sacrifice was according to his volition. Also, that his self-sacrifice is to be understood in terms of a "ransom" (ἀντίλυτρον) conveys that his death was both a payment and substitution, namely as the means through which freedom was acquired "on behalf of all" who were imprisoned (2:6).[57] Where "the human Christ Jesus . . . gave himself as a ransom," the payment price equates to the substitution of one human life for another—the life of "one mediator on behalf of all" (2:5b–6). To be sure, Christ's death on the cross is in view, and with the movement of the first microchiasm to the second, the audience are to understand that "Christ Jesus came into the world to save sinners" (1:15) by dying on their behalf (2:6).[58] Moreover, given this connection, the audience

---

56. For more extensive analysis on Paul's apparent use of Mark 10:45, see Towner, *Letters*, 183–84; Knight, *PE*, 121–23; Marshall, *PE*, 431–32.

Paul's reference to Mark and Matthew's Gospels seems to indicate that his Ephesian audience were familiar with Jesus's statement. Proposed dates for manuscript composition leave the possibility open that the Ephesian church were exposed to the written narratives. However, presumably the oral tradition—which preceded their composition—was at least made known to them by Paul. For a timeline of manuscript composition, see Carson and Moo, who suggest: Mark, late fifties or sixties; Matthew, prior to seventy; 1 Timothy, mid-sixties (*Introduction*, 182, 156, 572, respectively).

Paul's statement here in 1 Timothy 2:6 would also have clear echoes to another letter he wrote to the Ephesian church:

1 Tim 2:5–6: "Christ Jesus, who (Χριστὸς Ἰησοῦς, ὁ) gave himself (δοὺς ἑαυτόν) as a ransom on behalf of (ὑπέρ) all";

Eph 5:25: "Christ (ὁ Χριστός) loved the church and gave himself (ἑαυτὸν παρέδωκεν) on behalf of (ὑπέρ) her."

57. Knight, *PE*, 121: "ἀντίλυτρον represents a price paid to free captives and thus means ransom." Belleville, "1 Timothy," 47: "The backdrop is Greco-Roman economics. 'Ransom' was the stipulated price to set captives free—whether they were prisoners of war or slaves." Morris, *Apostolic Preaching*, 48: "In meaning it does not seem to differ from the simple λύτρον, but the preposition [ἀντί] emphasizes the thought of substitution; it is a 'substitute-ransom' that is signified." For further analysis on the substitutionary use of the preposition ἀντί, see Davies, "Christ in Our Place," 72–81. See also Edwards, "Reading the Ransom Logion in 1 Tim 2,6," 264–66.

58. Davies, "Christ in Our Place," 72–73: "The normal meaning of ἀντί is 'instead of', or 'in exchange for', and so this passage appears to teach that the purpose of Jesus' coming into the world was to give up His life, *i.e.* to die . . . and that this would be

understand that the imprisonment from which Christ saves sinners by giving his himself as a ransom (1:15; 2:6) must have in view the consequences of sin—the just judgment of the law upon those for whom the law is laid, namely sinners (1:8–10).[59] The freedom acquired by the "ransom," then, is multifaceted. It is freedom from the commendable law, which when used lawfully executes just judgment upon humans who are "without-law and without-obedience" (1:8–9a). At the same time, it equates to entering into an entirely new standing before the law: they are now "the just" for whom "the law is not laid" (1:9), that is, they are now Christians—those in the first microchiasm whose existence is "in faith" (1:2, 4) and "in Christ Jesus" (1:14).[60] Such freedom, therefore, is entirely defined by sinners's relation to the "one mediator of God and humans, the human Christ Jesus, who gave himself as a ransom" (2:5b–6)—it equates to standing in relation to a new authority, namely "Christ Jesus our Lord" (1:2, 12; cf. 1:14). The audience are thus to understand "ransom" as a simultaneous release from one realm of existence—"in unfaithfulness" (1:13)—and entrance into another, the realm "in Christ Jesus" (1:14)—"in faith" (1:2, 4).

The second half of Paul's declaration in 2:6 of the C' element—"on behalf of all"—is no less significant than the first. It punctuates the flow of the second microchiasm and brings to the fore several aspects of Christ's self-sacrifice. First, that Christ Jesus gave himself as a ransom "on behalf" (ὑπέρ) of all underscores the substitutionary quality of Christ's ransom payment, his death.[61] The death that he died was as a human and in their place. Second, given that "ransom" connotes freedom from sin, his ransom "on behalf" of all is to be understood as a substitution for sinners, namely those like Paul, who was formerly a blasphemer, living "in unfaithfulness," and liable to God's just judgment according to the commendable

---

accepted as the ransom price in the place of, and in exchange for, the lives of others."

59. The audience may also infer that Christ's ransom frees sinners from the power and authority of Satan in their lives (cf. 1:20).

60. Where freedom from Satan's power and authority is inferred, those for whom Christ gave himself as a ransom would also have a new standing in relation to Satan.

61. The connotation regarding "on behalf" (ὑπέρ) is debated. In favor of substitution, see Belleville, "1 Timothy," 48; Davies, "Christ in Our Place," 89–90; Patterson and Kelley, "1 Timothy," 662. In favor of representation, see Marshall, PE, 432; Knight, PE, 122. Arguments on both sides are compelling, yet Gaffin's comments seem to be especially helpful: "Christ's death is 'for' (ὑπέρ) others . . . Christ may be said to be the representative of those in union with him, but he is more than that . . . Particularly in his death, his representative role has an aspect . . . that is not adequately termed other than 'substitutionary' . . . we must account for both the exclusive or strictly substitutionary and the inclusive or representative aspects" ("Atonement in the Pauline Corpus," 144–45). Along with Gaffin, my translation intends both.

law. Here, then, it is emphasized to the audience that Christ Jesus as "mediator" is not merely a person who seeks to arbitrate between two parties. Rather, he directly acts "on behalf" of one of the parties—"all" sinners, humans—by giving himself as a ransom payment to the other party—the "one God" (2:5a). Like Moses who beseeched God on behalf of Israel, "But now, if you will forgive their sin—but if not, please blot me out of your book that you have written" (Exod 32:32 ESV), Christ surrenders his life for the sake of such sinners.

Finally, Paul makes clear that the ransom payment by Christ—his sacrificial death—is available to "all." Given its general placement in the second microchiasm, "all" (πάντων) in 2:6 is an obvious reference to "all humans" (πάντων ἀνθρώπων, 2:1; πάντας ἀνθρώπους, 2:4), which is further highlighted by its immediate placement after "humans, the human" (ἀνθρώπων, ἄνθρωπος, 2:5) within the C' element. This, of course, includes even those who are currently excluded from the realm "in faith"—both those "without-knowing . . . in unfaithfulness" (1:13) and "some" who "regarding the faith have become-shipwrecked" (1:19b). Indeed, where "Christ Jesus . . . gave himself as a ransom on behalf of all (πάντων)" in 2:6 echoes the phrase "Christ Jesus might display all (ἅπασαν) patience" in 1:16, the audience understand that Paul himself is the prime example of the application of Christ's activity: Christ inclusively "gave himself on behalf of all"—even on behalf of a blasphemer, persecutor, and hubristic-person (1:13) who directly persecuted Christ himself (Acts 9:4–5). Significantly, then, the inclusive scope of the Savior God's desire for "all (πάντας) humans to be-saved" (2:3–4a) is specifically defined and demonstrated by the act in which Christ Jesus "gave himself as a ransom on behalf of all (πάντων)" (2:6). In this way, the audience fully understand how the collaborative desire and activity of God and Christ Jesus (2:3–6) inform Paul's initial exhortation to the Ephesian church (2:1–2). That is, the dual fact that God desires "all humans (πάντας ἀνθρώπους) to be-saved" (2:4a) and that the "mediator of God and humans (ἀνθρώπων), the human (ἄνθρωπος) Christ Jesus . . . gave himself as a ransom on behalf of all (ὑπὲρ πάντων)" (2:5b–6) provides the entire basis to pray "on behalf of all humans" (ὑπὲρ πάντων ἀνθρώπων)" as the "first," lead activity of the church.[62] As the only mediator of God and humans, Christ Jesus has made salvation possible for all humans (2:4–6); such is the reason why those who have already been saved by Christ are to salvifically pray that all humans would-inevitably-come to have-faith upon

---

62. Long, *1 & 2 Timothy*, 67: "'*who gave himself a ransom for all*'—The emphasis here falls on the phrase 'for all,' which connects this christological claim with the earlier exhortation to pray for 'everyone.'" See Knight, *PE*, 122.

Christ (1:16; 2:1).[63] In short, the audience are to pray for the possibility of salvation for all humans to become a reality for all humans. Moreover, for the audience to maintain any arbitrary elitism and exclusivism toward any person at all—especially toward the false teachers who are opposing Paul and the gospel—contradicts the logical outworking of Christ's own work. Rather, in order to pray for "all" (2:1), the audience are exhorted to pray all the more for the salvation of "some" among them, by name, Hymenaeus and Alexander (1:20). Thus the interconnectivity of the final verse of the first microchiasm (1:20) with the first verse of the second microchiasm (2:1) is yet again heard by the audience, further reinforcing the function and impact of the transitional words (1:20; 2:1).

Verse 2:6 of the C' element concludes with the comment, "the testimony at his own times." Although the *grammatical* relation to the preceding clause is somewhat unclear due to the asyndeton,[64] the *meaning* of the phrase itself is clear due to the consistent progression of the macrochiasm thus far. The term "testimony" (μαρτύριον) refers to a proof and can carry both a subjective sense—one's own actions as proof—and an objective sense—proving another's actions.[65] Both are certainly present here. The advancement of the person "Christ Jesus" (Χριστοῦ Ἰησοῦ, 1:1–2) from the beginning of the first microchiasm to this point in the second microchiasm has provided the underlying context for the entire letter. The audience are thus to understand that Christ's personal entrance into the world—his personal activity in history to bless Paul (1:12–14), to patiently save sinners (1:15–16), and to give himself as a ransom (2:6)—is the "testimony" (μαρτύριον). Still, the emphasis on Paul's appointment as an "apostle of Christ Jesus" (ἀπόστολος Χριστοῦ Ἰησοῦ, 1:1; cf. 1:12) has also advanced through the first and second microchiasms to denote "the sound teaching" (1:10) that "Christ Jesus came into the world to save sinners" (1:15) by giving "himself as a ransom" (2:6). Thus both Christ's activity to save and Paul's duty to preserve the teaching concerning Christ's activity—not one or the other—are equally bound within the "testimony." As a corollary, the polemic against the false teachers who oppose Paul's teaching in the first microchiasm is certainly present

---

63. Rather than an immediate universal salvation for all humans, the emphasis of Christ Jesus's ransom in 2:6 is the universal offer for all humans to be-saved by Christ Jesus's sacrificial action. Such was evident from Paul's statements in the first microchiasm, namely that Christ Jesus came into the world to save sinners (1:16), and, to be sure, sinners are saved when they come to have-faith upon him for life eternal (1:16). For further discussion, see Schreiner, *Paul*, 182–86.

64. For various interpretations, see Dibelius and Conzelmann, *PE*, 43; Kelly, *PE*, 64; Guthrie, *PE*, 72–73.

65. See Couser, "'Testimony About the Lord,'" 296–98; Belleville, "1 Timothy," 48; Collins, *1 & 2 Timothy*, 198.

here: to reject Paul's "testimony" is certainly to reject Christ's "testimony." Such a connection between Christ and Paul and the resulting polemic against the false teachers was also the case for "the gospel" in 1:11 of the first microchiasm, which was concerned both with God's own self-disclosure of his radiant glory and the fact that Paul "was counted-faithful" to preserve it. In short, the movement of the macrochiasm has progressed "the gospel," likely to include "the testimony."[66]

Paul also states that the testimony is "at his own times" (καιροῖς ἰδίοις)—"his" referring to God. The emphasis here is on the sovereignty of God's plan of salvation in relation to Christ—that the testimony is given according to God's will and timing—"at his own times."[67] Where the testimony implies both Christ's entrance into the world and Paul's sound teaching thereof, the notion of sovereignty is extended not only to God's decision as to when Christ would come to give himself as a ransom (1:15) but also to Paul's appointment to teach about Christ (1:1, 12).[68] As the C' element of the second microchiasm comes to a close, the thrust of the overall macrochiasm continues: the audience are to cling to "the testimony" of God that focuses on the person and work of Christ Jesus, not to "some-thing different" that concentrates on myths and genealogies without-limit and thus lies-opposed to the sound teaching, the gospel (1:4a, 10b–11a).[69]

---

66. The apparent association (uniqueness of the article τό) between τὸ εὐαγγέλιον ("the gospel") and τὸ μαρτύριον ("the testimony") may be worth noting. For further analysis on the relation of εὐαγγέλιον and μαρτύριον, see Couser, "'Testimony About the Lord,'" 297–306.

67. Couser, "Sovereign Savior," 119: "Paul further connects the work of Christ with God by specifying that this 'testimony' of Christ, this self-giving ransom for *all*, occurred at 'God's own right time' (καροῖς ἰδίοις)." Marshall, *PE*, 432–33: "καιροῖς ἰδίοις functions here . . . to underline the fact that the time in view is the time appropriate in God's plan for 'the testimony' . . . a development in God's redemptive history." For further discussion regarding the plural use of "time" (καιροῖς) in 1 Timothy 2:6, see Knight, *PE*, 123–24.

68. Couser, "Sovereign Savior," 133: "the gospel and its proclamation are made manifest at God's own right time (καίροις ἰδίοις)."

69. Long captures the contrast well: "The gospel is not the private narrative of some local Roman deity nor is it the abstract answer to some mystical spiritual puzzle. It is a public event, performed by the human Jesus—visible, embodied, historical, and universal" (*1 & 2 Timothy*, 67).

1 Timothy 2:7: I-Myself Was Appointed Proclaimer, Apostle, Teacher

(B' Element)

In the B' element of the second microchiasm, Paul reiterates his unique authority: "To this I-myself was appointed" (2:7). The phrase "To this" (εἰς ὅ) relates directly to "the testimony" in 2:6b of the C' element. The obvious aural similarity between εἰς ("To," 2:7) of the B' element and εἰς ("one," 2:5a) and εἰς ("one," 2:5b) of the C and C' elements would be heard by the audience, strengthening the connection to what was said immediately prior while also advancing the flow of the microchiasm. The first person pronoun "I-myself" (ἐγώ) clearly recalls Paul's declarations in the first microchiasm: "I-myself (ἐγώ) was counted-faithful" (1:11); "I-myself (ἐγώ) am the first" of sinners (1:15).[70] As the third time that the audience have heard Paul say "I-myself" (2:7), the emphasis would no doubt invite their attention to Paul's personal statement. Furthermore, the passive verb "was appointed" (ἐτέθην) here in the second microchiasm recalls Paul's use of the verb in the first microchiasm regarding the activity of Christ Jesus who considered Paul faithful, "appointing" (θέμενος) him for service (1:12). This not only further strengthens the sustained flow and development of the macrochiasm but also reiterates that Paul's authoritative place in the history of salvation is ordained by the direct activity of God (1:11) and Christ Jesus (1:12).[71] The emerging pattern in the letter is that any explicit mention of the gospel (1:11) or any outline of its content (1:15; 2:6) is immediately followed up with an emphatic statement of Paul's credentials.[72] In effect, the audience's acceptance of Christ is demonstrated by their acceptance of Paul; their compliance with Paul's authoritative teaching and instructions represents a consistent response to his divine calling.

Paul's credentials in the B' element are listed as a triplet: "proclaimer and apostle . . . teacher" (2:7). This certainly echoes Paul's earlier triplet in the first microchiasm, referring to his former life "in unfaithfulness" wherein he was "a blasphemer and a persecutor and a hubristic-person" (1:13).[73] The contrast is obvious, not only highlighting the developmental

---

70. As in 1:11 and 1:15, the inclusion of the first-person pronoun "I" (ἐγώ) is grammatically unnecessary and, therefore, intentional. The translation "I-myself" captures the nuance.

71. Couser, "Sovereign Savior," 120: "Paul has been appointed by God (noting the divine passive, ἐτέθην)."

72. See Knight, *PE*, 124.

73. See Witherington, *Letters*, 217.

flow of the macrochiasm but also advancing the basic implication of the gospel: if Paul was granted-mercy and came to faith, then anyone can (1:16) because the Savior God desires all to be-saved (2:3–4a). The triplet in 2:7 therefore points to an outworking of Christ's ransom payment in 2:6 and a movement in the letter.

Beginning with "proclaimer" (κῆρυξ), in 2:7 of the C' element Paul makes clear that his appointment is to publically announce the testimony concerning Christ Jesus in 2:6 of the B' element.[74] Given Paul's concern to underscore his apostolic authority throughout the first microchiasm (1:1, 11, 12), it may seem somewhat surprising that Paul mentions "proclaimer" prior to "apostle" (ἀπόστολος). Yet, the sense likely rests in the cumulative sequence of both terms: the testimony in 2:6 has been proclaimed—not by anyone ordinary—but by the authorized apostle himself. Furthermore, by stating that he was appointed as an apostle to proclaim "the testimony" of 2:6, the audience would likely hear a missional overtone—the testimony being that Christ "gave himself as a ransom on behalf of *all*." That is, the audience are to understand that Paul's proclamation as an apostle is directly related to the Savior God's desire for "*all* humans to be-saved" (2:4a). Not only, then, are the earlier connotations of the second microchiasm propelled forward but also Paul's apostleship from the first microchiasm is now qualified with a missional purpose toward "all."

The next phrase the audience hear is "the truth I am saying, I am not falsifying." By itself, there is ambiguity. On the one hand, if the statement pertains to what precedes it, it could be understood as a defense of his apostleship. In this case, it seems that Paul is intimidating the false teachers: because he is, in fact, an apostle according to the command of God, the truth will prevail against those who oppose him—the sense being, "I will fight for the truth until my last breath."[75] On the other hand, the statement could be taken with what follows, namely Paul's credentials as a "teacher."[76]

---

74. Ibid.: "A herald [κῆρυξ] in a city such as Ephesus was a person who announced public auctions and sales, new taxes, the manumission of slaves, the beginning of public games, the order of kings, and the onset of religious ceremonies ... The basic task of the herald was to publicly announce something to people who had not yet heard the news." Barcley, *1 & 2 Timothy*, 83: "one who proclaims a message." See Marshall's comments (*PE*, 434).

75. Barcley, *1 & 2 Timothy*, 84: "In the Western world today, such an oath would raise much suspicions ... But in Roman legal practice in Paul's day, swearing such an oath was an indication that a person was willing to back up his assertions in court. This statement puts Paul's opponents on notice that he is not prepared to back down from his claim to apostleship, and he can provide the proof to support it."

76. See Fee, *1 & 2 Timothy*, 67; Roloff, *Der Erste Brief an Timotheus*, 112; Marshall, *PE*, 434.

Hearing Paul's statement in this way would likely be a polemic against the false teachers.[77] Still, another interpretation is possible when hearing the overall flow of the microchiasm and the meaning conveyed in its arrangement. In the B element of the second microchiasm, Paul expressed that it is God's desire for all humans "to come to a knowing-embrace of truth" (ἀληθείας) (2:4b). Paul's parallel declaration in the B' element, "the truth (ἀλήθειαν) I am saying" (2:7), indicates that he, uniquely and authoritatively, is the human means through which all humans come to a knowing-embrace of truth. The implication for the audience is significant: to not embrace Paul's speech as "truth" is to not "come to a knowing-embrace of truth" at all. What is more, given that "a knowing-embrace of truth" in the B element denoted "to be-saved" in the A element, for anyone in the audience to think that Paul is "falsifying" denotes that such a person is not saved. Because Paul says the "truth," the further implication is that his opponents do not; rather they are the ones who are "falsifying" (ψεύδομαι). Also worth noting, the verb "saying" (λέγω) in 2:7 of the second microchiasm recalls its earlier cognate "word" (λόγος) in 1:15 of the first microchiasm. That is, where the "word . . . [is] worthy of all acceptance" (1:15), the audience are to equally hear that what Paul is "saying" is worthy of all acceptance. The cascading effect of the macrochiastic progression thus emphasizes for the audience not only the validity of Paul's apostleship but also the content thereof: Paul's testimony that Christ Jesus came to save sinners (1:15) by mediatorially giving himself as a ransom for all (2:5b–6) is the truth (2:7), that is, the truth that saves humans (2:4a–b).

To conclude the B' element, Paul mentions his third credential: "a teacher of the Gentiles." In the immediate context of Paul's other credentials—namely his missional, apostolic authority based on truth—the term "teacher" (διδάσκαλος) would recall "the sound teaching (διδασκαλίᾳ)" in 1:10 of the first microchiasm. It is thus explicit: Paul is the "teacher" (διδάσκαλος) of "the sound teaching (διδασκαλίᾳ)" (1:10b). Moreover, then, where "the sound teaching" referred to "the gospel" (1:10–11a), the audience understand that Paul is, in effect, the "gospel-teacher." What is more, as much as "the sound teaching" and the gospel are "of God" (1:11a), Paul equally underscores that he "was appointed . . . teacher" (2:7); that is, Paul was passive in the divine activity of God to appoint him as a "teacher" of "the sound teaching." Still, Paul's designation as "teacher" is not merely affirmational; rather it is simultaneously polemical. The term "teacher" (διδάσκαλος) in 2:7 of the second microchiasm recalls "some" who "teach-different" (ἑτεροδιδασκαλεῖν, 1:3) and who are desiring to be "law-teachers" (νομοδιδάσκαλοι, 1:7) in the first

---

77. See Belleville, "Christology, Greco-Roman," 234.

microchiasm. In other words, while "some" teach "some-thing different" that "lies-opposed to the sound teaching ... the gospel" (1:10b–11a) and do so while "not understanding either what they-are-saying or regarding some-things they-are-insisting" (1:7), the proclaimer and apostle Paul was appointed as a "teacher" (2:7) of "the sound teaching" that "some" oppose (1:10b). By way of contrast, Paul's rhetorical use of "teacher" in the second microchiasm advances what the audience heard in the first microchiasm: to be sure, the false teachers—"some"—are not gospel-teachers. Indeed, unlike Paul, they are not divinely appointed.

The qualification that Paul is a teacher "of the Gentiles" deserves attention. "Gentiles" (ἐθνῶν) refers to non-Jewish people;[78] the term would certainly resonate with Paul's Ephesian audience, many if not most of whom were Gentiles who had come to have-faith upon Christ as a result of Paul's missionary journey at least ten years prior.[79] On the one hand, the phrase "teacher of the Gentiles" would remind Paul's audience that their salvation is directly attributed to him—such would be a call to loyalty and gratitude. On the other hand, that Paul is "teacher of the Gentiles" in the context of being an "apostle" would remind his audience that their allegiance to his authority is not merely appreciative but is required.[80] More than likely, Paul's statement "teacher of the Gentiles (ἐθνῶν)" had in view Jesus's own stated purpose for appointing Paul for service: "he [Paul] is to me a chosen vessel to bear my name in the sight of the Gentiles (ἐθνῶν) and kings and the sons of Israel" (Acts 9:15). Certainly, then, the audience are reminded that their allegiance to Paul is connected directly to Christ, whom Paul respresents (1:1). Furthermore, the phrase "of the Gentiles" advances the salvific thrust of the microchiasm. God desires "all humans"—not only Jews but also Gentiles—to be-saved (2:4a).[81] Paul's divine appointment as a "teacher of the Gentiles" is therefore an expression of God's desire. In this way, too, "of the Gentiles" emphasizes the missional quality of Paul's appointment as "proclaimer and apostle," which held the specific purpose of authoritatively

---

78. Knight, *PE*, 127: "Plural ἔθνη, which means 'nation' in the singular, is not usually used by Paul to mean 'nations' . . . but rather, and especially when it is anarthrous as here, as the designation for non-Jews, the 'Gentiles.'"

79. See discussion in chapter 1.

80. Marshall, *PE*, 433: "since the Ephesian church came within the orbit of this mission to the Gentiles, such a statement might at the same time contribute to the overall assertion of Paul's apostolic authority in a situation in which it was being challenged."

81. Knight, *PE*, 127: "the ambivalence of ἔθνη as 'Gentiles/heathens' or as 'nations' is significant because the term connotes on either view concern for 'all people.'" Long, *1 & 2 Timothy*, 67: "he [Christ] initiated the saving action as a gift, and his gift was not for some tribe or nation or class of religious elites but for every human being everywhere—for all."

and publically making known the testimony that Christ gave himself as a ransom for "all" (2:6).[82] At the same time, given the sustained polemic against the false teachers, the audience would likely hear Paul's statement "of the Gentiles" not only directed against the different teaching of "some" (1:3, 10b) but also—and more specifically—indicative that their teaching attempted to limit the scope of the gospel.[83]

Paul adds the further qualification "in faith and truth." The phrase "in faith" (ἐν πίστει) recalls its earlier occurrences in the first microchiasm (1:2, 4), referring to the sphere in which a person exists and operates upon receiving God's salvific blessings, namely grace and mercy (1:2, 1:13, 14, 16). That is, although the focus is on Paul's appointment as a "teacher," the specification "in faith" indicates that Paul's life and behavior are equally in view. Such is corroborated by the rhetorical impact of the contrasting triplets (1:13; 2:7), which distinguished two different modes of operation—Paul's movement from formerly being "in unfaithfulness" (1:13) to Paul now being "in faith" (2:7). Moreover, as part of the B' element, the qualification "in . . . truth" (ἀληθείᾳ, 2:7) recalls the parallel B element wherein "a knowing-embrace of truth" (ἀληθείας, 2:4b) was the outworking—the appropriate behavior and conduct—of what it means "to be-saved" (2:4a). Paul is not merely concerned with a cognitive acceptance of the gospel; rather, those actually "in faith" are to pursue a life that accords with the truth of the gospel—the sound teaching. Thus while the prepositional phrase "in faith and truth" may lend to some ambiguity, the structured progression of the overall macrochiasm suggests a clear, integrated message: Paul—unlike "some"—is living faithfully and truthfully in line with his apostolic appointment to proclaim and teach the truth to the Gentiles and all humans.[84] In short, the audience understand that Paul's life conforms to his missional message. Thus at the conclusion of the B' element, Paul pushes forward and ties together the earlier thrust of the microchiasm: in allegiance to his missional appointment as a proclaimer, apostle, and teacher of the Gentiles, and in line with his corresponding lifestyle "in faith and truth," the audience are to live missionally, making the gospel attractive to those who are yet to be-saved.

---

82. Knight, *PE*, 127: "Although ἐθνῶν most evidently goes with διδάσκαλος, the nearest word, it is likely that it qualifies the other two words."

83. See Schreiner, *Paul, Apostle of God's Glory*, 185; Marshall, *PE*, 425–26.

84. A few commentators understand the phrase as a reference to the content of Paul's teaching—that he teaches truth (e.g., Fee, *1 & 2 Timothy*, 67)—while others understand it as an expression of Paul's fidelity to his divine calling—that he ministers as a faithful and true teacher of the Gentiles (e.g., Hanson, *PE*, 70).

1 Timothy 2:8–15: Instructions for the Men and Women[85]

(A' Element)

In the concluding A' element of the second microchiasm (2:8–15), Paul begins: "I want, therefore, men to pray in all place lifting reverent hands without anger and word-quarreling" (2:8). The conjunction "therefore" (οὖν) here in 2:8 of the A' element recalls "therefore" (οὖν) in 2:1 of the parallel A element, clearly indicating for the audience that the two sections are interrelated and frame Paul's discussion. Where the "first," lead activity for the church in the A element was missional prayer and godliness for the salvation of all humans (2:1–4), the audience are thus to hear the A' element as having the same concern in the same way. Moreover, the conjunction "therefore" is further significant because it indicates that what Paul says now in the A' element is to be understood in light of its immediate context, namely his credentials as proclaimer, apostle, and teacher (2:7; B' element) which itself is in the context of Christ Jesus giving himself as a ransom on behalf of all (2:6; C' element). With this, the audience hear Paul's statement, "I want, therefore, men to pray in all place" (2:8). By stating, "I want" (βούλομαι), he is not merely expressing a personal inclination. Rather, Paul's expectation is for the audience to carry out his instructions as a way of acknowledging his authority as an "apostle of Christ Jesus" (1:1) according to the command of God and Christ Jesus (1:1) and thus of acknowledging the authority of "Christ Jesus our Lord" (1:2). This is corroborated by Paul's immediately prior statement about his credentials in 2:7, namely that he "was appointed" by God as a proclaimer, apostle, and teacher. In effect, then, Paul's statement "I want, therefore," would be heard by the audience in a much fuller sense: "As proclaimer, apostle, and teacher by divine appointment, I authoritatively instruct . . ."

It is possible that the audience would be unclear about Paul's meaning in regard to "men" (ἄνδρας). The Greek term ἄνδρας could refer both

---

85. In passing, it may be worth noting that Paul's instructions for the men (2:8) are far shorter than his instructions for the women (2:9–15). However, it is equally worth noting that in Paul's other letter to the Ephesian church, which was likely prior to 1 Timothy (see chapter 1), the instructions for the women—particularly married women (Eph 5:22–24)—are far shorter than his instructions for the men—particularly married men (Eph 5:25–33). Significantly also, whereas Paul instructs the married women to submit to their own husbands as to the Lord (Eph 5:22), Paul effectively instructs the married men to sacrifice themselves for their wives as Christ did for the church (Eph 5:25). To argue that Paul's instructions in 1 Timothy 2:8–15 are imbalanced toward women must be considered in view of Paul's instructions to the same Ephesian church in Ephesians 5:22–33.

to "men" in general or specifically to "husbands" among the audience.[86] Yet, given that he is addressing the entire Ephesian church and has not yet distinguished one kind of man from another, it would be restricting and rhetorically odd for Paul to suddenly refer only to the married men.[87] The generic label "men" would be most appropriate.[88] At the same time, given that familial language was associated with those who are "in faith" in the first microchiasm (1:2, 4) and that "in faith" continues in the second microchiasm (2:7), it seems that Paul would indeed have some kind of family connotation in mind. To be sure, the audience have heard the second microchiasm move from addressing the audience in general in the A element—men and women in the church without distinction or specification—to addressing only the "men" in the A' element. It is likely, then, that what Paul wants is for the men among the audience—relative to the women—to understand their unique role—specifically as men—as part and parcel of living and operating within the realm "in faith." With this distinction, the audience are to understand that the macrochiastic family theme "in faith" pertaining to "men"

---

86. Towner, *Letters*, 201, esp. n. 23; Ellis, *Pauline Theology*, 72–75.

87. More than likely, not all men were married in the audience; given the universal, inclusive nature of the microchiasm, it would be unfitting for Paul to suddenly exclude non-married men from praying. Witherington appropriately observes that "it would be strange for Paul to argue for husbands everywhere, rather than men in general, to pray in Christian worship" (*Letters*, 222). See Schreiner, "Interpretation of 1 Tim 2:9–15," 94.

Staton comments on the literary movement to suggest that husbands are in view: "Prior to 2:9, Paul addressed men with the Greek word *anthropos*. Paul then switched to *aner* in verse 8. Elsewhere in 1 Timothy [Staton is referencing 3:2, 12; 5:9], *anthropos* was used to refer to the male gender, or to people without being gender specific, while *aner* to husbands . . . My contention is that Paul shifted from men (males or generic people) to husbands specifically by shifting from *anthropos* to *aner* in 2:8 and 2:12" (*Biblical Liberation of Women*, 122). While Staton's interpretation of "*anthropos*" as a gender reference to "men" (instead of gender neutral "humans") is incorrect, he is correct that there is a linguistic movement in the microchiasm.

Staton's observations support the actual movement of Paul's rhetoric, however, his conclusion disrupts the flow and arrangement within second microchiasm. Notably, there is a sustained, unified rhetorical movement from all men and women among the audience (2:1–2) in the A element to all men (married and unmarried) (2:8) and all women (married and unmarried) (2:9–15) among the audience in the parallel A' element. Staton's suggestion creates a rhetorical disjunction, arguing that Paul guides the audience from a discussion about all the men and women in general (2:1–2) to specific men only (married). Indeed, the fact that Paul's rhetorical arrangement in the second microchiasm is a self-contained unit pertaining to men and women in general (2:1–15) is corroborated by the third microchiasm, wherein Paul's rhetorical arrangement is equally self-contained in regard to specific men only (married) and specific women only (married) in both the parallel A and A' elements; see volume 2, chapter 2.

88. This interpretation would also be supported by the absence of a modifying possessive pronoun.

does not refer to general family relations—husband and wife—but rather to "in faith" family relations—those who exist within "the household-law of God in faith" (1:4). In other words, for the "household" existing in the realm "in faith" to operate according to the "law" "of God," Paul wants the "men" to take specific action.

That Paul wants the men "to pray" (προσεύχεσθαι) in 2:8 of the A' element suggests that he wants the men to play a unique role in regard to the prayers (προσευχάς) that were described in 2:1 of the parallel A element.[89] In the A element, the entire audience—men and women—are exhorted to pray as the "first," leading activity of the church; the progression of the microchiasm here in the A' element now qualifies that the men in the audience—relative to the women—are instructed to pray, presumably, as the men's first, leading activity in the church. In sum, the implication from the microchiastic arrangement is that men and women will equally share in prayer (2:1), and men specifically will lead this shared activity (2:8).[90] The prepositional phrase "in all place" underscores that the men in the Ephesian church are to lead such prayers with a full appreciation of the salvific, missional emphasis in the microchiasm thus far.[91] Prayer "in all (παντί) place" in 2:8 of the A' element recalls the parallel prayer "on behalf of all (πάντων) humans" in 2:1 of the A element. It would also recall God's desire for "all (πάντας) humans to be-saved" in 2:4a of the A element. Thus the phrase is certainly a succinct restatement of the missional force of the A element. Yet, its placement within the concluding A' element naturally entails a movement toward a climax from its parallel introductory A element. Having pivoted around the C and C' elements concerning the one God and the fact that Christ Jesus "gave himself as a ransom on behalf of all (πάντων)" (2:5–6), the audience hear a developed progression regarding prayer. That is, while in the A element the church should pray on behalf of "all" humans (2:1) because the

---

89. Marshall, *PE*, 443: "The conjuction οὖν resumes the teaching on prayer in 2.1f."

90. To be sure, "prayer is not limited to men" (Patterson and Kelley, "1 Timothy," 662). Rather, the specification here in 2:8 suggests that the men in the Ephesian audience are called to promote such missional activity.

91. The translation of the singular noun "place" (τόπῳ) is intentional. Combined with Paul's address to the plural noun "men" (ἄνδρας), the sense seems to connote a collective disposition of unity—"all." Cf. Fee, who suggests the possibility that "corporate life in the church in Ephesus was not experienced in a large Sunday gathering in a single sanctuary but in many house churches . . . If so, then 2:8 is a word for each of these house churches: 'I want the men in every place (*en panti topo* = in every place where believers gather in and around Ephesus) to pray (= while in the gathered assembly) . . .'" (*Listening to the Spirit in the Text*, 152–53). Ibid. n. 12: "Furthermore to universalize the prepositional phrase ["everywhere" (*NIV*)] when the rest of the sentence so clearly fits the specific situation in Ephesus makes little sense."

Savior God *desires* "all" humans to be-saved (2:3b–4a), in the A' element the men must guide the church in prayer because now *in fact* the one mediator of God and humans has made it possible to be-saved by giving himself as a ransom for "all" (2:5b–6). Moreover, the phrase is likely borrowed from LXX Malachi 1:11: "For from the rising of the sun even to the going down thereof my name has been glorified among the Gentiles; and in every place (ἐν παντὶ τόπῳ) incense is offered to my name, and a pure offering: for my name is great among the Gentiles, says the Lord Almighty."[92] The OT allusion enhances the macrochiasm's overall progression in regard to salvation: not only does the gospel showcase God's glory so that people would bless God (1:11), but because the gospel is rooted in a factitive historical event—the testimony (2:6)—the clear implication is that "the Gentiles (2:7) and "all humans" (2:1, 4a) are presented with the opportunity to behold God's glory and bless him.

In 2:8b Paul states in positive and negative terms the way in which the men are to pray. Positively, the phrase "lifting reverent hands" has two aspects. The Jewish practice of "lifting" (ἐπαίροντας) hands in prayer was a way of expressing worship and solemnity (see Luke 24:50).[93] Similarly, the phrase "reverent hands" (ὁσίους χεῖρας) seems to reference the priestly practice of washing hands before entering the Tent of Meeting to reflect an inward start of purity (Exod 30:19–21).[94] Heard together, then, the phrase highlights not only the men's total focus on the person to whom they are praying—God—but also a comprehensive devotion to him while they are praying—an external and internal readiness to participate in what he desires, namely the salvation of all humans. Moreover, where the adjective "reverent" (ὁσίους) recalls Paul's identification of "the without-reverence" (ἀνοσίοις) as those for whom the law is laid (1:9), the clear implication is that the men are to pray as those for whom the law is not laid, namely as "the just" (1:9a). In other words, Paul's instruction to the "men" is calling upon them to live in a manner that is consistent with their existence "in faith."

Negatively, therefore, the men are to pray "without anger and word-quarreling." The term "anger" (ὀργῆς) contains the nuance of retribution;

92. See Towner, *Letters*, 203–4 for a fuller discussion on the use here of Malachi 1:11.

93. Lifting hands was most likely a Jewish practice; see Witherington, *Letters*, 223. By referring to OT and Jewish practices, Paul seems to assume that the non-Jewish Ephesian converts in the audience would understand the meaning conveyed by "lifting reverent hands," presumably by his own teaching. Cf. Gloer, *1 & 2 Timothy*, 140: "The lifting of hands while praying was the usual posture for praying in Paul's time for both Jews and Genitles (see Pss 141:2; 143:6)."

94. It is worth noting that the term "reverent" (ὁσίους) here would refer to a cultic, religious-ethical practice; see Marshall, *PE*, 445; Knight, *PE*, 129.

the audience would clearly hear that this stands in opposition to the peaceful and quiet life in 2:2 of the parallel A element that is intended to attract others to the gospel. Given this missional thrust, Paul likely has in mind anger specifically toward those who are "in faith"—certainly an angry household is not appealing to outsiders. Moreover, rather than displaying that the men's attention is focused on God—"lifting reverent hands," thus pointing others toward God—"anger" among the men would draw attention toward themselves, effectively nullifying the church's mission. Clearly, the men in the audience understand that they are not to harbor bitterness nor refuse to reconcile among themselves. The men are also to pray without "word-quarreling" (διαλογισμός); the term recalls Paul's use of prior cognates, namely the "useless-words" (ματαιολογία) to which "some" have turned-aside (1:6) and the "word" (λόγος) concerning Christ Jesus that is faithful and worthy of all acceptance (1:15). For the audience, Paul's implication would be clear: just as turning-aside for "useless-words" indicated a departure from a pure heart, good conscience, and a without-hypocrisy faith (1:5–6), so too does "word-quarreling" (2:8); conversely, the men's activity to pray "without word-quarreling" would conform with an acceptance of the "word" and thus an existence "in faith." Still, the polemical implication against the false teachers would not go unnoticed: just as turning-aside for "useless-words" characterizes "some" in the first microchiasm, so too does "word-quarreling" here in the second microchiasm. Thus Paul is not merely prohibiting disputes with respect to prayer among the men; rather, he is effectively instructing the men within God's household to be nothing like "some" whose attitudes and teachings not only bring-about controversial-speculations (1:4) but also result in shipwrecked faith (1:19). Moreover, given that Paul's specification to "men" in 2:8 was aimed at the proper "household-law of God in faith" (1:4), the need to mention "without anger and word-quarreling" is telling: the behavior associated with the false teachers is having the opposite effect as "men" in the church should have, namely division and the improper functioning of God's household.[95] Thus the corrective action that Paul wants is for the behavior of men to bring-about the household-law of God, and this starts with the men focusing on God's agenda and leading missional prayer as accords with the realm "in faith." The audience understand that the different teaching of "some" (1:3, 10b) will ultimately hinder the missional work of the church to pray on behalf of all humans, both on account of its exclusive scope (cf. 2:1, 4, 6, 7) and divisive effect (1:4). Paul, therefore, is calling to action those "in faith"—the

---

95. Witherington, *Letters*, 223: "This suggests a situation in which men are vying for the privilege of praying in the congregation, or there is some sort of honor-and-shame rivalry situation."

entire audience—who want salvation for all: the men need to step up and live as men "in faith," but simultaneously—and equally vital for the mission of the church—this requires the cooperation of the women to enable these men to do as Paul wants.

1 Timothy 2:9–15: A Minichiastic Unit[96]

Within the A' element of the microchiasm, the audience hear verses 2:9–15 as a minichiasm in itself. Verses 2:9–15 are composed carefully of four subelements ("a"-"b"-"b'"-"a'"); linguistic parallels identifying chiastic arrangements are indicated by the Greek text:

> "a". ⁹ likewise also women to cosmetic themselves in cosmopolitan apparel with modesty and self-control (σωφροσύνης), not in braids and gold or pearls or rich attire;
>> "b". ¹⁰ rather what is proper (πρέπει) for women who profess godliness, consistent-with good works. ¹¹ A woman in quietness (ἐν ἡσυχίᾳ) must learn in all submissiveness;
>> "b'". ¹² but I do not permit (ἐπιτρέπω) a woman to teach nor to govern a man; rather to be in quietness (ἐν ἡσυχίᾳ). ¹³ For Adam was formed first, then Eve. ¹⁴ And Adam was not deceived, but the woman being-deceived in transgression became;

---

96. Much attention and criticism has been focused on this section of 1 Timothy, primarily due to the potentional for its misuse and misapplication to discriminate and oppress women in various capacities in and outside of the church. Long, *1 & 2 Timothy*, 69: "Even if this text was originally designed as a wrench to repair an emergency problem, we need to face up to the unfortunate fact that it has often been used as a sledgehammer against women." As I intend to demonstrate, the language and rhetorical structure of Paul's speech in 1 Timothy 2:9–15 does not in any way condone inequality or mistreatment against women but rather upholds and draws from God's original design before sin, where no discrimination, inequality, or oppression existed.

Furthermore, consistent with the missional impetus of 1 Timothy 2, and particularly of the parallel A element (2:1–4a), I also intend to demonstrate that Paul's purpose for his instructions to the Ephesian women here in 2:9–15 is missional in nature, that is, intends to attract others to Christ. Malherbe's comments are helpful to establish the context: "The exhortation to pray (vv. 1–2) and the theological affirmation that follows (vv. 3–4) introduce terms that will be significant in vv. 9–15: quiet (ἡσύχιον), godliness (εὐσέβεια), and salvation (σωτήρ, σώζω). The first two describe conduct or demeanor, the third is part of the theological motivation for that conduct" ("The *Virtus Feminarum*," 48).

For an overview of historic and modern interpretations of 1 Timothy 2:9–15, see Brown, *An Historian Looks at 1 Timothy 2:11–14*, 1–65.

"a'".¹⁵ but she will be-saved consistent-with child-parenting, if they remain in faith and love and holiness with self-control (σωφροσύνης).

The first and only minichiasm of the 2:1–15 microchiasm is framed by the "self-control" exhibited by women within the Ephesian church in the "a" and "a'" sub-element. The minichiasm gravitates around what is "proper" and permissible for women in the Ephesian church, which Paul summarizes as a peaceable, non-confrontational disposition "in quietness" in the "b" and "b'" sub-elements.

1 Timothy 2:9: Women to Cosmetic Themselves with Modesty and Self-Control

("a" sub-element)

The "a" element of the minichiasm begins with the adverbial phrase "likewise also", picking up on the verb "I want" in 2:8.⁹⁷ The adverb "likewise" (ὡσαύτως) communicates that just as Paul had specific concerns and distinct commands for the men in general (2:8), so now he has specific and distinct concerns for the "women" (γυναῖκας) in general (2:9).⁹⁸ Again, what is in view is the distinct role that each gender has in the household of God—the realm "in faith"—in order to participate in and advance God's desire for all humans to be-saved. As with the men, Paul expects that the women will recognize Paul's unique identity as proclaimer, apostle, and teacher concerning the testimony about Christ Jesus that saves humans (2:6–7) and will respond to him accordingly. In short, what is necessary for the audience to bear in mind at the outset of the 2:9–15 minichiasm is its placement within the second microchiasm, which moves toward and centers upon God's purpose to save all humans. That is, the interpretation of any verse in the minichiasm must be consistent with the emphases and themes of the

---

97. See Knight, *PE*, 132; Marshall, *PE*, 446.

98. See discussion above regarding 2:8 and the rhetorical movement of Paul's language in the second microchiasm. In the A element, Paul addresses all married and unmarried men and women of the church (2:1–2); here in the parallel A' element, Paul addresses all married and unmarried men (2:8) and all married and unmarried women (2:9–15). Paul is not addressing only the married women ("wives") but all the women in the congregation, even if wives comprised the majority of the women. The strong presence of unmarried women in 1 Timothy 5 and Paul's similar concern for their "good work" (5:10) indicate that his instructions in the second microchiasm are no less applicable to unmarried women.

entire microchiasm. As with the men, heeding Paul's instructions has direct salvific implications.

Matching what was said to the men, Paul states in positive and negative terms the way in which the women are be missional. Positively, Paul wants the women among the audience to "cosmetic (κοσμεῖν) themselves," that is, to dress, ornament, and decorate themselves in "cosmopolitan (κοσμίῳ) apparel" (2:9). The play on words accentuates Paul's concern for proper attire. The verb "cosmetic" has the nuance "to be orderly." This same sense applies to the cognate adjective "cosmopolitan," meaning "appropriate, fitting, proper." The use of the term "apparel" (καταστολῇ) may have been intentional, given the contrast during this period between the *stola* (στολή), a heavy garment that signaled fidelity, and the *toga*, the gaudy attire of prostitutes.[99] Paul further specifies the meaning of "cosmopolitan apparel" through the prepositional phrase "with modesty and self-control" (μετὰ αἰδοῦς καὶ σωφροσύνης) to express a sense of restraint and propriety. These terms were current in Paul's time as references to self-controlled wives who sought to honor their husbands.[100] Ancient writers did not view dress-code as a neutral matter. Rather, they saw it as an expression of one's deeper values. The apostle assumes the same, however for Paul the values are not grounded in Greco-Roman culture but in the content of the gospel. As indicated by the movement of the microchiasm from the C and C' elements, proper clothing, modesty, and self-control are informed by "the testimony" that "there is one God and one mediator of God and humans, the human Christ Jesus, who gave himself as a ransom on behalf all (2:5–6)." Such grounding in the gospel would be further evident by its correspondence with "godliness and respectability" in 2:2 of the parallel A element.[101] In short, Paul is instructing the women in the audience to consider how they ought to "cosmetic" themselves in light of their own salvation, Christ's self-sacrifice (2:6), and the church's missional calling to do what is commendable and acceptable in sight of the Savior God, who desires to all humans to be-saved (2:1–4a).

Negatively, the women are to cosmetic themselves "not in braids and gold or peals or rich attire" (2:9). Immediately, the negative particle "not" (μή) would recall its earlier occurrences in the first microchiasm regarding "some" whom Timothy must charge to "not" (μή) teach-different (1:3), "nor" (μηδέ) to hold-toward myths (1:4), who are "not" (μή) understanding "either" (μήτε) what they-are-saying "or" (μήτε) regarding some-things

---

99. Winter, *Roman Wives*, 42–43.

100. Ibid., 101–2.

101. Tellbe, *Christ-Believers in Ephesus*, 190: "the main reason for this concern seems to be, not a general aspiration for acculturation or assimilation, but a concern for the respectable reputation of the community of believers in the wider society."

they-are- insisting (1:7), and whom Paul has given-over to Satan, that they might be-disciplined "not" (μή) to blaspheme (1:20). The rhetorical implication is that any activity of women in the Ephesian audience to cosmetic themselves "in braids and gold or pearls or rich attire" is that which associates them with the negative impact of "some," namely *not* bringing about the household-law of God in faith (1:4). Indeed, the further implication is by their activity to cosmetic themselves "in braids and gold or pearls or rich attire," the women in the Ephesian church are declaring their adherence to the different teaching of "some." The audience thus understand that Paul wants the women "not" to cosmetic themselves "in braids and gold or pearls or rich attire" not only because it would have a negative impact on the missional activity of God's household but also because it would have severely disastrous consequences for the women's own salvation—the final result of the activites of "some" is shipwrecked faith (1:20).

In the context of the first-century Greco-Roman world, Paul appears to be drawing from well-known portrayals of ostentatious women who disregarded "sumptuary laws" designed to promote frugality.[102] "Braids" (πλέγμασιν), the hairstyle adopted by wealthy women, stood in stark contrast to the simple styles associated with the model Imperial woman. "Gold or pearls" (χρυσίῳ ἢ μαργαρίταις) can be taken together as a reference to jewelry, which was the embodiment of flamboyance.[103] In addition, gold was the accessory of expensive prostitutes. Finally, "rich attire" (ἱματισμῷ πολυτελεῖ) was the opposite of simple clothing expected of the model Imperial woman. Such attire was often associated with promiscuous women.[104] In short, as much as women can cosmetic themselves to attract people to the testimony concerning Christ (2:9a), so too can they make the testimony unattractive (2:9b). For onlookers in the Greco-Roman world, braided hair, gold, pearls, and rich attire were all marks of the kind of woman who represented the abandonment of traditional Roman values.[105] Such would be the interpretation by those outside of the church; in this way, "the testimony" (2:6) would be seen as attack on what both

---

102. Towner, *Letters*, 208; Winter, *Roman Wives*, 104–7. My comments on the various accessories and clothing are taken mostly from Winter's own analysis.

103. More than wealth, the underlying concern seems to be regarding the Christian's way of life. Beattie, *Women and Marriage in Paul*, 92–93: "it is the way of life associated with these things that is the real issue here."

104. See Schreiner, "Interpretation of 1 Tim 2:9–15," 95.

105. See Beattie, *Women and Marriage in Paul*, 93–94. Scholer, "1 Tim 2.9–15," 105: Paul is "affirming high standards of cultural decency so that the church will be above reproach."

men and women esteemed in the Greco-Roman world.[106] Moreover, as with the men's anger and word-quarreling (2:8), these adornments would draw attention to the women rather than to the one God and the one mediator Christ Jesus (2:5), effectively nullifying the mission of the church. The rhetorical impact would be heard: rather than corresponding to the missional lifestyle of "godliness and respectability" in the A element (2:2), "braids and gold or pearls or rich attire" in the A' element would signify the opposite.[107] Given their call to live as the missional household of God, the entire audience understand that Paul's instructions to the women express not only a concern to disassociate themselves from any lifestyle that would hinder the progress of the gospel but also to live in a manner that is "cosmopolitan," fitting for those who exist "in faith."

It would be a mistake to assume that Paul was simply aligning himself with Greco-Roman standards of decency. Nor should it be supposed that the apostle held that fancy hairstyles, jewels, and rich attire were inherently wrong. Rather, Paul's twofold perspective in the second microchiasm regarding the salvation of all humans—missions—and the testimony concerning Christ Jesus forms the basis for his instructions to the women in the Ephesian church. In the A element of the second microchiasm, as the "first," lead activity, Paul exhorts the church to pray on behalf of all humans in accordance with God's desire for all humans to be-saved (2:1–4a). The priority of missions, therefore, dictates the daily conduct and behavior of both the men and women in the church.[108] If any semblance of immodesty hindered that priority—as would the men's anger and word-quarreling (2:8) and the women's decision to not cosmetic themselves with self-control (2:9)—then there was no doubt that those "in faith" should set aside anything that disrupted the progress of the gospel and thus the salvation of others.[109] Also,

---

106. Towner, *Letters*, 209: "The critique is precise. It prohibits the kind of dress and adornment that would associate Christian women with the revolutionary 'new woman' already in evidence in the East. Were that connection to be made, the church would be open to allegations of endorsing this departure from traditional values."

107. Marshall, *PE*, 451: "Thus women are called to substantiate their claim to faith by exhibiting the appropriate adornment, which is nothing other than the Christian character and practice expected of all believers."

108. Wall with Steele, *1 & 2 Timothy*, 86: "the ideal [Christian] woman's public life is prompted more by theological motive than by social propriety: God's desire to save every woman . . . is realized by the witness of influential Christan women who exemplify God's saving grace to outsiders . . . By so doing, not so much by spoken word as by prudent deed, they provide an apt illustration of Paul's apostolic mission in the world."

109. E.g., Richards, "(Mis)Reading Paul through Western Eyes," 256, translates the phrase in 2:9 as, "'Women should dress *sexually* modestly.'" In this case, Paul's point, at least in part, may be that provocative dress could hinder people from looking toward Christ Jesus.

given that Christ Jesus became a human—surrendering all his wealth and status—in order to give himself as a ransom on behalf of all, those "in faith" (1:2, 4; 2:7) who "have-faith" upon Christ (1:16) are to follow him as "Lord" (1:2, 12, 14) by foregoing whatever luxuries they might otherwise enjoy here and now for the missional purpose of salvation for all humans. Indeed, rather than spending money on "rich attire" (2:9), such money could be used to participate with God's missional desire for all humans to be-saved (2:4a). Certainly, the women who are "in faith" may do so in full conviction of their "knowing-embrace of truth," namely of "the testimony" (2:7) that "life eternal" (1:16) was secured for them by Christ's ransom payment on their behalf (2:6).[110] To be sure, Paul is not instructing the women to cosmetic themselves in a particular way as ambassadors for Greco-Roman culture—nor would the audience perceive his instructions as such. Instead, the unity, flow, and parallelism within the microchiasm clearly convey that—as an apostle of Christ Jesus, that is, as a person who was appointed to proclaim and teach the gospel (2:7)—Paul wants the women to be missional in the same way that their "Savior God" is missional (2:3), in the same way that Christ Jesus "who came into the world to save sinners" is missional (1:15). It is, therefore, within the missional context of Paul's letter that the rhetorical purpose of Paul's statement to the women in 2:9 is clear: Paul wants the women "to cosmetic themselves in cosmopolitan apparel," namely that which attracts others to Christ.[111]

---

110. Most likely there were wealthy women in the church. Witherington, *Letters*, 217–18: "One need not urge the poor to refrain from wearing luxurious clothing and fancy jewelry, for they have none"; see Bassler, "Limits and Differentiation," 137.

Wagener suggests that because "these women were well-to-do and economically independent . . . the author is taking direct aim at these women's focus on social status and trying to force them back into the restrictive framework of their domestic roles as wives" ("PE," 837). The missional intension of the microchiasm, however, recommends that suppression is not in view; rather than a call for the women to abandon their material wealth and social status, the audience would likely hear Paul's statement as a call to abandon anything that promotes themselves more than it promotes Christ Jesus.

111. For further discussion regarding the missional connotation of "to cosmetic" (κοσμεῖν) and "cosmopolitan" (κοσμίῳ), see Plummer, *Paul's Understanding of the Church's Mission*, 98–105.

1 Timothy 2:10–11: What is Proper for Women Who Profess Godliness, Good Works

("b" sub-element)

In the "b" element of the minichiasm (2:10–11) Paul continues his instructions to women: "rather what is proper for women who profess godliness, consistent-with good works" (2:10). The term "rather" (ἀλλ') signifies a contrast to the preceding statement. In effect, having stated how the women should not cosmetic themselves in 2:9b—"not in braids and gold or pearls or rich attire"—Paul in 2:10 further elaborates on his positive instructions for how the women are to cosmetic themselves in 2:9a—"in cosmopolitan apparel with modesty and self-control."[112] Paul's specification in 2:10 for women to cosmetic themselves with "what is proper for women who profess godliness, consistent-with good works" affirms that—much more than their outward appearance—the observable lifestyle of the women is in view. The verb "proper" (πρέπει) carries the sense of what is fitting or of what corresponds to something else. Here, "what is proper" concerns "women who profess godliness." The repetition of "women" (γυναιξίν) in 2:10 after Paul had already specified that his instructions are to "women" (γυναῖκας) in 2:9a not only reiterates that Paul is addressing all women in the Ephesian church—married and umarried women in general—but also highlights the "proper" way that the women in the church are to missionally attract others to Christ. The participle "who profess" (ἐπαγγελλομέναις) denotes a serious public claim; in effect, where the public claim is "godliness," Paul is underscoring that "women who profess godliness" ought to, in fact, substantiate their claim. The term "godliness" (θεοσέβειαν) is a composite of "God" (θεός) and the verb "to worship, venerate, adore" (σέβω)—the latter describing those who were genuinely devoted and associated with Jews (see Acts 17:17).[113] To be sure, "godliness" (θεοσέβειαν) here in 2:10 of the A' element recalls the cognate noun "godliness" (εὐσεβείᾳ) in 2:2 of the parallel A element. Where "godliness" in 2:2 was applied to the entire congregation—both men and women—in reference to a missional life that outwardly demonstrates one's existence "in faith," the audience understand that "godliness" in 2:10 carries the same missional implication. In this way,

---

112. Marshall, *PE*, 451: "ἀλλ' introduces the contrast to the kind of decoration rejected in v. 9. The construction is elliptical as there is no expressed antecedent to ὅ we are to supply κοσμεῖν and read 'not with braided hairstyles . . . but [adorn themselves with that] which befits . . . namely by means of good deeds."

113. The verb σέβω was a technical term used to describe Gentiles who accepted Jewish adherence to monotheism and attended synagogue but refused circumcision; see Friberg 24319 (BW).

the qualifying phrase "what is proper" would undoubtedly intend a salvific impact. Heard in full, then, Paul's Ephesian audience understand that "what is proper for women who profess godliness" in 2:10 is a specific articulation of the way that women in the Ephesian church are to express the cumulative message of the microchiasm: the Savior God desires all humans to be-saved (2:3–4a); Christ Jesus gave himself as a ransom on behalf of all so that all could be-saved (2:6); the church, as it aligns to Paul's apostolic proclamation and teaching (2:7), is called to be the conduit—prayer and godliness (2:1–2)—through which all humans come to a knowing-embrace of truth (2:4b); all men in the church are to pray with reverence (2:8); and all women in the church are to exhibit their profession of godliness (2:10).

Paul goes on to specify what is proper for women who profess godliness: they are to cosmetic themselves "consistent-with good works" (2:10). The phrase conceptually echoes the "peaceful and quiet life" described in 2:2 of the parallel A element. Such a life, the audience now perceive, is anything but passive. Rather, the progression of the microchiasm indicates that "a peaceful and quiet life" must exude a sense of purpose and a refusal to partake in what is improper for those who exist "in faith" (1:2, 4; 2:7). The women who profess godliness are not to cosmetic themselves in "rich attire" (2:9) because their money is used "consistent-with good works" instead (2:10). The preposition "consistent-with" (δι') connotes the sense of "in keeping with" and recalls its occurrence in the prior microchiasm: Paul was granted-mercy "consistent-with" (διά) both his status as the first, lead of sinners (1:15b, 16a) and the fact that Christ Jesus came into the world to save sinners (1:15a). Thus in the same way that Paul's salvation was "consistent-with" (διά) Christ's saving purposes, so also are the "good works" of the women "consistent-with" (δι') what is proper for their profession of godliness (2:10). In other words, the "good works" function as an organic demonstration of the women's salvation *and* of their missional role within the church. The adjective "good" (ἀγαθῶν) recalls Paul's description of "the charge" in 1:5 of the first microchiasm, the goal of which is "love from a pure heart and a good (ἀγαθῆς) conscience and a without-hypocrisy faith." Furthermore, "good" (ἀγαθῶν) in 2:10 recalls the manner in which Timothy is to carry out "the charge," namely to war the commendable war while "holding faith and a good (ἀγαθήν) conscience" (1:18–19). The clear connotation of the "good works" in which the women are to cosmetic themselves (2:10), therefore, represents their mutual participation with Paul and Timothy in the charge to preserve the sound teaching against the different teaching of "some" (1:3, 10b). Indeed, the "good works" of the women would not only demonstrate their allegiance to Paul and Timothy but also their deliberate refusal to be influenced by "some" who have turned-aside from a "good conscience" (1:5-6), who by rejecting a "good conscience" have become-shipwrecked regarding the faith (1:19), and whose activities clearly hinder God's missional purposes, bringing about controversial-speculations rather than the household-law of God in faith (1:4b). Notably also, given that neutrality in the "war" against the false teachers is not an option (1:18), the audience would likely hear an implicit undertone: to not cosmetic themselves with "good works" would represent an active allegiance with "some."

The term "works" (ἔργων) connotes tangible action—an active participation in what is good, and thus a life that demonstrates one's existence "in faith." Paul's instructions for the women to cosmetic themselves "consistent-with good works," then, is a salvific and missional summons to make visible what is invisible, that is, to display the impact of the sound teaching, the gospel, on their lives—the spiritual renovation that God has accomplished in their now "pure heart" and "good conscience" (1:5, 19).[114] By allowing others to see the the sound teaching in this way, the women effectively become a missional conduit through which God exhibits his glory through the gospel (1:11). Moreover, such a missional aspect suggests that these "good works" are not to be limited to the members of God's household but are to extend to all humans so that all might come to a knowing-embrace of truth (2:4). In short, Paul emphasizes the highly essential role of the Christian women in the audience to bring-about the household-law of God in faith (1:4b), that is, to ensure that God's missional household attracts all humans to Christ Jesus.[115]

Continuing the missional theme—and to avoid any misunderstanding about what comprises "good works"—Paul instructs the women in the church: "A women in quietness must learn in all submissiveness" (2:11).[116] Here, Paul's specification of "A woman" (γυνή) in 2:11 after already conveying that his instructions are to "women" (γυναῖκας) in 2:9a and to "women" (γυναιξίν) in 2:10 would not go unnoticed. To be sure, the sustained linguistic emphasis on women (2:9a, 10, 11) would communicate that Paul has

---

114. Wall with Steele, *1 & 2 Timothy*, 87: "Paul's purpose is simply this: the congregation's worship practices, down to the individual believer, should personify the redemptive purpose of God our Savior set out by the preceding theological formulation [2:5a–6]."

115. Scholer rightly observes that "there is no exegetical, historical, and hermeneutical basis to regard 2.9–10 as normatively different from 2.11–12" ("1 Tim 2.9–15," 106). Indeed, the missional lifestyle of godly women is equally normative for the entire 2:9–15 minichiasm.

116. Moo's analysis ("1 Tim 2:11–15," 182–83) is an example of balanced, careful, and insightful exegesis. While I do not agree fully with the practical applications of his analysis, his reading of this much debated section of 1 Timothy is helpful.

all of the women in view—both married and unmarried.[117] Moreover, the rhetorical chain of "women" (2:9a), "women" (2:10), and "woman" (2:11) would convey the inseparable connection of Paul's instructions in each occurrence. That is, Paul's instruction that "A woman in quietness must learn in all submissiveness" (2:11) has in view the same salvific and missional intention as the "good works" that are "proper for women who profess godliness" (2:10) and the "cosmopolitan apparel with modesty and self-control" in which the women are "to cosmetic themselves" (2:9a).

The sequential position of the prepositional phrase "in quietness" prior to the verb "must learn" suggests that Paul's emphasis is not on the fact that women ought to learn but on the manner and disposition that they are to exhibit when learning.[118] While the term "quietness" (ἡσυχίᾳ) has two meanings—one pertaining to "silence" in an absolute sense and the other pertaining to "a disposition of tranquility"—the audience would not be unclear about which meaning Paul intended.[119] The term "quietness" (ἡσυχίᾳ) here in 2:11 of the A' element recalls its adjectival cognate "quiet" (ἡσύχιον) in 2:2 of the parallel A element; in 2:2, "quiet" is applied to the entire church—men and women—and denotes the missional disposition that pertains to "a peaceful and quiet life . . . in all godliness and respectability" (2:2). Undoubtedly, then, the adjective "quietness" in 2:10 would be understood to denote the same missional disposition, that is, of peaceableness, godliness, and respectability—*not* absolute silence.[120] Indeed, not only Paul's language but his deliberate organization thereof to frame and

117. See discussion above regarding 2:8 and the rhetorical flow of Paul's general language. In the context of Paul's general instructions to all women, the specification "A woman" would not signify "wives."

118. Barcley, *1 & 2 Timothy*, 90: "The emphasis in this verse is on the *manner* in which women are to 'learn', and not on the learnig itself." Moo, "1 Tim 2:11–15," 183: "But this does not mean that Paul's desire for women to learn is the main point being made here. For it is not the *fact* that they are to learn, but the *manner* in which they are to learn that concerns Paul: 'in quietness' and 'with full submission.'"

119. On the term "quietness," see the discussion between Moo and Payne: Moo, "1 Tim 2:11–15"; Payne, "A Response to Douglas J. Moo's Article"; Moo, "A Rejoinder"; Payne, "A Surrejoinder." Moo, in my opinion, presents a more persuasive position. See also Spencer, *Beyond the Curse*, 74–80.

120. Blomberg, *From Pentecost to Patmos*, 363: "The word for 'quietness' does not mean 'without speaking;' the same root also appears in 2:2 in which believers are to live 'peaceful and *quiet* lives.'" Staton, *Biblical Liberation of Women*, 129: "Internal evidence also supports that *esuchia* . . . does not suggest a total lack of verbalization because of its use in 2:2 which is paralleled with being tranquil (*eremos* for 'peaceful' and *esuchios* for 'quiet'—v.2)." Malherbe, "The *Virtus Feminarum*," 49–50: "Like v. 10, vv. 11–12 also pick up from v. 2b, 'a calm and quiet life with all godliness and dignity' . . . which suggests that quietness is a quality of behavior defined by godliness." Cf. Zamfir, *Men and Women*, 226.

hinge the second microchiasm upon the theme of salvation and missions would be apparent:

> A element: "I exhort, therefore... that a peaceful and quiet (ἡσύχιον) life we might lead-through in all godliness (εὐσεβείᾳ) and respectability... our Savior God, who desires all humans to be-saved" (2:1-4);
>
> C element: "For there is one God" (2:5a);
>
> C' element: "and there is one mediator of God... Christ Jesus, who gave himself as a ransom on behalf of all" (2:6);
>
> A' element: "I want, therefore... what is proper for women who profess godliness (θεοσέβειαν), consistent-with good works. A woman in quietness (ἡσυχίᾳ) must learn...." (2:8-11).

The explicit missional purpose of Paul's exhortation to the church in the A element and instructions to the women in the A' element not only provides the framework for understanding the microchiasm, but the explicit missional activity of God and Christ Jesus in the pivot C and C' elements grounds the framework of the A and A' elements. To be sure, the audience are to understand Paul's instructions in 2:11 of the A' element—"A woman in quietness must learn"—as a specific articulation of his general exhortation to men and women in the A element: the particular outworking of "a peaceful and quiet life... in all godliness and respectability" (2:2) by the women is through a peaceable temperament "in quietness" when learning.[121] Over and against mute silence, clearly a disposition of tranquility—peaceable, not argumentative—was capable of winning the admiration of those outside the church.

The historic nature of Paul's letter suggests that Paul is responding to some sort of situation, that is, he is not speaking in a vacuum. The very fact that Paul the "teacher" (διδάσκαλος, 2:7) indicates that women "must learn" (μανθανέτω, 2:11) is itself not insignificant. Likely at least some women were

---

121. Wall with Steele, *1 & 2 Timothy*, 90: "the term used, ἡσυχία (*hesychia*, 'quietly'), repeats the disposition of the entire worshiping congregation described earlier in v. 2b. This repetition creates an intertext that implies that a 'quiet and submissive' woman during instruction personifies the quiet disposition of the entire congregation in its civic relations." Jones, "Women, Teaching, and Authority," 145: "Paul's instruction to Timothy is that women should learn without causing disturbance or turmoil, just like the men should avoid anger and disputing in their prayer."

objecting to or in some way becoming unruly towards Paul's teaching.[122] Given the definite presence and influence of "some" in the Ephesian church (1:3–7), such women may have aligned themselves with the false teachers and were thus not doing what is proper for women who profess godliness (2:9–10). Certainly, intending the same missional impact that Paul highlighted in the parallel A element, the disposition with which the Christian women "must learn" in the church, for the sake of the watching world, was of paramount importance.[123]

Given the phrase "in quietness must learn," the inclusion of the prepositional phrase "in all submissiveness" (1:11) alerts the audience to both the gravity of this specific instruction and the possibility of a more fundamental issue, namely one's disposition toward authority. While the term "all" (πάσῃ) may simply be a point of emphasis—"in total submissiveness"—such does not correspond to Paul's use of "quiet" and "in quietness" in the A and A' elements, which refers not to total silence but rather to an observable, peaceable disposition. Specifically, Paul's use of "in all (ἐν πάσῃ) submissiveness" here in 2:11 of the A' element recalls and demonstrates its connection to "in all (ἐν πάσῃ) godliness and respectability" in 2:2 of the parallel A element. Certainly in 2:11, then, that a woman must learn "in all submissiveness" would be a tangible demonstration of "godliness and respectability"—here, toward teachers in the church. Paul himself epitomizes the point. Paul is Christ Jesus's very own personal representative, an "apostle" (1:1, 12); he is such "according to the command of God our Savior" (1:1), and he "was appointed" by God as a "proclaimer, apostle . . . teacher . . . in faith and truth" (2:7); thus, Paul's instructions that "A woman . . . must learn" would have significant implications. The juxtaposition of Paul's divine appointment as "teacher" (διδάσκαλος, 2:7) and that he was divinely counted-faithful with

---

122. A brief note on the social context in Ephesus may be relevant. Witherington, *Letters*, 218: "we are dealing here with women who have some social status and probably some education as well. Ephesus was a cosmopolitan city full of people of high status and rank, and some of them . . . had become Christians. Such people naturally would expect to lead and to be spokespersons in the new community. They would not be inclined to be quiet and listen and learn, but that is precisely what Paul says must happen at this point."

123. Shreiner, "Interpretation of 1 Tim 2:8–15," 97: "The focus of the command is not on women learning, but *the manner* and *mode* of their learning." Not a few commentators suggest that Paul's instruction about women learning would have resonated with Jewish converts, given that learning was not generally promoted by the Jews (e.g., Moo, "1 Tim 2:11–15," 183; Payne, *Man and Woman*, 314; Celoria, "1 Tim 2," 20). Others are less certain that Paul is contrasting Christianity with restricting aspects of Judaism (e.g., Marshall, *PE*, 452). Still, others reject this view altogether (e.g., Gench, *Tyrannical Texts*, 7–8). For further discussion on women's education in the first century, see Baugh, "Foreign World," 33–35.

"the sound teaching (διδασκαλίᾳ)" (1:10b–11) in relation to his instructions that a woman "must learn" (μανθανέτω, 2:11) clearly specifies both the content and the source thereof, namely "the sound teaching" by Paul the "teacher."[124] Furthermore, as a divinely appointed "teacher . . . in faith and truth" (2:7), the definite suggestion is that any woman "in faith" (1:2, 4) and thus who has come to "a knowing-embrace of truth" (2:4) would want to "learn" from Paul, including his instructions. Still, due to Paul's overarching concern in the first microchiasm about the different teaching of "some" that lies-opposed to the sound teaching (1:3, 10b), it would simultaneously be evident to the audience that a deliberate choice by "a woman" to not "learn" from Paul the "teacher" delineates her alignment with "some" who "teach-different" (1:3, 10b). Such would delineate a woman's personal rejection of Christ Jesus, whom Paul represents as an apostle (1:1, 12; 2:7), and of "the sound teaching," the gospel, that concerns him (1:10b–11a). Thus as much as Paul's statement that "A woman must learn . . . in all submissiveness" (2:11) intends a tangible demonstration of "all godliness and respectability" (2:2) toward teachers in the church, it more basically identifies a personal disposition toward authority—certainly Paul's authority to represent Christ Jesus according to the command of God (1:1), and certainly Christ Jesus's authority as "Lord" (1:2). Emphasizing this point, the term "submissiveness" (ὑποταγῇ) itself expresses an awareness and appropriate response to the structures of authority that God has established, whether that authority is between God and mankind, rulers and constituents, or husbands and wives.[125] Here, then, the audience understand that Paul is not merely concerned with submitting to teachers but—more basically—with submitting to authority.

1 Timothy 2:12–14: Adam Was Formed First, Then Eve

("b'" sub-element)

In the "b'" sub-element of the 2:9–15 minichiasm (2:12–14), Paul continues his salvific, missional instructions to the women in the church: "but I do not permit a woman to teach nor to govern a man" (2:12).[126] Given Paul's

---

124. The passive verbs "was counted-faithful" (1:11) and "was appointed" (2:7) are divine passives and imply that God is the active participant.

125. See e.g., Romans 13:1 ("All souls must be-submissive (ὑποτασσέσθω) to authorities who are holding-above"); Ephesians 5:21, 22 ("Submitting ('υοτασσόμενοι) to one-another in fear of Christ . . .").

126. Verse 2:12 of the "b'" sub-element, which appears to restrict women in the church from teaching and governing men in the church, has generated much debate.

sustained attention to the missional lifestyle of the women, the disjunctive "but" (δέ) functions not as a strong contrast but as a transition.[127] In effect, where the women were to positively exhibit the missional qualities of the entire church—"a peaceful and quiet life . . . in all godliness and respectability" (2:2)—through their disposition "in quietness . . . in all submissiveness" (2:11), Paul's instructions are now stated as a negative prohibition in 2:12. Notably, whereas Paul had individually addressed the particular role of "men" (ἄνδρας, 2:8) in distinction from "women" and "a woman" (γυναῖκας, 2:9; γυναιξίν, 2:10; γυνή, 2:11), here in 2:12 Paul describes the interactive roles of women and men together—specifically, the role of teaching and governing by "a woman" (γυναικί) in relation to "a man" (ἀνδρός) in the church. Furthermore, throughout the A' element of the microchiasm, Paul has consistently been referring to men and women in general. Consistent, therefore, with Paul's general reference to "men" (ἀνδρός, 2:8) and "women" and "a woman" (γυναῖκας, 2:9; γυναιξίν, 2:10; γυνή, 2:11), the audience would hear Paul's instruction in 2:12 as pertaining to "a woman" (γυναικί) and to "a man" (ἀνδρός) in the same way—not to husbands and wives.[128] Indeed, given Paul's sustained, general address in the A and A' elements to both married and unmarried men and women—the entire congregation of men and women in general (2:1-4), the men in general (2:8), and the women in general (2:9-11)—it would certainly be odd for Paul or the audience to suddenly intend and hear 2:12 as a specific instruction to individual households. To be sure, Paul's prohibition regards the dynamic of "a woman" and "a man" in the church, that is, "in faith"—not husbands and wives.[129]

Given Paul's continued emphasis on salvation (2:3-6) and the church's collaborative missional activity to be a conduit thereof (2:1-2, 7-11), it would be clear to the audience that Paul's instructions pertaining the

---

Gench, *Tyrannical Texts*, 3: "It has frequently been used to silence all women, to exclude them from leadership, to confine them to domestic roles, to legitimate hierarchical relationships. Indeed, to this day, it is the pivotal biblical text in ongoing ecclesial controversies over the role of women in church and society, in many quarters still justifying the church's exclusion of women from leadership roles."

While this study's examination of the 1 Timothy text will demonstrate that the apostle Paul—on the basis of Genesis—does actually exclude women from teaching and governing men in the church, I do sympathize with those who have suffered unduly from a misapplication of this biblical text, which was meant to protect women, not oppress them, as will be discussed below.

127. Cf. Knight, *PE*, 140: "δέ is used here to indicate the contrast, 'learn but not teach.'"

128. The absence of a definitive article (e.g., Eph 5:22; Col 3:18), which would have made clear that Paul was speaking about the relation between a husband and wife, is notably absent. See Knight, *PE*, 140, 142. Contra Long, "Christ's Gifted Bride," 99.

129. See Bassler, *1 & 2 Timothy*, 59-60.

integrated dynamic of "a woman" and "a man" in the church (2:12) is intended to be a missional conduit of salvation. To be sure, where the Savior God desires "all humans to be-saved" (2:3–4a)—irrespective of background and without regard to gender—it is clear that from God's perspective, that is, "in the sight of the Savior God" (2:3), all humans are equally valuable without distinction. Thus for Paul is who "was appointed proclaimer and apostle . . . teacher" (2:7) "according to the command of God our Savior" (1:1), his instructions here in 2:12 for the dynamic between "a woman" and "a man" in relation to teaching and governing in the church are clearly informed by God's paradigm of universal human equality, without any distinction in value, and by God's desire for all humans to be-saved.

Although not a cognate, the aural similarity of the verb "I . . . permit" (ἐπιτρέπω) here in 2:12 of the "b'" sub-element echoes the verb "is proper" (πρέπει) in 2:10 of the parallel "b" sub-element. In effect, the rhetorical connection conveys that "what is proper (πρέπει) for women who profess godliness . . . good works" (2:10) is what "I . . . permit" (ἐπιτρέπω) for women (2:12). That is, given the linguistic and conceptual arrangement of the "b" and "b'" sub-elements, 2:10 and 2:12 would convey the sense of good works are proper for women who profess godliness (2:10), but for a woman to teach or to govern a man is improper (2:12)." Clearly, Paul is still concerned with the proper conduct of women who are "in faith" and the missional impact thereof. Furthermore, combined with the negative particle "not" (οὐκ), Paul's prohibitive phrase "I do not permit" would not be heard by the audience as a mere suggestion; rather, where Paul clearly identified that he "was appointed"—divinely—"proclaimer and apostle . . . teacher" (2:7) and that he authoritatively represents Christ Jesus as an apostle "according to the command of God our Savior and Christ Jesus" (1:1), the audience would hear his instructions "I do not permit" as an authoritative statement precisely because it is divinely sanctioned.[130] Undoubtedly, then, as emphasized throughout the entire performance of the letter thus far, Paul's Ephesian audience understand that to reject his authoritative instructions as an "apostle of Christ Jesus" (1:1) would be tantamount to rejecting the One whom Paul respresents and who appointed Paul for service, namely "Christ Jesus our Lord" (1:12).[131]

---

130. Knight, PE, 140: "Some have suggested that Paul conveys here only a note of personal disinclination . . . But such a suggestion misunderstands the authoritativeness of ἐπιτρέπω when used by Paul."

131. It may be worth noting that the audience would not have heard the present tense aspect of the verb "I . . . permit" (ἐπιτρέπω) in a limited and temporary way but rather that Paul was simply insisting on the prohibition. See Moo, "1 Tim 2:11–15," 185. Cf. Marshall, PE, 454–55: "Nothing can be determined from the aspect or from the

The grammatical construction of 2:12 clearly directs the audience's attention toward the verb "to teach."[132] Indeed, Paul's rhetorical use of cognate terms relating to teaching have shaped the overarching concern of his letter: "some" in the Ephesian church "teach-different" (ἑτεροδιδασκαλεῖν, 1:3); specifically, "some" who are desiring to be "law-teachers" (νομοδιδάσκαλοι, 1:7) are teaching some-thing different that lies-opposed to "the sound teaching (διδασκαλίᾳ)" with which Paul was counted-faithful by God (1:10b–11) and to which Paul was appointed as a "teacher" (διδάσκαλος, 2:7).[133] Certainly, Paul's prohibitive statement "I do not permit a woman to teach (διδάσκειν)" (2:12) would be heard in this sustained emphasis. While the immediate implication of Paul's instruction to not permit a woman "to teach" (διδάσκειν) suggests a connection to "some" who "teach-different" (ἑτεροδιδασκαλεῖν, 1:3) and are desiring to be "law-teachers" (νομοδιδάσκαλοι, 1:7), the degree thereof is undefined. Given the presence of "some" who "teach-different" in the Ephesian church, namely two men publically identified as Hymenaeus and Alexander (1:3, 20), the different teaching of "some"—particularly these men—may have influenced women in the church to abandon "the sound teaching" of Paul by influencing them "to teach" men in the church. Certainly, Paul's instruction here in 2:12 would be consistent with "the sound teaching" (1:10b); thus the prohibition for a woman not "to teach" would be a summons for any and all women in the church to realign themselves with that which Paul was counted-faithful—"the sound teaching," the gospel (1:10–11). Furthermore, where Paul makes explicitly clear that "some" who "teach-different" (1:3) are men (1:20), it is unlikely that the audience hear Paul's instructions as a concern that women in the church are the group of "some" who are teaching different. Rather, by indicating that he does not permit a woman "to teach" (2:12), the audience would understand that Paul's instructions apply to teaching in general, that is, not to the content of teaching, nor to the danger of teaching some-thing different, but to the fact of teaching itself.[134] At the same time, by specifying "a man" (ἀνδρός) as the object

---

verb itself as to the length of time that the injuction would be in effect." See Williams, *The Apostle Paul and Women in the Church*, 112; Schreiner, "Interpretation of 1 Tim 2:9–15," 99–100.

132. The verb is announced at the beginning of the statement; a more literal but less intelligible translation would be: "But to teach, a woman I do not permit, nor to govern a man" (διδάσκειν δὲ γυναικὶ οὐκ ἐπιτρέπω οὐδὲ αὐθεντεῖν ἀνδρός).

133. As divine passives, the verbs "was counted-faithful" (ἐπιστεύθην, 1:11) and "was appointed" (ἐτέθην, 2:7) denote Paul's passivity and God's activity; see chapter 3; see also above.

134. The verb "to teach" (διδάσκειν) in 2:12 does not specify any object of teaching (see *italics*)—neither "different" (ἕτερον) teaching (1:3, 10b), nor "sound" (ὑγιαινούσῃ)

of the verb "to teach," the audience would positively understand that Paul is not prohibiting women from all teaching in general; rather, the teaching in view is only in relation to men.[135] That is, women were permitted to teach other women, as Paul makes clear in his other letters (e.g., Titus 2:3–4).[136] In the case that women in the church were taking the position "to teach" men, Paul's instruction in 2:12 makes clear to the audience that such is contrary to the sound teaching with which he was counted-faithful (1:10b–11) and to which he himself was appointed as a teacher by God's divine activity (2:7). Consequently, where women were teaching men in the Ephesian church, they were actually engaged in some-thing different that lies-opposed to the sound teaching (1:10b), not because the content of the women's teaching was different, but because the act of their teaching men—as indicated by Paul's prohibitive statement in 2:12—was a misapplication of the sound teaching.[137] Still, given that Paul's instructions are

---

teaching (1:10).

This is contra interpretations that Paul's prohibition is not concerned with women teaching in general but only with women who teach false doctrine. Marshall, "Women in Ministry," 67: "The use of the verb *teach* rather than 'teach false doctrine' does not rule out the possibility that false teaching may have been the issue." See Celoria, "1 Tim 2," 21; Scholer, "1 Tim 2.9–15," 107; Payne, *Man and Woman*, 299. Though these interpretations are plausible, the literary context recommends that general teaching is in view, not different teaching by women; further explication is provided below.

135. Though the noun "man" (ἀνδρός) is the immediate object of the verb "to govern" (αὐθεντεῖν), it is also the object of the verb "to teach" (διδάσκειν). Hamilton, "What Women Can Do in Ministry," 24, 41: "both infinitives are modified by ἀνδρός. . . . As it is, the text reads, 'But I do not permit for a woman to teach [a man] or to exercise authority over a man.'"

136. See Schreiner, "Interpretation of 1 Tim 2:9–15," 101. Cf. D'Angelo, "Εὐσέβεια," 160.

137. This is not to suggest that Paul's prohibition here is limited only to the women who were influenced by "some" who "teach-different" (1:3, 10b). While Paul may have had this particular group in mind, the immediate context of the A' element makes clear that Paul has in mind exhortations for both men in general and women in general.

More than likely, women were teaching in Ephesus. Gench, *Tyrannical Texts*, 5: "You don't command them not to teach unless they are, in fact, teaching." See Wagener, "PE," 837; Eisen, *Women Officeholders*, 102; Dowling, *Taking Away the Pound*, 39. Hearon and Maloney rightly state that it "is difficult to reconstruct what the women are teaching, since the author is careful to give no voice to their words" ("Listen to the Voices of the Women," 44). However, in the case that women were teaching, Paul's focus is not that they are false teachers—"some" who teach-different (1:3)—but rather that they are teaching, which itself may have been the result of the different teaching of "some." The nuance is important. Quite unlike his polemic against "some"—namely men, Hymenaeus and Alexander (1:20)—wherein the different content of their teaching is the focus (1:3, 4, 10), Paul's concern with the women is not the content of their teaching but the fact of it (2:12). Moreover, the consistent use of the polemical term "some" to speak of the false teachers throughout the first microchiasm (1:3, 6, 8, 19)

being publically announced in front of the entire Ephesian church, it is unlikely that Paul is referring to matters of women teaching men in private. Instead, Paul not only conveyed that teaching is a public matter capable of influencing the entire church—either to accept "the sound teaching" or to accept "some-thing different" (1:10b)—but also that it is an authoritative matter—either from Paul the divinely appointed "teacher" (2:7) or from "some" who "teach-different" and are desiring to be "law-teachers" (1:3, 7). In other words, Paul's instructive statement "I do not permit a woman to teach . . . a man" (2:12) would denote the prohibition of "public authoritative teaching" in the church.[138]

In this context, the final clause of Paul's instructive statement is heard: "nor to govern a man" (2:12). To be sure, the audience understand that the verbal phrase "I do not permit a woman to teach . . . a man" equally applies to the latter half of the clause, the sense being, "nor do I permit a woman to govern a man."[139] The verb "to govern" (αὐθεντεῖν) conveys that Paul has a woman's authority in view, specifically in relation to a man in the church.[140] The notion of authority would certainly recall the letter's overall

---

is noticeably absent from Paul's instructions to the women in the A' element of the second microchiasm. Furthermore, the explicit identification of the false teachers as men ("Hymenaeus and Alexander," 1:20) in first microchiasm is also worth noting. All of this corroborates that Paul viewed the fact of women teaching and governing men as the result and influence of false teaching—by men (1:20)—rather than viewing the women as the false teachers themselves.

138. The modern analogy to what Paul has in mind is likely preaching. That the verb "to teach" (διδάσκειν) refers to an authoritative function by church leaders in the NT, see Schreiner, "Interpretation of 1 Tim 2:9–15," 101–2; Moo, "1 Timothy 2:11–15," 185.

The observation that "to teach" refers to "public authoritative teaching" may raise the question of whether Paul would have permitted women to teach other topics that did not primarily involve the proclamation of the gospel itself (e.g., the topic of marriage) (see Holmes, *Text in a Whirlwind*, 17). This is a tantalizing question, but one consideration to keep in view is that any single Christian teaching is organically tied to a coherent Christian doctrinal system. In this sense, it is impossible "to teach" on any particular topic without also teaching, whether directly or indirectly, on the whole topic itself. While this is not to say that women should never teach, according to Paul it appears that women's teaching authority should be limited to the instruction of other women (see Titus 2:3–4). Paul's concern, therefore, is not to stifle women's participation in God's missional household; rather, Paul's prohibition must be heard in light of the microchiasm's concern for all people to be-saved (2:4), a task for which he was appointed as a teacher by God (2:7).

139. See note above regarding "man" (ἀνδρός) as the object of both verbs "to teach" and "to govern."

140. Although the topic is of ongoing debate, any attempt to render the infinitive verb αὐθεντεῖν other than "to govern" or "to have authority over"—particularly through a precarious etymological analysis—is mistaken, as Moo observes ("1 Tim 2:11–15," 186). Specifically, αὐθεντεῖν does not connote a negative manner of governing, such as

emphasis not only on Paul's authority as an apostle who fully represents Christ Jesus (1:1) but also—and more significantly—that Paul's authority comes directly from God's authority (1:1, 11; 2:7). As such, for the women who exist in the realm "in faith" (1:2) and thus seek to bring-about the household-law of God "in faith" (1:4), Paul's instruction to not permit a woman "to govern" a man in the church (2:12) would be understood as part of "the household-law of God" where Paul, derivatively, and ultimately God the Father and Christ Jesus the Lord are the authority (1:2). In short, authority in the church, and thus Paul's instructions pertaining to the men and women in the church, is to be seen as part of God's household design that accords with his desire for all humans to be-saved. Significantly, as the audience understand that Paul's instructions are from God, they are to hear that it is part and parcel of their salvation.

The conjunction "nor" (οὐδέ) functions to clarify rather than qualify Paul's instruction; that is, in addition to not teaching men, women are not "to govern a man."[141] In effect, the audience understand that Paul is delineating the two verbs "to teach" and "to govern" as two connected

---

domineering authority (e.g., Belleville, "Teaching and Usurping Authority," 209). That is, Paul in 2:12 is not prohibiting a *negative* form of women governing men but rather a *neutral* form of women governing men in general within the church. Köstenberger's comments are helpful: "The meaning of διδάσκειν in 1 Timothy 2:12 is therefore an important preliminary issue in determining the meaning of αὐθεντεῖν... διδάσκειν, when used absolutely, in the New Testament always denotes an activity that is viewed positively by the writer, to be rendered 'to teach'... If the writer had intended to give the term a negative connotation in 1 Timothy 2:12, he would in all likelihood have used the term ἑτεροδιδασκαλειν (as in 1 Tim. 1:3; 6:3) or some other contextual qualifier specifying the (inappropriate or heretical) content of the teaching... Since the first part of 1 Timothy 2:12 reads, 'But I do not permit a woman to teach,' and the coordinating conjunction οὐδέ requires the second activity to be viewed correspondingly by the writer, αὐθεντεῖν should be regarded as viewed positively as well and be rendered 'to have (or exercise) authority,' and not 'to flout the authority of' or 'to domineer'" ("Complex Sentence," 74). Cf. Marshall, "Women in Ministry," 59, 68. For further analyses on the the use and meaning of αὐθεντεῖν, see Baldwin, "Αὐθεντέω, in 1 Tim 2:12," 39–51; Hübner, "Translating αὐθεντέω," 16–26; Decker, *Evaluation*, 441.

141. Moo provides a more exegetical response ("1 Tim 2:11–15," 187): "While the word in question, *oude* ('and not,' 'neither,' 'nor'), certainly usually joins 'two *closely related* items,' it does not usually join together words that restate the same thing or that are mutually interpreting, and sometimes it joins opposites (e.g., Gentile and Jew, slave and free; Galatians 3:28). Although teaching in Paul's sense here is authoritative in and of itself, not all exercising of authority in the church is through teaching, and Paul treats the two tasks as distinct elsewhere in 1 Timothy when discussing the work of elders in the church (3:2, 4–5; 5:17). That teaching and having authority are 'closely related' is, of course, true, as it is true that both ministries often are carried out by the same individuals, but here and elsewhere they are nonetheless distinct, and in 1 Timothy 2:12, Paul prohibits women from conducting either activity, whether jointly or in isolation, in relation to men." See Köstenberger, "Complex Sentence," 54–56.

but distinct categories and activities. Thus while "to teach" undoubtedly represents an authoritative function, the sense being "public authoritative teaching," it would be equally clear to Paul's audience that "to govern" is not limited to a teaching function. In other words, the audience would not hear the two verbs "to teach" and "to govern" forcibly merged together to mean "authoritative teaching"—the construction of Paul's statement is certainly not communicating, "but I do not permit a woman to authoritatively-teach a man."[142] Much rather, Paul's use of the conjunction "nor" is clearly instructing the Ephesian church that a woman is not permitted "to teach nor to govern a man" (2:12). The audience understand that Paul is plainly prohibiting all the women from both teaching all the men and from having authority over them.[143]

142. It has been suggested that Paul is only prohibiting authoritative teaching (e.g., Jones, "Women, Teaching, and Authority," 146; Blomberg, *From Pentecost to Patmos*, 363–64; Payne, "*Oude* in 1 Timothy 2:12"). However, this interpretation not only seems to confuse Paul's grammar but also reduces Paul's instruction beyond his original intentions, forcibly collapsing two distinct verbs into one.

143. Contra Payne, *Man and Woman*, 444.
Paul's instruction here in 2:12 certainly might sound jarring and even offensive to a modern Western audience; however, as I will demonstrate below regarding 2:13–14, Paul's prohibitive instruction is not only derived from God's creational design that intended safety and joy for humans (2:13) but also from matters of salvation (2:14). In passing, it may be worth noting that Paul's statement might have been equally jarring to some of the Ephesian women in the audience, some (if not many) of whom were likely wealthy, educated, and enjoyed a privileged social standing (see Witherington, *Letters*, 217–21).

Modern scholarship tends to view Paul's teaching here in 2:12 as misogynistic, that is, anti-woman. However, as 2:13–14 will demonstrate, this is clearly not the case. Furthermore, as will be discussed in volume 2, chapter 2, the relationship of Paul's teaching in 2:12–14 to the male leadership role described in 3:2 removes any hint of misogyny. Barcley's comments are helpful: "Indeed, many have called Paul a misogynist (a hater of women). But Paul's letters make clear that many women ministered alongside him and that he had a tender relationship with many women (cf. Phil. 4:2–3; also Rom. 16:1–4, 6, 12–13, and the other women listed in this greeting section). But it is not clear that any of the women mentioned in Acts or in Paul's letters were involved in doing what Paul forbids in 1 Timothy 2" ("1 Timothy," 365).

It may also be worth noting that modern interpretations of 2:12 and the subsequent dismissal thereof seem to represent a deeper issue, namely a personal dismissal of God's own revelation of himself. Ruether, "Feminist Theology," 191: "The critique of such misogynist passages in the Bible presuppose a critical shift of consciousness that has major implications for the authority of the Bible. By naming such a passage as 'misogynist,' one rejects it as authoritative for revealing the will of God and the true nature of God's will for humanity and creation." Genest, "Feminist Theories," 45: "What happens when feminist exegesis questions this Bible from the viewpoint of the dominated? . . . according to the model of hermeneutical operation proposed . . . a passage such as 1 Tim 2:11–15 does not question the present situation from which its questioning has sprung but the biblical text itself . . . In view of all of this, feminist exegetes are contesting, in

Paul immediately presents a positive contrast to his prior instruction: "rather to be in quietness" (2:12). The term "rather" (ἀλλ᾽) here in 2:12 of the "b'" sub-element recalls its occurrence in 2:10 of the parallel "b" sub-element as a positive contrast to the negative activities that hindered the missional activity of the church: "rather (ἀλλ᾽) what is proper for women who profess godliness." Furthermore, what Paul means when he instructs women "to be in quietness" would not be unclear to the audience. The term "quietness" (ἡσυχίᾳ) here in 2:12 of the "b'" sub-element recalls it occurrence in 2:11 of the parallel "b" sub-element to describe the peaceable disposition in which women in the church are to cosmetic themselves: "A woman in quietness (ἡσυχίᾳ) must learn in all submissiveness." That is, where Paul's instruction in 2:11 of the A' element—"A woman in quietness (ἡσυχίᾳ) must learn"—was a specific articulation of his general, missional exhortation to both men and women in 2:2 of the A element—"a peaceful and quiet (ἡσύχιον) life . . . in all godliness and respectability"—the audience understand that Paul's instruction in 2:12 of the A' element—"rather to be in quietness (ἡσυχίᾳ)"—also expresses a particular outworking of the entire church's missional purpose to attract others to Christ for salvation. Moreover, as in 2:2 and 2:11, Paul's use of the term "quietness" clearly does not intend or refer to absolute, mute silence but a disposition of tranquility and peace.[144] Thus the main point that Paul appears to be highlighting is not that a woman "must learn" (2:11) and not teach (2:12) but rather that a woman should cosmetic herself with a disposition that aligns with those who profess godliness (2:10).[145]

Notably, because the cognate terms "quiet" (2:2) and "quietness" (2:10, 12) are clearly applied both to all Christians (2:2) and to women Christians (2:2), the audience understand that Paul is not instructing "quietness" only for women (2:10, 12) but rather a disposition of "quiet" that all Christians—men and women in general—are called to exude (2:2). Indeed, Paul inclusively applies the same standard to himself and to Timothy (see *italics*): "that a peaceful and quiet life *we* might lead-through" (2:2). In other words, even though Paul has provided individual instructions within

---

various degrees, the very notions of canon, revelation, and inspiration." Analogously, if Paul's first-century audience were to willfully disregard the revelatory teaching in 2:12 by the apostle Paul who was completely passive in God's authoritative activity to command and appoint him as an authorized apostolic teacher (1:1; 2:7), then the necessary implication would be a willful disregard of God's own teaching in 2:12 and thus God himself. As will be discussed in 2:13–14 and 3:2, God's teaching here is emphatically and entirely intended to uphold, protect, and cherish women.

144. See May, "Apostle Paul," 84.

145. Much discussion on these controversial verses tends to miss this important observation regarding Paul's strategic placement of the phrase "in quietness" within the rhetorical arrangement of the letter.

the A' element to the men (2:8) and to the women (2:9-12), both sets of instructions reinforce that Paul intends both the men and women in the church—to be sure, everyone "in faith," including Paul and Timothy—to equally share the same peaceable demeanor. Just as Paul wants "men to pray in all place lifting reverent hands without anger and word-quarreling" (2:8), so too Paul wants "women to cosmetic themselves in . . . what is proper . . . in quietness . . . to be in quietness" (2:10, 12). The same was also true of "godliness," which Paul applied to both men and women in the church— "that a peaceful and quiet life we might lead-through in all godliness (εὐσεβείᾳ) and respectability" (2:2)—and was to be specifically exhibited by "women who profess godliness (θεοσέβειαν)" (2:10). Thus pertaining to Paul's instruction for a woman "to be in quietness" (2:12), the audience understand that the unique way in which women in the congregation are to exhibit the disposition of the entire church is not merely in the context of learning (2:11) but in the specific context of learning from the men in the church who teach and govern (2:12). The net effect of Paul's general exhortations to the church (2:1-2) and his specific instructions directed thus far to men and women (2:8-12) within the second microchiasm reflect the apostle Paul's view—to be sure, Christ Jesus's view, whom Paul represents (1:1, 12)—that men and women are to play corresponding and harmonized roles that bring-about the household-law of God in faith (1:4b), namely with both men and women in the church equally and uniquely expressing their alignment with "God our Savior and Christ Jesus our hope" (1:1), that is, with the "Savior God" who desires all humans to be-saved (2:3-4a) and thus with "Christ Jesus, who came into the world to save sinners" and "gave himself as a ransom on behalf of all" (1:15; 2:7).

In summary of Paul's instruction in 2:12, the women in the Ephesian audience who profess godliness (2:10)—that is, who exist "in faith" (1:2, 4; 2:7) and thus "in Christ Jesus" (1:14) as a result of coming to a knowing-embrace of truth (2:4), namely the sound teaching (1:11a) to which Paul was divine appointed as "teacher of the Gentiles in faith and truth" (2:7)— are to recognize the unique roles of teaching and authority that are proper for men and women in the church and bring-about the household-law of God "in faith" (1:4). Given that Paul's authoritative exhortations both generally and individually to men and women in the A and A' elements (2:1-2; 8-12) hinge upon the saving purposes of the one God and one mediator Christ Jesus in the C and C' elements (2:5-6), it is clear to the audience that the dynamic roles of teaching and authority by women in relation to men in the church (2:12) does not assume an intrinsic difference in value but in function, which is to be understood as the congregation's collaborative participation within God's overall plan and purpose of salvation for all humans

(2:4). Where the emphasis in the second microchiasm is that salvation has been made available to all humans through the human Christ Jesus, the emphasis is equally that all—irrespective of background and without partiality or distinction—are to be-saved if they come to a knowing-embrace of truth (2:4). It is within this paradigm of universal human equality without distinction in value—as evidenced by the Savior God's desire for all humans to be-saved, irrespective of background or gender (2:3–4)—that Paul's instructions to men and women in the congregation (2:8–15) are to be understood. Furthermore, it is within this framework that Paul places a special emphasis on men and women accepting and fulfilling their equal and harmonizing roles that will not only bring-about the household-law of God in faith (1:4) but also the salvation of humans.

Due to the structure of the minichiasm, the audience understand that "what is proper (πρέπει) for women who profess godliness" in 2:10a of the "b" sub-element corresponds to why Paul does "not permit" (οὐκ ἐπιτρέπω) a woman to teach nor to govern a man" in 2:12 of the parallel "b'" sub-element. While Paul makes clear that this is proper for women "in faith," he has yet to provide the ultimate basis and reason thereof. Given that Paul is Christ Jesus's very own personal messenger, an apostle (1:1, 12), and that Paul is only an apostle by divine initiative (1:1; 2:7), the audience understand that the ultimate basis cannot and would not originate from Paul. Indeed, the ultimate basis would exclusively originate from God and Christ Jesus.

In the latter half of the "b'" element, Paul declares the ultimate basis: "For Adam was formed first, then Eve" (2:13). As the audience heard in 2:5, the conjuction "For" (γάρ) marks the basis for the preceeding statement. In effect, the audience understand that the reason why Paul does not permit a woman in the church to teach nor to govern a man (2:12) is because "Adam was formed first, then Eve" (2:13).[146] Throughout the 2:9–15 minichiasm and in the 2:1–15 microchiasm, Paul's reasoning for men and women's behavior has been grounded in God's desire for all humans to be-saved (2:3–4) and the corresponding divine activity of the one mediator Christ Jesus, who gave himself as a ransom on behalf of all (2:5–6). Similarly in 2:13, rather than turning to a personal conviction or cultural norm, Paul grounds his instruction in God's divine activity in the creation of humans, namely the

---

146. See Knight, *PE*, 142. Moo fairly observes: "There is a more serious problem with the viewpoint according to which verse 12 may be applied only to women who are seeking to teach falsely: verse 13. It is telling that most of the advocates of this general approach pass over verse 13 very quickly, explaining it as simply as an 'introduction' to verse 14, or ignoring it entirely. Yet this verse provides the first reason ('for' [*gar*]) for the prohibitions in verse 12" ("1 Tim 2:11–15," 190); Moo cites the examples of Spencer, *Beyond the Curse*, 89–91 and Evans, *Women in the Bible*, 104.

narrative of Genesis 2:7-23. In reference to the same "Adam" (Αδαμ) whom the Lord God commanded (LXX Gen 2:16), Paul observes: "Adam ('Αδάμ) was formed first, then Eve (Εὕα)" (2:13).¹⁴⁷ To be sure, that Paul has the creation narrative in view is clearly communicated by the passive verb "was formed" (ἐπλάσθη), indicating Adam and Eve's complete passivity in the matter; that is, they were created by God in the exact manner that God himself determined: "Adam . . . first, then Eve" (2:13). Paul's rhetorical use of "first" (πρῶτος) and "then" (εἶτα) deserves explicit attention.

The movement of the overall macrochiasm is telling. In the concluding A' element of the first microchiasm, the audience heard Paul's use of "first" (πρῶτός, 1:15b; πρώτῳ, 1:16a) to connote his "lead, foremost, prominent" status among sinners—not his temporal sequence in history as a sinner.¹⁴⁸ In the introductory A element of the second microchiasm, the audience heard Paul's use of "first" (πρῶτον, 2:1) to communicate the "lead, foremost, prominent" activity of the church, namely missional prayer and godliness (2:1-2). Here, then, in the concluding A' element of the second microchiasm, the audience again hear Paul use the term "first" (πρῶτος, 2:13). To be sure, the interconnected macrochiastic progression from the A' element of the first microchiasm to the A element of the second microchiasm—via transitional words—then to the A' element of the second microchiasm—via chiastic parallelism—not only indicates that the audience would understand Paul's use of "first" (πρῶτος, 2:13) in the same, consistent way as "first" (πρῶτός, 1:15b; πρώτῳ, 1:16a; πρῶτον, 2:1), but it also strengthens and affirms that

---

147. Moo's comments here are especially astute: "For by rooting these prohibitions in the circumstances of creation rather than in the circumstances of the fall, Paul shows that he does not consider these restrictions to be the product of the curse and presumably, therefore, to be phased out by redemption. And by citing creation rather than a local situation or cultural circumstance as his basis for the prohibitions, Paul makes it clear that, while these local or cultural issues may have provided the *context* of the issue, they do not provide the *reason* for his advice. His *reason* for the prohibitions of verse 12 is the created role relationship of man and woman, and we may justly conclude that these prohibitions are applicable as long as this reason remains true" ("1 Tim 2:11-15," 190-91). See also Moo's response to the counter position (ibid., 191). Merkle, "Paul Arguments from Creation," 548: "It is based on creation and therefore transcends cultures."

It may be worth noting that in the relevant portions of LXX Genesis to 1 Timothy 2:13-14 (LXX Gen 2:7—3:24; cf. 1:26-27), the name "Adam" (Αδαμ) occurs nearly twenty times (2:16, 2:19, 20, 21, 22, 23, 25) while the name "Eve" (Ευαν) does not occur at all until after the relevant portions (LXX Gen 4:1). Clearly, the LXX Genesis narrative places a literary emphasis on "Adam," not only regarding *creation* (2:7-25) but also regarding *sin* (3:1-24). In 1 Timothy 2:13-14, Paul's rhetorical emphasis is likewise placed squarely on "Adam" both in regard to creation and to sin; see discussion below.

148. Recall Knight's comment: "Paul does not mean the "first" in a sequence, since he was not the first one saved by Christ" (*PE*, 102).

Paul himself intends for his audience to understand the four occurrences of the same word in the same, consistent way: "lead, foremost, prominent" in status, degree, or importance—*not* sequence in history. Significantly, then, the audience clearly understand that Paul is not merely concerned in verse 2:13 to speak about the sequential order in which Adam and Eve were created—Adam first, then Eve (e.g., Gen 2:7, then 2:21–22).[149] Much rather, Paul is clearly concerned to highlight how prominence and the order thereof relates to teaching and authority between men and women—Adam first, then, Eve (e.g., Gen 2:15–17, then 2:19–20a, 23).[150] In sum, where Paul was the "first"—lead, prominent—of sinners (1:15b, 16a) and Paul's exhortation for prayer and a life of godliness is the "first"—lead, prominent—activity of the church (2:1), so too is Adam the "first"—lead, prominent—in creation. It is in this context that Paul's next words—"then Eve"—would be clearly interpreted by his audience.

Paul has provided consistent, prior context to not only define but also affirm Paul's use of "first" (1:15b, 16a; 2:1; 2:13). Conversely, the audience have no prior context to interpret Paul's use of "then" (εἶτα) except for its specific occurrence here in connection with "first." Thus, given Paul's reliable employment of "first" in reference to that which is "lead" or "prominent," it would not only be wildly unfitting for him to suddenly introduce "then" as a temporal marker of sequence, but it would also be equally unfitting on the part of his audience to perceive such a sudden, ungrounded change in meaning. The understanding would clearly be that "then" is a qualification of Adam's prominence as "first." Where Adam is "first," the phrase "then Eve" is unambiguous: Eve is second to Adam's lead. Thus in 2:13 Paul is clearly distinguishing Adam as the human whom God formed to lead— "first"—and Eve as the human whom God formed to follow—"then."[151]

---

149. In view of Genesis 2:7, then Genesis 2:21–22, the narrative communicates that Adam was created *sequentially* prior to Eve.

150. In view of Genesis 2:15–17, then Genesis 2:19–20a, 23, it is clear that Adam alone was given a specific purpose to guard the garden (2:15), Adam alone was commanded directly by the Lord God and told the consequences thereof (2:16–17), and Adam alone was given authority to name all living creatures (2:19–20a), which included the naming of Eve, whom he named "woman" (2:23). In this way, the narrative communicates that Adam was created with *prominence* in regard to Eve.

151. The observation regarding Paul's consistent use of the term "first" as indicative of *prominence* rather than *sequence* does not undermine traditional interpretations of 2:13. Not a few commentators conclude that Adam's authority in relation to Eve is based on timing, that is, a creational sequence, e.g., Long, *1 & 2 Timothy*, 76: "since Adam was created first and then Eve second (2:13), the order of creation establishes males as authoritative teachers over females." Yet, rather than concluding that Adam's *prominence* is the result of his *sequence*—the traditional interpretation—it is apparent that the audience would understand Paul's statement as much more direct and streamlined: Adam's

Paul's use of "first" and "then" deserve two further observations. While the consistent use of "first" clearly conveys that Adam was created in a position of prominence relative to Eve, the term "first" is quite specific, therefore, that Adam's position was only one of *prominence*—note, *not dominance*—in relation to Eve. Second, the phrase "then Eve" is rhetorically unnecessary for Paul to make his point. That is, the simple phrase "For Adam was formed first" would have sufficiently communicated that Adam was formed to be the lead.[152] Paul's deliberate inclusion of the phrase "then Eve" would therefore be intentional and heard with a definite rhetorical emphasis (see *italics*), the sense being, "Adam was formed *first, then* Eve." That Paul felt compelled to emphasize this point likely indicates its corrective function for the audience; more than likely, there was a misunderstanding in Ephesus regarding God's purpose of creation and men and women's roles therein. The polemical context of the letter further suggests that such a misunderstanding may have been the result of "some" who teach "some-thing different" that lies-opposed to the sound teaching (1:3, 10b). In response to the presence and influence of "some" in the mid-sixties Ephesian church, Paul has demonstrated in his 1 Timothy letter to the church that only the sound teaching with which he was counted-faithful (1:10b–11) and to which he was appointed as a teacher (2:7) is apt to correct the different teaching of "some" (1:3, 10b). Paul's statement in 2:13—indeed, in the entire 2:9–15 minichiasm—is therefore part of the sound teaching, the gospel that exhibits God's radiant glory and results in blessing toward him (1:10b–11a). In short, the audience understand that Paul's corrective teaching for the church in Ephesus has God in view from beginning to end.

---

prominence is simply the result of his *prominence*—"first," lead, foremost, prominent (1:15b, 16a; 2:1).

Exegetical objections to Adam's prominence are often based on the sequence of creation. For example, Orlemanski suggests—albeit incorrectly—that the sequential creation narrative of Genesis 1 and 2 undermines Adam's prominence: "The first creation story in Genesis [1:27] gives man and woman a simultaneous moment of birth, and, 'male and female,' they share dominion over the earth. Within this first iteration, there is no basis for establishing the priority of one sex over the other. Only the second account establishes Eve's secondary and dependent status. In order to produce the priority of man over woman, the reader must forget the ambiguity at the root . . . temporal succession is the principle that grounds Adam's superiority to Eve, as at 1 Timothy 2:12–13" ("A Silence in the Family Tree," 41). To be sure, I disagree with Orlemanski's exegesis of Genesis 1 and 2; yet, her point is worth noting because where *sequence* is not Paul's principle, there are no exegetical grounds to reject that *prominence*—regardless of *sequence*—is Paul's point in 1 Timothy 2:13. All responsibility, therefore, clearly falls upon Adam; see below in regard to 2:14.

152. The simple phrase "For Adam was formed first" would also be consistent with the LXX Genesis creation narrative, which names Adam nearly twenty times but does not name Eve until after the creation and sin narrative; see note above.

Given that Paul's statement in 2:13—"For Adam was formed first, then Eve"—marks the basis for his instruction in 2:12—"I do not permit a woman to teach nor to govern a man"—it is clear to the audience that Adam's prominence, his creational role as the "first," lead, prominent human in relation to Eve, is the basis for Paul's prohibitive instruction for a woman to teach and to govern in relation to a man. In other words, Paul is clearly identifying that God created Adam "to teach" and "to govern" as "first" in relation to Eve. To be sure, where 2:12 distinctly concerns both teaching and governing, the fact that 2:13 is presented as the basis for 2:12 makes clear that Adam's prominence as "first" ought to be understood in relation both to teaching and to governing.[153] The positive basis for why it is proper for women who profess godliness (2:10; "b" sub-element) not to teach nor to govern a man (2:12; "b'" sub-element) is because it was proper for Adam to both teach and govern as "first" (2:13). Heard together, therefore, the rhetorical implication of Paul's statements in verses 2:12 and 2:13 would be heard positively, the sense being: "I permit a man and to teach and to govern a woman, for Adam was formed first both to teach and to govern, then Eve."

Moreover, the arrangement of 2:12–13 within the linguistic arrangement of the 2:9–15 minichiasm would carry forward a further indication. The parallel organization of the "b" sub-element (2:10–11) and "b'" sub-element (2:12–14) makes clear to the audience that Paul's main concern is *not* that women "in quietness must learn" (2:11) while men are permitted "to teach" and "to govern" (2:12); rather, Paul's main point to the audience is explicitly in regard to what is proper for women who reside in the realm "in faith" and thus live according to and bring-about "the household-law of God in faith" (1:4). Paul's concern and reason for referencing Adam as "first" is therefore directly tied to his concern for women to live out their unique and necessarily role as women in the missional household God—positively, to do what is proper for women who profess godliness (2:10, 12b); negatively, to avoid what is improper (2:12a). Thus where 2:13 is the basis for why women "must learn" from men in the church, the clear indication is that Adam was intended by God—"formed first"—to support, foster, and encourage what is proper for Eve. In other words, Eve's godliness and proper conduct was directly tied to Adam being "first" in teaching and authority. As noted above, for Paul to convey his point regarding Adam's prominence as "first," the statement in 2:13 does not require the

---

153. The Genesis narrative itself implies that Adam's role was to teach Eve. Witherington, *Letters*, 229: "That story is quite clear that Adam alone was formed and was present for God's original instructions about what was prohibited. Eve was not there for proper divine instruction." Presumably, Eve learned about God's commands (Gen 2:16–17) through Adam's teaching.

mention of Eve. Here, then, Paul's inclusion of the qualifying clause "then Eve" not only functions for rhetorical emphasis but also—and far more significantly—further explains why Adam was "first" as teacher and authority, namely to ensure that Eve did "what is proper for women who profess godliness" (2:10). In short, it was Adam's creational role to safeguard Eve's godliness—"Adam was formed first" for this very purpose. Simultaneously, therefore, as much as Adam was the "first" (2:13) in regard to teaching and governing (2:12), it could be said that Eve was the "first" in regard to learning and submissiveness (2:11). In this way, Eve was the "first"—lead—of what is proper for women who profess godliness (2:10). Notably, Adam did not impose this arrangement on Eve, nor did Adam decide his role thereof; rather both she and Adam were passively "formed" (ἐπλάσθη), created by God to be in this dynamic.[154] It was God's original design and intention that for Eve's benefit Adam was formed "first" (2:13) "to teach" and "to govern" (2:12) for the promotion of her godliness (2:10). The application to Paul's Ephesian audience would be apparent: a woman in the church who professes godliness (2:10) learns in the same way that Eve was created to learn from Adam. Indeed, where 2:13 is the basis for 2:12, Paul's statement would apply equally to the women and men: the women in the audience are intended to do what Eve was formed to do, namely learn from Adam; the men in the audience are intended to do what Adam was formed to do, namely to teach and to govern the women in order to foster, encourage, and promote the women's godliness. In a word, "Adam was formed first" to protect Eve; the men in Ephesus are supposed to protect the women.

In the concluding verse of the "b'" sub-element (2:14), Paul states: "And Adam was not deceived, but the woman being-deceived in transgression became." The audience would understand 2:14 as a clear reference to humanity's sin in Genesis 3 after the creation narrative in Genesis 2. While Paul's allusion to humanity's sin in 2:14 (Gen 3) after his reference to the sinless creation account in 2:13 (Gen 2) is sequentially fitting, its significance within Paul's sustained focus on salvation is far greater. By referring to the entrance of sin into the world in 2:14, Paul provides the reason why Christ Jesus came into the world in 1:15—to save sinners—and thus why Christ Jesus gave himself as a ransom on behalf of all in 2:6. To be sure, it is Paul's statement of the event of sin here in 2:14 of the A' element that

---

154. The passive form of the verb "was formed" (ἐπλάσθη) both conveys Adam and Eve's lack of participation and God's full activity in the matter; see above. Barcley, *1 & 2 Timothy*, 93: Paul's "appeal to creation indicates to us that this command has a universal and abiding validity. It points to the way God intended human beings to function from the beginning, before the Fall, before the corrupting influence of sin in human relationships."

provides all relevance for Paul's discussion of the "Savior God, who desires all humans to be-saved" in 2:3–4a of the parallel A element.

Given Paul's clear emphasis on Adam's creational role as the "first," lead, prominent human (2:13), the meaning of Paul's statement "Adam was not deceived" would not be unclear. Undoubtedly, Paul's statement is not excusing Adam from the events in Genesis 3; much rather, Paul is indicating the opposite.[155] A few observations are worth mentioning. First, within the current "b'" sub-element, Paul specified Adam's creational role as having a "first"—prominent, foremost, leading—quality and purpose. Thus as "first," all responsibility falls upon Adam—not Eve. Paul is emphatic that this was an inherent part of God's design: "Adam was formed first, then Eve" (2:13). Second, as noted, the movement of the minichiasm indicates that Adam was not merely formed by God to simply be "first" in regard to teaching and governing; much more, God formed Adam in order that Adam would carry out his purpose for being "first" in regard to teaching and governing. In other words, God created Adam with the full ability to complete and perform his role as "first." Were anything to go wrong, it would not be an inherent inability in Adam to teach and govern. Furthermore, as the "first," lead teacher who received all instructions directly from God (Gen 2:16–17), and as the "first," lead authority who was appointed directly by God (Gen 2:19–20a, 22–23), were anything to go wrong, it would not be due to an inherent insufficiency in the content or quality of Adam's teaching and governing that he received.[156] Therefore when Paul says "Adam was not deceived" (Ἀδὰμ οὐκ ἠπατρήθη), this is clearly quite true. Paul's statement plainly indicates that any failure by Adam to carry out his creational role as "first" could only be due to a voluntary abdication of the role for which he was directly created and equipped by God. In other words, where 2:14 refers to the act of humanity's sin, the clear sense is that Adam knew better but chose otherwise.[157] Moreover, certainly the one to suffer from

---

155. It has been suggested that Paul's statement in 2:14 intends to place the blame for sin on Eve; such an interpretation, however, is neither supported by the 1 Timothy text nor by Paul's other letters. For example, Keegan suggests that 1 Timothy 2:14 indicates that Adam is not to blame and, therefore, concludes that such "is contrary to Paul's teaching, for Paul clearly speaks of Adam's sin, not Eve's (Rom 5:12–19)" (*First and Second Timothy*, 16). To be sure, Paul's teaching in 1 Timothy 2:14 is fully consistent with his other teaching: Adam is to blame; see discussion below.

156. This goes against the notion that Eve's deception resulted from Adam's inept instruction (e.g., Witherington, *Letters*, 231; McCabe, "Answers," 4–5).

157. Blomberg aptly observes: "if Adam was not deceived, then it means that he sinned 'with his eyes wide open,' so to speak" (*From Pentecost to Patmos*, 364). It may be worth noting that Blomberg goes on to indicate that such is "scarcely a reason for giving him [Adam] and his progeny a leadership role!" (ibid.). Similarly, Schreiner suggests

SALVATION FOR ALL THROUGH PRAYER AND GODLY CONDUCT

such willing abdication by Adam would be Eve, who was formed to learn from and be led by Adam (2:13).

It is within this context that Paul's concluding statement in 2:14—"but the woman being-deceived in transgression became"—would be heard by the audience. It was not Adam's deception or ineptitude—"Adam was not deceived" (Ἀδὰμ οὐκ ἠπατρήθη)—but rather Adam's rejection of his creational role to be "first"—his refusal to teach and to govern Eve—that led to "the woman being-deceived" (ἡ . . . γυνὴ ἐξαπατηθεῖσα) in 2:14. In other words, where Eve was "being-deceived," it was precisely because Adam allowed it to happen.[158] Heard together, then, Paul's statement "Adam was not deceived, but the woman being-deceived" does not indicate that Eve was primarily to blame but rather positively indicates that Adam, who was competent, lucid, and equipped by God to teach and to govern as "first" (2:13), was both primarily and directly to blame for the event in 2:14.[159] For sure, Paul's main point effectively concerns abdication by Adam, not usurpation by Eve.[160] Thus in 2:14 of the "b'" element, the audience hear and are emphatically reminded that Adam was indeed "first"—lead, foremost, prominent—in regard to sin.[161] For the men in the Ephesian church listen-

---

that "it is hard to see how this argument would function as a reason for men teaching women" ("Interpretation of 1 Tim 2:9-15," 113). However, rather than implying a flaw in God's design or that men are unqualified to teach women, Paul's point is to highlight that Adam's active decision to reject God's design is what led to sin and endangered Eve; in effect, therefore, Paul is calling upon the men in the church to live according to their creational design. Indeed, the activity of men abdicating their creational role is the activity and situation that neither Paul nor God want the men in the Ephesian church to repeat; hence, the men are to teach and to govern.

158. This is corroborated by the Genesis narrative, as Scholer aptly puts it: "Gen. 3:6 states that the man was with the woman in the event" ("1 Tim 2.9-15," 113). Merkle, "Paul Arguments from Creation," 543: "apparently Adam was with Eve during the temptation . . . Adam should have intervened and spoiled the serpent's plan. That Adam watched the event and yet did not intervene points to the active abdication of his lead-role to teach and to govern." Contra Tamez, *Struggles for Power*, 42.

159. Knight, *PE*, 143-44: "καὶ Ἀδὰμ οὐκ ἠπατρήθη is not meant to deny Adam's sin or participation in the fall . . . but to indicate, as the Genesis narrative does, that he sinned willfully, not as a result of deception (Gn. 3:6, 12)." Merkle, "Paul Arguments from Creation," 543: "According to Gen 3:13, Eve exclaims, 'the serpent deceived [ἠπάτησέν, LXX] me.' Adam, however, could make no such claim since the serpent did not directly deceive him."

160. Contra Wagener, "PE," 837. What is clear from the text is that Adam's personal decision to reject his role as "first" is in view. To be sure, the emphasis is on Adam, as Merkle states: "His failure . . . allowed Eve to be deceived and, at the same time, become the leader in their relationship" ("Paul Arguments from Creation," 543).

161. Gench aptly asserts: "Genesis . . . by no means absolves Adam" (*Tyrannical Texts*, 7). Such is precisely Paul's point in 1 Timothy.

Keegan suggests that Paul's statements in 1 Timothy 2:13-14 is an "unusual

ing to the performance of Paul's letter, the apostle's statements in 2:13–14 would likely be heard as a subtle rebuke, the sense being that they had, to a degree, abdicated their creational role as teachers and authorities, effectively causing the need for Paul to address the situation in in 2:12. More specifically, had the men who were responsible for teaching and governing in the Ephesian church actually taught and governed the congregation as they were intended to do—to be sure, in keeping with "the sound teaching" (1:10b)—then there would be no need for Paul's corrective instructions nor an explanation thereof (2:12–14). Significantly, given that Paul's letter was occasioned by "some" who "teach-different" in the Ephesian church (1:3), particularly "some-thing different" that lies-opposed to "the sound teaching" with which Paul was counted-faithful (1:10b–11) and to which Paul was appointed as a "teacher" (2:7), the audience would likely understand that Paul's corrective statements in 2:12–14 are not primarily aimed the women but rather at "some"—of whom are men, namely Hymenaeus and Alexander (1:20). In other words, where Paul is clearly using 2:13–14 to highlight the role of men to teach and govern in the church, the rhetorical force of Paul's statement would be specifically intended for the men who both "teach-different" and govern inadequately in the mid-sixties Ephesian church. Indeed, the inadequacy of "some" who teach and govern in the church—those whom Timothy must charge (1:3)—is Paul's overarching concern.

Still, the women in the audience would likely hear a subtle rebuke as well. By implying that women who profess godliness (2:10) are supposed to be like Eve in her creational role (2:13), Paul would clearly intend for them not to repeat Eve's mistake (2:14). In Genesis 3, as much as Adam is to blame for abdicating his role, Eve is to blame for abdicating hers. On the one hand, her error was that she assumed Adam's vacant role as "first," thus "being-deceived," that is, taught and governed by the serpent rather than by Adam, and thus "in transgression became" Adam's teacher and authority.

---

interpretation of the Adam and Eve story" and thus an example of "1 Timothy's inventive interpretation of Genesis" (*First and Second Timothy*, 16). Keegan's conclusion, however, stems from an incorrect exegesis of the 1 Timothy 2:13–14 text and a subsequent methodology thereof. Ibid.: "One needs to go beyond the original meaning of [1 Tim] 2:11–12 by reading this passage with a hermeneutic of suspicion . . . a method that questions the validity of these cultural presuppositions and seeks a deeper meaning in the text. This method enables contemporary readers to arrive at fresh meanings of the text that are free from the cultural assumptions of the past." Keegan's comments are significant, not only highlighting his own "inventive interpretation" of biblical texts—which he himself calls a "hermeneutic of suspicion"—but also highlighting the fundamental distortion of Paul's point, namely that God's creational design is not a human, cultural presupposition but is a God-presupposition.

On the other hand, therefore, Eve's error was that she abondoned the purpose for which she was formed in relation to Adam.[162] The first sin, then, as articulated in 2:14, would be understood by the audience as the dual and improper exchange of both teaching and authority: not only did Adam give up his creational design and Eve abandon hers, but also each one assumed the other's—Adam, of course, leading this exchange as "first." Thus in the "b'" sub-element, where Paul's basis for women not teaching nor governing men in 2:12 was positively stated as "Adam was formed *first, then* Eve" in 2:13, the audience hear Paul's basis for 2:12 stated negatively the same way in 2:14, the sense being: "but Adam chose to be *then*, and Eve became *first*." It is for this reason—both positively (2:13) and negatively (2:14)—that Paul, who is an authoritative proclaimer, apostle, and teacher according to the command and divine appointment of God (1:1; 2:7) decidedly instructs the women in the audience not to teach nor to govern men (2:12). Paul does not want the men and women in the church—those who exist "in faith" (1:2, 4; 2:7) that is, "in Christ Jesus" (1:14)—to reenanct the entrance of sin into the world (2:14) but rather to live in view of Christ Jesus's entrance into the world to save them (1:15), and thus live to bring-about the household-law of God in faith (1:4).

Because Christ Jesus came into the world to save sinners (1:15) from the results of 2:14, it certainly would not be fitting nor proper for the men and women in the audience to ignore Paul's instructions—he fully represents Christ Jesus according to the command of Christ Jesus (1:1) and by Christ Jesus's very own personal appointment of Paul for service (1:12). Certainly, then, the phrase "the woman being-deceived" would be a warning for the women in the audience not only to listen to the sound teaching of the authoritative, apostolic teacher Paul (1:10b; 2:7) but to do so over and against the different teaching of "some" in the Ephesian church. In sum, 2:14 of the "b'" sub-element would be heard by the Ephesian audience as a tangible example of what happens when God's creational design for teaching and authority among men and women is not accepted, namely the result is that humans "being-deceived in transgression became."[163] Significantly, then, given that Paul has described the possibility of existing in two oppos-

---

162. Witherington, *Letters*, 232: "This situation Paul may see as a violation of the creation order, but even more to the point, he sees it as an abuse or an unauthorized use of power." Cochran, *As Though It Were Actually True*, 214: "Unlike the husband, however, the wife does have a mitigation on this responsibility [to lead]. If her husband leads her to sin, she is to obey God rather than man." In this way, where Adam functionally led Eve to sin by abdicating his leadership role, Eve was to remind Adam to resume his responsibility for which he was created.

163. Schreiner, "Interpretation of 1 Tim 2:9–15," 145: "Thus, the appeal to Genesis 3 serves as a reminder of what happens when God's ordained pattern is undermined."

ing realms—"in faith" (1:2, 4; 2:7), that is, "in Christ Jesus" (1:14) versus "in unfaithfulness" (1:13)—Paul's application of the phrase "in transgression (ἐν παραβάσει) became" to his Ephesian audience would likely be understood as a synonym for the latter—an existence "in unfaithfulness" (ἐν ἀπιστίᾳ). In other words, the sense of becoming "in transgression" would be tantamount to the shipwrecking of their faith (1:20). Thus the implication of not adhering to Paul's instructions in the "b'" sub-element (2:12–14) is straight-forward, not only conveying a rejection of faith and salvation but also a willful alignment and acceptance of sin and its entrance into the world—the definitive antithesis of holding grace to Christ Jesus as Lord (1:12), the mediator who came into the world to save sinners (1:15) and gave himself as a ransom on their behalf (2:6).

1 Timothy 2:15: She Will Be-Saved, If They Remain In Faith

("a'" sub-element)

In the concluding "a'" sub-element of the 2:9–15 minichiasm and concluding verse within the A' element of the second microchiasm, Paul declares: "But she will be-saved consistent-with child-parenting, if they remain in faith and love and holiness with self-control" (2:15). The passive verb "will be-saved" (σωθήσεται) here in 2:15 of the A' element recalls Paul's earlier assertion in 2:3–4a of the parallel A element that the "Savior" (σωτῆρος) God desires all human "to be-saved" (σωθῆναι). Notably, the passive verbs "to be-saved" (σωθῆναι, 2:4a) in the A element and "will be-saved" (σωθήσεται, 2:15) in the A' element highlight God's divine activity: neither "all humans" in the A element nor any woman in the A' element can "be-saved" (2:4a, 15) apart from God's saving activity. Indeed, the verb "will be-saved" (σωθήσεται) in 2:15 not only recalls that God desires all humans "to be-saved" (σωθῆναι) in 2:4a but specifically that the "Savior" (σωτῆρος) God" desires such (2:3). It is for this reason that Paul states, "For there is one God, and there is one mediator of God and humans" (2:5)—God is the active participant in the salvation of humans. Significantly, then, both in the linguistic framing of the A and A' elements and in the conceptual framing of the pivotal C and C' elements, Paul's emphasis on God's divine concern for the salvation of humans in the second microchiasm would be apparent:

> A element: "our Savior (σωτῆρος) God, who desires all humans to be-saved (σωθῆναι)" (2:3–4a);
>
> C element: "For there is one God" (2:5a);

C' element: "and there is one mediator of God and humans, the human Christ Jesus, who gave himself as a ransom on behalf of all" (2:5b–6);

A' element: "she will be-saved (σωθήσεται)" (2:15).

The entire microchiasm is both framed by and hinges upon God's divine activity to save humans. Moreover, "she will be-saved" in 2:15 functions as the climactic summation of God's divine activity in the literary unit. Further still, due to the progression of the microchiasm, the placement of the phrase "she will be-saved" in 2:15 of the concluding A' element brings fuller meaning to the parallel verb "to be-saved" in 2:4a of the A element: God's desire is not for all humans to be-saved from an abstract danger but from the specific consequence of Adam and Eve's active rebellion against their creational design, and thus against their creator, God himself. In this way, the microchiasm advances the audience's understanding of who their Savior God is: the very God who was sinned against by humans (2:14) is the same God who desires humans to be-saved from such sin (2:4a), hence Paul climactically concludes that "she will be-saved" (2:15). Indeed, such is possible because the mediator of God and humans, the human Christ Jesus came into the world "to save" (σῶσαι) sinners (1:15; 2:5b).[164]

Paul goes on to state that a woman will be-saved "consistent-with child-parenting, if they remain in faith and love and holiness with self-control" (2:15). The preposition "consistent-with" (διά) in 2:15—the sense being "in keeping with"—recalls its prior occurrence in 2:10 wherein Paul specified that the proper manner for women who profess godliness to cosmetic themselves is "consistent-with (δι') good works." Here in 2:15, then, Paul's statement "she will be-saved consistent-with" clearly has in view the missional lifestyle of women in the church who profess godliness and thus exist in the realm "in faith." What is more, "consistent-with" (διά) in 2:15 also recalls its occurrence in 1:16 wherein Paul declared that "consistent-with" (διά) his status as the "first," lead of sinners (1:15b, 16a) and the fact that Christ Jesus came to save sinners (1:15a), he was granted-mercy. Notably, in both these

---

164. To be sure, Paul's Ephesian audience would understand that "will be-saved" in 2:15 refers specifically to salvation—not physical well-being. Contra MacArthur, *1 & 2 Timothy*, 28: "In this context this is better translated 'will be preserved.' The Greek word can also mean 'to rescue,' 'to preserve safe and unharmed,' 'to heal,' or 'to deliver from.' It appears several times in the New Testament without reference to spiritual salvation (see Matt. 8:25; 9:21–22; 24:22; 27:40, 42, 49; 2 Tim. 4:18)." Here in 1 Timothy, however, it is evident that the sustained context of Paul's use of "will be-saved" (σωθήσεται) is the same spiritual, eternal salvation referred to in 1:1 ("Savior"; σωτῆρος), in 1:15 ("to save"; σῶσαι), in 2:3 ("Savior"; σωτῆρος), and in 2:4a ("to be-saved"; σωθῆναι). See discussion in Knight, *PE*, 144–47. See also discussion in Cohick, *Women*, 138.

occurrences, Paul's use of "consistent-with" is heard within the specific context of salvation—"Christ Jesus came . . . to save sinners . . . consistent-with this, I was granted-mercy" (1:15–16a); "she will be-saved consistent-with . . ." (2:15). Thus as much "consistent-with" in 2:15 conveys that the missional activity of the women is in view, the indication is also that such activity will result in the salvation of others.

The term "child-parenting" (τεκνογονίας) denotes "childbearing."[165] On the surface, this seems to suggest that women must marry, conceive, and bear children in order to "be-saved."[166] However, Paul has made clear throughout the second microchiasm that all human salvation only comes through the divine activity of the one God, particularly the activity of the "one mediator of God and humans, the human Christ Jesus, who gave himself as a ransom on behalf of all" (2:6).[167] To be sure, no amount of "child-parenting" is a means of salvation—Paul made clear in the first microchiasm that only by humans coming to have-faith upon Christ Jesus is what takes hold of his coming to save them (1:15–16).[168] Given Paul's allusion to the Genesis narrative in the immediatlely prior verses (2:13–14), it seems that the audience might hear "she will be-saved consistent-with child-parenting" as a further allusion to Genesis, namely LXX Genesis 3:15 wherein Eve's seed—the seed of "the woman" (τῆς γυναικός)—will defeat the seed of the serpent. In this case, Paul would likely be making a reference to Mary and the birth of Christ Jesus who came into the world to, as it were, defeat the serpent—bruising the serpent's head, while having his heel bruised by the serpent (Gen 3:15).[169] Yet, given the progression, flow, and rhetorical

---

165. It may be worth noting the jarring impact of the term "child-parenting" upon the audience. Osiek and Balch, *Families in the New Testament World*, 139: "Many women in Greco-Roman society died in childbirth." See Cohick, *Women*, 135.

166. See Keegan, *First and Second Timothy*, 16. Wagener, "PE," 838: "the promise of salvation, spoken in the indicative, has an immense prescriptive role: it eliminates a woman's freedom and compels women to fulfill their reproductive role." Gench, *Tyrannical Texts*, 7: "1 Timothy 2:15 . . . is unique in the New Testament in suggesting that salvation for women is different from that of men, requiring adherence to domestic, maternal roles." Tamez, "1 Timothy," 511: "The phrase 'she will be saved through child-bearing' (2:15) is thus best understood as an argument used to convince women to continue in their assigned traditional roles." See Portefaix, "'Good Citizenship,'" 155; Upton, "Feminist Theology," 109.

167. The passive verbs "to be-saved" (2:4a) and "will be-saved" (2:15) convey that humans do not act to save themselves but rather are passive in regard to God's activity to save them. See discussion above.

168. Payne, *Man and Woman*, 418: "Unless 1 Tim 2:15 is the only exception, each of the twenty-nine occurrences of the verb σῴζω in the Pauline corpus refers to spiritual salvation from sin that comes through Christ."

169. See Knight, *PE*, 146–47; Oden, *First and Second Timothy*, 101–2; Witherington,

unity of the overall macrochiasm thus far, the audience would likely hear Paul's statement in another way. Without dismissing the vital role that women have in propagating the human race or the fact that Christ Jesus indeed came into to the world to save sinners through the child-parenting of Mary, Paul's use of the term "child-parenting" (τεκνογονίας) recalls for the audience his earlier use of "child" (τέκνῳ, 1:2; τέκνον, 1:18) in the first microchiasm to explicitly refer to his familial relationship with Timothy in the realm "in faith" (1:2), his shared duty with Timothy to bring-about the household-law of God "in faith" (1:4), and through their common reception of grace from Christ Jesus (1:2) his shared existence with Timothy "in Christ Jesus" (1:14). Here in 2:15, then, just as "genuine child (τέκνῳ) in faith" (1:2) and "child (τέκνον) Timothy" (1:18) were understood by the audience not in reference to Paul's literal, biological child-parent relationship, neither would Paul's use of "child-parenting" (τεκνογονίας) refer to a literal, biological child-parent relationship. Indeed, such is corroborated (see *italics*) by Paul's qualifiying phrase, "if they remain *in faith*" (2:15). Thus where "child-parenting" occurs within the framework of Paul's broader understanding of family as the household of God "in faith" (1:2, 4; 2:7, 15), the audience would understand that Paul is referring to "child-parenting" as a human's entrance into the familial realm "in faith." In other words, Paul is refering to the missional activity of the women in the audience to enable sinners to enter into the realm of "in faith," namely by doing what is proper for women who profess godliness (2:10), that is, to cosmetic themselves "consistent-with good works" (2:10)—a missional lifestyle that attracts others to have-faith upon Christ Jesus (1:16). The clear implication of the phrase "consistent-with child-parenting" (2:15), therefore, is that the women in the Ephesian church are to play a crucial role in the missional purpose of the church and thus the salvation of humans by adhering to Paul's instructions in the 2:9–15 minichiasm.[170] In short, "child-parenting" is the missional outworking of what is proper for the women in the Ephesian church. Thus the movement of the 2:9–15 minichiasm from the missional concern in the "a" sub-element for women "to cosmetic themselves" in a way that attracts people to Christ Jesus (2:9) becomes explicit and

---

Letters, 230.

170. This chiastic understanding effectively resolves the exegetical conundrum, which Knight aptly describes: "It would be contrary to Paul's teaching elsewhere and to the emphasis of this letter (cf. 1 Tim. 1:15, 16; 2:3–6) and the other PE . . . to understand σωθήσεται as referring to spiritual salvation if διὰ τῆς τεκνογονίας is taken as referring to childbearing in general. This would make salvation for women conditional on a work, and specifically a work not all are able to perform" (*PE*, 145). Furthermore, any tension pertaining to the dangers of physical childbirth in the first-centery Greco-Roman world is removed.

reaches a climax in the parallel "a'" sub-element. Indeed, the "women who professes godliness" and abide by Paul's instructions "to cosmetic themselves . . . consistent-with good works" (2:9–10) will attract many to Christ Jesus—such is "consistent-with child-parenting" (2:15).

Given that Paul has reminded the audience in his letter that salvation for humans is exclusively through the one God and particularly through the one mediator of God and humans, the human Christ Jesus, who came into the world to save sinners (1:15; 2:5a–b) *and* is by coming to have-faith upon him (1:16) thereby entering the realm "in faith," which is "in Christ Jesus" (1:2, 4, 14; 2:7, 15), it is unmistakable to Paul's audience that the phrase "if they remain in faith" (2:15b) correspondingly specifies the way in which women will be-saved. That is, Paul's statement "if they remain in faith (ἐν πίστει)" in 2:15 clearly refers to the women's continued existence with Paul and Timothy in the familial realm "in faith" (ἐν πίστει) wherein Timothy is Paul's "child" (1:2), their continued familial lifestyle to bring-about "the household-law of God in faith (ἐν πίστει)" (1:4) by living according to the rules of "God the Father" (1:2), and their continued adherence to the instructions of Paul, who was divinely appointed a proclaimer, apostle, and teacher of the Gentiles "in faith (ἐν πίστει) and truth (2:7). Paul's specifying statement "if they remain in faith" (2:15), therefore, not only affirms that the audience are to understand the term "child-parenting" (2:15) as a missional activity to bring humans into the familial realm "in faith" but also emphasizes that the phrase "she will be-saved consistent-with child-parenting" (2:15) articulates that such missional activity is borne out of the women's own salvation. In other words, "consistent-with child-parenting" is a demonstration that the women "remain in faith" and thus "will be-saved" (2:15).[171] As such, "if they remain in faith" (2:15) is a rhetorical restatement of Paul's concern in the 2:9–15 minichiasm: "women who profess godliness" (2:10)—those who profess to be "in faith"—"will be-saved . . . if they remain in faith." That is, the women's activity to "remain in faith" would be evidenced by doing "what is proper" for their profession of godliness (2:10), namely "to cosmetic themselves" (2:9) in a manner "consistent-with good works" (2:10) and "consistent-with child-parenting" (2:15).[172] In short, Paul is climactically identifying the missional lifestyle of women in the church that attracts others to have-faith upon Christ Jesus (1:16).

Significantly also, the implication of Paul's statement "if they remain in faith" (2:15) advances the audience's understanding of the relation between

---

171. Cf. Knight, *PE*, 147: "διά with the genitive is used here to express means, instrument, or agency." The "agency" here is their new mode of existence "in faith."

172. Similarly, Schreiner, "Interpretation of 1 Tim 2:9–15," 118–19.

proper behavior and salvation in the second microchiasm: "godliness" (2:2) in the A element and "godliness" (2:10) in the A' element is not only a missional instrument through which other humans are "to be-saved" (2:4a) by God in the A element but also a personal indicator that oneself "will be-saved" (2:15) by God in the parallel A' element. Positively, then, the audience understand that the women's unique role in "child-parenting," that is, bringing humans into "the household-law of God in faith" (1:4) is not only "what is proper" for those living in God's missional household but also is evidence that they are existing and operating in the realm "in faith" and thus "will be-saved." In climactic fashion, therefore, as the second microchiasm concludes, Paul emphasizes the missional aspect of the household of God in which they live: just as Timothy became a "child in faith" (τέκνῳ ἐν πίστει, 1:2), the audience are to see many more come "to have-faith" upon Christ Jesus (1:16) through the missional "child-parenting" (τεκνογονίας) of the women who "remain in faith (ἐν πίστει)" (2:15). What is proper for women who profess godliness (2:9–15) will in fact bring-about "the household-law of God in faith (ἐν πίστει)" (1:4) by an active participation with the "Savior God, who desires all humans to be-saved" (2:3–4a).

Still, the verb "they remain" (μείνωσιν) recalls its prior occurrence in 1:3 of the first microchiasm wherein Paul exhorted Timothy "to remain" (προσμεῖναι) in Ephesus, that he might charge "some" not to teach-different. Notably, in the same way that Timothy is expected to adhere to Paul's authoritative exhortation as an apostle of Christ Jesus "to remain" in Ephesus (1:3), so also the women are expected to adhere to Paul's instructions and thereby "remain" in the realm "in faith" (2:15). Indeed, in the same way that Timothy must adhere to Paul's exhortation for the sake of preserving the sound teaching and thus the salvation of those within the Ephesian church (1:10b; 2:4b), so also must the women adhere to Paul's instructions for the same salvific, missional purpose. Furthermore, just as Timothy's adherence "to remain" in Ephesus (1:3) will undoubtedly result in difficult circumstances—for sure, a "war" with "some" (1:18–19)—Paul's use of the verb "remain" in 2:15 would likely indicate that the women's adherence to Paul's instructions will also result in challenging circumstances, particularly brought on by those in the church who adhere to "some-thing different" that lies-opposed to "the sound teaching" of Paul and thus his instructions to the women (1:10b–11; 2:9–15). That is, the macrochiastic connection suggests that both Timothy and the women in the Ephesian church will share in the common struggle to preserve the sound teaching against the different teaching of "some" and to promote godliness as part of their existence "in faith," that is, as part of the missional household of God.

Paul's concluding list in verse 2:15—"in faith and love and holiness with self-control"—would carry forward further significance for Paul's instructions to the women. Specifically, the contrast between the lifestyle qualities of the women who are "in faith" (2:15) and the false teachers who are "in unfaithfulness" (cf. 1:13) would be apparent. While the women are to remain "in faith (πίστει) and love (ἀγάπῃ) and holiness" (2:15), "some" have not only turned-aside from "love" (ἀγάπη) and "a without-hypocrisy faith (πίστεως)" (1:5-16) but also—by rejecting "faith" (πίστιν)—"regarding the faith (πίστιν) have become-shipwrecked" (1:19). In short, for the women in the Ephesian church to remain "in faith and love and holiness" (2:15) is to do exactly the opposite of what the false teachers have done: by not shipwrecking their faith (1:19), the women will be-saved (2:15).

Moreover, the term "love" (ἀγάπη) in 2:15 recalls that the end of Paul's charge in 1:5 for Timothy to stop the false teachers is "love" (ἀγάπη). In this way, Paul's use of "love" in 2:15 suggests that he intends for the women to be fully aligned with the goal of Paul's charge—"love" (1:5)—and thus with Timothy, who must carry out the charge (1:3). That is, by remaining in "love" (2:15), the women will functionally assist Timothy in their respective roles to bring-about the household-law of God "in faith" (1:4). Still, combined with the phrase "in faith" (ἐν πίστει, 2:15), Paul's specification that the women are to remain "[in] love" (ἀγάπῃ) affirms that faith and love are inseparable—to exist "in faith" is to exist "in love."[173] Such was already implied in Paul's discussion of the charge in 1:5, wherein he conveyed that "love" (ἀγάπη) comes from "a without-hypocrisy faith" (πίστεως). Given the rhetorical chain of datives in Paul's statement in 2:15, the same implication would be heard for the term "[in] holiness" (ἁγιασμῷ); that is, to exist "in faith" is not only inseparable from existing "[in] love" but also from existing "[in] holiness."[174] Still, where the term "holiness" is connected to an existence in the realm "in faith" and "love" (2:15), the significance of Paul's statement would not go unnoticed. The term "holiness" (ἁγιασμῷ) derives specifically from the unique attribute of God, who alone is "holy, holy, holy" (ἅγιος ἅγιος ἅγιος, LXX Isa 6:3). Thus where the women—indeed all humans—exist "in faith . . . [in] holiness" (2:15), Paul is highlighting the climactic reality of what it means to exist "in faith," namely living in the perfect presence of the one God who is "holy."[175]

---

173. The dative form of the noun "love" (ἀγάπη) carries forward the preposition "in" (ἐν).

174. The dative form of the noun "holiness" (ἁγιασμῷ) carries forward the preposition "in" (ἐν).

175. The emphasis of God's holiness is worth noting. In LXX Isaiah 6:3, the repetition that God is "holy, holy, holy" (ἅγιος ἅγιος ἅγιος) highlights its importance.

The closing noun "self-control" (σωφροσύνης) here in 2:15 of the "a'" sub-element recalls its earlier occurrence in 2:9 the parallel "a" sub-element wherein Paul instructed "women to cosmetic themselves . . . with modesty and self-control (σωφροσύνης)." Due to the progression of the 2:9–15 mini-chiasm, the sense of the term "self-control" is both affirmed and expanded for the audience. On the one hand, the interconnected aspects of a missional lifestyle and one's own salvation are heard in the parallelism: "women to cosmetic themselves . . . with modesty and self-control" in the "a" sub-element (2:9) means that "they remain in faith . . . with self-control" and thus "will be-saved" (2:15) in the "a'" sub-element. On the other hand, therefore, the term "self-control" in 2:15 also expresses what is proper for women who profess godliness (2:10), which includes the acceptance and adherence to Paul's instructions for gender dynamics among men and women regarding teaching and governing in the church. That is, to remain "in faith . . . with self-control" provides the positive basis that upholds God's creational design for men and women (2:13) by enabling men to teach and to govern in the church (2:12). Furthermore, heard within the overall concern and framing arrangement of the microchiasm, the quality of "self-control" as the concluding, climactic statement of the A' element is to be appreciated for its missional and salvific purpose, particularly in view of the "Savior God, who desires all humans to be-saved" in 2:3–4a of the introductory A element. Indeed, all humans who are spectators of the women's commitment to remain "in faith and love and holiness with self-control" (2:15) may tangibly observe the reality of what it means to have-faith upon Christ Jesus for life eternal (1:16), that is, the reality of salvation here and now. The proper conduct of women who profess godliness punctuates the missional force of the second microchiasm.[176]

That the godly women are "in holiness" undoubtedly underscores their existence in the realm where God is present.

176. The verse immediately following 2:15—"Faithful is the word" (3:1a)—is sometimes interpreted in connection with the A' element of the second microchiasm. For further discussion, see volume 2, chapter 2.

Bibliography

Volume 1

Aageson, James W. *Paul, the Pastoral Epistles, and the Early Church*. LPS. Grand Rapids: Baker Academic, 2008.

Agnew, Francis H. "The Origin of the NT Apostle-Concept: A Review of Research." *JBL* 105/1 (1986) 75–96.

Akin, Daniel, L. "The Mystery of Godliness Is Great: Christology in the Pastoral Epistles." In *Entrusted with The Gospel: Paul's Theology in the Pastoral Epistles*, edited by Andreas J. Kostënberger and Terry L. Wilder, 137–52. Nashville: B&H, 2010.

Amundsen, D. W., and C. J. Diers. "The Age of Menopause in Classical Greece and Rome." *HB* 42 (1970) 79–86.

Assis, Elie. "Chiasmus in Biblical Narrative: Rhetoric of Characterization." *Prooftexts* 22/3 (2002) 273–304.

Aune, David E. *The New Testament in Its Literary Environment*. Cambridge: James Clarke, 1987.

———. *Prophecy in Early Christianity and the Ancient Mediterranean World*. Eugene, OR: Wipf & Stock, 1983.

Bailey, Kenneth E. *Paul Through Mediterranean Eyes: Cultural Studies in 1 Corinthians*. Downers Grove, IL: InterVarsity, 2011.

Barcley, William B. *1 & 2 Timothy*. Webster, NY: Evangelical, 2005.

———. "1 Timothy." In *A Biblical-Theological Introduction to the New Testament: The Gospel Realized*, edited by Michael J. Kruger, 357–75. Wheaton, IL: Crossway, 2016.

———. "Introduction to the Pastoral Epistles." In *A Biblical-Theological Introduction to the New Testament: The Gospel Realized*, edited by Michael J. Kruger, 349–56. Wheaton, IL: Crossway, 2016.

Barrett, C. K. *The Pastoral Epistles*. NCBNT. Oxford: Clarendon, 1963.

———. *The Signs of an Apostle*. London: Epworth, 1970.

Bassler, Jouette M. *1 & 2 Timothy and Titus*. ANTC. Nashville: Abingdon, 1996.

———. "Limits and Differentiation: The Calculus of Widows in 1 Timothy 5.3–16." In *Feminist Companion to Paul: Deutero-Pauline Writings*, edited by Amy-Jill Levine with Marianne Blickenstaff, 122–46. New York: T. & T. Clark, 2003.

Bauckham, Richard. "Pseudo-Apostolic Letters." *JBL* 107 (1988) 469–94.

———. *The Testimony of the Beloved Disciple: Narrative, History, and Theology in the Gospel of John*. Grand Rapids: Baker, 2007.

Bauer, Walter, et al. *A Greek-English Lexicon of the New Testament and Other Early Christian Literature* (BDAG). 3rd ed. Revised by F. W. Danker. Chicago: University of Chicago Press, 2000.

Baugh, S. M., "A Foreign World: Ephesus in the First Century." In *Women in the Church: An Interpretation and Application of 1 Timothy 2:9–15*, edited by Andreas J. Köstenberger and Thomas R. Schreiner, 13–38. 2nd ed. Grand Rapids: Baker, 2005.

Beattie, Gillian. *Women and Marriage in Paul and His Early Interpreters*. LNTS. New York: T. & T. Clark, 2005.

Becker, Eve-Marie. "The Person of Paul." In *Paul: Life, Setting, Work, Letters*, edited by Oda Wischmeyer, 121–32. Translated by Helen S. Heron. New York: T. & T. Clark, 2012.

Belleville, Linda L. "1 Timothy." In *1 Timothy, 2 Timothy, Titus, Hebrews*, edited by Philip W. Comfort, 25–60. CBC 17. Carol Stream, IL: Tyndale, 2009.

———. "Christology, Greco-Roman Religious Piety, and the Pseudonymity of the Pastoral Letters." In *Paul and Pseudepigraphy*, edited by Stanley E. Porter and Gregory P. Fewster, 221–44. PS 8. Boston: Brill, 2013.

———. "Christology, the Pastoral Epistles, and Commentaries." In *On the Writing on New Testament Commentaries: Festschrift for Grant R. Osborne on the Occasion of his 70th Birthday*, edited by Stanley E. Porter and Eckhard J. Schnabel, 317–38. Boston: Brill, 2013.

———. "'Son' Christology in the New Testament." In *The New Evangelical Subordinationism? Perspectives on the Equality of God the Father and God the Son*, edited by Dennis W. Jowers and H. Wayne House, 59–79. Eugene, OR: Pickwick, 2012.

———. "Teaching and Usurping Authority: 1 Timothy 2:11–15." In *Discovering Biblical Equality: Complementarity Without Hierarchy*, edited by Ronald W. Pierce and Rebecca Merrill Groothuis, 205–23. Downers Grove, IL: InterVarsity, 2005.

Bird, Michael F. *The Gospel of the Lord: How the Early Church Wrote the Story of Jesus*. Grand Rapids: Eerdmans, 2014.

Blass, F., and A. Debrunner. *A Greek Grammar of the New Testament and Other Early Christian Literature* (BDF). Translated by R. W. Funk. Chicago: University of Chicago Press, 1961.

Blomberg, Craig L. *From Pentecost to Patmos: An Introduction to Acts Through Revelation*. Nashville: B&H, 2006.

———. "The Structure of 2 Corinthians 1–7." *CTR* 4 (1989) 3–20.

Botha, Pieter J. J. "The Verbal Art of the Pauline Letters: Rhetoric, Performance, and Presence." In *Rhetoric and the New Testament: Essays from the 1992 Heidelberg Conference*, edited by Stanley E. Porter and Thomas H. Olbricht, 409–28. JSNTSup 90. Sheffield: JSOT, 1993.

Bowman, Robert M., Jr., and J. Ed Komoszewski. *Putting Jesus in His Place: the Case for the Deity of Christ*. Grand Rapids: Kregel, 2007.

Breck, John. "Biblical Chiasmus: Exploring Structure for Meaning." *BTB* 17 (1987) 70–74.

———. "Chiasums as a Key to Biblical Interpretation." *SVTQ* 43 (1999) 249–67.

———. *Scripture in Tradition: The Bible and Its Interpretation in the Orthodox Church*. Crestwood, NY: St. Vladimir's Seminary, 2001.
Brinks, C. L. "'Great is Artemis of the Ephesians': Acts 19:23–41 in Light of Goddess Worship in Ephesus." *CBQ* 71/4 (2009) 776–94.
Brookins, Timothy A. "'I Rather Appeal to *Auctoritas*': Roman Conceptualizations of Power and Paul's Appeal to Philemon." *CBQ* 77/2 (2015) 302–21.
Brouwer, Wayne. *The Literary Development of John 13–17: A Chiastic Reading*. Atlanta: SBL, 2000.
Brown, J. G. *An Historian Looks at 1 Timothy 2:11–14: The Authentic Traditional Interpretation and Why It Disappeared*. Eugene, OR: Wipf & Stock, 2012.
Brox, Norbert. "Zu den persönlichen Notizen der Pastoralbrief." *BZ* 13 (1969) 76–94.
———. *Die Pastoralbriefe: 1 Timotheus, 2 Timotheus, Titus*. 5th ed. RNT. Regensburg: Fredrich Pustet, 1989.
Bruce, F. F. "Myth." In NIDNTT, edited by C. Brown, 2:643–47. Grand Rapids: Zondervan, 1978.
Bufe, Chaz. *Provocations: Don't Call Them Libertarians, AA Lies, and Other Incitements*. Tuscon: See Sharp, 2014.
Campbell, R. Alastair. "Identifying the Faithful Sayings in the Pastoral Epistles." *JSNT* 54 (1994) 73–86.
Carson, D. A., and Douglas Moo. *An Introduction to the New Testament*. 2nd ed. Grand Rapids: Zondervan, 2005.
Caulley, Thomas Scott. "The Title *Christianos* and Roman Imperial Cult." *ResQ* 53/4 (2011) 193–206.
Celoria, Heather. "Does 1 Timothy 2 Prohibit Women from Teaching, Leading, and Speaking in the Church?" *PP* 27/3 (2013) 20–23.
Cochran, Matthew E. *As Though It Were Actually True: A Christian Apologetic Primer*. Eugene, OR: Resource, 2010.
Cohick, Lynn H. *Women in the World of the Earliest Christians: Illuminating Ancient Ways of Life*. Grand Rapids: Baker, 2009.
Coiner, Harry G. "The Secret of God's Plan: Guidelines for a Theology of Stewardship." *CTM* 34/5 (1963) 261–77.
Collins, Raymond F. *1 & 2 Timothy and Titus: A Commentary*. NTL. Louisville: Westminster John Knox, 2002.
Couser, Greg A. "The Sovereign Savior of 1 and 2 Timothy and Titus." In *Entrusted with The Gospel: Paul's Theology in the Pastoral Epistles*, edited by Andreas J. Kostënberger and Terry L. Wilder, 105–36. Nashville: B&H, 2010.
———. "'The Testimony About the Lord', 'Borne by the Lord', or Both? An Insight into Paul and Jesus in the Pastoral Epistles (2 Tim 1:8)." *TynBul* 55/2 (2004) 295–316.
Dalbert, Peter. *Die Theologie der hellenistisch-jüdischen Missions-Literatur unter Ausschluss von Philo und Josephus*. ThF 4. Hamburg: Volksdorf, 1954.
D'Angelo, Mary R. "Εὐσέβεια: Roman Imperial Family Values and the Sexual Politics of 4 Maccabees and the Pastorals." *BibInt* 11 (2003) 139–65.
Dart, John. *Decoding Mark*. Harrisburg, PA: Trinity, 2003.
———. "Scriptural Schemes: The ABCBAs of Biblical Writing." *CC* 121/14 (2004) 22–25.
Davidson, Jo Ann. *Toward a Theology of Beauty: A Biblical Perspective*. New York: University Press of America, 2008.

Davies, R. E. "Christ in Our Place—The Contributions of the Prepositions." *TynBul* 21 (1970) 71–91.

Decker, Rodney J. "An Evaluation of the 2011 Edition of the New International Version." *Themelios* 36/3 (2011) 415–56.

Deppe, Dean B. *All Roads Lead to the Text: Eight Methods of Inquiry into the Bible.* Grand Rapids: Eerdmans, 2011.

———. *The Theological Intentions of Mark's Literary Devices: Markan Intercalculations, Frames, Allusionary Repetitions, Narrative Surprises, and Three Types of Mirroring.* Eugene, OR: Wipf & Stock, 2015.

DeSilva, David A. "X Marks the Spot? A Critique of the Use of Chiasmus in Macro-Structural Analyses of Revelation." *JSNT* 30/3 (2008) 343–71.

De Vries, Pieter. "The Glory of YHWH in the Old Testament with Special Attention to the Book of Ezekiel." *TynBul* 62/1 (2011) 151–54.

Dewey, Joanna. "Mark as Aural Narrative: Structures as Clues to Understanding." *STR* 36 (1992) 45–56.

———. *The Oral Ethos of the Early Church: Speaking, Writing, and the Gospel of Mark.* BPC 8. Eugene, OR: Cascade, 2013.

De Young, James B. "The Source and NT Meaning of ARSENOKOITAI, with Implications For Christian Ethics and Ministry." *MSJ* 3/2 (1992) 191–215.

Dibelius, Martin, and Hans Conzelmann. *A Commentary on the Pastoral Epistles.* Philadelphia: Fortress, 1972.

Dodd, C. H. "The Gospel of the Glory of the Blessed God: 1 Tim 1:11." *USQR* 6/1 (1950) 6–10.

Donelson, Lewis R. "The Structure of Ethical Argument in the Pastorals." *BTB* 18 (1988) 108–13.

Douglas, Mary. *Thinking in Circle: An Essay on Ring Composition.* New Haven, CT: Yale University Press, 2007.

Douma, Jochem. *The Ten Commandments: Manual for the Christian Life.* Phillipsburg, NJ: P&R, 1996.

Dowling, Elizabeth V. *Taking Away the Pound: Women, Theology and the Parable of the Pounds in the Gospel of Luke.* LNTS. New York: T. & T. Clark, 2007.

Doxiadis, Apostolos, and Michalis Sialaros. "Sing, Muse, of the Hypotenuse: Influence of Poetry and Rhetoric on the Formation of Greek Mathematics." In *Writing Science: Medical and Mathematical Authorship in Ancient Greece*, edited by Markus Asper, 367–410. Boston: de Gruyter, 2013.

Dunn, James D. G. *Jesus, Paul, and the Gospels.* Grand Rapids: Eerdmans, 2011.

Easton, Burton Scott. *The Pastoral Epistles: Introduction, Translation, Commentary and Word Studies.* New York: Scribner's, 1947.

Edwards, J. Christopher. "Reading the Ransom Logion in 1 Tim 2,6 and Titus 2,14 with Isa 42,6–7; 49,6–8." *Bib* 90/2 (2009) 264–66.

Ehrensperger, Kathy. "Speaking Greek Under Rome: Paul, the Power of Language and the Language of Power." *Neot* 46/1 (2012) 9–28.

Eisen, Ute E. *Women Officeholders in Early Christianity: Epigraphical and Literary Studies.* Translated by Linda M. Maloney. Collegeville, MN: Liturgical, 2000.

Elliot, Neil, and Mark Reasoner, eds. *Documents and Images for the Study of Paul.* Minneapolis: Fortress, 2011.

Ellis, E. Earle. *Pauline Theology: Ministry and Society.* Eugene, OR: Wipf & Stock, 1997.

Engel, William E. *Chiastic Designs in English Literature from Sidney to Shakespeare*. New York: Routledge, 2009.
Ermatinger, James W. *Daily Life of Christians in Ancient Rome*. DLTH. Westport, CT: Greenwood, 2007.
Evans, Mary J. *Women in the Bible: An Overview of All the Crucial Passages on Women's Roles*. Downers Grove, IL: InterVarsity, 1984.
Fairbairn, Patrick. *Commentary on the Pastoral Epistles*. Lafayette, IN: Sovereign Grace, 2001.
Fay, Ron C. "Greco-Roman Concepts of Deity." In *Paul's World*, edited by Stanley E. Porter, 51–80. Boston: Brill, 2008.
Fee, Gordon D. *1 & 2 Timothy, Titus*. NIBC 13. Peabody, MA: Hendrickson, 1988.
———. *Listening to the Spirit in the Text*. Grand Rapids: Eerdmans, 2000.
Ferguson, Everett. *Backgrounds of Early Christianity*. 2nd ed. Grand Rapids: Eerdmans, 1993.
Forster, Arthur Haire. "The Meaning of Δόξα in the Greek Bible." *ATR* 12/4 (1930) 311–16.
Fowler, Robert M. "Why Everything We Know About the Bible Is Wrong: Lessons from the Media History of the Bible." In *The Bible in Ancient and Modern Media: Story and Performance*, edited by Holly E. Hearon and Philip Ruge-Jones, 3–18. BPC. Eugene, OR: Cascade, 2009.
Friberg, B., and T. Friberg. *Analytical Greek New Testament*. Grand Rapids: Baker, 1981.
Gaffin, Richard B., Jr. "Atonement in the Pauline Corpus: 'The Scandal of the Cross.'" In *The Glory of Atonement: Biblical, Historical and Practical Perspectives: Essays in Honor of Roger Nicole*, edited by Charles E. Hill and Frank A. James III, 140–62. Downers Grove, IL: InterVarsity, 2004.
———. *By Faith, Not By Sight: Paul and the Order of Salvation*. 2nd ed. Phillipsburg, NJ: P&R, 2013.
Gench, Frances Taylor. *Encountering God in Tyrannical Texts: Reflections on Paul, Women, and the Authority of Scripture*. Louisville: Westminster John Knox, 2015.
Genest, Olivette. "Feminist Theories in the Interpretation of the Bible." In *Women Also Journeyed with Him: Feminist Perspectives on the Bible*, 25–50. Translated by Madeleine Beaumont. Collegeville, MN: Liturgical, 2000.
Gill, Malcolm. *Jesus as Mediator: Politics and Polemic in 1 Timothy 2:1–7*. New York: Peter Lang, 2008.
Glahn, Sandra L. "The First-Century Ephesian Artemis: Ramifications of Her Identity." *BSac* 172 (2015) 450–69.
———. "The Identity of Artemis in First-Century Ephesus." *BSac* 172 (2015) 316–34.
Gloer, W. Hulitt. *1 & 2 Timothy–Titus*. Macon, GA: Smyth & Helwys, 2010.
Grant, Robert M. *Augustus to Constantine: The Thrust of the Christian Movement into the Roman World*. New York: Harper & Row, 1970.
Gray, Patrick. *Opening Paul's Letters: A Reader's Guide to Genre and Interpretation*. Grand Rapids: BakerAcademic, 2012.
Grothe, Mardy. *Never Let a Fool Kiss You or a Kiss Fool You: Chiasmus and a World of Quotations That Say What They Mean and Mean What They Say*. New York: Penguin, 1999.
Guthrie, Donald. *The Pastoral Epistles: An Introduction and Commentary*. TynNTC 14. Grand Rapids: Eerdmans, 1990.

Hamilton, James M., Jr. "What Women Can Do in Ministry: Full Participation Within Biblical Boundaries." In *Women, Ministry and the Gospel: Exploring New Paradigms*, edited by Mark Husbands and Timothy Larsen, 32–52. Downers Grove, IL: InterVarsity, 2007.

Hanson, Anthony Tyrrell. *Studies in the Pastoral Epistles*. Eugene, OR: Wipf & Stock, 1968.

Harding, Mark. *What Are They Saying About the Pastoral Epistles?* Mahwah, NJ: Paulist, 2001.

Hariman, Robert. "What Is a Chiasmus? Or, Why the Abyss Stares Back." In *Chiasmus and Culture*, edited by Boris Wiseman and Anthony Paul, 45–68. New York: Berghahn, 2014.

Harris, Geoffrey. *Paul*. London: SCM, 2009.

Harris, Murray J. *The Second Epistle to the Corinthians: A Commentary on the Greek Text*. NIGTC. Grand Rapids: Eerdmans, 2005.

Harrison, James R. "The Brothers as the 'Glory of Christ' (2 Cor 8:23): Paul's *Doxa* Terminology in Its Ancient Benefaction Context." *NovT* 52/2 (2010) 156–88.

―――. "Family Honour of a Priestess of Artemis." In *A Review of Greek and Other Inscriptions and Papyri Published between 1988 and 1992*, edited by S. R. Llewelyn et al., 30–36. NDIEC 10. Grand Rapids, Eerdmans, 2012.

Harvey, John D. *Listening to the Text: Oral Patterning in Paul's Letters*. Grand Rapids: Baker, 1998.

Hasler, Victor. *Die Briefe an Timotheus und Titus*. Zürich: Theological, 1978.

―――. "Epiphanie und Christologie in den Pastoralbriefen." *TZ* 33 (1977) 193–209.

Haufe, Günter. "Gnostische Irrlehre und ihre Abwehr in den Pastoralbriefen." In *Gnosis und Neues Testament: Studien aus Religionswissenschaft und Theologie*, edited by Karl-Wolfgang Tröger, 325–39. Gütersloh: Gütersloher Verlagshaus Mohn, 1973.

Hearon, Holly E. "The Implications of Orality for Studies of the Biblical Text." In *Performing the Gospel: Orality, Memory, and Mark: Essays Dedicated to Werner Kelber*, edited by Richard A. Horsley et al., 3–20. Minneapolis: Fortress, 2006.

Hearon, Holly E., and Linda M. Maloney. "Listen to the Voices of the Women." In *Distant Voices Drawing Near: Essays in Honor of Antoinette Clark Wire*, edited by Holly E. Hearon, 33–56. Collegeville, MN: Liturgical, 2004.

Heil, John Paul. *1–3 John: Worship by Loving God and One Another to Live Eternally*. Cambridge: James Clarke, 2015.

―――. *The Book of Revelation: Worship for Life in the Spirit of Prophecy*. Eugene, OR: Cascade, 2014.

―――. "The Chiastic Structure and Meaning of Paul's Letter to Philemon." *Bib* 82/2 (2001) 178–206.

―――. *Colossians: Encouragement to Walk in All Wisdom as Holy Ones in Christ*. ECL 4. Atlanta: SBL, 2010.

―――. *Ephesians: Empowerment to Walk in Love for the Unity of All in Christ*. SBL 13. Atlanta: SBL, 2007.

―――. *The Gospel of John: Worship for Divine Life Eternal*. Eugene, OR: Cascade, 2015.

―――. *Philippians: Let Us Rejoice in Being Conformed to Christ*. ECL 3. Atlanta: SBL, 2010.

―――. *The Letter of James: Worship to Live By*. Eugene, OR: Cascade, 2012.

―――. *The Letters of Paul as Rituals of Worship*. Eugene, OR: Cascade, 2011.

―――. *Worship in the Letter to the Hebrews*. Eugene, OR: Cascade, 2011.

Herrick, James A. *The History and Theory of Rhetoric: An Introduction*. 5th ed. New York: Routledge, 2013.
Ho, Chiao Ek. "Mission in the Pastoral Epistles." In *Entrusted with The Gospel: Paul's Theology in the Pastoral Epistles*, edited by Andreas J. Köstenberger and Terry L. Wilder, 241–67. Nashville: B&H, 2010.
Holland, Glenn S. "'Delivery, Delivery, Delivery': Accounting for Performance in the Rhetoric of Paul's Letters." In *Paul and Ancient Rhetoric: Theory and Practice in the Hellenistic Context*, edited by Stanley E. Porter and Bryan R. Dryer, 119–40. New York: Cambridge University Press, 2016.
Holmes, J. M. *Text in a Whirlwind: A Critique of Four Exegetical Devices at 1 Timothy 2.9–15*. SNTG 7. JSNTSup 196. Sheffield: Sheffield Academic, 2000.
Hooker, Morna D. "Artemis of Ephesus." *JTS* 64/1 (2013) 37–46.
Horsley, Richard A. "Introduction." In *Performing the Gospel: Orality, Memory, and Mark: Essays Dedicated to Werner Kelber*, edited by Richard A. Horsley et al., vii–xvi. Minneapolis: Fortress, 2006.
———. *Jesus and Empire: The Kingdom of God and the New World Disorder*. Minneapolis: Fortress, 2003.
———. *Text and Tradition in Performance and Writing*. BPC 9. Eugene, OR: Cascade, 2013.
Hübner, Jamin. "Translating αὐθεντέω *(authenteō)* in 1 Timothy 2:12." *PP* 29/2 (2015) 16–26.
Hughes, R. Kent, and Bryan Chapell. *1-2 Timothy and Titus: To Guard the Deposit*. Wheaton, IL: Crossway, 2012.
Humphries, Mark. *Early Christianity*. New York: Routledge, 2006.
Hutson, Christopher E. "Ecclesiology in the Pastoral Epistles." In *The New Testament Church: The Challenge of Developing Ecclesiologies*, edited by John P. Harrison and James D. Dvorak, 164–88. McMBSS. Eugene, OR: Pickwick, 2012.
Hutson, Christopher R. "'Saved through Childbearing': The Jewish Context of 1 Timothy 2:15." *NovT* 56/4 (2014) 392–410.
Iersel, Bas M. F. van. *Mark: A Reader-Response Commentary*. Translated by W. H. Bisscheroux. JSNTSup 164. Sheffield: Sheffield Academic, 1998.
Irons, Kendra Weddle, and Melanie Springer Mock. *If Eve Only Knew: Freeing Yourself from Biblical Womanhood and Becoming All God Means for You to Be*. St. Louis: Chalice, 2015.
Ito, Akio. "Paul the 'Herald' and the 'Teacher.'" In *Sacred Words: Orality, Literacy and Religion*, edited by A. P. M. H. Lardinois et al., 351–70. OLAW 8. Boston: Brill, 2011.
Jeon, Paul S. *To Exhort and Reprove: Audience Response to the Chiastic Structures of Paul's Letter to Titus*. Eugene, OR: Pickwick, 2012.
———. *True Faith: Reflections on Paul's Letter to Titus*. Eugene, OR: Wipf & Stock, 2012.
Jeremias, Joachim. "Chiasms in den Paulusbriefen." *ZNW* 49 (1958) 145–56.
———. *Die Briefe an Timotheus und Titus*. NTD 9. Göttingen: Vandenhoeck & Ruprecht, 1963.
Jervis, L. Ann. *The Purpose of Romans: A Comparative Letter Structure Investigation*. JSNTSup 55. Sheffield: JSOT, 1991.
Jewett, Robert. *Paul's Anthropological Terms: A Study of Their Use in Conflict Settings*. AGAJU. Leiden: Brill, 1971.

Johnson, Luke Timothy. *Contested Issues in Christian Origins and the New Testament.* SNT 146. Boston, MA: Brill, 2013.

———. "First Timothy 1,1–20: The Shape of the Struggle." In *1 Timothy Reconsidered,* edited by Karl Paul Donfried, 19–39. COP 18. Leuven, Belgium: Peeters, 2008.

———. *Letters to Paul's Delegates: 1 Timothy, 2 Timothy, Titus.* Bloomsbury Academic, 1996.

———. "The Social Dimensions of Sōtēria in Luke-Acts and Paul." In *The SBL 1993 Seminar Papers,* edited by E. H. Lovering, 520–36. Atlanta: Scholars, 1993.

Jones, Hefin. "Women, Teaching, and Authority: A Case for Understanding the Nature of Congregational Oversight as Underlying 1 Timothy 2:11–12." In *The Gender Conversation: Evangelical Perspectives on Gender, Scripture, and the Christian Life,* edited by Edwina Murphy and David Starling, 143–54. Eugene, OR: Wipf & Stock, 2016.

Keegan, Terence J. *First and Second Timothy, Titus, Philemon.* NCBC 9. Collegeville, MN: Liturgical, 2006.

Kelly, J. N. D. *A Commentary on the Pastoral Epistles.* HNTC. Peabody, MA: Hendrickson, 1987.

Kim, Sang-Hoon. *Sourcebook of the Structures and Styles in John 1–10: The Johannine Parallelisms and Chiasms.* Eugene, OR: Wipf & Stock, 2014.

Kittel, Gerhard. "Genealogia des Pastoralbriefe." *ZNW* 20 (1921) 49–69.

Knight, George W., III. *The Faithful Sayings in the Pastoral Epistles.* Kampen: J H Kok, 1968.

———. *The Pastoral Epistles: A Commentary on the Greek Text.* NIGTC. Grand Rapids: Eerdmans, 1992.

Köstenberger, Andreas J. "A Complex Sentence: The Syntax of 1 Timothy 2:12." In *Women in the Church: An Interpretation and Application of 1 Timothy 2:9–15,* edited by Andreas J. Köstenberger and Thomas R. Schreiner, 53–84. 2nd ed. Grand Rapids: Baker, 2005.

———. "Hermeneutical and Exegetical Challenges in Interpreting the Pastoral Epistles." In *Entrusted with The Gospel: Paul's Theology in the Pastoral Epistles,* edited by Andreas J. Kostënberger and Terry L. Wilder, 1–27. Nashville: B&H, 2010.

Köstenberger, Andreas J., and Richard D. Patterson. *Invitation to Biblical Interpretation: Exploring the Hermeneutical Triad of History, Literature, and Theology.* ITS. Grand Rapids: Kregel, 2011.

Krause, Deborah. *1 Timothy.* RNBC. London: T. & T. Clark, 2004

Kuruvilla, Abraham. *Text to Praxis: Hermeneutics and Homiletics in Dialogue.* New York: T. & T. Clark, 2009.

Laale, Hans Willer. *Ephesus (Ephesos): An Abbreviated History from Androclus to Constantine XI.* Bloomington, IN: WestBow, 2011.

Lieu, Judith M. "'Grace to you and Peace': The Apostolic Greeting." *BJRL* 68 (1985) 161–78.

Lock, Walter. *A Critical and Exegetical Commentary on the Pastoral Epistles.* ICC. Edinburgh: T. & T. Clark, 1924.

Long, Fredrick J. "Christ's Gifted Bride: Gendered Members in Ministry in Acts and Paul." In *Women, Ministry and the Gospel: Exploring New Paradigms,* edited by Mark Husbands and Timothy Larsen, 98–123. Downers Grove, IL: InterVarsity, 2007.

———. "Roman Imperial Rule under the Authority of Jupiter-Zeus: Political-Religious Contexts and the Interpreation of 'the Ruler of the Authority of the Air' in Ephesians 2:2." In *The Language of the New Testament: Context, History, and Development*, edited by Stanley E. Porter and Andrew W. Pitts, 113–54. LBS 6. Early Christianity and Its Hellenistic Context 3. Boston: Brill, 2013.

Long, Thomas G. *1 & 2 Timothy and Titus*. BTCB. Louisville: Westminster John Knox, 2016.

Longenecker, Bruce W. *Rhetoric at the Boundaries: The Art and Theology of the New Testament Chain-Link Transitions*. Waco, TX: Baylor University Press, 2005.

López, René A. "A Study of Pauline Passages with Vice Lists." *BSac* 168 (2011) 301–16.

MacArthur, John. *1 & 2 Timothy: Encouragement for Church Leaders*. Nashville: Nelson, 2007.

———. *1 Timothy*. MNTC. Chicago: Moody, 1995.

Malherbe, Abraham J. "The *Virtus Feminarum* in 1 Timothy 2:9–15." In *Renewing Tradition: Studies in Texts and Contexts in Honor of James W. Thompson*, edited by Mark W. Hamilton et al., 45–65. PTMS. Eugene, OR: Pickwick, 2007.

Man, Ronald E. "The Value of Chiasm for New Testament Interpretation." *BSac* 141 (1984) 146–57.

Mappes, David A. "The Heresy Paul Opposed in 1 Timothy." *BSac* 156 (1999) 452–58.

Marshall, I. H. "The Christology of Luke-Acts and the Pastoral Epistles." In *Crossing Boundaries: Essays in Biblical Interpretation in Honor of Michael D. Goulder*, edited by Stanley. E. Porter et al., 167–82. Leiden: Brill, 1994.

———. *The Pastoral Epistles*. ICC. Edinburgh: T. & T. Clark, 1999.

———. "Women in Ministry: A Further Look at 1 Timothy 2." In *Women, Ministry and the Gospel: Exploring New Paradigms*, edited by Mark Husbands and Timothy Larsen, 53–78. Downers Grove, IL: InterVarsity, 2007.

Matera, Frank J. *God's Saving Grace: A Pauline Theology*. Grand Rapids: Eerdmans, 2012.

Maxey, James A. *From Orality to Orality: A New Paradigm for Contextual Translation of the Bible*. BPC 2. Eugene, OR: Cascade, 2009.

May, Grace. "Appreciating How the Apostle Paul Champions Men and Women in Church Leadership." In *The Quest for Gender Equity in Leadership: Biblical Teachings on Gender Equity and Illustrations of Transformation in Africs*, edited by KeumJu Jewel Hyun and Diphus C. Chemorion, 77–95. Eugene, OR: Wipf & Stock, 2016.

McCabe, Elizabeth A. "Answers to Unresolved Questions: A Closer Look at Eve and Adam in Genesis 2–3." In *Women in the Biblical World: A Survey of Old and New Testament Perspectives*, edited by Elizabeth A. McCabe, 1–20. Lanham, MD: University Press of America, 2009.

McEleney, Neil J. "The Vice Lists of the Pastoral Epistles." *CBQ* 36/2 (1974) 203–19.

Meiser, Martin. "Timothy in Acts: Patristic Reception." *ASE* 32/2 (2015) 325–32.

Merkle, Benjamin L. "The Biblical Qualifications for Elders." In *Baptist Foundations: Church Government for an Anti-Institutional Age*, edited by Mark Dever and Jonathan Leeman, 253–70. Nashville: B&H, 2015.

———."Eccesiology in the Pastoral Epistles." In *Entrusted with The Gospel: Paul's Theology in the Pastoral Epistles*, edited by Andreas J. Kostënberger and Terry L. Wilder, 173–98. Nashville: B&H, 2010.

———. "Paul's Arguments from Creation in 1 Corinthians 11:8–9 and 1 Timothy 2:13–14: An Apparent Inconsistency Answered." *JETS* 49/3 (2006) 527–48.
Metzger, Bruce M. *A Textual Commentary on the Greek New Testament* (*TCGNT*). 2nd ed. Stuttgart: Deutsche Bibelgesellschaft, 1994.
Mihoc, Vasile. "The Final Admonition to Timothy." In *1 Timothy Reconsidered*, edited by Karl Paul Donfried, 135–52. COP 18. Leuven: Peeters, 2008.
Miller, Colin. "The Imperial Cult in the Pauline Cities of Asia Minor and Greece." *CBQ* 72/2 (2010) 314–32.
Miller, James D. *The Pastoral Letters as Composite Documents*. SNTSMS 93. Cambridge: Cambridge University Press, 1997.
Mitchell, Margaret M. "Corrective Composition, Corrective Exegesis: The Teaching on Prayer in 1 Tim 2, 1–15." In *1 Timothy Reconsidered*, edited by Karl Paul Donfried, 41–62. COP 18. Leuven: Peeters, 2008.
———. "New Testament Envoys in the Context of Greco-Roman Diplomatic and Epistolary Conventions: The Example of Timothy and Titus." *JBL* 111/4 (1992) 641–62.
Montague, George T. *First and Second Timothy, Titus*. CCSS. Grand Rapids: BakerAcademic, 2008.
Moo, Douglas J. "1 Timothy 2:11–15: Meaning and Significance." *TrinJ* 1 (1980) 62–83.
———. "The Interpretation of 1 Timothy 2:11–15: A Rejoinder." *TrinJ* 2 (1981) 198–222.
Morgan-Wynne, John E. "Attitudes towards Erring Brothers and Sisters in Early Christianity as Reflected in the New Testament." In *Ecumenism and History: Studies in Honor of John H. Y. Briggs*, edited by Anthony R. Cross, 225–53. Eugene, OR: Wipf & Stock, 2002.
Morris, Leon. *The Apostolic Preaching of the Cross*. Grand Rapids: Eerdmans, 1955.
Moulton, J. H., and G. Milligan. *The Vocabulary of the Greek Testament from the Papyri and Other Non-Literary Sources* (MM). 2nd ed. Grand Rapids: Eerdmans, 1963.
Mounce, William D. *Pastoral Epistles*. WBC 46. Nashville: Thomas Nelson, 2000.
Mournet, Terence C. *Oral Tradition and Literary Dependency: Variability and Stability in the Synoptic Tradition and Q*. WUNT 2/195. Tübingen: Mohr Siebeck, 2005.
Muddiman, John, and John Barton, eds. "The Pastoral Epistles." In *The Pauline Epistles*, edited by John Muddiman and John Barton, 244–62. OBC. New York: Oxford University Press, 2001.
Nässelqvist, Dan. *Public Reading in Early Christianity: Lectors, Manuscripts, and Sound in the Oral Delivery of John 1–4*. Boston: Brill, 2016.
Neyrey, Jerome H. "'First', 'Only', 'One of a Few', and 'No One Else': The Rhetoric of Uniqueness and the Doxologies in 1 Timothy." *Bib* 86/1 (2005) 59–87.
———. *Give God the Glory: Ancient Prayer and Worship in Cultural Perspective*. Grand Rapids: Eerdmans, 2007.
Nystrom, David. "We Have No King But Caesar: Roman Imperial Ideology and the Imperial Cult." In *Jesus Is Lord, Caesar Is Not: Evaluating Empire in New Testament Studies*, edited by Scot McKnight and Joseph B. Modica, 23–37. Downers Grove, IL: InterVarsity Academic, 2013.
O'Connor, Jerome Murphy. *St. Paul's Ephesus: Texts and Archaeology*. Collegeville, MN: Liturgical, 2008.
Oden, Thomas C. *First and Second Timothy and Titus*. Interpretation. Louisville: Westminster John Knox, 1989.

Orlemanski, Julie. "A Silence in the Family Tree: The Genealogical Subject in Heldris of Cornwall's *Silence*." In *Individualism: The Cultural Logic of Modernity*, edited by Zubin Meer, 33–46. New York: Lexington, 2011.
Oropeza, B. J. *Jews, Gentiles, and the Opponents of Paul: The Pauline Letters*. Apostasy in the New Testament Communities 2. Eugene, OR: Cascade, 2012.
Osiek, Carolyn, and David L. Balch. *Families in the New Testament World: Households and House Churches*. Family, Religion, and Culture. Louisville: Westminster John Knox, 1997.
Osiek, Carolyn, et al. *A Woman's Place: House Churches in Earliest Christianity*. Minneapolis: Fortress, 2006.
Pate, C. Marvin. *Apostle of the Last Days: The Life, Letters and Theology of Paul*. Grand Rapids: Kregel, 2013.
Patterson, Dorothy Kelley, and Rhonda Harrington Kelley, eds. "1 Timothy." In *Women's Evangelical Commentary: New Testament*, edited by Dorothy Kelley Patterson and Rhonda Harrington Kelley, 654–90. Nashville: B&H, 2006.
Paul, Anthony. "From Stasis to Ékstasis: Four Types of Chiasmus." In *Chiasmus and Culture*, edited by Boris Wiseman and Anthony Paul, 19–44. New York: Berghahn, 2014.
Paul, Anthony, and Boris Wiseman. "Chiasmus in the Drama of Life." In *Chiasmus and Culture*, edited by Boris Wiseman and Anthony Paul, 1–18. New York: Berghahn, 2014.
Payne, Philip B. "The Interpretion of 1 Timothy 2:11–15: A Surrejoinder." In *What Does The Scripture Teach about the Ordination of Women? Differing Views by Three New Testament Scholars*, 96–107. Minneapolis: Evangelical Free Church of America, 1986.
———. "Libertarian Women in Ephesus: A Response to Douglas J. Moo's Article, '1 Timothy 2:11–15: Meaning and Significance.'" *TrinJ* 1 (1981) 169–97.
———. *Man and Woman, One in Christ: An Exegetical and Theological Study of Paul's Letters*. Grand Rapids: Zondervan, 2009.
———. "*Oude* in 1 Timothy 2:12." Unpublished paper presented at the Evangelical Theological Society, Atlanta. 1986.
Petersen, W. L. "Can ARSENOKOITAI Be Translated by 'Homosexuals'? (1 Cor. 6:9; 1 Tim. 1:10)." *VC* 40 (1986) 187–91.
Pfitzner, V. C. "Office and Charism in Paul and Luke." *Colloquium* 13/2 (1981) 28–38.
Phillips, Thomas E. *Paul, His Letters, and Acts*. LPS. Grand Rapids: BakerAcademic, 2009.
Plessis, Paul du. *Borkowski's Textbook on Roman Law*. 5th ed. Oxford: Oxford University Press, 2015.
Plummer, Robert L. *Paul's Understanding of the Church's Mission: Did the Apostle Paul Expect the Early Christian Communities to Evangelize?* PBM. Milton Keynes: Paternoster, 2006.
Portefaix, Lilian. "'Good Citizenship' in the Household of God: Women's Position in the Pastorals Reconsidered in the Light of Roman Rule." In *Feminist Companion to Paul: Deutero-Pauline Writings*, edited by Amy-Jill Levine with Marianne Blickenstaff, 147–58. New York: T. & T. Clark, 2003.
Porter, Stanley E., and Sean A. Adams. "Pauline Epistolography: An Introduction." In *Paul and the Ancient Letter Form*, edited by Stanley E. Porter and Sean A. Adams, 1–8. PS 6. Boston: Brill, 2010.

Porter, Stanley E., and Bryan R. Dyer, eds. *Paul and Ancient Rhetoric: Theory and Practice in the Hellenistic Context*. New York: Cambridge University Press, 2016.

Poythress, Vern S. "The Church as Family: Why Male Leadership in the Family Requires Male Leadership in the Church." In *Recovering Biblical Manhood and Womanhood*, edited by John Piper and Wayne Grudem, 233–47. Wheaton, IL: Crossway, 1991.

Puskas, Charles B., and Mark Reasoner. *The Letters of Paul: An Introduction*. 2nd ed. Collegeville, MN: Liturgical, 2013.

Quinn, Jerome D. *The Letter to Titus: A New Translation with Notes and Commentary and an Introduction to Titus, I and II Timothy, The Pastoral Epistles*. AB 35. New York: Doubleday, 1990.

Reasoner, Mark. *Roman Imperial Texts: A Sourcebook*. Minneapolis: Fortress, 2013.

Resseguie, James L. *Narrative Criticism on the New Testament: An Introduction*. Grand Rapids: Baker, 2005.

Reumann, John. "Oikonomia = 'Covenant': Terms for *Heilsgeschichte* in Early Christian Usage." *NovT* 3/4 (1959) 282–92.

Rhoads, David. "The Art of Translating for Oral Performance." In *Translating Scripture for Sound and Performance: New Direction in Biblical Studies*, edited by James A. Maxey and Ernst R. Wendland, 22–48. BPC 6. Eugene, OR: Cascade, 2012.

———. "Performance Events in Early Christianity: New Testament Writings in an Oral Context." In *The Interface of Orality and Writing: Speaking, Seeing, Writing in the Shaping of New Genres*, edited by Annette Weissenrieder and Robert B. Coote, 166–93. BPC 11. Eugene, OR: Cascade, 2015.

Rhoads, David, and Joanna Dewey. "Performance Criticism: A Paradigm Shift in New Testament Studies." In *From Text to Performance: Narrative and Performance Criticisms in Dialogue and Debate*, edited by Kelly R. Iverson, 10–21. BPC 10. Eugene, OR: Cascade, 2014.

Richards, E. Randolph. "(Mis)Reading Paul through Western Eyes." In *Paul as Missionary: Identity, Activity, Theology, and Practice*, edited by Trevor J. Burke and Brian S. Rosner, 247–63. New York: T. & T. Clark, 2011.

———. *Paul and First-Century Letter Writing: Secretaries, Composition, and Collection*. Downers Grove, IL: InterVarsity, 2004.

Ridderbos, Herman. *Paul: An Outline of His Theology*. Translated by John Richard De Witt. Grand Rapids: Eerdmans, 1975.

———. *Redemptive History and the New Testament Scriptures*. Translated by H. De Jongste. 2nd ed. Revised by Richard B. Gaffin Jr. Phillipsburg, NJ: P&R, 1988.

Robinson, Anthony B., and Robert W. Wall. *Called to Lead: Paul's Letters to Timothy for a New Day*. Grand Rapids, Eerdmans, 2012.

Rodríguez, Rafael. *Oral Tradition and the New Testament: A Guide for the Perplexed*. New York: Bloomsbury, 2014.

Roloff, Jürgen. *Der Erste Brief an Timotheus*. EKK 15. Zürich: Neukirchener, 1988.

Rotenberry, Paul. "Blessing in the Old Testament: A Study of Genesis 12:3." *ResQ* 2/1 (1958) 32–36.

Ruether, Rosemary Radford. "Feminist Theology." In *Resistance: The New Role of Progressive Christians: Progressive Christians Uniting*, edited by John B. Cobb Jr., 186–205. Louisville: Westminster John Knox, 2008.

Saarinen, Risto. *The Pastoral Epistles with Philemon and Jude*. BrazTCB. Grand Rapids: Brazos, 2008.

Salisbury, Kevin. "Paul's First Letter to Timothy: An Example of Missonal Contextualization." *Colloquium* 44/1 (2012) 78–101.
Sampley, J. Paul. "Ruminations Occasioned by the Publication of These Essays and the End of the Seminar." In *Paul and Rhetoric*, edited by J. Paul Sampley and Peter Lampe, ix–xvii. New York: T. & T. Clark, 2010.
Sandiyagu, Virginia R. "ʹΕΤΕΡΟΣ and ʹΑΛΛΟΣ in Luke." *NovT* 48/2 (2006) 106–30.
Schlarb, Egbert. *Die gesunde Lehre: Häresie und Wahrheit im Spiegel der Pastoralbriefe*. Marburg: Elwert, 1990.
Schlatter, A. *Die Kirche der Griechen im Urteil des Paulus: Eine Auslegung seiner Briefe an Timotheus und Titus*. Stuttgart: Calwer Vereinsbuchhandlung, 1936.
Schnabel, Eckhard J. "Paul the Missionary." In *Paul's Missionary Methods: In His Time and Ours*, edited by Robert L. Plummer and John Mark Terry, 29–43. Downers Grove, IL: InterVarsity, 2012.
Scholer, David. "1 Timothy 2.9–15." In *Feminist Companion to Paul: Deutero-Pauline Writings*, edited by Amy-Jill Levine with Marianne Blickenstaff, 98–121. New York: T. & T. Clark, 2003.
Schreiner, Thomas R. "An Interpretation of 1 Timothy 2:9–15: A Dialogue with Scholarship." In *Women in the Church: An Interpretation and Application of 1 Timothy 2:9–15*, edited by Andreas J. Köstenberger and Thomas R. Schreiner, 85–120. 2nd ed. Grand Rapids: Baker, 2005.
———. *Interpreting the Pauline Epistles*. Grand Rapids: BakerAcademic, 2011.
———. *Paul, Apostle of God's Glory in Christ: A Pauline Theology*. Downers Grove, IL: InterVarsity, 2001.
Seo, Pyung Soo. *Luke's Jesus in the Roman Empire and the Emperor in the Gospel of Luke*. Eugene, OR: Pickwick, 2015.
Shiner, Whitney Taylor. *Proclaiming the Gospel: First Century Performance of Mark*. Harrisburg, PA: Trinity, 2003.
Shively, Elizabeth E. *Apocalyptic Imagination in the Gospel of Mark: The Literary and Theological Role of Mark 3:22–30*. Boston: de Gruyter, 2012.
Siew, Antoninus King Wai. *The War Between the Two Beasts and the Two Witnesses: A Chiastic Reading of Revelation 11.1—14.5*. New York: T. & T. Clark, 2005.
Smit, Peter-Ben. *Paradigms of Being in Christ: A Study of the Epistle to the Philippians*. LNTS. New York: Bloomsbury, 2013.
Smith, Claire S. *Pauline Communities as "Scholastic Communities": A Study of the Vocabulary of "Teaching" in 1 Corinthians, 1 and 2 Timothy and Titus*. WUNT 2/335. Tübingen: Mohr Siebeck, 2012.
Smith, Craig A. *Timothy's Task, Paul's Prospect: A New Reading of 2 Timothy*. NTMono 12. Sheffield: Sheffield Phoenix, 2006.
Spencer, Aída Besançon. *1 Timothy: A New Covenant Commentary*. NCCS. Cambridge: Lutterworth, 2013.
———. *Beyond the Curse: Women Called to Ministry*. Peabody, MA: Hendrickson, 1989.
Spicq, C. *Saint Paul: Les Épîtres Pastorales*. 2 vols. EBib. Paris: Gabalda, 1969.
Staton, Knofel. *The Biblical Liberation of Women for Leadership in the Church As One Essential for the Spiritual Formation of the Church*. Rev. ed. Eugene, OR: Wipf & Stock, 2003.
Stelzenberger, Johannes. *Syneidesis im Neuen Testament*. Paderborn: Schöningh, 1961.
Stirewalt, Luther M. *Paul: The Letter Writer*. Grand Rapids: Eerdmans, 2003.

Stock, Augustine. "Chiastic Awareness and Education in Antiquity." *BTB* 14 (1984) 23-27.
Stout, Stephen O. *The "Man Christ Jesus": The Humanity of Jesus in the Teaching of the Apostle Paul.* Eugene, OR: Wipf & Stock, 2011.
Strange, William A. "'His letters are weighty': Text and Authority in Early Christianity." In *Honouring the Past and Shaping the Future: Religious and Biblical Studies in Wales: Essays in honour of Gareth Lloyd Jones*, edited by Robert Pope, 112–32. Herefordshire: Gracewing, 2003.
Swinson, L. Timothy. *What Is Scripture? Paul's Use of* Graphe *in the Letters to Timothy.* Eugene, OR: Wipf & Stock, 2014.
Tamez, Elsa. "1 Timothy." In *Global Bible Commentary*, edited by Daniel Patte, 508–15. Nashville: Abingdon, 2004.
———. *Struggles for Power in Early Christianity: A Study of the First Letter to Timothy.* Translated by Gloria Kinsler. Maryknoll, NY: Orbis, 2007.
Tellbe, Mikael. *Christ-Believers in Ephesus: A Textual Analysis of Early Christian Identity Formation in a Local Perspective.* WUNT 242. Tübingen: Mohr Siebeck, 2009.
Thompson, James W. *Preaching Like Paul: Homiletical Wisdom for Today.* Louisville: Westminster John Knox, 2001.
Thomson, Ian H. *Chiasmus in the Pauline Letters.* JSNTSup 111. Sheffield: Sheffield, 1995.
Tomlinson, F. Alan. "The Purpose and Stewardship Theme within the Pastoral Epistles." In *Entrusted with The Gospel: Paul's Theology in the Pastoral Epistles*, edited by Andreas J. Köstenberger and Terry L. Wilder, 52–83. Nashville: B&H, 2010.
Towner, Philip H. *1-2 Timothy and Titus.* IVPNTC. Downers Grove, IL: InterVarsity, 1994.
———. *The Goal of Our Instruction: The Structure of Theology and Ethics in the Pastoral Epistles.* JSNTSup 34. Sheffield: JSOT, 1989.
———. *The Letters to Timothy and Titus.* NIGTC. Grand Rapids: Eerdmans, 2006.
———. "Pauline Theology or Pauline Tradition in the Pastoral Epistles: The Question of Method." *TynBul* 46 (1995) 287–314.
Trebilco, Paul. *The Early Christians in Ephesus from Paul to Ignatius.* Grand Rapids: Eerdmans, 2004.
Twomey, Jay. *The Pastoral Epistles Through the Centuries.* Oxford: Wiley-Blackwell, 2009.
Upton, Bridget Gilfillan. "Feminist Theology as Biblical Hermeneutics." In *The Cambridge Companion to Feminist Theology*, edited by Susan Frank Parsons, 97–113. Cambridge: Cambridge University Press, 2002.
Van Neste, Ray. *Cohesion and Structure in the Pastoral Epistles.* JSNTSup 280. New York: T. & T. Clark, 2004.
———. "Cohesion and Structure in the Pastoral Epistles." In *Entrusted with The Gospel: Paul's Theology in the Pastoral Epistles*, edited by Andreas J. Köstenberger and Terry L. Wilder, 84–104. Nashville: B&H, 2010.
Vegge, Tor. "Baptismal Phrases in the Deuteropauline Epistles." In *Ablution, Initiation, and Baptism: Late Antiquity, Early Judaism, and Early Christianity*, edited by David Hellholm et al., 497–556. BZNW 176. Berlin: De Grutyer, 2011.
Vena, Osvaldo D. *Jesus, Disciple of the Kingdom: Mark's Christology for a Community in Crisis.* Eugene, OR: Pickwick, 2014.

Viviano, Benedict T. *Matthew and His World: The Gospel of the Open Jewish Christians Studies in Biblical Theology*. NTOASUNT 61. Göttingen: Vandenhoeck & Ruprecht, 2007.
Wagener, Ulrike. "Pastoral Epistles: A Tamed Paul—Domesticated Women." In *Feminist Biblical Interpretation: A Compendium of Critical Commentary on the Books of the Bible and Related Literature*, edited by Luise Schottroff and Marie-Theres Wacker, 830–47. Grand Rapids, Eerdmans, 2012.
Wall, Robert W. "Empire, Church, and Missio Dei: On Praying for Our Kings (1 Timothy 2:1-2)." *WesTJ* 47/1 (2012) 7–24.
Wall, Robert W., with Richard B. Steele. *1 & 2 Timothy and Titus*. Grand Rapids: Eerdmans, 2012.
Wallace, Daniel B. *Greek Grammar: Beyond the Basics: An Exegetical Syntax of the New Testament*. Grand Rapids: Zondervan, 1996.
Ward, Richard F. "Pauline Voice and Presence as Strategic Communication." *Semeia* 65 (1994) 95–107.
Welch, John W. "Chiasmus in the New Testament." In *Chiasmus in Antiquity: Structures, Analyses, Exegesis*, edited by John W. Welch, 211–49. Hildesheim: Gerstenberg, 1981.
———. "Criteria for Identifying and Evaluating the Presence of Chiasmus." In *Chiasmus Bibliography*, edited by John W. Welch and Daniel B. McKinlay, 157–74. Provo, UT: Research, 1999.
Wendland, P. "Σωτήρ: Eine religionsgeschichtliche Untersuchung." *ZNW* 5 (1904) 335–53.
Westgate, Ruth. "Greek House and the Ideology of Citizenship." *WA* 39/2 (2007) 229–45.
White, John L. "Apostolic Mission and Apostolic Message: Congruence in Paul's Epistolary Rhetoric, Structure and Imagery." In *Origins and Method: Towards a New Understanding of Judaism and Christianity: Essays in Honuor of John Hurd*, edited by Bradley H. McLean, 145–61. JSNTSup 86. Sheffield: Sheffield Academic, 1993.
———. "Saint Paul and the Apostolic Letter Tradition." *CBQ* 45/3 (1983) 433–44.
Wieland, George M. *The Significance of Salvation: A Study of Salvation Language in the Pastoral Epistles*. Eugene, OR: Wipf & Stock, 2006.
Wilder, Terry L. "Pseudonymity, the New Testament, and the Pastoral Epistles." In *Entrusted with The Gospel: Paul's Theology in the Pastoral Epistles*, edited by Andreas J. Kostënberger and Terry L. Wilder, 39–51. Nashville: B&H, 2010.
Williams, Don. *The Apostle Paul and Women in the Church*. Glendale, CA: Regal, 1977.
Wills, Garry. *What Paul Meant*. New York: Viking, 2006.
Winter, Bruce W. *Roman Wives, Roman Widows: The Appearance of New Women and the Pauline Communities*. Grand Rapids: Eerdmans, 2003.
Wiseman, Boris. "Chiastic Thought and Culture: A Reading of Claude Lévi-Strauss." In *Culture and Rhetoric*, edited by Ivo Strecker and Stephen Tyler, 85–103. New York: Berghahn, 2009.
Witherington, Ben, III. *Letters and Homilies for Hellenized Christians*. Vol. 1, *A Socio-Rhetorical Commentary on Titus, 1–2 Timothy and 1–3 John*. Downers Grove, IL: IVP Academic, 2006.
———. *New Testament Rhetoric: An Introductory Guide to the Art of Persuasion in and of the New Testament*. Eugene, OR: Cascade, 2009.

Witherington, Ben, III, with Darlene Hyatt. *Paul's Letter to the Romans: A Socio-Rhetorical Commentary*. Grand Rapids: Eerdmans, 2004.

Wright, David F. "Homosexuals or Prostitutes? The Meaning of ARSENOKOITAI (1 Cor. 6:9; 1 Tim. 1:10)." *VC* 38 (1984) 125–53.

———. "Translating ARSENOKOITAI (1 Cor. 6:9; 1 Tim. 1:10)." *VC* 41 (1987) 396–98.

Wright, N. T. *What Saint Paul Really Said: Was Paul of Tarsus the Real Founder of Christianity?* Grand Rapids: Eerdmans, 1997.

Yarbrough, Mark M. *Paul's Utilization of Preformed Traditions: An Evaluation of the Apostle's Literary, Rhetorical, and Theological Tactics*. New York: T. & T. Clark, 2009.

Zamfir, Korinna. *Men and Women in the Household of God: A Contextual Approach to Roles and Ministries in the Pastoral Epistles*. NTOASUNT. Göttingen: Vandenhoeck & Ruprecht, 2013.